SCHOENBERG REMEMBERED

Diaries and Recollections

Arnold Schoenberg

SCHOENBERG REMEMBERED

Diaries and Recollections (1938-76)

Dika Newlin

Pendragon Press *New York*

Library of Congress Cataloging in Publication Data

Newlin, Dika, 1923-
  Schoenberg remembered.

    1. Schoenberg, Arnold, 1894-1951. 2. Composers—United
States—Biography. 3. Newlin, Dika, 1923- I. Title.
ML410.S283N5   780',92'4 [B]   79-19128
ISBN 0-918728-14-2

To the memory of
ARNOLD SCHOENBERG,
1874-1951
without whom this book wouldn't be

Contents

Illustrations

Foreword

One does not bear witness to the times because one has decided to do so. One may, perhaps, turn out to have been a witness, if posterity thinks one worthy of the title.

René Clair

During the period covered by these diaries, I wrote something in them every day, a practice I still follow. While the notebooks contain much material about Los Angeles of the '40s which might be of interest to the social historian or the nostalgia buff, including all of it would have made a book of unwieldy size. Therefore I have confined myself, in the main, to those daily entries or parts of entries which are directly or indirectly concerned with Schoenberg. The ellipses are of matter considered trivial, repetitive, or not relevant to the main topic of the entry.

A grave decision had to be made early in the editing: how to handle Schoenberg's talk. In the diaries, I had transcribed as accurately as possible the sounds of his rich Viennese accent. However, I felt that the many distortions of spelling caused by this practice would, in the long run, irritate and distract the reader. Therefore, for the most part I have restored normal English spelling, keeping only Schoenberg's often idiosyncratic word-choice and word-order. I feel certain that he would have approved of this. As he wrote in a famous letter which I quoted in my foreword to the first edition of *Style and Idea*, "I do not plan to hide the fact that I am not born in this language."

In many instances, the names of Schoenberg's students have been replaced by initials or pseudonyms. The reason becomes clear in the text: some people might not appreciate being immortalized as the butts of Schoenberg's often cruel classroom jokes.

Other than these changes, the diaries are as I originally wrote them. When I first broached to Schoenberg the idea of writing his biography, he approved of it vigorously, "because," he said, "you will tell the truth." I have tried to do that, then and now. Then and now, I have not wanted to "prettify" anything about Schoenberg, his family, his friends, or myself. Such falsification would only do a disservice to a great man and his associates.

THANKS

... for the memory
(Leo Robin)

Because of the nature of this book, there will not be the usual lengthy list of acknowledgments. Nonetheless, a few thank-you's are in order: Clara Steuermann, archivist of the Arnold Schoenberg Institute, diligently sought out the Schoenberg family photos I wanted. Drew University Library, the Madison (New Jersey) Public Library, and the Art and Music Room of the Richmond (Virginia) Public Library were pleasant havens for checkkng details in the lives of some of my minor characters (and handy hideouts for peaceful proofreading, far from frenetic felinity). The staff of the Interlibrary Loan Department of James Branch Cabell Library, Virginia Commonwealth University was able to secure Julius Toldi's elusive memoires from the El Paso (Texas) Public Library—a happy find.

The selections from Roy E. Carter's translation of Schoenberg's *Harmonielehre* are reprinted by permission of Faber and Faber Ltd., London, and the University of California Press, Berkeley and Los Angeles.

Excerpts from this book were previously published in the *Journal of the Arnold Schoenberg Institute*, June, 1977, and the *Musical Newsletter*, Fall, 1977.

Prologue
Before Schoenberg

Luck is a heavenly gift.
                    Arnold Schoenberg

"Come to our house tonight for a party!" Ann Howe cried intensely. "We're having over some of the Cincinnati Symphony people."

It sounded good to me. I, eleven years old this summer of 1935, was enthusiastic about most things, but especially about musical parties. I loved to mingle with musicians, hear their shop-talk and anecdotes. I could participate, too. After all, hadn't I been composing since I was eight years old? Hadn't I had lessons with the famous Arthur Farwell, who'd worked so hard to promote American music with his Wa-Wan Press? Hadn't I, even, won some prizes for my composing and piano-playing? (The best part of the prize, I always thought, was the banquet at which it was presented.)

This summer, Mamma, Papa, and I had come up from East Lansing, Michigan, where Papa was professor of English at Michigan State College, to spend two weeks at Diamond Park on Green Lake.

Ann, a gifted young violinist who studied with Michael Press at the College, had suggested this resort. She was here now with her adopted mother, the elegant Polish lady Beatrice Perutz. Here, too, were many members of the Cincinnati Symphony, who taught and performed, summers, at the National Music Camp (Interlochen) across the lake. Most nights, you could hear music wafting across from the rustic open-air auditorium. One could, of course, drive around the lake to reach the camp, but it was far more romantic to row across at night for a concert!

Ann was talking now about people I'd meet at the party:

"You'll like Bak especially—"

"Bak?"

"Vladimir Bakaleinikoff."

"Wow! What a name! Who's *he*?"

"Our associate conductor. He's a wonderful man, with all kinds of stories to tell. Get him to tell you about the time he played viola d'amore before the Czar—"

Now that was more like it. I *loved* Czars! A few years ago, I'd had quite a crush on the Romanoff family. I'd even disconcerted my parents one night by constructing a mock coffin for the late Czar Nicholas II and insisting on carrying out my version of a Russian funeral service in the living-room. I wasn't quite that obsessed with the Russian royal family any more; but still, it looked as if I were in for an interesting evening. Better think what pieces of mine I might play. (I was *sure* to be asked.)

"Why don't you play *Cradle Song*?" Mamma suggested.

"Oh, but that's so *old*—I wrote it three years ago! Don't you think some of the newer pieces—"

"Well, sure, dear, but don't leave out *Cradle Song*. You know it's one of your best."

It was, I agreed. I hadn't been composing long when I wrote it; in fact, I'd just acquired some music paper after having, for some months, written in robin's-egg-sized notes on my father's lined school tablets. One day, a simple rocking pattern in thirds, in C-sharp minor, occurred to me. I wrote it down, added a poignant little melody, brought the whole thing to a climax. Recapitulating the beginning, I suddenly felt the urge to turn to G major for the piece's close. Why? It just sounded right! And there was nobody to tell me "It shouldn't be done" (thank God!) *Cradle Song* seemed like the right name for the piece. Later, unwittingly emulating Mahler (of whom I had not yet heard), I'd add a program after the fact, delineating a touching tale of a mother who rocks her child in its cradle, dreams of the future glory it may enjoy (that was the boffo climax), then returns to her quiet rocking. A bit of unconscious autobiography, perhaps?

Now, after supper, we strolled over to Ann and Beatrice's attractive, airy cottage. Several other guests were already there. I noticed a man of medium height with graceful hand movements, swarthy features, and striking silver hair. Ann introduced me. So *this* was the great Vladimir Bakaleinikoff! I was struck by his gentle yet intense manner and his interest in what I had to tell him of my work. When, at the end of the evening, I played—*Cradle Song*, of course!—I observed his special attentiveness. "I like that piece a great deal," he told me, as we walked back to our cottages. "When you return to East Lansing, could you, perhaps, send me copy?"

I could; I did. And thought not much more about it. I was too busy, back home, with the activities of the last year of high school. (I'd been "kicked upstairs" after three years of grade school on the advice of a concerned sixth-grade teacher, who secretly gave me the high-school entrance exams. Much later, I learned the real reason: my diminutive presence in the sixth-grade classroom had angered, not my classmates, but some of their parents, who feared that I might give their children an "inferiority complex." It wasn't the last time I would be perceived as a threat . . .)

One day in early December, a letter arrived from Bak in Cincinnati. I opened it casually, expecting not much more than a pre-Christmas greeting. Then I let out a whoop: "Mamma! Papa! Come here! You won't believe this! Bak has orchestrated my *Cradle Song* and is going to conduct it with the Cincinnati Symphony!"

In my wildest dreams, I hadn't hoped for this. Now I longed to go to Cincinnati for the performance. To my everlasting disappointment, we didn't go. I no longer remember why; most likely, we felt we couldn't afford the trip. In any event, the concert took place in Emery Auditorium, on December 28th. My piece, I heard later, had been much liked. Also enjoyed was another première: *Sketches of the City*, by young Gardner Read.[1]

---

[1]Gardner Read, b. 1913, had composed *Sketches of the City*, a symphonic suite based on Carl Sandburg's Chicago poems. Its première had in reality taken place at the Eastman School of Music in Rochester, N.Y., on April 18, 1934. Read subsequently went on to a distinguished career as composer and author. He was composer-in-residence at Boston University College of Music from 1948 to 1978. See *Baker's Biographical Dictionary of Musicians*, 6th ed., rev. by Nicolas Slonimsky (1978), pp. 1400-1401.

Four days before, Alban Berg had died in a Vienna hospital. I didn't know that. I also didn't know that, when I'd sent Bak the *Cradle Song*, I'd taken my first steps toward studying with Arnold Schoenberg.

Vladimir Bakaleinikoff, a brilliant viola and viola d'amore player as well as an excellent conductor, was one of a family of musicians. His brothers Constantin (Kostya) and Mischa, whom we would later meet in Hollywood, were to become prolific film composers. Kostya scored fourteen films, including one good one (Clifford Odets' *Clash By Night*, 1952, with Robert Ryan, Paul Douglas, Barbara Stanwyck and Marilyn Monroe). The more prolific Mischa accounted for 110, mostly on the order of such cinematic masterpieces as *Harem Girl, Voodoo Tiger*, and *Creature with the Atom Brain*.[2] Vladimir would later join them in the studios as an orchestral musician and even, briefly, enacting the role of a conductor in *Wife, Husband and Friend* (1939, with Loretta Young and Warner Baxter). As associate conductor to Eugene Goossens in Cincinnati and later to Fritz Reiner in Pittsburgh, he was often given the assignment of conducting young people's concerts. Such tasks suited him well, for Bak had a lifelong concern for young people and an interest in spotting and furthering talent among them. He was a pretty good spotter, too; two of his later protegés were Patrice Munsel, the sparkling young coloratura soprano star of the Met, and Lorin Maazel, the kiddie conductor who later rose to world fame with his assignments in Berlin, Cleveland, and elsewhere.[3]

After the performance of *Cradle Song*, Bak became a man with an obsession where I was concerned. He wrote to my parents about it. The one man in the world with whom I must study, he decreed, was Arnold Schoenberg. In fact, if Schoenberg lived in China, I would have to find a way to get there and study with him. Why Bak felt this way, I did not (and still do not) fully understand. The 19th-century Russian musical tradition in which he had been reared had nothing to do with Schoenberg. To my knowledge, he never conducted Schoenberg's music or even particularly liked it. What told him how gloriously right the chemistry between me and Schoenberg

[2]James Limbacher, *Film Music, From Violins to Video* (Metuchen, N.J., Scarecrow Press, 1974), pp. 537-38.
[3]Recently (1979) named the rather improbable successor to Gustav Mahler as director of the Vienna State Opera.

would be—who knows? In any event, he was vehement on the subject.

As for me, I knew little of Schoenberg. When he came to America in 1933, there had been a flurry of broadcasts of his music. I seem to remember hearing him talk on a broadcast from the Library of Congress and being impressed with some of his ideas, even though I couldn't understand everything he said. I had heard *Verklärte Nacht* and, being a thoroughgoing romanticist, loved it. But all this didn't bring studying with Schoenberg any closer. The idea seemed bizarre and impractical. Clearly, I was too young to go and live in Los Angeles without supervision; we had no friends or family in Los Angeles with whom I might stay; Papa didn't want to give up his position at Michigan State; and a professorial salary wouldn't cover the maintenance of two households. So, for the time being, Schoenberg was a distant dream—if that.

None of this, however, fazed Bak. To whoever would listen, he would talk about the wonder-girl who ought to be sent to Schoenberg for study, and who badly needed the money to finance such a venture. One evening, at a reception after a Cincinnati Symphony concert, he began to talk to a Russian colleague about this favorite topic. At the supper-table, neither of them paid the slightest attention to the inconspicuous woman who had been seated between them. Dramatic Russian sentences flew through the air; hands waved in vivid illustrative gestures. Finally, she could stand it no longer. "Excuse me," she blurted, "but I don't speak Russian. I just *have* to know what you gentlemen are so excited about!" Apologizing for their rudeness, Bak proceeded to explain.

Thus, there entered into my life a new character: Henriette Voorsanger. Wife of a prominent Cincinnati rabbi and sister of a New York municipal judge, she'd long been active in all sorts of good works. As she listened to Bak's story about me, her imagination was captured. Here, she knew, was a good work that would really be worth doing!

Without ever having seen me or my family (we corresponded, but weren't to meet until the summer of 1939), Henriette now proceeded to explore every possible source for the money I needed. She had a quality indispensable to a fund-raiser and promoter: a sublime inability to accept or even acknowledge rebuff. After three years, her tireless wheeling and dealing would pay off for me. From 1939 until 1945, I received generous grants from Independent Aid,

Inc., a private foundation sponsored (very quietly) by tobacco heiress Doris Duke, and wisely directed by Marian Paschal. Whatever my later differences with Henriette and Marian may have been, I never did, and never shall, forget their help at a crucial point in my career. They richly deserve the joint dedication of my book *Bruckner-Mahler-Schoenberg.*

But all this was in the future. Right now, life in East Lansing went on pleasantly enough. By special dispensation (the school had never admitted anyone so young before), I had entered Michigan State. I was studying not only music, but also French, German, geology, botany. I loved it all, especially the scientific field trips which were a welcome diversion from hours at the piano or writing-board. In music, Leonard Ellinwood, later known for his edition of Landini's works, offered wise guidance in theory, harmony and counterpoint. His concept of counterpoint teaching was a historical one; he asked us to compose in all contrapuntal styles that had existed in Western tradition, beginning with organum. A chromatic madrigal I wrote, *The Nightingale*, remains in my memory. I was doing a lot of free composition, too, especially of piano music and songs; my piano and orchestra piece, *Dirge* (which Bak later conducted in Moscow, Idaho), was written during this time.

Cradle Song, in Bak's orchestration, was having a career of its own. Bak conducted it at Interlochen on August 5, 1936; there I finally heard it—an unforgettable thrill! I no longer remember how it got onto the WPA circuit and was played by a number of WPA orchestras. In later years, the Works Progress Administration would be criticized, with some justification, for its many expensive and useless boondoggles. But its contributions to the arts were of inestimable value; this was just one small example. Izler Solomon, later to succeed Fabien Sevitzky as conductor of the Indianapolis Symphony, conducted the work with his Lansing Symphony, the excellent civic orchestra of Michigan's state capitol.

A new member had joined the family: black and brindled Tammy (Inverary Tam O'Shanter), a self-willed Scottie, my high-school graduation present. Summers we'd all pile into the elderly Chevrolet *Empress of Blandings* (after P.G. Wodehouse's immortal pig) and drive up to Interlochen for a few weeks' fun. There was swimming, rowing on the lake or up mysterious creeks, hiking, and wildflower-gathering; and always nearby, Bak, who'd listen to my newest pieces, ask me shrewd questions about my work, and make helpful comments and suggestions.

Summer of '38; things suddenly became serious! In July, Papa had travelled to Sarah Lawrence College for a brief workshop offered to college teachers of English literature. He'd visited with Marian Paschal in New York; she'd been interested in what he had to say, but had made no financial commitment. I'd spent a quiet summer in East Lansing taking a few summer courses, steeping myself in Flaubert in preparation for a French literature course I planned to take in the fall, playing ball with Tammy and his Scottie girlfriend Bunty, going to every new movie that came along, gathering fruit in the garden, collecting fossils and stamps, and feeding the resident chipmunk. It was a typical carefree Midwestern summer. In a sense, it would be the last summer of my childhood.

At the beginning of August, we drove to Diamond Park. Bak, fresh from his first year in Hollywood, was already there. He looked at my new compositions, wore a grave expression, and said little. Later, he spoke seriously to my parents: "She must go to Schoenberg *now*. It's exactly the right time. If you wait longer, you will regret it." He'd already met Schoenberg, told him of me and my work; Schoenberg was definitely interested. "But how can we do it? We've made no arrangements, no extra money has come in, she's already registered at Michigan State for the fall . . ." "Borrow, take savings, do anything, but GO! Do it for the sake of American music!"

They were convinced. On September 9, Mamma and I boarded a train at the old Grand Trunk station in Lansing, on the first leg of a journey into the unknown. It would be the first of my many flights forward into a new life.

The author in front of her home in Westwood Village, Easter, 1939.

The author scans her first book, East Lansing, Mich., 1947.

The Meeting
The First Months

In the happy confusion of the first three months in Los Angeles, I kept no diary. What follows is based upon my vivid memories only.

After a few days in a hotel, we'd found a home which would be ours for the duration of our stay in Los Angeles: 476 Landfair Avenue (*Anarkali Arms*), a Spanish-style, balconied, red-tile-roofed apartment house in the hills above Westwood Village. The house still stands, though the view from it is not as spectacular as it used to be. On clear days (this was before the smog era), I used to sit on the front balcony and see Catalina Island in the distance as I composed. The apartment's manager, Mrs. Frank Laverty, her daughter Pearl, son-in-law Mahns and neurotic dachshund Brünnhilde or Hiddy (who immediately attached herself to Mamma with a passion!) would prove to be good friends.

Admission to UCLA, even at a late date, had been no problem, because of my near-perfect academic record. But, as soon as we were well settled, it was urgent that I see Schoenberg to find out what courses of his I should take. An appointment was duly made. "Try to look older," counselled Mamma; "He may not like your being just fourteen. Don't tell him your age unless you have to!"

So, in a rather dressy dress, medium-high heels, with my long hair dressed in an old-fashioned style (those earphone-coiled braids on either side of the head which Nuria Nono-Schoenberg told me, nearly forty years later, she'd envied!), I went over to school one afternoon to meet Schoenberg. "Come in!" a soft, yet penetrating voice called as I knocked on the office door. I entered, saw a diminutive bald-headed man with an enchanting smile and bright brown (sometimes shading to hazel) intensely gazing eyes. Quickly he put me at my ease, began to ask me the necessary questions about my work. I spoke fluently of my career and accomplishments. Suddenly, something seemed to strike him: "May I ask you a very personal question? How old are you?" Well, here it comes, I thought. "Fourteen." A great light flashed over his face. "Aha, *now* I know who you are! You are the girl of whom told me *Mister Kukuloff!*"

This version of "Bakaleinikoff" was typical of Schoenberg's treatment of names. My classmate Simon Carfagno was variously known as "Trafaglio," "Kabutchum," and, in a bilingual triumph, "MacFagno." Horace Ferris also had some problems: "Mr. Harris— Mr. Ferris—oh well, it does not matter, *you* know who you are!" Fortunately, there wasn't too much he could do with "Newlin."

My identity settled, Schoenberg had to decide where to place me in the classes. His decision: I should register for everything he offered on a senior level, and audit all the other courses that he and his assistants gave. Great!

The fall sped swiftly by. I loved the classes, even though I found Schoenberg sometimes inexplicably severe with me. I sensed that he felt early success as a *Wunderkind* might have spoiled me. He wanted to "put me in my place," to make sure that I didn't overvalue what I'd already accomplished to the possible detriment of what I might accomplish in the future. Admittedly, this hurt a little. But, I rationalized, as he came to know me and my work better, he'd realize that I was capable of sane self-criticism perhaps even more severe than *his* strictures upon me.

I enjoyed most of the California life: the acrid-spicy scent of eucalyptus, the swaying feathery palms, the sea-bathing and beach-combing, the oranges, avocados, dates and figs fresh from the tree, the eclectic-exotic architecture which often reminded me of Chicago's Century of Progress Midway. Social life at school abounded, too; UCLA had, in those years, the not-undeserved reputation of a country-club college. For Christmas, there'd be a special treat; Papa would travel to Los Angeles for our first reunion in three months.

Christmas morning: "Open this last," Mamma requested as I went for my heap of presents. She indicated a slim, flat package. I finally opened it, found a green spiral school composition book. "Why this?" I asked. "You should start keeping a regular diary now, and saving all your concert programs, too. Important things are happening to you; in the future you'll be glad you did this. So many things I threw away from my school days. I've always regretted it!"

Well, that sounded sensible, and fun too. What better time to begin such a project than New Year's Eve? So, on December 31, 1938, I sat down with my new green notebook and a freshly filled pen. I began to write:

Nuria, Trude holding Larry, and Arnold holding Ronnie,
early 1941

Book I
December, 1938 - June, 1939

Austrian army sergeant: *"Are you really the famous composer Arnold Schoenberg?"*
Schoenberg: "Well, nobody else wanted to be, so I had to take on the job."

December 31, 1938

The year of 1939 is going to open for me under conditions very different from those I expected a year ago. Of course, at that time I dreamed of coming to California to study with Arnold Schoenberg —as I have dreamed for the past three years—but I was afraid that this would never take place, as I knew it would be practically impossible for us to finance the venture ourselves. And, in spite of Mr. Bakaleinikoff's unflagging efforts to obtain financial aid for me, the prospects of getting it were not very bright at that time. However, even the impossible can be accomplished, I see, if there is a strong enough will behind it. Last summer ('38), when we were, as usual, at Interlochen so that I could see Mr. Bakaleinikoff and show

13

him my latest work, he said that it was absolutely necessary that I should come to Los Angeles this fall, as I was now at the right stage of musical development to get the most out of Schoenberg's instruction. So we came home as fast as possible, packed our bags, made hasty arrangements, and left East Lansing on September 9th. We arrived here the 12th in a very dishevelled and confused condition, but in spite of our complete unfamiliarity with the area we were able to find an apartment which has been very satisfactory to us ever since.

I find Schoenberg a very inspiring teacher. He is all of 64 and does not enjoy the best of health, but he is vigorous, both in mind and body. Very self-centered, of course, just as one might expect; very few people of his reputation can escape being egocentric. I believe he has very little sentiment or sentimental leanings; I think this characteristic could be deduced from his music, as it, in its later growth (I exclude *Verklärte Nacht*), is nothing so much as intellectual gymnastics. Not that I think music should be simply a spontaneous overflow of personal feeling but the heart has more place in it than he allots, I hope! . . . One of his chief characteristics is his sardonic and somewhat ill-natured sense of humor, which is, nevertheless, tempered with enough *Gemütlichkeit* that his personal jokes do not so much insult as amuse the recipient. He teaches very methodically and concisely, partly by lecturing, partly by getting the students to discuss questions, partly by criticism of students' work in class, and partly by writing his own examples and asking for suggestions, criticisms, etc. All written work must be of the greatest strictness. If someone says, "Can we do so-and-so?", he replies, "Yes, in 10 years." Of course, just this sort of instruction is what I have needed for a long time. S's attitude toward me has been very favorable; he always holds up my work as an example to the others of what should be done. He promised Joseph Achron,[1] whom Mr. Bakaleinikoff sent to ask him for a letter of recommendation for me, that he would give me any sort of letter I wanted if I would just say the word. So I have nothing to complain of! My main projects for him now are a triple fugue for 5 strings and a set of variations for string quartet. I am in all of his courses: two in composi-

---

[1] The Russian-Jewish composer (1886-1943), a good friend of the Schoenbergs. He wrote many compositions on Jewish themes.

tion, three in counterpoint, and form and analysis. Officially I don't have to work for three of these, but of course I do. In addition to this work I am auditing first-year counterpoint and attending, for credit, a piano class, an orchestration class, and three French courses—17th century, 16th century, French composition.

I must terminate this little disquisition or it will never stop. Schoenberg would say, "You make epic poem!" Nothing more to do but wish myself a Happy New Year and tie into a book for the evening.

January 3, 1939

Well, I started back to school today! Schoenberg gave me back a paper graded A. I made an appointment for 2:30 on Thursday to ask him about the letter of recommendation. I surely hope he hasn't forgotten that he promised to give it to me. He seemed in very good humor and made quite a few jokes. Apropos of the usual literal definition of fugue as a flight, he said, "In my opinion, the only time the second voice will 'fly' from the theme is when the theme is very bad." He derives the word from, or relates it to, the German *Gefüge*: composition. "Of course," he continued, "all compositions are not fugues and there are—ahem—*some* fugues which are not compositions!" Again he got off a joke at my expense. I was writing on the board and he asked me to erase something, which I did. Then he said, "It is good, Miss Newlin, that you get practise erasing at the board so that you will be able to erase your papers clean!" He never forgets a mistake!

January 5, 1939

I had my interview with Schoenberg this afternoon; he was supposed to come at 2:30 but showed up about ten minutes of 3 instead, saying that his car had broken down. All I had time to discuss with him, therefore, was the letter of recommendation, but of course that was the important thing. He said that he would write it tomorrow and give it to me in the afternoon if I would call him up and remind him of it some time between 9:30 and 10 tomorrow morning. He asked what he should say in it, and I gave him some general idea of the sort of thing I wanted, allowing him, of course, plenty of leeway to add whatever commendation he felt I deserved. In class today he did not get to my variations but I was able to let him know that I had written some—and there was only one other student who had. As usual he was very humorous. The student who had written the variations had considerable trouble playing them and finally said, "I can't do it." "But you have two hands, I see!" exclaimed Schoenberg. Later he flicked some cigarette ashes into the piano and could not blow them out, as they stuck to the felts. "Oh well," he said, "this is not a very good piano, and maybe they will help it somewhat. At least they'll probably keep the moths out."

January 6, 1939

As Schoenberg had told me to call him in the morning and remind him to write my letter of recommendation, I did so. I didn't get him, but his wife answered and told me that he was writing it just then. Naturally I expected that he would stop me after one of the afternoon classes to deliver it to me, but he didn't, and I was terribly afraid that he had forgotten to bring it. But just as I was leaving the Music Building, I heard an automobile horn behind me, looked around—and there he was with the family! He asked why I hadn't stopped him for the letter, and I told him that I had tried to get him after the last class but had been held up by collecting my graded papers from over the holidays. (I got three back, one ungraded, two A's.) He gave me the letter and further offered me a ride into the village, so I went with them as far as Leconte and Westwood. Much to my surprise, he has a little girl who can't be more than 6, if that old.[2] I had seen her at a university concert before and had suspected that she might be a relative, but of course never dreamed that he would have a daughter that age. She is very cute-looking (dark hair with bangs and brown eyes) and, as little a thing as she is, I suppose she realizes that she has a rather important father. I had met the wife before but got a better look at her than I had. She is quite a bit younger than he—I would say in her late forties; tall, gaunt and

---

[2]Nuria, later married to the Italian dodecaphonist Luigi Nono, was born on May 7, 1932.

rather bedraggled-looking—I dare say domestic life with him is not of the happiest as he seems the type to rule his household with an iron hand.

As for the letter, much to my surprise, he spoke of my abilities with considerable force—said that in all the forty years of his teaching he had never had a pupil who at so early an age was as promising as I.

Odds and ends: Schoenberg showed us his Suite for String Orchestra (first movement, Overture and Fugue) in Special Studies. It is a remarkable piece of constructive contrapuntal technique, of the greatest strictness and yet far from lacking interest aside from that of a mathematical problem. His best joke of the day, on M. (an assistant whom he dislikes), who came late: "Ah, so you think you don't need me any more? You've learned it all, have you?"

January 10, 1939

Mr. Schoenberg was simply *full* of fun this afternoon in double counterpoint class. (We are starting fugues now, and learning the best ways of writing a subject.) As usual, he had to have a joke at my expense. He asked for volunteers to write canonic fugue subjects on the board. I and three others offered to do so, so he sent us all up and told us to divide the board space evenly. When I started to write, I found that I was encroaching on another girl's space—or, rather, *he* did. Before I could do a thing, he exclaimed, "See how little consideration Miss Newlin has for the rights of others! *Miss* Newlin, I told you to divide the space *honestly*, like brothers would!" And of course I was subjected to the combined laughter of twenty Bruins. Really most embarrassing, these situations! Other witty sallies of his during the day: in answer to a student who asked if we could use eighth notes: "No, especially if you want to. If you don't want to, it will be all right." He told another boy to tie over a note which he had written on the board; the young fellow was rather slow in catching on, and finally asked, "You mean tie it to *this* note?" "Well," Schoenberg answered, "if you can think of anything else to tie it to, that's all right. Perhaps you would like to tie it to my office?" The same student had inadvertently written parallel seconds. "It is not allowed," admonished S., "to write parallel dissonances. (Except, of course, fifths!!!)" When the class was a little slow in copying down something he had put on the board, he proclaimed, "A musician should be able to write music as fast as he uses the typewriter. Of course, I don't know how fast you type; about twenty words per hour, I suppose."

January 12, 1939

Well, Mr. Schoenberg is sick again today! I don't know what is the matter with him; a cold, I suppose. He has probably been cavorting around the tennis court in shorts during the recent cold spell. One of the assistants met the composition class and perfunctorily glanced at our variations.

January 13, 1939

I had not expected that Schoenberg would be back today, but much to my surprise, he was. He said that he had had a terrible cough the past two days and it had been such a great strain on his heart (which is weak anyway, I guess) that the doctor had had to prescribe a special cardiac medicine. I don't like the sound of any of this; at his age he ought not to try to be as active as he is. In spite of having been so sick, though, he seemed quite as chipper as ever and came through with a great many good jokes—none at my expense, for a wonder. He sent his assistant M. out to find a passkey to his office. As M. left, Schoenberg said to the rest of the class with his usual ironic intonation, "Oh, I'm sure that he will be able to get the keys; he is *so smart!*" In the first-year composition class, he wanted to blue-pencil part of a girl's Minuet and found that the point of his blue pencil was broken off. "Oh, but don't think for a minute that that will help you," he exclaimed, "I will *make* point!" Thereupon he produced a large knife and proceeded to sharpen the pencil. His usual comment on the students' exercises is, "This could be little more *fantastical!*" One of the students, therefore, handed in a piece called *Unfantastico Menuetto*. S. looked at it and from time to time asked, "Would it have been *too* fantastic to write the correct harmonies here?" At the end, he stated, "Well, you certainly succeeded in writing what you set out to write!" Funniest of all were his experiences as a young man playing chamber music with his friends. He was a violinist then, and decided to learn to play the viola. This was rather difficult because he couldn't read the alto clef, but he finally caught on to it. At first, when the group wanted 'cello parts they put bass zither strings on the viola and played the lower voice on the altered instrument, but finally that would no longer do. So S. saved and saved till he had five dollars, bought a second-hand 'cello on a Saturday, and started playing it in ensemble that Sunday. He didn't even know that it had to be played with different fingering from the violin or viola! I would have liked to hear that quartet play . . . or would I?

January 16, 1939

I had planned to ask Mr. Schoenberg if I could bring Mamma to class sometime this week, but unfortunately it slipped my mind, so I'll have to attend to it tomorrow. He seems to have quite recovered from his sickness and was just as funny as ever today. Some of his better remarks: in the Form and Analysis class he asked on what degree of the original key a certain part of the piece we were analyzing ended. As nobody could answer, he said, "Well, I suppose we will have to count a little. Let us throw dice, if you think that will help." Later in the hour he asked five students to come to the blackboard to write harmonic analysis, and said very elaborately, "Now, Mr. So-and-So, you will write on the *first fifth* of the board. Miss Blank, you will write on the *second fifth*," etc. One of the students could not think of very much to write; S. asked him, "Well, can't you think of enough to fill up the *whole fifth* of the blackboard I let you have?" The same student started by mistake to write on four staves instead of two. Schoenberg's comment: "Piano music is *usually* written on two staves instead of four—or would you like to write string quartets?" In the first-year composition class he started to explain the Scherzo form (although we'll still be writing minuets till the end of this term), and was discussing the middle section, or *part of elaboration* as he likes to call it. "Now first," he explained, "you will write four measures and then make a sequence of four. Then you will make sequence of two measures. Then you will make terrible mess!"

He sent Mr. Stein,[3] one of the assistants, out to get some music, and of course gave him the keys so that he could get into the office.

---

[3]Leonard Stein, who became a faithful and considerate editor of most of Schoenberg's theoretical works (cf. below, pp. 363-64). He is now Director of the Arnold Schoenberg Institute in Los Angeles.

When Stein came back with the music, he inadvertently kept the keys. Schoenberg asked him, "Ah, you need these keys?" When Stein replied that he didn't, Schoenberg rejoined, "Well, then, it will be better if you give them to me. I would like to be able to get into my house." A girl in the front row remarked, "Well, maybe *he* would, too!" Schoenberg looked at Stein and inquired, "Well, *would* you?" (No answer.)

January 17, 1939

In the double counterpoint class this afternoon Schoenberg continued to explain and write examples of two-voiced fugues. As usual, he was very witty. At the beginning of the class, he asked if anyone had had any trouble with the assignment (canonic fugue subjects), and asked one girl in particular who hardly ever does any work. She said she had had no trouble, but he took her right up on that—"Ah! I know why you had no trouble! You did not do the assignment!" (She had, though, for a change.) Speaking about the cadence of the fugue, he said, "Now it is true that the petrified animals [dinosaurs] have very long tails, and also the alligators, but that is no reason why the tail of the fugue should be longer than its body." He stated, while writing his fugue example on the blackboard, that he would like very much to make a certain modulation in the second section, and asked, "Now, why do I want to do this?" Everybody thought and thought, but nobody could see why. All of a sudden he burst out laughing and cried, "Because it is impossible!"

Of course, as usual, he had to have his little joke on M. The latter's duty is to play what Schoenberg writes on the board, and this he does very badly. He made even more mistakes than usual today. Schoenberg stopped him and exclaimed, "Oh, *please* play this again! This more than mistakes, this is *murder!*"

I was finally able to stop S. long enough to ask if I could bring Mamma to class this week, and he said I could, so that's settled.

January 19, 1939

Schoenberg looked at my five Mozart variations this afternoon and, as I expected, had a good deal to say about my way of writing for string quartet. On the whole, he thought the variations pretty good, but some of the effects I had used, double-stops in inner parts, doubling in octaves, etc., while quite legitimate under certain circumstances, were rather inappropriate for the particular character in which I used them. Naturally he recommended that I study many string quartet scores (which I do, and always have done, but, I suppose, not always knowing exactly the things to look for). All this is good advice . . . but the unfortunate thing was that, as I brought Mamma along to visit the class, he decided to put all his criticisms, which were really not such serious ones, in the most insulting way possible. He usually does not act like this to me, and, as I know he just did it because Mamma was there, it does not improve my opinion of his character. (Which I never did admire, by the way. I always thought him mean, though I hesitate not at all to recognize him as a great teacher and composer and a great wit, too!) To add insult to injury, he acted entirely too nice to my classmate Connie, who hardly ever does any work and who usually doesn't know what's going on, but who makes up for it by putting on the sweet smile of injured innocence when he criticizes her, looking at him very hard and powdering her nose in a marked manner . . . I suppose she flatters his ego—as if it needed it! Mamma says I am unfair and jealous, but I think for the most part I see pretty clearly.

He had a funny remark to make about my missing accidentals. I'd left out only one, but he noticed it and said, "I think I will buy you a little package of flats, sharps, and naturals to sprinkle among your works!"

January 20, 1939

A rather choice bit of luck came my way this afternoon. As there was no particular work to be done in the Special Studies class, Schoenberg talked with the assistants and me about our future plans. He happened to mention the fact that M.'s and St.'s work had much improved since they had had the opportunity of doing assistant's work. Then he said to me, "Miss Newlin, I want you to do that kind of work for me next year—grading papers, playing in the classes, and so forth." Well now, that is *something*! Assuredly there must be pay for such jobs, and I had often thought of asking him about the possibility of my doing the work, but never thought that he would offer it of his own accord. My age will be a problem, but as I will be almost sixteen and through school by next fall, I don't think much negative action could be taken.

S. told one wonderful joke today. In the first-year composition class, he was showing that one should often, in score-reading, play certain parts in different octaves to bring them within the range of the hands. He said that Mozart once presented to a pianist one very low note, one very high note, and two in the middle register, and asked him to play them all at once. Of course, the answer was that the pianist played the two middle notes with his nose! S. tried to demonstrate this at the piano—amid howls of laughter in which I joined—and finally admitted, "This man must have had longer nose as I!" In Special Studies, he said to his assistants, "If you wanted to be music critics, you should have stopped studying five years ago!"

January 23, 1939

Had my first examination this morning: Form and Analysis. I had expected that the questions would be a little changed from those Schoenberg had given us, but they were the identical ones. S. himself came to the examination, but only long enough to go about the room, see how the students were doing, and say, "Ah, I see we are already wandering a little!"

January 26, 1939

Just for fun, I thought I'd look up some of the facts of Schoenberg's life (his birthday, etc.) in *Grove's Dictionary*, but this idea was spoiled by the fact that he does not figure in it (at least, not in the 1927 edition, and I couldn't get the newest. We have it at home and I think I'll ask Papa to look him up in it). The only musical encyclopedia that even mentioned him was an obscure dictionary of Pratt's, and the first remark it made about him was "Eccentric Austrian composer."[4] This made Mamma a little indignant but I think it is funny. (Wonder if he knows he hasn't "made" *Grove's*?)

---

[4]Waldo Selden Pratt (ed.), *The New Encyclopedia of Music and Musicians* (New York, Macmillan, 1924), p. 734. The continuation of the article on Schoenberg lives up to its opening: ". . . many of his attempts to expand structural procedure in novel ways seem more bizarre than successful . . . his whim-

Today was a rather hectic day, as I had two examinations—advanced composition and double counterpoint—and they were not very well managed, to say the least. In substance they were easy enough and I know I wrote fairly good papers in both courses, but one thing after another kept happening as I tried to concentrate on pure counter-point. It would have been funny if it hadn't been so nerve-racking.

I arrived for the advanced composition examination at ten, and Mr. Stein, the assistant in that course, duly showed up with a sealed envelope supposed to contain individual examinations for each person. First off, no examination for me! A hurried telephonic conference about this matter took place between Stein and Schoenberg; Schoenberg said I could have Mr. T.'s examination and he would arrive in fifteen minutes with another paper for T. So far so good. Schoenberg did show up in fifteen minutes but he insisted that there were examinations for *everybody* in the envelope, and that Mr. Stein had made a mistake! Characteristically, S. had forgotten to bring T.'s examination, so I had to share my questions with T., and I had time to copy down only one of the two before he asked if he could have them. This was all right with me, as I assumed we would all be working in the same room and I could ask for them back when I wanted them.

Just about then, things began to happen. At eleven, with officially one hour to go and with me half through, Schoenberg saw something on my paper that could be changed. I started to change it. "Oh no, Miss Newlin, don't erase any more; better copy over!" he said with a seraphic smile that made me want to strangle him. I copied over. While I did this, he decided to look at the sheet from which I was copying, and took it for about ten minutes, standing right behind me and breathing heavily in my right ear, while I hoped and prayed that he would leave me alone. However, at the end of this little perusal, he came up with another bright idea. "It is good that you write without using piano, but I think it would be nice that

---

sicality and straining after startling effects provoke serious question. His text-book in harmony is challenged as a crude mixture of obsolete theories and impatience with all restraint. His boast that he has never read a music-history perhaps offers an explanation."

you play what you have written over and see how you like it." This little piece of advice was the beginning of my troubles. I went into a room and wrote, for the first and last time, for five uninterrupted minutes. Soon a class filed in. It was Schoenberg's first-year composition class, but it should not have been in this room, which was reserved for Nelson's[5] first-year composition class. Schoenberg's first-year class had to meet in the room where we were at first, so I couldn't go back in there. I went into another room which was already occupied by my classmate C. I could write there, but I couldn't play, because C. can't think when I play. Mr. Stein popped in and I told him to go and get the rest of my examination questions from T. Needless to say, I never saw any more of Mr. Stein, T., or the examination questions. Mr. Nelson popped in to tell us to play quietly, as his composition students can't concentrate. Schoenberg's students popped in at regular intervals. Some went away, some stayed and insisted on playing. As for Uncle Arnold himself, the last I saw of him was a glimpse of him frantically skittering up and down the hall looking for rooms with piano in which to house his Bruins. Finally I handed in the examination without the second question and Mr. Stein said it would be all right, as I'd written so many variations. By this time the third floor of the Education Building had begun to take on the air of a rather cheerful madhouse, what with dear old Uncle Arnold, who was quite potty this morning, and me and the other Bruins rushing around like headless chickens.

Well, I think that in fairness to the truth I should state that I finally got hold of the missing question after the double counterpoint examination. I found it in Mr. Stein's papers and was able to do it up in short order. Schoenberg said I ought to do it, but I don't suppose he will ever realize all the pottering I did and how nervous I got. This afternoon, for a wonder, I was able to get a vacant practice-room—vacant, that is, except for Uncle Arnold, who kept popping in and out at the quaintest times. One just gets started writing some rather fluent counterpoint and—pouf!—there he is, breathing hard at you and making his little suggestions before you can say a word. The examination was just one verse of a chorale prelude with three different endings.

[5] Robert U. Nelson (b. 1902), author of *The Technique of Variation* (Berkeley, University of California Press, 1948) and of the important article "Schoenberg's Variation Seminar," *Musical Quarterly*, April, 1964, pp. 141-65.

Got two first-year comp. papers back this afternoon; both A. Schoenberg had graded one himself.

Schoenberg showed up this afternoon as chipper as ever, not having been killed off by dust-storms, rains, and other such little treats, though he was coughing away as is his wont. He gave us back our examination papers and I was pleased to note that I had an A, the only one in the class. He spent the time discussing the scherzo form and illustrating with appropriate examples. We are to continue writing string quartet variations for a little while, though.

He made one very good joke at the expense of Mr. Stein. Stein went out with the keys to get some music from the main office, and after a while came back to report that he couldn't get the door unlocked. Schoenberg said, "So? But that's easy; just do this—" and twiddled his fingers appropriately. When Stein insisted it was the wrong key, he went out, tried it himself, and came in with his arms full of music, saying triumphantly, "You see?" One would give much for a candid camera to catch his wonderful facial contortions at such times! He was very pleasant to me today, told the class that I had written a very good examination, and when I happened to mention the fact that I'd written six sets of variations last term, looked surprised and then said to the others, "Why do you not do this too?" I think he'll *die* when he sees my twenty fugues approaching on Tuesday!

Our Uncle Arnold was in top form this afternoon. When I came into class late, he was delivering a harangue to the Bruins about how he just *loved* to teach, and made the following remark: "Of course, I am *not* ordinary teacher; perhaps some of you have already realized this—hm?" I had brought all the piano sonatas I possess—all of Beethoven, Mozart, and Schubert—to class. No one else had done this, however, and when some of them protested that so much music was too heavy to carry (I can testify to the truth of this; I kept dropping it all the time going from one class to another, and kept hoping that he'd offer a few words of sympathy for my sorry plight; none came, though), he asked, "Why, are you afraid your cars will break down?"

In Special Studies, Mr. Stein presented some sketches for a double fugue subject which were rather illegible, to say the least. Schoenberg protested, "You never wrote like this before, Mr. Stein; I think you learn this from Mr. M, yes?"

In the first-year composition class, he was talking about a feature which appeared twenty measures later than another, and said by mistake "Twenty *days*". Of course everyone laughed a little at this. He, however, laughed so hard that he had to sit down and hold his sides, and then said, "I don't know why I said that—you know, *I am very funny sometimes!*" But the funniest, most marvelous, most sublime incident of the afternoon will live forever in the memories of UCLA music students as the Big Log Jam of 1939. The Special Studies class, it seems, is a class *to be arranged*. As such, it has no definite room assigned to it; we have been meeting in one certain room all during the last semester, but this is not official and was only done because S. can't hear people practising when he is in there. Well, when M. and I went to the room we found another class, officially scheduled in that room, meeting there, so we went post-haste after Uncle Arnold. He immediately began to fuss, fume, fret, and storm, and cried out, "Where is Mr. Allen?[6] I must see Mr. Allen *at once!*" Mr. Allen was duly sent for, obtained, and apprised of the situation—though it was rather hard for him to find out much, for every time he asked a question in reference to the matter, Uncle Arnold all but stamped his feet, and yelled, "This is *my* classroom! This is where my class *belongs*! This is where my class has *always* met!" By this time he, M., St. and I, in appropriate poses of dramatic defiance, were holding at bay a whole corridor full of students and the entire music faculty who'd come out to see the fun! Finally the offending class was removed . . . The twenty students belonging to it marched out and we four marched in like triumphant conquerors of an enemy fort. The only thing lacking to make this incident utterly pure and perfect comedy was the presence of one Mrs.

[6]Leroy W. Allen was then head of the music department. I vividly remember his discussion, in orchestration class, of the opera which he called "Tan Howzer."

D., a music-education hag who has a bee in her bonnet about hygienic conditions in the classroom. Every now and then she pops into one of Uncle Arnold's classes, turns on the lights in the room, and emerges with the grimly determined smile of one who has saved the eyesight of twenty Bruins. Her function at this affair would have been to take Uncle Arnold's temperature, mop his brow, or something of the sort. But even without that crowning touch, the affair was wonderful farce. I don't think I'll ever forget the unbelievable expression he wore!

February 20, 1939

Schoenberg was certainly full of beans this afternoon! In Special Studies, where we have now started to write Rondos, M. presented the beginning of one which was "a leetle poor" in more than one respect. When S. called his attention to his mistakes, M. observed (I sometimes marvel at his gift for always saying the tactless thing!), "You know, the theme of that is more or less derived from the last movement of your Third String Quartet." To which Uncle Arnold replied, "Yes, *very* distantly, I *hope*!" In Form and Analysis, when repeating his usual joke about the aspirin-harmonies,[7] he apologized. "Of course, all of you have heard this joke before, but I can't keep inventing new ones all the time, it would wear me out!" But, as usual, his wittiest remarks were made in the first-year composition class, where we are now writing Scherzos. It happened that I had written quite a long one—four pages with Trio—and, as soon as he saw its extent, he exclaimed, "Ah, Miss Newlin, I see you invested

---

[7]The "aspirin" joke dates back to the third edition of *Harmonielehre* (1922, p. 239): "One rule we shall most strictly observe: we shall not use the diminished seventh chord as it is commonly used, as a panacea out of the medicine cabinet, for example aspirin, which cures all ills." (*Theory of Harmony*, tr. Roy E. Carter, Berkeley, University of California Press, 1978, p. 196.) Curiously, aspirin isn't mentioned in the first edition (1911), though the drug had been known since 1899; perhaps it hadn't yet entered Schoenberg's personal pharmacopoeia. Doubtless, by 1939, Schoenberg's exposure to the works of Hollywood composers of the '30s had intensified his sensitivity to the diminished seventh chord's misuse.

too much in this!" When Mr. Stein had finished playing it, Schoenberg commented, "You know, there is one good thing about Czerny —*he is short!*" One student had made a sudden and incorrect modulation from F minor to C major. Uncle Arnold asked, as is his wont, "What is this?" and the student replied, "I modulate to the dominant major here." S. thereupon inquired, with an expression of benign sweetness behind which he conceals his sharpest barbs, "And what is it that you want to do there?" The student's answer to this was, "I got tired of writing out four flats all the time!" S., who will have the last word at all costs, finished off the little conversation by saying, "Ah, you will have to have a transposing piano, so that you need only write in one key."[8] This same student had written a very poor melody in one piece. S. immediately exclaimed, "Oh, is this not sweet!" and proceeded to play it with that perfectly idiotic expression which he is so clever in assuming. This furnished the cue for him to tell his standard joke about poor melodies; he always declaims the alphabet in the most dramatic manner possible, singing it on just one note (usually slightly off key). Mr. Y., a professional violinist who is taking the course, also came in for a good bit of ridicule. The first part of his Scherzo consisted of a very banal, broken-chord figure. When it came back, S. started to sing it, then remarked, "I think we have all heard this before, yes?" The second part was mostly in unisons; before half a bar of it had been played, S. piped up, "You know, this is the best-harmonized thing you ever wrote!" Y., always a little slow on the uptake, answered, "But it isn't harmonized at all!" The whole episode amused our Uncle Arnold so intensely that he had to sit down, hold his sides, and quiver like jelly, with the result that the unfortunate opus was drowned in screams of laughter. And of course he had to finish with a devastating comment! He said that the exercises weren't bad on the whole. One of the girls retorted, "But I thought you said quite a few bad things about them!" His answer to this was, "Oh, but I

---

[8]Perhaps Schoenberg had heard about the transposing piano of his fellow ASCAP member Irving Berlin, which had a special device enabling one to transpose any piece of music into F sharp (the only key in which the popular composer could play).

expected them to be *much worse*!" I pass all these remarks by without comment because it would only spoil their effect. Of course one must see him in action to appreciate how truly, excruciatingly funny he is.

February 21, 1939

As usual on schooldays, there isn't much to write except what Schoenberg did and said, which, today, was surely plenty! This afternoon was the double-counterpoint class; I handed in twenty fugues and I guess he must have thought I was putting on too many airs, because he certainly exerted himself to lay me low! Alas, I gave him the opportunity to lay into me by offering to write on the board. The following then occurred:

> Schoenberg: Ah, now Miss Newlin will show us how nicely she can write. You see, she does not have to use a paper and eraser, and so her writing will be very clean. Yes, Miss Newlin?
>> (This little preamble has made me a bit nervous. I start to write, however, and promptly incur the professorial vengeance by starting to write on the second stave instead of on the first.)
> S.: No, no, no, Miss Newlin! There are only four staves, you know! You are too, *too* economical!
>> (I sigh resignedly and write one [1] note.)
> S. One moment, Miss Newlin. Now, class, can she do this? Yes or no?
> Bruin A: I think —
> S.: No, no, no words, write it on the board. (Bruin A proceeds to board.)
> Bruins B, C, D, and E:————(As they open their mouths to speak, Schoenberg shouts, "Write on board, please — pictures, no words!")
>> (Bruins B, C, D, and E proceed to board. The congestion is terrible. In the confusion resulting from a tussle between Bruins B and D for board space, I try to write a second note.)
> S.: *Please*, Miss Newlin, don't write any more! Now, class, can she do this? Yes or no?

30 Bruins (giving up hope of breaking the impasse other-wise): NO!

S.: Thank you. Now, Miss Newlin, you will make the best use of your counterpoint—namely, erase it.

> (I stifle an impulse to brain *le cher maître* with the nearest object handy, and erase the offending note. I proceed with the writing, and actually get through a measure without incident. Just about now, I add a pair of 8th notes for variety.)

S.: Class, can she—(etc. as before).

30 Bruins (having learned their lesson well): NO!

S.: All right, Miss Newlin (with a stubborn toss of the head), take away these eighth notes.

I: Can't I possibly use them here?

S.: Well, I suppose no one will kill you. (To class) Do you know why I do not let her use eighth notes? (No answer. He starts to shake all over laughing.) Why, because she *wants* to use them!—Oh, Miss Newlin, you might add a passing-note at the end of this measure.

> (The measure is too crowded anyway, so I start to erase with the intention of putting in the note after-wards.)

S.: Miss Newlin! I told you to *put in*, not take out! Do you always put in your notes with an eraser? (Sighting a Bruin who doesn't appear to be looking very hard at the blackboard) Oh, Mr. Fordham, what do you think of this counterpoint?

F.: I'm sorry, Professor, but I'm having trouble with my eyes today; I can't see the board.

S.: Oh, you should *at least* wear glasses in the second year of counterpoint. Miss Newlin, I don't like the shape of the notes you are making. Please make nice large round ones!

> (By this time, I am a complete nervous wreck. S. senses this and decides to heckle T., who wrote a really terrible final examination and has some sort of punishment coming to him.)

S.: All right, Mr. T, you may continue this fugue. You won't have to write very much—you see, Miss Newlin just couldn't stop writing! Now, explain the steps you take as you go—think aloud!—Oh, I don't hear anything, Mr. T! Can it be that you are not thinking? Mr. T!

> (T. writes a while, then regards the board in silence.)

T: You see, I've come up against a sort of problem here.
S.: Oh, so! (Observes problem—a question of the entrance of fugue voices—and points it out to the class.) Now, who can solve this problem? (No one answers.) Professor Quiz speaking—Five Dollars![9]
I: Well, you could change the order of the voices.
S.: Yes, and you could change to another class, too—perhaps this would be best. (I subside.) Well, let us not continue with this any longer. Now I shall talk about church modes. Oh, but before I forget it, I want you all to write 3 fugues for next time. *Three* fugues, yes, Miss E? One, two, three? (Holding up 3 fingers. — The experienced reader of Thurber[10] will remember Bolenciewicz, the star football player "not any dumber than an ox, but not much smarter," whom all the professors tried to push through for the sake of dear old Alma Mater. S. is always trying to do this with Miss E., desperately hunting for questions to which she might know the answers.) Now, about the church modes. Oh, Mr. Carr (a deep bow in his direction), I should be so greatly honored if you would give me your attention.

(Follows a long discussion of the church modes. Soon S. comes to the point about the major-like and minor-like modes.)

S.: Now, what are the other major-like modes, besides the Ionian?
I: (making one last feeble fling) Mixolydian and Lydian.

---

[9]*Professor Quiz* was a tremendously popular radio quiz show of this period, along with *Information Please, Kay Kyser's College of Musical Knowledge,* and others. Even a "Professor Quiz" movie was planned, but to my knowledge nothing came of this. See Erik Barnouw, *The Golden Web (A History of Broadcasting,* Vol. II, 1933 to 1953; New York, Oxford University Press, 1968), pp. 102, 104. Schoenberg was much aware of such popular entertainment forms—as, later, of television.

[10]James Thurber (1894-1961), brilliant American humorist and cranky stylist. His *My Life and Hard Times* (New York, Harper, 1933), from which the Bolenciewicz story comes, is indispensable to the full appreciation of Columbus, Ohio. Bolenciewicz was later unforgettably impersonated by Jack Oakie in *Rise and Shine* (1941). Ralph Rainger, who wrote its songs, including the comic "Hail to Bolenciewicz", was one of Schoenberg's Hollywood pupils.

S.: *Please*, Miss Newlin, give them in *logical* order! First Lydian, *then* Mixolydian, yes?

(I retire into hibernation. It is just about time.)

February 23, 1939

As I had to present my variations for string quartet this afternoon (I brought the number up to seven; no one else had more than three), I was afraid that Schoenberg might explode all over the place, but, much to my surprise, he did nothing of the sort. In fact, his only important criticism was that I didn't use enough features of the theme in my variations. I think he might have made some comment about my writing for string quartet if it hadn't been that the time was up before he got to do much more than hear what I had written. He spent the first hour showing us examples of elaboration sections for a Scherzo based on an Adagio theme from one of Beethoven's piano sonatas. All this is for the new textbook on composition which he is now starting to write. (By the way, the *Harmonielehre* translation is coming out in a few months.)[11] Of course, as usual he had to have his little joke at my expense. He wanted a bookmark for his notebook, and, seeing my folder, asked if he might borrow it for that purpose. At first I didn't understand what he wanted or even that he was addressing me. I suppose he must have thought that I was reluctant to let him have it, because when I finally handed it over he said, "You will get it back, Miss Newlin. I think you could safely take out insurance on it!"

Along this same line was a joke he made at the expense of Miss E. As usual, she had nothing this time, but told him that she had written some variations for string quartet the last time and that she thought he had them. He drew himself up to his full height (if you can say he has a full height) and announced, "I do *not* steal manuscripts! At least, not usually." I might have commented that he

[11]My prediction was just nine years off. Robert D.W. Adams' condensed translation finally appeared in 1948. Roy E. Carter's complete translation came thirty years later (see above, footnote 7).

wouldn't get much out of *her* manuscripts, but confined myself to saying that, as much as I remembered, we had not handed in our variations on that day. At that, I think she would have liked to kill me! But the thing he said that amused me most was in connection with my first variation. In it, there was a long and difficult broken-octave passage for first violin. Taking note of this, he asked, "Miss Newlin, are you much of an octave-player on the violin?" I answered, truthfully enough, "Why, no, I'm not much of a violin-player at all!" Schoenberg: "Well, then, why should you expect anyone else to be more of a violin player as you? When you are a renowned composer, violinists will play your octaves, your tenths, yes, even your twelfths. But now that you are a beginner, you must avoid them." This amused me terribly in the light of his declaration that violinists would have to grow a sixth finger in order to be able to play his violin concerto, and that he would patiently wait for them to do so! [12]

February 24, 1939

Uncle Arnold was full of tantrums and notions this afternoon. His top performance was, as it so often is, a verbal flaying of Mr. M. We were supposed to have written Rondos for Special Studies, but M. had given up his Rondo theme and started on a poorish set of variations. Schoenberg's response to this: "Oh! Why you not take advantage of what I teach you? I do not understand you! You must realize that I am the greatest teacher in the whole world. I am certainly the greatest in this country and if there's one in Europe to equal me I do not know about it. Why don't you take advantage of this? Why you not come to second-year composition—you *should* come, you *should* work in it! (Looks over the exercise) Oh, Mr. M., this *so* poor!" (Tears his hair—oh, I forgot, he can't do that very well, but anyway he goes on ranting and raving.) He kept on in this style for

[12]He *really* hoped that violinists would eventually grow a longer little finger— but the "sixth-finger" story has stuck!

practically all the rest of the hour, except when he was showing us Rondo examples from his book, but his parting shot was, to my mind, the best of all. He'd just been playing the abovementioned examples (very badly, as usual) and said, "Oh, the students in the composition class will certainly laugh when they hear me playing! Mr. M., you must tell them that it was you! If you tell on me, I'll tell how you compose! (With a playful wave of the hand, almost shaking his finger) So—goodbye, all!" M. stalked out with a vengeful expression, muttering to me, "*What* a dirty trick!"

Composition class was also pretty lively today. For the first time he saw what bad condition my Beethoven sonatas were in, and scolded me: "Ah, Miss Newlin, you should not treat them like your manuscripts. They do not deserve it so much!" He spent part of the class time writing a different continuation for a Scherzo by one of the students. When the Muse didn't visit him quite as soon as he had expected, he got out his cigarettes, as he so often does, and remarked, "I think I will smoke now for inspiration!" He took a puff and then proceeded to write for quite some time. Finally he exclaimed, "See how inspiring that was!" I dare say the whole class will take up smoking extensively now! Also in this class, he showed us examples from his book, this time a large number of short, characteristic variations on a simple broken-chord motive. While we were gathering around the piano to see the material, one girl dropped all her books with a considerable clatter. Schoenberg came flouncing up with a great fuss and bustle (probably he thought that I was the miscreant and was determined to have one more joke at my expense), and shouted, "Oh, who is the unfortunate person? Are my notebooks all right? (Seeing the precious documents safe and sound) Oh, if my things are all right, it does not matter!" (General riot!)

♭ *February 27, 1939*

This afternoon, I presented a part of my new Rondo and a Scherzo, and was told to rewrite both! At first I thought that all would be well with the Rondo. Schoenberg spent a long time making suggestions for the rhythmic improvement of the motives, harmonic content of the transitions, etc., and I was sure that with the suggested changes I could go on with it. But, instead of that, when he had finished his criticisms he assumed that angelic smile which he always wears when about to make a particularly dirty dig, and said, "Ah, Miss Newlin, you write fast. You will make other thing, on other theme, for next time, yes? It will be good experience for you, yes?" I see plainly that the only way I'll ever finish a Rondo is to up and *finish* one! The revision of the Scherzo won't be much trouble, as there is just one little thing to change.

Comic relief from Uncle Arnold: speaking to M., about his Rondo: "Of course, you need not always use the harmony of Czerny, Mr. M.; you should sometimes use the harmony of Brahms, but *never* the harmony of M., which, if rich, is too rich!"

I've started a most daring project for this Thursday, which will probably succeed in getting me annihilated, but will be good fun while it lasts. For my set of variations for that day, I've decided to choose one of Schoenberg's own themes, a selection from the Adagio of the D-minor Quartet. [Measures 51-58, p. 60 of the Dreililien edition.] I got it from Egon Wellesz' biography, which I've just taken out of the library and which I haven't had a chance to read yet, but from which I played several musical excerpts this evening. I was so much taken with this little 8-measure passage (it's in E major, and rather reminds me of the ending of the second movement of my second string quartet in B major) that I decided to write on it and take the consequences—which will be plenty! I'll start the variations tomorrow.

February 28, 1939

I wrote the first Schoenberg variation this morning, and it really went much more fluently than I had expected. To facilitate the understanding of the rather complicated harmony—and to let him know that I had understood it—I wrote out a harmonic excerpt of the eight measures. I think this will be quite a help to me in constructing further variations.

Nothing especially noteworthy happened in Double Counterpoint this afternoon. S. discussed at some length the six church modes and their use in the writing of two-part fugues, and then wrote out part of one such fugue for us. (We'll continue with the regular two-voice fugues in major, though, till further notice.) He did have one small joke at my expense. He was discussing a cadence to the fifth degree of Dorian, and asked whether a C sharp or C natural would be better. First he had Mr. M. (who miraculously escaped unscathed) play the cadence with a C sharp, and then asked us one by one how we felt about this. When it came to me, I started to say, "I think—" Schoenberg: "No, no, we want to know *not* what you think, but what you *feel!*" Then the C natural ending was played, followed by the same procedure except that he asked me, "Now, Miss Newlin, what do you *think?*" I replied, "I *think* it's a little weak!" Schoenberg: "Good. Now, what do you *feel?*" I: "The same thing, of course!" Just another of his little tricks to embarrass me. Really, though, I shouldn't complain, as it will be nothing to what I get on Thursday! By the way, he told us, à propos of not being able to understand something I said (a frequent occurrence), that he was in Spain with his wife once and had a terrible time getting along, because, though he spoke Spanish *perfectly* (if he speaks it as perfectly as English, it must be *something!*), he couldn't understand a word! I like to make note of these facts, even the most trivial, because they could one day serve as notes to a book which would be great fun writing and would fill a need, for so far as I know there is no really detailed biography of *le maître* (ahem!). Armitage's book is only a series of sketches and Wellesz' is mostly concerned wtih cursory discussion of his works, as much as I've seen of it.

March 2, 1939

The last laugh in the affair of the Schoenberg variations was on me —but not, alas, in the way I'd expected. Before the class started, I amused myself telling the other students about my *wonderful* joke, with the inevitable result that everyone anxiously looked forward to the beginning of the fray. And what happened? Uncle Arnold bounced in, favored everyone with a sweet smile, and the first thing he said was this: "Well, I think we should discuss the Scherzo form today, no? You will hand in your variations for me to look at *at home!*" At that, he almost forgot to take them at the end of the class, and I had to run frantically after him with them. Had he seen the knowing snickers run around the class, he would have known something was up, but he didn't notice anything. As my paper was the only one handed in, I suppose he'll manage to lose it within the week. We spent most of the time analyzing the second movement of Beethoven's first Rasumovsky Quartet, which I was very glad to have done, as I own the score of the work and have always considered it one of the finest of his string quartets. As usual, we got quite a few jokes doled out to us, together with much information about the enigmatic form of the piece. About an analysis appended by the editors to the score—"I would not call this *analysis*, but *paralysis*!" On the same subject: "I see the editors have called this a sonata form—they should have asked me first!" All this, though, is pretty flat compared to the sublime scrap that I'd been expecting. I dare say that, if he remembers to correct my variations, the comments of his vitriolic pen will equal those of his sharp tongue; but, with him, the spoken word is funnier—for obvious reasons!

Finally tonight I finished my Rondo! S. will be much surprised, I expect. If he started looking over the famous variations this evening, he may not want to see anything else I've written!

March 3, 1939

We had a famous visitor in Schoenberg's classes, the Austrian composer Ernst Krenek.[13] I guess S. wanted to show K. what a wonderful teacher he is, for he insisted, an unusual thing with him, on calling on all the *best* pupils to recite, write on the board, etc. Irony of fate; this was the day I had decided to be a shrinking violet and not put myself forward as much as I customarily do. Instead of that, I was actually called on to come to the board twice in an hour, and was asked all the hard questions. Fortunately, I came out with flying colors. Even my newly completed Rondo, which I presented in Special Studies, was not criticized very severely except from the

---

[13]Ernst Krenek (b. 1900), eclectic Austrian, later American, composer who has written in most genres and styles. His greatest success was the jazz opera *Jonny spielt auf (Swing It Johnny!*, 1927). His textbook *Studies in Counterpoint* (New York, G. Schirmer, 1940) is a manual of twelve-tone technique for beginners, a concept of which Schoenberg disapproved.

standpoint of some easily corrected irregularities in form. But that didn't exempt me from my share of ridicule! Three incidents in particular stand out. In Special Studies, I had kept a pencil by me while I was playing the Rondo, and when I got up to leave the piano I forgot to retrieve it. Schoenberg noticed it, picked it up, and asked, "This is yours?" When I replied that it was, he continued, in his usual vein, "I would not want to rob you of such a valuable article. (Holding it up in front of the group) I think she uses this when she is hungry. You *do* like to eat your pencils, yes, Miss Newlin?" When I put an end to this sportive interlude by asking whether I should revise this Rondo, with the greater subordination of the second theme, the rewriting of the middle section with a more distinct, étude-like character, the omission of the transition in the recapitulation, and the addition of an extended coda, or whether I should start all over again with a new theme, he answered, succinctly, "Both!"

Other remarks I considered worth noting:

Form and Analysis: (In answer to a girl who had used the term "musical idea") "We have not used once the term *idea* in this class. Not one of us knows what is an idea. Perhaps some of us have had one, but if we did, we did not know about it, yes?" This should have given me the cue to bring up his picture of an idea which he showed us in second-year composition yesterday, but I didn't think of it. The first block represents the statement of a model, the second a repetition, and the tail a liquidation.

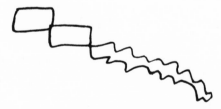

———(Complaining about the noise of the construction of the new Life-Science building next door) "Of course, I would not mind this noise so much if it would be a music department, but I see no reason why we should suffer for other departments, no?"

———(Criticizing Schirmer's thumbnail analyses of sonata form) "Of course, Schirmer did not make these himself. One of his boys did it. In this case I can excuse it. Not otherwise!!"

Special Studies: (In answer to Mr. Stein, who said that he had no work because he had been moving) "I think you have been moving all year, yes?"

Oh, and I got a kickback about the variations, but not a very serious one. He simply said that it "had no sense" for me to try to write variations on his theme. I may get a severer reprimand in the composition class, but I don't much care. He showed a perfectly reasonable attitude and didn't seem angry at all.

March 6, 1939

In Special Studies, Schoenberg asked me if I had heard from Miss Paschal yet, and added, "I hope you will not be disappointed, yes?" I considered this very thoughtful, and am glad he hasn't forgotten the matter. He says Bruckner is not enough recognized in this country, also Reger and Mahler. (All three are enough recognized for me, but let that pass!) He happened to speak of the *Gurre-Lieder*, a strange coincidence, as we were just reading aloud a detailed account of them in Wellesz' biography last night. He says they were a great success when he conducted them in London, Amsterdam and Vienna, and he always had to take bows for at least half an hour after the performances. He wishes Klemperer would do them, and so do I, as I would be interested to hear them after having read all about them. Perhaps a petition of the students addressed to K. would be effective, but S. might be afraid that people would think he'd put us up to it.[14] What is a *Gurre*, anyway? My German dictionary tells me it may be a horse, a screw, or a shad, and none of these seems to fit the plot. Perhaps it doesn't really matter.[15]

March 7, 1939

I finally got my twenty fugues back in Double Counterpoint, only half read, I think, as there were no corrections on the latter part

[14]Klemperer never did.

[15]*Gurre* is, of course, the Danish castle which is the seat of much of the action.

and I know I must have made a few mistakes! The grade was A- (the minus, I suspect, is because of the large number of fugues, but of course I can't prove this).

Schoenberg continued discussing two-voice modal fugues this afternoon, finishing the Dorian one which he began last time, and writing a new Phrygian one. His always active mind has a new bee in its bonnet (beautiful mixed metaphor, *n'est-ce pas?* but mixed metaphors seem to fit our Uncle Arnold's personality). Well, anyway, he has a new idea, which is the organization of a student contest for recognizing music played on records. He would have prizes totalling, say, a hundred dollars, with a fifty-dollar first prize, and the rest distributed proportionally. The students would be prepared for the examination by being given an opportunity to hear a certain amount of selected recorded music each day. The examination would consist of filling out blanks in answer to the following questions: Name of piece? Composer? Time of writing? Key of piece? Number of measures of selection? Position of selection in composition? and so on. I think this is a very nice idea and I certainly think it would further the interest of the students in really knowing classical music better than they do.

🖉 *March 10, 1939*

Oh, but Schoenberg was in top form this afternoon! The effect, by the way, wasn't at all diminished by the fact that he wore two unmatched shoes, with one untied shoestring, and that his clothes were covered by a species of sticky white dust. I was afraid he might be cross because the Form and Analysis class had resolutely refused to buy two books of Beethoven variations, and he had finally to be satisfied with their getting the thirty-two in C minor. But evidently he realizes that a lot of them really can't afford to buy so much expensive music (when he asked the class who was in a position to buy it, I alone raised my hand), as he wasn't angry about it at all. He finally let me go on to a new Rondo theme, though not without a good many criticisms of what I'd already written, chiefly on the grounds of insufficient variety in the accompaniment figures. He spent practically a whole hour showing me examples of many such figures in Brahms, for which I was very grateful, as I realize my acquaintance with B.'s piano works is insufficient and I welcome any opportunity to extend it. Also in the Rondo: "For next time you will put in the accidentals you left out this time—I'm sure that will keep you busy till Monday, yes?"

And we did have a *wonderful* time in composition class, chiefly as the result of his suggestion that we write our next Scherzos for string quartet. On this, one girl spoke up, "There are so many of us who play strings, why couldn't we play the Scherzos in class, just for fun?" He approved of the idea; he's always urging us to do much ensemble work, and if we say there's no time, he invariably retorts, "Is twenty-six hours in day!" But he pounced on the word "fun": "I do not think this for fun, this for correction, and this not so much fun for author. Well, I admit it *is* fun for the others in class, yes?" Then he began a canvass of class members to find out who played what, and, much to his consternation, there was no 'cellist in the group. Thereupon, pointing to a student in the back of the room, he exclaimed, "Mr. Bell, why you not play 'cello?" Bell answered, "Oh, that would be too much." Schoenberg: "Perhaps too much for audience, yes?" And so it went during the whole class. Yes, we learned something, too. He started to discuss the form of the Andante movement of a sonata, which we'll write after the Scherzo.

March 11, 1939

Went downtown to buy music and look for a present for Tammy's 3rd birthday . . . I bought Schoenberg's *Drei Klavierstücke*, Op. 11. I played them through when I got home, and think them *terrible*. Every time I see his later works I wish that he'd kept on in the tradition of *Verklärte Nacht*, the First String Quartet, and the early songs. Of course, it isn't fair to judge such music just by one playing. I intend to make a thorough study of it, especially of No. 2, which I liked best or disliked least. But I don't think I'll ever grow to really like it wholeheartedly. It amuses me when I see his occasional marking of a very angular melody, *Sehr zart*! Wellesz always speaks, too, of his tender themes, but I don't see it. I'm glad to have the music, though. Also, we bought a 5-cents short outline of Schoenberg's life[16] with a terrible picture of him on the cover. It must have been taken in his forties. In addition to having the most daft smile I've ever seen on a human face, he has his right hand up behind his ear in a gesture which looks peculiarly like a cross between *Heil Hitler* and *le pied au nez* [nose-thumbing] . I've stood it up beside Tammy's picture, where it is singularly fitting, I think.

March 12, 1939

A drive to the Santa Monica beach. On the way home we took a brief turn up North Rockingham Drive to see Schoenberg's house. It is the very first one off Sunset, and is an extremely pleasant-looking spot, a two-story white stucco house with red tile roof set back in a lovely long garden, and with an extensive fenced yard behind containing, of all things, a dog house and an Irish setter! The proprietor was not in evidence . . . All the Brentwood residential section looks especially pretty now that the acacias and the smoky blue wild lilacs are in full bloom.[17]

Afterwards I sketched the beginning of a Rondo (I don't like it a bit and have a good mind not to show it to Schoenberg) and did a Scherzo and Trio in the most wonderful handwriting with all its sharps and flats, for string quartet. I call this little masterwork Op. 0, *Hommage à Czerny*, hoping thereby to suitably tickle our Uncle Arnold. Oh yes, and I worked some more on Op. 11 no. 2 today and find that I almost like it. I guess it only takes getting used to.

March 13, 1939

We spent most of the time analyzing in all of Schoenberg's classes this afternoon: the 32 Variations in C minor in Form and Analysis,

[16]By Frederick Martens (New York, Breitkopf and Härtel "Little Biographies" Series, 1922).

[17]Shirley Temple lived across the street. Schoenberg was incensed when guides on the frequently-passing tour buses would point out her home and not his. Private cars, too, would crawl by, their tourist-drivers having discovered the location of one of the "Guides to the Movie Stars' Homes" which were peddled on street-corners. (Schoenberg was quite taken with this "art-form;" see below, p. 165.)

Rockingham Avenue (the street's correct name), like Brentwood in general, was a favorite residential area for Hollywood personalities. A little later, the supremely sophisticated songwriter Cole Porter lived at 416 N. Rockingham.

the Rondos of the Brahms Piano Trios and Quartets in Special Studies, and various Andantes of Beethoven Sonatas in first year composition. Nothing particularly eventful happened in any of the classes, unless one might call the return of M. to Special Studies after a two-week absence for the purpose of finishing his Rondo (he didn't finish it, by the way) an Event. We all thought that Schoenberg would be terribly angry with him, but all he did was to make a deep, ceremonious bow before him and say, "Ah, how honored we are to have you back with us today! And what eternal works have you created?"

🖋 *March 14, 1939*

Schoenberg was supposed to have returned our double counterpoint papers to us this afternoon, but, as usual, he'd forgotten to do it. He spent the afternoon finishing the Phrygian two-voice fugue and starting a three-voice one. Again there's nothing special to record, except one rather rococo joke on M. When S. had finished the Phrygian fugue, he had M. play it, as is customary. During this performance, S. noticed a mistake in the counterpoint. At once he changed it on the board, and then said, "Of course, it is not really as bad as it sounds when this man with the long legs puts his big feet on the pedal!" Of course, M. looked pretty sick about it. Our Uncle Arnold doesn't care much what he says, does he now?

🖋 *March 16, 1939*

Schoenberg's reaction to my Scherzo for string quartet (based on the theme of the Scherzo of my 1st string quartet) was pretty favorable on the whole. Naturally, he had to have his little quip with respect to the six sharps—he said, "You want to make it possible for the instruments to use all their open strings, yes?" On coming to a passage which I had written with innumerable double-sharps, in E sharp major, and on observing said double-sharps (the cross with 4 dots; he always writes just the cross), he remarked, "These are either too double or too sharp—I don't know which!" After many futile attempts to read the passage, he added, "As a punishment for this, you must play this piece!" For the rest, his criticisms were not numerous: the theme should be more melodically interesting in

various ways, I should use a strict sequence in the part of elaboration
and extend it, etc. But he's just acquired the craziest idea! I
happened to mention, I don't remember how or why, that I was
taking eleven subjects, and at once he became perturbed: "But this
too much for you! You will wear yourself out! Why you not stop
working in my Special Studies, and just work in few of my classes?"
And so on and so on, all with the greatest consideration and sweetness, which was really too funny to be imagined, considering the
large amount of work which he has asked of me in the past. Ironically enough, he then asked me to do two or three Scherzos for next
time, the others just one, as it was their first attempt this year.
Actually, I've been a little tired lately and if he realizes this and
takes such a kind attitude about it, it's a good thing. Of course I
won't stop working in Special Studies unless he presses the matter,
but if I ever have to make a temporary defection, at least I know
that he appreciates my position.

We analyzed some more Brahms quartets (after everyone's exercises had been looked over) for the sake of deriving ideas from their
great thematic richness. Next time we have been promised a going-
over of the second movement, in particular, of the A-minor Quartet,
which I am glad of as I know and love the work, and, in addition,
own the score. Of course, Schoenberg may forget all about it, as
usual, before next Thursday rolls around.

March 17, 1939

Spring is definitely here—and it isn't just the flowers that show it,
or the weather (which is a bit chilly & foggy), but the strange garb
in which our Uncle Arnold has suddenly blossomed forth. For,
though his shoes matched (for a change) and the shoestrings were
tied, and though his customary suit of black was actually clean, all
this was made up for by the lavishness of the rest of his costume.
He wore a brilliant blue shirt, which had a detachable collar, pinned
to a flowing sky-blue tie with large white polka-dots, but otherwise
just hanging loose around his neck, and which didn't come up high
enough on him to cover his chest completely. This was topped off
by a white waistcoat with stripes of the same vivid sky-blue. But even
this wouldn't have amused me so much if it hadn't been that I was
wearing the identical colors in all my clothes, and even had a white

sweater with blue embroidered stripes which could have been made to match the remarkable waistcoat. I hardly think, though, that we would have been mistaken for the Heavenly Twins!

His mood, not surprisingly, matched the gaiety of his clothes. He was full of fun, especially in Form and Analysis. Just as he had gotten off to a good start discussing (again) the 32 Variations, an airplane flying low overhead started to make such a terrible noise that none of us could hear a word he said. "Well," he shouted, "we will have to stop this at once. Who of you has brought his anti-aircraft artillery with him so that we can shoot this terrible thing down?" Later, I offered to write a harmonic analysis of certain measures of the 3rd Variation on the board. When I was about half-way through, he came up to me and asked, "Miss Newlin, can you read this?" I was feeling quite brave, so I answered, "Yes, I can." Whereupon he retorted, "Well, then, I envy you, for I cannot!" This might have been the end of the incident if, at this juncture, some half-dozen of my fellow-workers hadn't chosen to sing out, "Why, Professor! *We* can read that perfectly well!" Uncle Arnold didn't get angry at this. He simply laughed and contented himself with making pointed remarks about the un-circular nature of the circles which I had put around my figured basses (to make it easier for him to read!)

I got off pretty easily with my Rondo in Special Studies (by the way, nothing more was said about my not working in the class). I was afraid that I hadn't done enough—I'd completed only the first theme, and sketches of the transition and second theme—but the amount, if not the content, appeared to suit him. He still thinks my themes old-fashioned (!) and not rich enough. However, he considers the material worth working over, and gave me a new version of the first theme (with a characteristic staccato chordal accompaniment instead of the semi-contrapuntal effect which I had tentatively tried) which he wants me to use. It was in this class that he gave us a more or less sketchy outline of his method of composing. He always conceives a theme complete at once with all its attributes—melody, harmony, rhythm, type of accompaniment, instrumentation, etc.—but he always makes many sketches before deciding on a permanent form. The first thirty or forty measures, say, of the first movement of a string quartet are always the hardest for him to write. From there on, he is likely just to write his ideas out as rough sketches on two lines only, but with the same clear conception of the orchestration and other attributes. He never writes a melody first and har-monizes it afterwards, or, as Tschaikovsky did, writes an orchestral piece for piano and then orchestrates it.[18] It takes him, on the average, about fifteen days to write a movement of a string quartet.

In 1st-year composition, we continued to analyze Adagios, which we will definitely write for next time. The feast of reason and the flow of soul continued unabated here. One girl asked if she might open the window, and if he would object to the draft. "Oh, no," replied Schoenberg, "I *like* drafts; it is only the noise of the building that I hate. This would be something to put in my biography, yes? or this would be good in an interview: 'Do you like drafts, Professor Schoenberg?' " This should have silenced her, but in about five minutes she was up again, this time to say that she wondered why Beethoven had used a certain figuration, because she didn't like it a bit! The answer, "Well, if you do not like, you make streamlined edition (what a terrible word this is) and maybe you will even find a publisher for it. If you did, I would like to see him in jail!" That, naturally enough, ended further comment on her part!

By the way, I read in the *Bruin* that he is giving all his works to the University library. According to the article, they already have one of the later string quartets and *Pierrot Lunaire*, but neither is catalogued. Also, I note that it was he who presented the library with the Armitage book. Pretty cute!

March 20, 1939

Schoenberg looked over the Andante which I had written for first-year composition and made many suggestions for its revision, including one distinctly nasty comment (well, I don't *really* mean "nasty"). When Mr. Stein had finished playing it, Schoenberg was silent for a long while, then, assuming his most benign look, said

---

[18]But Tschaikowsky wrote, "You ask how I work in regard to orchestration. I never compose in the abstract—never does the musical idea come to me except with suitable exterior form. So I find the musical thought simultaneously with the orchestration." (quoted by Martin Cooper, "The Symphonies," in *The Music of Tschaikowsky*, ed. Gerald Abraham, New York, W.W. Norton, 1946, reprinted 1974 in the Norton Library, p. 32.) Schoenberg wasn't always guilt-less of revising history, as he often accused musicologists of doing.

simply and almost demurely, "You know, I rather liked those last two chords!" He didn't get to my Rondo in Special Studies, for, as he so often does in that class, he launched into a long drawn-out monologue touching upon his own merits. He talked at length about the *Art of Fugue* and the proper method of performing Bach's ornamentation (he believes that all the appoggiaturas should be played short). He described the arrangements he made when he was president of the *Verein [für musikalische Privatauffuhrungen].* It was about one of these arrangements, of a Mahler symphony, I believe, that he said, "This was so perfect that those who knew the original, said that they would hardly have known them apart!" He told of his relations with Busoni and the late composer and writer, van Dieren.[19] It seems, and I was interested to learn this, that Busoni considered Op. 11, no. 2 (which I'm learning now) unpianistic and wanted to make an orchestration of it.[20] "It was then," said Schoenberg, with obvious delight in the remembrance, "that we had the big fight!" Busoni, however, finally backed down. S. admires him very much and thinks his work should receive more attention.

His vernacular vocabulary, incidentally, increases daily. Today, his newest acquisition seems to be "So what?" which I suppose he regards as the American equivalent of his beloved "So!" Another of his favorites is "Step on it!" It is touching to see how proud he is of himself when he manages to work such an expression into his lecture.

March 23, 1939

My three new Scherzos were pretty well received on the whole. Of course, Schoenberg was able to find many weak points in them, and

[19]Bernard van Dieren (1884-1936), Dutch composer and writer who worked mainly in England; best-known for his once-controversial book of critical essays, *Down Among the Dead Men* (Oxford University Press, 1935; reprinted, Freeport, N.Y., Books for Libraries Press, 1967). It includes an excellent essay on Busoni.

[20]Ferruccio Busoni (1866-1924), the brilliant pianist, composer, editor and teacher, did not make an "orchestration" of Op. 11 no. 2, but a "concert version" for piano, with many Lisztian flourishes. After an exchange of letters between Schoenberg and Busoni, the arrangement was published by Universal-Edition in spite of Schoenberg's severe reservations. However, the two men later became good friends.

to point out ways for improvement, but, after all, that's what I really want! However, an incident which happened just after I had finished playing them was unbelievably embarrassing to me. Each hour is marked by the buzzing of a buzzer which sounds twice in ten minutes to indicate the end of one class and the beginning of the next. Our class lasts two hours. At the ringing of the second four o'clock bell, just as I had finished my pieces, Schoenberg leaped up, bounded toward the door, and cried, with an expression of seraphic joy, "So, good-bye!" Of course, we all exclaimed in consternation, "But you're not leaving now, are you—it's only four o'clock!" In spite of his efforts to keep a straight face, one could instantly feel his spirits dropping a few degrees (just a few, for he really does enjoy teaching when he's not too tired). To Mr. Stein's amused query as to whether the class had been so tedious that he'd taken one hour for two, he answered "No," but his tone hardly carried conviction. When he came to my second Scherzo and saw that I'd written a third one, too, he sighed and remarked resignedly, "Well, at least this will give us something to discuss, yes?" For the rest, he analyzed the second movement of the Brahms A-minor Quartet, and spent quite a little time talking about the *Harmonielehre*. Altogether, he says, it was more than two years in preparation; every time the publisher would get the new proofs out, S. would decide that he wanted to do it all over again. He was fortunate to have had a patient publisher! But his eloquence soared to new heights when he described the reception of the book. He told of the many letters he had received, "treating him as Hitler is now treated in Germany," and climaxed his account by telling us how much correspondence had come to him over the years, mostly worded as follows, "I find your wonderful *Harmonielehre* the only consolation to me here in the trenches. Every night I sleep with it under my pillow and it gives me new hope for life!" etc. etc.

Odds and ends of his remarks: to a student whose piano Scherzo was "not very rich": "I would characterize this as fluent futility." This is as good a place as any to note an especially clever remark he made last Monday, which I quite forgot to put down at the time. He was critical of a "leetle poor" Adagio and asked the class, "Now, what would you do if you were so unfortunate as to have no more of an idea than this?" One girl piped up, "I would study examples of Beethoven." Schoenberg: "You mean *steal*, yes? Well, perhaps you are right. I always say, 'Well stolen is half composed.' "

I missed a fine chance to hear Schoenberg's Second Quartet after class. Stein had the records with him and was playing them through, but I had to hurry home to finish an Adagio and a Rondo, so I simply couldn't afford the time to stay for more than the first few measures. But oh, it's beautiful, what I heard of it! It is strangely reminiscent of César Franck in parts, I think. A footnote on the work: the rhythm of its opening measure ♩ ♪♪♪♩ is the signal his wife uses to let him know when she has come for him with the car! I always like to note these little things.

March 24, 1939

Well, as usual, I must "make other thing" for Monday! Schoenberg looked at my sketches for the Rondo. While he thought that there was some good in them, he found that some of my modulations were a little too sudden (on this he remarked, "This what happens when one tries to apply Alchin harmony!")[21], and that my harmonic structure subsequent to the theme was more complicated than any which the theme would justify. So, I have to start over again. Besides, he still thinks my string quartet style a little too pianistic. I said, "Of course, I realize it isn't the best string quartet writing." He, taking me up on that, as I should have expected, replied, "No, it is not the best—nor even the second best—perhaps the fiftieth best, yes?" But at least I had the advantage of having done some work, whereas the others are so afraid of criticism that they never write anything. Schoenberg takes a very reasonable view of this situation, much more so than I would have expected of him. He never becomes angry about it, but always tells them that it doesn't matter whether what they have written is good or not, so long as they write, *write* and WRITE! I'm always held up as the shining example in this, and I dare say they aren't very happy about that. "Of course," he said

---

[21]I.e., the rules expounded in *Applied Harmony* (Los Angeles, L.R. Jones, 1935) by Carolyn Alchin, longtime professor of harmony at the University of Southern California.

to M. today, "the first theme of your Rondo was poor; the second theme was also poor; the harmony was also poor; but you should have finished writing it, all the same!" A little more tact could be used to advantage in the enunciation of this principle, but the basic idea is certainly right enough.

I forgot to mention the defect of my string quartet style which amused him the most—my totally inadvertent use of a low F-sharp in the second violin part. I was afraid that he might really blow up at this, but, surprisingly enough, he admitted having made such errors himself—in the *Gurre-Lieder*, where he wrote low B's for the 'cello and viola—and so was ready enough to forgive me. But there must always be the little tang of sarcasm. After having described the care he always took to mentally "feel" the fingerings of the stringed instruments, which was easy for him because he played them all, he observed, "Of course, your case is little different, I think!" Even so, it was rather magnanimous of him to admit ever having made such mistakes himself, an admission which he need not have made at all.

March 27, 1939

Schoenberg came to his classes today as usual, but he certainly shouldn't have, because, he told us, he had been in bed the whole weekend as the result of a terrible heart-attack Saturday morning. He said that just while he was breakfasting he was taken with a coughing spell, followed by a violent palpitation of the heart—so violent that, when the doctor arrived some time later, his heartbeat was more than twice its usual speed. Of course, after such an attack, he has no business to be on his feet at all for the next week at least. But here he was, as white as a sheet and not able to keep his mind on what he was doing for five consecutive minutes, yet actually claiming that, aside from these occasional unfortunate occurrences, he has a *strong heart*! The doctor had insisted on his giving up smoking, which he did, but I dare say he won't stick to that resolution long, as his hand kept straying to his pocket all afternoon. I don't think he would have resisted temptation had he had his cigarettes with him! No use talking, the man's simply committing suicide by refusing to take better care of himself and, in his present condition, I wouldn't lay odds on his lasting the year out. Despite his exhaustion, he still seemed in good humor—so much so, in fact, that he actually let my new Rondo sketch get by without many corrections. But this may simply have been because he didn't feel able to do anything with it; for some ten minutes after I'd played it, I didn't think he was going to make any comment on it at all. He just sat there looking at it and breathing stertorously. I was even afraid that he might be having another attack, and God knows I'd have no idea what to do for him if he did. He thought one of my transitions too long and, after having cut out the superfluous measures, remarked, "I do not think we lose anything very valuable, no?" I was obliged to agree. Then, in first-year composition, he repeated his old joke about my lending accidentals, with a new variation: next time, it seems, I am to bring a large sack full of flats, sharps, and naturals, taken from the secret hiding-place where I store them, "and then everyone will help himself to all he wants." It's almost pathetic to see the poor old man trying to be as gay as ever when he's just risen from what might have been his deathbed.

March 28, 1939

I'd been afraid that Schoenberg might not be able to come today, but he did, still a little shaky and having difficulty concentrating (he insisted on making wrong cadences in his three-voice fugue, which he practically finished) but otherwise much better. As I predicted, he's already broken the no-smoking rule. That will probably mean an attack for him tomorrow, if he's not careful! . . . He had a good deal to say on the subject of some people who were noisily moving chairs about next door. "Is this, perhaps," he inquired, "some new activity of music department?" His newest grammatical construction is, I think, worth noting. It is "more slowlier!"

March 30, 1939

On Tuesday I had thought Schoenberg was looking better, but he has certainly suffered a relapse since! I think he was worse today than he's been in a long time: bad color, a constant tic in his left cheek, and a tendency for his hand to shake violently when writing.

I'm really afraid that he's leading up to a stroke. Why, why doesn't he have the sense to stay at home? Obviously he was feeling terrible, as he let our works by with comparatively few criticisms, and even failed to scold the unfortunate C. as much as usual. But that didn't prevent him from being as *gemütlich* as ever. When showing us the elaborate extensions of the cadences in the *Eroica*, he said, "This very different from what most composers would do. When they come to the cadence, they say, 'Ah, now I am at home, I can take off my clothes' "—and started to suit the action to the word! . . . I was much amused by his disquisition on Beethoven's "harp quartet without the harp" [Op. 74]. The point of the story is that on a program it was listed as "quartet with harp" and some wit asked where the harp was. "Of course, you know, " he continued, "this could really happen, that Beethoven wrote such a work of which no one ever heard. For example, there are his pieces for violin and viola;[22] I have heard of them, but I never heard, never saw them! So, Beethoven *could* have written quartet with harp. He *did* not, but he *could* have!"

March 31, 1939

For a time I was afraid that Schoenberg really was sick this afternoon, as he didn't show up for the Form and Analysis class and came half an hour late to Special Studies. However, all that had held him up was some luncheon or other from which he had had to walk over here—and I don't imagine that's very good for him! But he seemed to feel better today than yesterday, though he still twitched and didn't have a very good color. I regret to have to say that, with the approach of spring, the fatal tennis urge is stirring in his heart. Just as he was leaving Special Studies, a bleached blonde with a tennis racket appeared, and how he did perk up! Though she isn't in any of his classes, and hence he can't know her very well, he came rushing up, asked, "Ah, so you play, too?", and instantly began demonstrating the correct backhand stroke, in which pleasant occupation I left him. I only hope the incident doesn't put nefarious ideas into

[22]Perhaps Schoenberg referred to the Duet for Viola and 'Cello "mit obligaten Augengläsern" (1796).

his head. It's bad enough breaking doctor's orders about smoking, but if he starts this tennis business again it's certain suicide. Why doesn't somebody keep a better eye on him?

As usual, he found plenty to amuse him in the afternoon's proceedings. For once, he didn't get to make fun of me. He didn't see my Rondo, and he actually liked the Adagio; but he did instruct me to go to a "musical filling station" when I came to continue the Rondo, and to tell the attendant to "fill it up with musical fluid." In conclusion, he ordered, "Get rhythm, Miss Newlin, get rhythm!" M. had a nine-measure start which he considered to be a three-part song form. When he asked S. if it could be treated as such, the latter replied, "Why, it is not even *one*-part song form!" Most of his sarcasm, though, was expended on our last term's three-part song forms. He wants us to bring them next time, so that he can choose some to *improve upon* (ahem!) in his new composition textbook. "You see," he explained, "I want an average form so that I can show how it could be made better; but I cannot write a *student's* three-part song form, so that is why I want you to bring yours. "But," exclaimed some of us, "we didn't save our last term's papers!" Schoenberg: "Oh, why not? Perhaps you could have found a publisher. Maybe once you could get them put out in the funnies, yes? But if you will look in large waste-box in the hall, perhaps there is still hope of finding them." Poor Mr. Bell had a rather embarrassing moment. As he was going through the group clustered about the piano to get his paper for the day, he tripped over somebody's feet and, with a loud crash, fell as flat as a flounder! Uncle Arnold, who had been absorbed in his work, turned around with a start when he heard the noise, and, on seeing what had happened, inquired, "Ah, Mr. Bell, what did you do? Could you perhaps do this twice? I did not see you the first time. How does one do these things?" Mr. Bell just blushed, picked himself up, and shuffled off to his seat, sadly rubbing his side. Uncle Arnold did, it is true, ask if he had hurt himself, but I suspect that there was more of sarcasm than of sympathy in the question!

April 3, 1939

Today I expected Schoenberg to murder me, no less, because I actually had the nerve to ask him to make suggestions about the interpretation of Op. 11 no. 2. But nothing of the sort happened; he didn't hear me play the piece (and a good thing, too!), but he was quite willing to discuss it at some length with us. As Mr. Stein plays it, and also the terribly difficult No. 3, he, too, was able to ask questions about their interpretation, so the session turned out to be a very interesting one. Of course, there had to be a joke at my expense. When I gathered up my courage and feebly quavered, "You know, Professor Schoenberg, I'm working on this piece and I would appreciate it ever so much if you would give me suggestions as to how it should be played," he answered, rocking with laughter the while, "Why, play it as it is written, of course!" There is a recording of it in existence, by a Catherine somebody-or-other,[23] but it, along with the *Verklärte Nacht* and the *Hanging Gardens*, is an illegitimate recording, and he thinks of suing the company (which one, I don't know).[24]

Another interesting matter, this time a question which came up in Form and Analysis. At the beginning of the class, he read us a letter from some music educator (the type is too well-known, or notorious, to need comment), asking whether he would approve the project of counting the proportions of chords in a long representative list of 18th and 19th century music, to determine which chords appeared most frequently. Well, of course, all this sort of thing, in music as in anything else, is the most arrant foolishness, and Schoenberg saw through it right away. After having read the letter, he turned to us and asked, "Well what do *you* think would be the most frequently used chords—of course, this term is nonsense, it should be *degrees*?" Naturally enough, the whole class chorused in unison, "Tonic, dominant, and subdominant!" Whereupon, assuming his most cherubic smile, he said, "You see, at once one knows it! What

[23]Katherine Ruth Heyman (1887-1944), American pianist, specialist in the music of Scriabin, and close friend of Ezra Pound. She wrote *The Relation of Ultramodern to Archaic Music* (Boston, Small, Maynard and Company, 1921). Her recording of Op. 11, no. 2 was paired with Scriabin's *Flammes sombres* (Friends of Recorded Music 9).

[24]The offending recordings were by Victor (Ormandy conducting the Minneapolis Symphony) and Columbia (Erica Storm singing songs 5 and 12 of the cycle, with Mosco Carner, biographer of Puccini and Berg, at the piano). Cf. David Hall, *The Record Book* (New York, Smith and Durrell, 1940), pp. 1075-76.

need is there to research to find out such a thing?" Then he read us his own reply; its idiom may have been a little halting, but it certainly was scathing!

April 9, 1939

We had an Easter treat of sorts. We walked down to San Vicente Boulevard to wait for streetcars. This sounds rather eccentric, but it had a very practical purpose. I am thinking of asking Schoenberg for an appointment some time this week to discuss the possibility of my having an assistantship next year. Of course, the appointment could be at the University, which would be much more convenient for me, but he never is in his office except from 2:30 to 3 on Tuesday and Thursday, and usually arrives a good twenty minutes late at that! Besides, when I have asked him for appointments before, he has always inquired rather wistfully, "At home?", so I assume he would rather have it there. Hence, our peculiar activities on San Vicente were natural enough. We had found by referring to the map and city guide that San Vicente and Burlingame was the nearest one could get to Rockingham Drive, so our problem was to find out how often the streetcars went on San Vicente. It seems that they come every half hour, if the schedule is always reliable. In any case, I have a pretty good idea that when I get out there he will probably be playing tennis or something, having failed to grasp the idea that I wanted to consult him about an important matter, or having completely forgotten my existence . . .

I finished *Harmonielehre* this afternoon. *Mon Dieu, quel livre!* I think I have never read anything that expressed so completely the personality as well as the ideals and concepts of its author. I certainly intend to tell him what I think of it when I see him again tomorrow!

April 10, 1939

I didn't get to ask Schoenberg for the appointment this afternoon, as he was unaccountably elusive after each class, and especially so at four o'clock. I know perfectly well that he saw me and realized that I was trying to catch his eye, but I guess he just decided to have a little fun with me. He sailed out of the classroom and down the hall (wearing, of course, his most seraphic smile) without giving the slightest sign that he even recognized my existence. I even followed him all the way downstairs and out to the car, giving vent to an occasional discreet cough, but did he look around once? No! Then, when I was safely ensconced in Miss R.'s car on the way home (she gave me a lift as far as Leconte) and he was driving right behind, he could afford to beam at me and wave ostentatiously, when he saw me looking out of the back window! Now what can you do with a man like that? I think the only course is for me to lie in ambush near his office, then, when he enters or exits, spring forth with wild animal cries and grab him by the coattail. Seriously, though, I didn't try too hard to stop him, because he had told us in the Special Studies class that his little boy had been terribly ill with pneumonia all last week (but is better now), and I simply didn't have the heart to bother him about my affairs, which may be all-important to me but, I suppose, can't mean much to him. I may speak to him tomorrow, however. It all depends on what opportunities I get.

Special Studies was a real treat today. He had brought his *Drei Satiren* and the Third String Quartet to show us. The quartet I'd seen before, but the Satires were new to me, and I guess to all the others. And oh, how clever they are! The one in which the "modernists" who smash all over the piano and then end up with a banal V-I are satirized is a real treat, as is the "kleiner Modernsky," which is an out-and-out takeoff on Stravinsky and his *Rhabarberkontrapunkt*.[25] Schoenberg told us that these works were written after a long silence as a reprisal against the attacks made on him by Stravinsky, Casella and others. "Of course," he said, "none of the great men would attack me; only these unimportant people like Stravinsky!" (I *like* Stravinsky's works, but let that pass.) Then he continued, in his best Napoleonic vein, "Long time I was silent. Then, one day, I lift up my hand (majestically suiting the action to the word), I *biff in*—and never more do these people bother me!" Well, he certainly did *biff in*! After the satires comes a series of canons invertible in all possible directions, to show what *real*

[25]Extras in the German theatre would yell "Rhabarber" (rhubarb) over and over again to give the effect of a large crowd. "Rhabarber counterpoint" is equally noisy, busy, and empty of content.

counterpoint is. Among them is one dedicated to Shaw on his 70th birthday. Shaw never acknowledged it and naturally Schoenberg was no little cut up about that. While playing them, he would keep saying, "This here very smooth, yes?" or, "Now comes a fugue; and this fugue, it is not bad." He certainly must have been born with an almost divine self-confidence!

April 11, 1939

Stein said that Constant Lambert[26] has written that Schoenberg *has no sense of humor*!! To which Schoenberg replied, "If I were you, I would not suggest to him that he expose himself to my sense of humor, because I do not think he would like!" I don't think so either.

Schoenberg never mentioned Bruno Walter's recent broadcast of Mahler's First. I'd pictured him with his ear glued to the radio in an attitude of rapt devotion; I'd thought he'd ask us who'd heard it and expect us all to burst forth in paeans of praise. Of course, Mahler may have been a great man personally, and we know he befriended Schoenberg in many ways, but I see no reason why a personal admiration for him should have to extend to his work. Still, that's but human nature . . .

April 13, 1939

The Advanced Composition class was unusually rewarding today, as Schoenberg spent practically all the time in analyzing, first, part of his *Verklärte Nacht* (near the end where a modulation is made from D flat to D, with the use of many sequences), and then the first movement of the First String Quartet. My, how good it made him feel to have a chance to analyze his immortal works for the students.

---

[26]The British conductor and composer (1905-51), proclaimed: "An atonal comic opera is a chimerical thought . . . He (Schoenberg) has the lack of humour of the diabolist . . ." Constant Lambert, "Schönberg and Official Revolution," *Music Ho! A Study of Music in Decline* (London, Faber & Faber, 1934), pp. 204-205.

When he was having the recording of *Verklärte Nacht* played, and when the climax came, he impulsively rushed over to the piano and started to pound out the chords (which were, fortunately, in tune), and to sing or scream at the very top of his voice! Mercy, what a noise! All the time he was analyzing the Quartet, he would keep making such remarks as these: "Now, is this not wonderful, this structural unity? Is not this counterpoint rather remarkable?—no, I will not say *rather*, but *very*. But this is not yet the best—better things yet are coming, wonderful things!" In any other person, such conceit would be merely obnoxious, but in him it is really endearing; at least I find it so.

Footnote to history: I almost forgot to record Schoenberg's *wonderful* costume! It consisted of a peach-colored shirt, a green tie with white polka-dots, a knit belt of the most vivid purple with a large and ostentatious gold buckle, and an unbelievably loud gray suit with lots of black and brown stripes. All he needed was flowers in his hair and plaid socks to be a *real* picture!

April 14, 1939

Schoenberg was full of plans for the publication of the *Harmonielehre*. It seems that he's going to have to put it out himself, as he hasn't found a publisher for it yet. Many publishers expressed great enthusiasm at first, but later were unable to take it, probably because they wrote to teachers to find out if use would be made of it and received unfavorable answers. Even the cheapest possible edition would cost him at least a thousand dollars to put out, and he doesn't want to do it unless he can be absolutely sure of covering the costs. He knows that this University would use it, and also (through friends of his at those places) USC, Pomona, and the junior college, but that wouldn't be enough. If he can get fifty sales apiece at ten universities (two dollars per copy; it would have to be abridged, of course), that would cover the costs; and he wants to be sure of at least that before taking any action. Once certain, the publication could be undertaken at once and completed in four weeks. It could be photographed from typed pages (the musical examples handwritten) and bound in spirals. Now, in ascertaining what universities he could depend on, I can be a definite help, for I can write to Ellinwood at Michigan State College and Stahl at University of Michigan, and sound them out. Or, I can write to Papa and ask him to speak to E. about it. And, for a sales talk, all I'd need would be a literal transcription of Uncle Arnold's remarks about his master-piece! Only today, he said that all of his pupils who had studied it harmonized *"like gods!!"*, and continued, "Not to learn from this wonderful book of mine would require a special kind of lack of talent! Why, even one who was deaf, dumb and blind could under-stand it, it is so wonderfully logical!" Oh, and he was still carrying on about *Verklärte Nacht*. Referring to the Kolisch performance of the sextet version at Denver two years ago, he said, or, rather, breathed ecstatically, "Oh, how noble this sounds, how pure, how wonderful!"

He did not spare us his sharp tongue in first-year composition, where he looked at our variations for the first time. Naturally enough, I got my share. I had left out quite a few accidentals and was having to stop poor Stein every other second to tell him that he was playing wrong. "Well," commented Schoenberg, "I think you should write commentary on this piece for the benefit of the unfor-tunate player, yes?" One of the girls had chosen for a theme, of all things, that of the 32 Variations! When Stein had finished playing it, Schoenberg beamed in his usual saintly fashion and said, "This good, yes?" Fortunately, he liked my variation and theme; as long as he confines his sarcasm to the sharps and flats, I really don't care much.

April 17, 1939

I certainly came to Schoenberg's classes in fear and trembling today. The reason? Simply that I'd had the unheard-of, phenomenal nerve to actually dare to show him some of my real music for a change. I simply decided that, if I wanted to learn anything about song-writing, I'd have to show him some songs. Anyway, he'd have to become aware of my own style sooner or later. So, I dusted off my fresh copies of *With Rue* [*With Rue My Heart is Laden*, A.E. Housman] and *Alysoun*, made motions at practising them, and packed them up with my Adagio and Variations to take to Special Studies. I was afraid that he might develop a slight case of spon-taneous combustion on hearing them (especially in view of my

terrible singing voice; the way I gently slither off the high F sharp in
Rue is really worth hearing!)—but, wonder of wonders, he actually
liked them! Naturally, he found things in the construction that were
faulty: the interludes, for example, were a little too long, and not
sufficiently connected with the preceding motives, but he felt that
they conveyed the spirit of the words well, and that they really had
"something in," which is more than he, or even I, can say for my
more formal academic efforts. This venture succeeded so well that I
plan to get at the long-deferred work of revising the second string
quartet, and show that to him by easy stages. Incidentally, everyone
else in the class enjoyed the songs too. M. thinks that the students
ought to get up a concert of my works. Not such a bad idea! I would
be really delighted if I could get the first quartet decently performed, as I have never once heard it done.

April 18, 1939

Summer heat was here in terrifying earnest this afternoon, unfortunately for poor dear Uncle Arnold, whose problem was made
worse by his suppressed desire to go and see the afternoon showing
of *La Grande Illusion.* [27] For a full ten minutes he stood in front of
the class debating with himself as to whether or not he ought to dismiss us and go. He asked those of us who had seen it if it was really
good (of course, we all replied in the affirmative!) and then made
wistful little motions towards the door. Everyone encouraged him
to go, as we could all see that the heat had exhausted him greatly
and that he was actually in no condition to be teaching. In fact, he
admitted that he was worn out and thought of leaving early, but he
finally won the battle with himself by deciding that we needed him
so much that it would be wrong for him to leave us. The whole thing
was utterly pathetic! All during the two hours, he was so tired that
he had to be continually stopping and sitting down to rest for a few
minutes at a time. But that didn't keep him from sharpening his
tongue on me; not at all! He wanted to ask me to write an analysis
of one of his themes (for the modal 3-voice fugues) on the board, so
he bowed deeply in my direction, and, with his most saintly smile,

[27]Jean Renoir's classic anti-war film (1938).

requested, "Miss Newlin, will you now write this example on the board, to make up to us *for all your many shortcomings?*" I suppose I really should have retorted, "*What* shortcomings, Professor?", but, when stepped on by Schoenberg, one does not attempt to get up. One simply tries to laugh it off the best one can. If that had been all, it wouldn't have been so bad, but that was *not* all. As he was finishing up the pedal-point of his three-voice fugue, M. called to his attention that he'd left out a sharp. He corrected the mistake, and then, with another bow in my direction, exclaimed, "Please excuse me, *Miss Newlin!*" Was ever an innocent person more unjustly persecuted?

April 20, 1939

I finally got to make my important appointment with Schoenberg! Since I wasn't feeling well, I'd stayed away from the first-year counterpoint class at two, but I arrived, on purpose, a little early for the three o'clock class so that I might have a chance to rest a little before starting in. Under the circumstances, I thought I might as well go to S.'s office to see if he were there, and sure enough, he was! He seemed pleased to see me, and readily gave me the appointment for Tuesday at 2:30. *Of course*, he says I'll have to call him up in the morning so that he won't forget it—quite a nuisance, as it's quite impossible to get him on the telephone, but it's better than having him breezing in twenty minutes late as he did last time! Even in such serious matters, he has to make fun of me. He happened to ask me if I'd heard from Miss Paschal yet about the money, and I replied that I hadn't—whereupon he said, "Well, if you do not hear from her, you write to her and tell her that she must send back my letter of recommendation at once. I will not let her have my valuable autograph if she does not do something for you!" A very touching demonstration, to my mind. I only hope he's favorably disposed on the day of the interview!

The composition class had the special treat of hearing the records of most of the 1st Quartet. Aside from a little trouble with the phonographs, which played flat or sharp but never quite right, it went very well, and is really beautifully played. Like most of his other work, it alternates passages of the most beautiful clarity with ones which, as he admits himself, are unintelligible without following the score. The Adagio is especially beautiful, as I had expected from the part on which I wrote those famous variations. Of all things, I'd arranged it wrongly for string quartet! I had given the 1st violin the melody, and it belongs in the viola! Well, how could I know? Naturally, the one who got the most pleasure from the afternoon's proceedings was Uncle Arnold. I'll never forget him perched on the desk as near to the phonograph as he could get, his head cocked appreciatively to one side for all the world like an alert robin or a Scottie! I think he was really relieved that I didn't show him my Scherzo (I put it off on the grounds of still being too weak to go through with it properly, which is quite true), though he seemed to be rather worried by my assertion that I'd been sick, as all during the two hours he periodically hovered over me in an anxious, avuncular manner. I suppose he thinks I'm heading for a complete nervous breakdown. He would!

April 21, 1939

Again today I missed out on showing the Scherzo to Schoenberg, which I had planned to do in the Special Studies class, because he had brought some of his earlier songs to show us and of course had no time or inclination to think of anything else. The songs are beautiful, I think, but oh dear, *such* words: Dehmel,[28] Keller,[29] all the neo-romantics. Not a first-rate one among the lot. But in any case, I was very glad to have a chance to see them, as I know I have

---

[28]Richard Dehmel (1863-1920), whose poem *Verklärte Nacht* was the inspiration for Schoenberg's string sextet. Schoenberg's early songs to his texts are *Erwartung* (Op. 2, no. 1), *Schenk mir deinen goldnen Kamm* (Op. 2, no. 2), *Erhebung* (Op. 2, no. 3), *Warnung* (Op. 3, no. 3) and *Alles* (Op. 6, no. 2).

[29]Gottfried Keller (1819-90), Swiss writer whose tale *Die Leute von Seldwyla* was the basis for Delius' opera *A Village Romeo and Juliet*. Schoenberg's early songs to his texts are *Die Aufgeregten* (Op. 3, no. 2), *Geübtes Herz* (Op. 3, no. 5), and *Ghasel* (Op. 6, no. 5).

In retrospect, I seem to have been unduly harsh on Dehmel's and Keller's poetry. In fact, their lyrics are among the better ones which Schoenberg chose for his songs.

a lot to learn about song-writing. As usual with him, he was over-flowing with praise of his own efforts. True enough, he rather be-littled one of the songs: "This one," he said, "I do not know so well—I wrote it one day very fast, because I had not enough music paper to finish my string quartet and I had to have something to do while I was waiting to get some!" But then he continued, to say that it was good too—"Of course!" But the thing that amused me most occurred near the end of the hour, after he'd said that he wouldn't have time to finish showing us all the songs today, but would do so Monday. Last time, he'd said that he would bring for analysis the songs of Brahms and Schubert—very cunningly avoiding his own name so that one of us would bring it up, as in fact we did. But did he have a single song by anyone but himself this time? No! Well, anyway, at the end of the hour, B. asked, "Weren't you plan-ning to analyze some of Brahms' and Schubert's songs next time, too?" Schoenberg simply put his head to one side, assumed a most quizzical expression, and, with that inflection peculiar to him, remarked, "*Brahms? Schubert?*" Nothing else was said—or needed!

I think he would have liked to get my appointment over with today, as, when he arrived at Special Studies early and found me there, he started to ask me about the Paschal business; but just then the rest of the class filed in, so he had to stop. Well, I wish I had it over with, too. I'm so afraid that he may manage to get sick or something over the weekend! In fact, he laid claim to being a "leetle tired" today, but this, it seemed, was because he had been out until two the night before and had gotten up at seven for some unknown reason—probably to play tennis. Well, I hope he keeps himself in trim till Tuesday, at least! In any case, he seems to be interested and sympathetically disposed, and I hope that that augurs some success on my part.

April 25, 1939

And now I finally have the load of worries about the assistantship off my mind! I certainly went for my appointment this afternoon in fear and trembling, even though I'd called to remind him of it in the morning, I was afraid he mightn't show up, and if he *did*, I was pretty well terrified at the thought of what he might say. Well, it all went off quite well. He said I couldn't be an assistant as I was too young and hadn't enough experience, but he was perfectly willing for me to be a reader. And as for the private lessons, he thinks that, if I come to the new courses that he'll be giving next year and to some of the old ones again, I'll get all I need without lessons. Of course I think that both classes and lessons would be advantageous, but then, that's up to him. He was much disturbed at my not having heard from Miss Paschal; in fact, he said he had a good mind to charge her $100 for his personal letter, and he's perfectly capable of doing it. He wants to try to get help for me himself, but believes that it's pretty hopeless to get the full sum of $2000. In fact, the amount rather horrified him; I suppose he thinks that we live like queens, but I tried to disillusion him, and I hope I succeeded. "But, Miss Newlin," he kept exclaiming, "*professors* get $2000 a year! Families of *four* live on that, I *know*!" Of course he realized that the crux of the problem is, in part, the expense of maintaining an establishment *à deux* here, and feels that it would be the best thing if I could live in some family, which I could do on $50 (?) or so. In fact, he even promised to investigate the matter for me. . . . It's very sweet of him to take the matter so to heart, and I hope that any efforts he makes will be successful. Incidentally, talking to me for a half-hour must have exhausted him terribly, for he was a good twenty minutes late to class. He spent most of the time today discussing double counterpoint.

April 27, 1939

Oh dear, oh dear, but our beloved Uncle Arnold was in a state today! I don't know just what was the matter with him. He didn't look very well, with a bad color and swollen eyes, but whatever it was, he was surely taking it out on *me*! I had to jump off on the wrong foot by coming some 10 minutes late. . . . He said not a word to that, but I guess he was just biding his time, for when I came to present my work the blows fell like hailstones. First off, I said that it would be better if I'd play the upper two parts and Stein the lower two. Now, always heretofore I've done the whole thing myself, usually pretty creditably, and could have done it today, but the piece is rather difficult and I simply thought it would sound better if done four-hands. But did Schoenberg take all this into account? Not for a minute! He just made explosive noises, and snorted, "Why you not practise these things so you can play? Why you not make your own piano score, at least? Look at all the others who do this, why not you too?" . . . I said nothing, and started to play, about a half-beat ahead of Stein. First thing on the page was a juicy pair of parallel fifths. Naturally, S. observed these right away, and asked if they were intentional. When I replied that they were, he retorted, "But why? Why you do these things? This only outlet of one who does not know to do better! It is so terrible that now everyone thinks he can do everything! When you will be Beethoven you can do these things. Not otherwise!" This was getting a bit too hot for human consumption, but I held my tongue and continued, now 3/4 of a beat ahead of Mr. Stein. This kept up for some five minutes more, when Schoenberg finally shouted, "No more, Miss Newlin, no more! It is no use, I cannot help you! I cannot read one word of these hieroglyphics!" And this, if you please, about my *copy*. He didn't even get down to the original manuscript! "I absolutely *refuse*," he went on, "to look at your music so long as it is like this. It is too much you ask of me, *too* much! You *must* once write a clear manuscript. Why you not write like Miss Temple, hm?" (A neat, but untalented student) This last was really the unkindest cut of all, but I kept holding my tongue as before, except that I was now biting it.

But I got some recompense for all this. During the second hour he showed us all the *wonderful finesses* of his Suite in Ancient Style. [30] Now, it happens that this edition is photographed from his own manuscript—a first draft, too—and not the least reason for his showing it to us was to give me an example of really beautiful handwriting. Well, after about five minutes he came to a passage which absolutely puzzled him. First he'd correct one note, then another; he'd play it over and over again, always muttering, "There must be

[30]The *Suite for String Orchestra*, Schoenberg's first American work, a tonal composition using old dance forms. Schirmer issued the beautiful facsimile score in 1935 and Klemperer premièred the work in Los Angeles on May 18 of that year.

something wrong," but as he literally didn't remember his own theme, he couldn't place the mistake in copying! Of course we all exchanged amused looks at this little episode, and Mr. Stein even ventured to remark, "Tut, tut!" For a moment, Schoenberg was really quite discomfited—this is the second time I've seen him so—but finally recovered himself with a jerk and said, "Well, at least I do not make two or three mistakes in a measure!" Anyhow, that brief period of confusion was well worth what I had to go through before! For the nonce I'm almost angry with him (fingers crossed, naturally), but I'll have forgotten about it tomorrow, so will he, and things will be as jolly as ever. Or will they, with the two songs (*Early Autumn*'s wilder, even, than I remembered it) and the viola variations confronting him?

April 28, 1939

Fortunately, Schoenberg was in much better humor today than yesterday, and was looking better, too. He didn't hear the viola variations (I handed them in and he promised that he'd look at them), and I didn't show him *Early Autumn* [Hsu Hun] because I want to recopy it, but I did play and sing *Let It be Forgotten* [Sara Teasdale] for him. Evidently he thought there was "something in," though he found the harmony not sufficiently related to any degrees, and didn't like the suddenness of the ending. "You see," he criticized, "you suddenly say, 'Enough—I will write no more!' and stop. Perhaps the listeners would have liked to stop some time before, but as they are not composing the piece there is no help for them, unfortunately!" Also he thought the style of accompaniment, particularly in those places where the left hand plays stretches of a tenth or more, rather unpianistic. "Of course this is not unplayable," he explained—"Why see, I have only a small hand and I can play this easily! (Pounding away happily) Can the others do this, hm?" His pride in his own accomplishments, even little ones like this, is certainly childish. But of epic simplicity and grandeur was his wonderful speech to M., who, as usual, hadn't done any work and was trying to excuse himself. Schoenberg interrupted him impatiently: "You will be so sorry for this in few years, *so* sorry! I am sixty-five now; I will only teach for five more years, if I can—and then all will be over, there will be nothing any more! And so you will have lost this wonderful opportunity!"

🖉 *May 1, 1939*

This surely wasn't much of a May Day; weather mostly dismal and foggy. To top things off, Schoenberg is sick again: the flu, with what Stein darkly describes as complications. Evidently he's planning to come back tomorrow if he can stand on his feet. I suppose he wants to enjoy the pleasure that our company gives him, but it's a shame he has to be afflicted this way.

🖉 *May 2, 1939*

Schoenberg was back again this afternoon, but certainly should not have been, as, though his manner was outwardly as carefree as ever, he was really inconceivably feeble. In the four-voice fugue in double counterpoint which he began for us, he made one mistake after the other, which ordinarily he never does. First he'd write a first theme with too many 8th notes, then he'd forget to make it in double counterpoint, and so on and so on *ad infinitum*. Worse yet, it seemed as if he dropped everything he touched. He could hardly hold his pencil in his hand, and, as for adjusting the writing-easel properly, why, he was simply helpless! After making a few ineffectual efforts to fix it, and dropping it on his foot a couple of times, he finally had to call on M. for help: "Will you once teach me how you do this? I cannot do it, I just cannot!" The whole thing was indescribably pathetic, and I could see that everyone was deeply affected by it. His cough, too, seems much worse than it has been. . .

🖉 *May 4, 1939*

As I'd expected, Schoenberg didn't even attempt to look at our work today. A cursory glance at Miss Temple's current masterpiece got him shuttled off to the discussion of chorale harmonization in the *Harmonielehre*. He spent all the rest of the two hours talking, first of that, then of his conception of opera. I was much amused by one point which came out in the latter. He believes, sensibly enough, that in composing music for the theatre one should have most vividly in mind at all times the exact scenic situation, the length of time each action will take, etc. Well, it seems that in one of his operas (he didn't mention which, but I believe it's *Von Heute auf Morgen*) a woman has to step behind a screen and change her clothes, during which time the stage is empty. "I absolutely refuse," he exclaimed, "to write in such a place one measure more than is necessary!" So what does he do but practise taking his clothes off two or three times to see how long it takes him?[31] And evidently it's the same with all his other operatic incidents; he mentioned, in particular, the scene in *Die Glückliche Hand* where somebody chases somebody with a bloody sword.[32] The image thus conjured up of his madly tearing around with a kitchen-knife after the nearest bystander in an attempt to find out how long the scene takes, is an irresistible one. ... Some wit should have asked him if he'd tried out all the action of *Verklärte Nacht* to see how long *that* took? I don't doubt for a moment that he did, but probably not in the spirit of disinterested scientific research. Ahem!

What he says about his method of songwriting I also find most interesting. Some of it (the idea, for example, that a composer may sometimes get the entire feeling of a poem from the first few lines and work from that alone)[33] I'd read previously, but most not. He says that his usual procedure has always been to repeat the poem over and over again until he gets a definite sensation of the rises and falls of the speech melody, which he then applies to the vocal melody. (He didn't say, but I take it this is the germ of the idea of *Sprechgesang*.) The melody and harmony are only details of the same concept, and not at all separate ideas. Well, that's not surprising, but I think it's a good idea to record these things. Oh yes; he made a wonderful remark about his themes! He had just said that getting good themes that have a logical connection is in part a matter of luck, and Stein asked him, out of curiosity, if he had ever been absolutely unable to find two themes that fit. "No," he answered after a very, very little reflection," I don't think, I *don't* think. My

[31]Obviously he overlooked the difference in time between male and female clothes-changing!

[32]The bloody sword appears in scene 3. Schoenberg's protagonist, The Man, climbs from a ravine carrying it (but not chasing anyone) as the celebrated light-show of this scene is foreshadowed.

[33]See his essay "The Relationship to the Text" (first published in *Der Blaue Reiter*, 1913), which I translated for *Style and Idea*.

themes, they *always* fit!" . . . His cough seems better but he still looks extremely feeble, and is full of nervous twitchings. He shook so when he was trying to cut the pages of the paperbound edition of *Harmonielehre* that I was terribly afraid he might cut himself, but fortunately he got through without accident. Really, though, he's in no condition to be teaching at all. I suppose that the reason for his gathering us about him and talking about himself was that he was feeling simply too tired to do anything else. It's a shame, but what can we do about it?

May 5, 1939

Schoenberg seems to be looking and feeling much better today than yesterday. I had *Early Autumn* and the beginning of a rondo to show him, but he didn't get around to looking at either, as he spent most of the time in Special Studies analyzing the last movement of the Mozart G-major Quartet [K. 387]. During first-year composition he showed us how the transition to the second theme of a rondo should contrast with the first theme. In explaining the modulation which occurs in the transition, he remarked, "I do not think you will try to go from F major to X minor; I would not go any further as *O* minor, then that will be O.K.!" How proud of himself he always is when he's managed to work some of his beautiful American vernacular into his conversation! Now I do hope, bless his dear heart, that he stays well over the vacation and doesn't contract any new ailments. Hilsberg[34] happened to say today that when Uncle Arnold isn't playing tennis on account of bad weather, he's playing ping-pong. If he has no more sense than that at sixty-four, where will he get any?

May 8, 1939

At long last Schoenberg looked at *Early Autumn* in the Special Studies class. He wasn't able to talk about it at much length, as he

---

[34]The Polish pianist Ignace Hilsberg, my piano teacher from 1938 to 1941.

remembered only in the last five minutes that we might possibly have something to show him, but nevertheless he had time to touch on all the important points. His only really decisive criticism was that the style of the accompaniment was not sufficiently pianistic; also, he thought that perhaps it was not advisable to place the main melody in the piano and allow the voice to take a subordinate semi-contrapuntal part, as it does in the second half. But that is only a suggestion on his part. I had the beginning of a rondo for him to look at, too (this in the first-year composition), but when he got to my paper, which was about in the middle of the heap, he simply handed it to me with the remark, "Well, Miss Newlin, I think yours will be all right—at least I hope it will!" And he looked at everybody else's! Actually, I don't blame him; I've written rondos before; he realizes that I know the form without any special need of further help with it, and, besides, he is terribly worn out these days. "You know," he complained to us in Special Studies, "ever since I gave up smoking, I am tired all the time!" That means *ever since he had his heart attack*, and I'm bound to say I don't like the look of it, not a bit! Though he didn't seem quite as broken-down today as he has the past week, he still gets all his words mixed up from time to time, and is always dropping things; and I keep noticing this new little tendency to save himself wherever he can, as in the case of his not looking at my rondo. It is absolutely right for him to do this, and if he'd do it more, so much the better it would be for him! It is all a terrible worry to us. . . .

In spite of his still-failing health, he's as witty as ever, particularly in Form and Analysis. To a student who was delivering a rather long-winded discourse on something or other, he said, "Oh, not so many words! Say it with flowers, rather!" I was most amused by his class-conscious distinction between those of us who claimed that a certain part of the 2nd movement of Op. 13 [Beethoven] was a "b" section and those who insisted it was a "B" section. To the partisans of the capital B, he said, "Now, will two representatives from the capitalists step to the board, please?" and two did. But the small "b" supporters were more bashful, and after a brief wait he remarked, "So, so, will no one come forward for the proletariat?" Suffice it to say that the representatives of the underdog got the upper hand and I, true to my liberal upbringing, was one of their supporters!

🎵 *May 9, 1939*

Nothing especially exciting happened in Double Counterpoint this afternoon. Schoenberg arrived nearly an hour late—just too tired to show up sooner, I suppose. He looked as if they'd put him out and forgotten to bury him, and seemed in quite a state of mental confusion, judging by the mistakes he insisted on making. But he was in time to look at most of my fugue. The points he criticized were just what I expected, namely, the places where I had accumulated too many cross-related tones, etc., for comfort. They're not wrong, but are awkward, and I was glad to have him show me less uncomfortable ways of getting out of them. Also he continued writing the four-voice fugue. We are to start one for the next time; it is to be finished by the first of June and will constitute the major part of our final examination.

🎵 *May 11, 1939*

Well, Schoenberg surely didn't spare me, or himself, today. I brought the first part of that Scherzo, which I suppose I should have known better than to do, but then I thought it good and rather wanted his opinion on it. WHICH I GOT! He kept pretty quiet while I was playing, but after I'd finished he gave me a fishlike look and demanded, "Why you write octet?" Frankly, I didn't get it, not even when he repeated the question a second time; but just as I opened my mouth to ask what on earth he was talking about, he cut in, "Yes, it is octet; four to play, and four to turn pages, because there are no posies [pauses] in; that makes octet, yes?" I replied, somewhat feebly, that I supposed it did. But from then on there was no opportunity for me to get in a word, the *bons mots* came so thick and fast. First, the tempo marking: "So, I see this is *Presto con fuoco!*" (I'd played it at about the tempo of a funeral march.) "*Fuoco* means fire, you know. Let us call the fire-engines, at once!" Then, the harmonies, which he thought too difficult for me to manage and inappropriate to the "leetle poor" melody: "You know, such a harmony is like Woostie [Worcestershire] sauce. One can put it on fish, one can put it on beefsteak, one can even put it on angel food cake. But this would not be so good, I don't think!" One measure after another he picked to pieces, and after each he said: "But suppose this is right. It is not right, but let us forget about it. But then we go on, and then what, what do we see?" New horrors in every note: "For you to try to do this is as if you would learn to dive by jumping out this window!" And then, of all times, some girl came barging into the classroom by mistake, bouncing out, visibly startled, as soon as she realized her error. With a puzzled smile, *le cher maître* remarked, "Why do they always look so scared when they see me? Is it because I look *so* terrible, hm?" I exercised laudable restraint and passed right over this lovely opportunity to tell him what was what. I don't blame him for having been rather cross today, anyway, as he has a terrible boil on his nose, and God knows I realize just how miserable that particular affliction can make a person.

His little daughter was waltzing all over the walk at 5 o'clock, showing off what appeared to be a brand-new white hat, coat, and dress. Oh, but he must be proud of her! I suppose that she is going with him to the Pro Arte concert at Pasadena this evening. He said he intended to be there.

May 16, 1939

Today I had thought that Schoenberg would look at the beginnings of our four-voice fugues, but instead he continued the writing of his model, which was really more advantageous to us. He had his usual troubles with adjusting the easel, and, in connection with this, got off a good joke on poor M. (whose playing is not improving). M., he remarked to the class at large, "is the only man in the world who can fix this thing; in this way he is the most valuable contrapuntal assistant!" I was terribly amused by Uncle Arnold's attempt to inject a little classical learning into his feast of reason. Having come to a tough spot in his fugue, he said, "And now I am between Scylla and Charybdis; you know, those little animals which bite!"

May 18, 1939

Schoenberg didn't look at my Adagio today, or, rather, I didn't let him, for I hadn't finished it and I wanted to make a clean copy of it in any case. However, I don't suppose he would have got around to it even if I had wanted to show it to him, for he spent most of the afternoon discussing Brahms' B-flat major and G-major Sextets. I was glad to hear his analysis of them, as they are hardly ever played. Also, he made some remarks on the A-minor Quartet; I was particularly amused by his comments on the string writing in it. "Now here," he said, referring to the opening broken-chord passages for viola, "this is just *awful* for viola, just *awful*! But (pointing to a place a few measures further on) here it already better; here it is pretty good, yes?"—and so on and so on in the same complacent vein.

Stein's plans and mine for having the classes jointly present him with a gift at his home, in a sort of surprise-party affair if possible, got a little further this afternoon through our taking the matter up with Strang.[35] He thinks it a fine idea, but doesn't know exactly what to give him. He told us that once he bought him a most expensive mechanical pencil with all sorts of contrivances for writing music (it must have cost six or seven dollars) which he couldn't work at all and had completely destroyed in a month. Just at this point Uncle Arnold interrupted, so we had to stop, but I think we can make the announcement in classes tomorrow.

May 19, 1939

At last I was able to get Schoenberg to look at my Rondo in Special Studies today; he thought it all right, but not very inspired. I more than agree with him, so I'll write another for Monday. He spent most of the time in this class analyzing the first and last movements of the Mozart D-major Quartet [K. 575]. I'd hoped that he would give me some help on the middle part of my other Rondo (for first-year composition) but he didn't look at it, on the grounds that I could help myself, but "others needed him more." Of course he is doubtless right in this, but all the same I would have liked to have his views on the piece. Incidentally, for the past week or so he is apparently looking and feeling much better, and hasn't been coughing nearly so much or complaining of fatigue—and this in spite of the recent fog and cold. I only hope that the fine weather doesn't tempt him to go out for tennis and lose all his gains.

---

[35]Gerald Strang (1908-   ) had been Schoenberg's assistant at UCLA since 1936; he subsequently taught at many Los Angeles-area colleges. His imaginatively-titled compositions include *Mirrororrim* (for piano) and *Compusition* (generated by computer).

Our plans for the presentation went a step further this afternoon. Stein told Abraham of them and asked him to announce them in the classes next week before Schoenberg's arrival. We're still undecided as to the details of the affair, but those will be cleared up next week—will have to be, in fact, as that's the last week of classes before examinations.

May 21, 1939

The alumni tea at which our beloved Uncle Arnold was the guest of honor was very enjoyable. Surprisingly enough, he didn't bring his wife or the children, either; he had some explanation for her absence, but I didn't hear it. Maybe he had a better time without her; not that he isn't obviously devoted to her and the family, but then the pleasure which he derives from the company of large numbers of pretty young ladies is well-known to all. As is his wont, he was in the highest good humor, all beams and bows and *Handküsse*, and dressed to the nines, even to a pair of striped trousers! He had prepared no set speech, but simply answered questions from the floor about his courses at the University, placing particular emphasis on how *con*tent (accent definitely on the first syllable) he was with his devoted pupils. After his speech, Mr. Allen got up to say a few words; he didn't come to the front of the room, but simply stood at his seat and made a few well-chosen comments on how much the students loved and respected Schoenberg. Well, the latter was so proud he could almost burst! When Allen sat down, Schoenberg was so touched that, beaming from ear to ear, he waved back at him (with that certain engaging little wave that he always gives us when leaving class) with a white handkerchief in his hand! Such a gesture, so naive yet so charming, is absolutely typical of him. Those taking ways just can't be put down on paper, and yet merely thinking about them makes one feel "all good inside." And when, after the *a cappella* choir had sung, all the lovely girls in their evening dresses mobbed him, his delight was immeasurable! It certainly is a genuine pleasure to see anyone so happy.

May 22, 1939

Well, today I collected the grand sum of 20 cents for Uncle Arnold's gift fund! This, however, represents only the collection from one class and a lot of other people in it who hadn't any money with them promised me some as soon as they could get it. Everyone to whom I've spoken thinks it a lovely idea and is sure that it'll please him no end. Now I do hope it comes off all right.

He was in the best of humor this afternoon, though I thought he looked a little feeble from his over-exertions among the pretty ladies yesterday. Unfortunately, he didn't get around to looking at any of my work, either in Special Studies or in first-year Composition, but then I suppose he will cover it before the end of the week and of the semester—at least, he'd better! Most of the time in Special Studies he spent talking about the *Gurre-Lieder*, especially the style of orchestration employed, in which he uses each instrument only as long as it expresses the mood he wants, changing color sometimes in the middle of a measure. This produces a somewhat choppy effect in the individual choirs of strings, wind and brass, but the general ensemble, he says, "sounds fine, yes, really *fine!*" However, he admits that with more experience he would have orchestrated it differently.

May 23, 1939

Today marked the last meeting of our Double Counterpoint class, and Lord, how Uncle Arnold did overflow with sentiment on such a sad occasion! He was able to hold up pretty well during the class time, while the arduous task of going on with his four-voice fugue kept his mind occupied, though he was terribly exhausted. He said he'd been standing up all morning constructing some diagrams for his composition book. But, when the time was up, he was really broken-hearted! "Just five minutes longer let me stay and work with you," he begged, "just five minutes more, if you are not too tired!" Of course, we gladly let him keep us the extra time; but all good things must come to an end, and, when he finally had to leave, he stood watching us a minute, half smiling and half crying, then quickly recovered himself and ran out the door, with a pitiful attempt at his usual debonair "Goodbye" and gay wave of the hand. Yes, he actually wept for us! The idea would be inconceivable to me if I didn't know him as I do. What a great heart he's got, for all of his weaknesses. In the last analysis, they, too, will be forgiven him—and why not, for they only add to the charm of his nature!

May 24, 1939

I collected 97 cents for the gift fund today in Stein's quiz section of Form. I didn't stay for the class, but simply made my announcement, collected my money, and departed. Of course, 97 cents is by no means all I'll get from that group; a great many of them were not there today, and most who were hadn't brought money. But I had promises aplenty for contributions this Friday, which will be soon enough if we buy the gift this weekend and present it some time next week. The total funds are now $1.41; we want to bring it up to five dollars, which we can easily do with the aid of the larger contributions that the five most advanced students will probably make.

May 25, 1939

The last class in second-year Composition this afternoon wasn't nearly as tearful an affair as I had expected, though Uncle Arnold did have considerable difficulty parting from us at the end. The poor man was obviously worn out, and no wonder, what with the broiling heat we've suffered these past two days. It was a pitiful sight to see him drag his weight along the Education Building walk as if he could hardly put one foot in front of another. I'm afraid, too, that my embryonic Adagio (the only work anybody'd done for today) did nothing to lighten the burden of his declining years. But he perked up right enough when we proceeded to the analysis of several of the Adagios of Beethoven Quartets, and even more so when showing us (complete with singing executed by himself) some of his earlier songs: *Geübtes Herz, Waldsonne*, and *Wie Georg von Frundsberg von sich selber sang*. The songs are really lovely, I think (without prejudice, naturally), and don't think for a moment that *he* doesn't realize their value. In pointing out all the wonderful details, he remarked, "Ach, these the things that really count, yes?" But he thinks that his later works are a vast improvement. I, personally, beg to disagree, but probably simply because I don't know the later things well enough. Time alone will tell. But oh, how he revelled in the Adagios! For a long time, while Mr. Stein was playing, he contented himself with conducting with one hand, singing with an expression of most perfect beatitude, and wiggling his hips back and forth in the stress of emotion. But finally he couldn't hold himself back any longer. "Please," he pleaded with Mr. Stein, "let me play the 'cello part. I like to so much!" Of course, Stein had to let him have his way, but the results certainly did Beethoven no good. Uncle Arnold, whose piano playing is really pathetic, but affecting withal because he is so sincere about being unable to do it, was constantly a half-beat late, and finally had to give up altogether. In spite of everything, though, he still thinks he can be justly proud of the pseudo-pizzicato effect he manages to produce with great bodily effort. But, perfection of interpretation aside, it's really a treat to see him get so much pleasure out of such little things.

I picked up another quarter for *ye gifte funde*. The bulk of the contributions will come in tomorrow, after which time I'll turn the money over to Stein, Strang, or somebody else, to do the gift shopping.

May 26, 1939

I'd planned to give the money to Stein today, as we have nearly 3 dollars, but so many contributions were promised for next Monday that I decided to wait till then. Besides, Stein disappeared into the room where Klemperer and somebody else were rehearsing the two-piano version of *Kammersymphonie*, right after my last class. So I simply couldn't get hold of him. Well, next Monday is soon enough, and the presentation can surely take place some time in the coming week. Mr. Stein and I, in any case, will have an easy entrée into his home during the time of examinations, for he wants both of us to write a rondo or a sonata form for Special Studies (I may write in my own style so long as I don't go harmonically beyond, say, Schoenberg's earlier works or those of R. Strauss) and to come to him with our sketches at various times before the term ends. A fine idea, I say!

Special Studies, incidentally, was most interesting today, as it always is. He got sidetracked into a lengthy discussion of Hindemith. He concedes Hindemith's talent and facility, but thinks that many of his experiments—for example, the complete divorcement of theatre music from what is happening on the stage—are simply *pour épater le bourgeois*. And besides, it seems, he has too much self-confidence (quite a criticism, coming from Schoenberg!) Schoenberg especially disapproves of Hindemith's and Stravinsky's use of old-fashioned pseudo-contrapuntal rhythmic figures with "modernistic" intervals. It happened that B. had a copy of Stravinsky's Piano Sonata with him, so Stein played most of it then and there. Schoenberg thought little of it except for the second theme of the Adagietto. I myself wasn't much impressed, though I am terribly fond of much of Stravinsky.

May 27, 1939

Went to see *Good-Bye, Mr. Chips.*[36] Lord, what a mess! Donat has certainly sold out to the sugar-and-tears trade. But *Donald's Penguin*[37] more than made up for our sufferings. He was the cutest thing I've seen on the screen—carried himself just as Uncle Arnold does, and was just about the same size.

I started my Special Studies sonata form (a *real* piece, for once) this morning, and so far am well pleased with the theme I found. (*Not* stole, though it sounds a *leetle* bit like the first theme of Schoenberg's first Quartet.) I did not write a great deal of it, as I want his approval before plunging too far ahead.

I spent the evening writing analyses of my examination pieces and putting in order all my existing Schoenberg papers of this year, which I want to keep for sentimental reasons. And practical ones, too, for they'll be of great value if I ever have to teach.

May 29, 1939

C'est la dernière classe, n'est-ce pas? Though Schoenberg didn't weep today, he did everything but. Of course, he was tremendously affected by the great ovation, complete with cheers, which we gave

[36]This sentimental favorite after James Hilton's popular novel, with Robert Donat and Greer Garson (1939), looks much better in retrospect, especially in comparison with the ridiculous musical remake of 1969.

[37]One of Walt Disney's deathless Donald Duck cartoons.

him in the two large classes (Form & Analysis and first-year Composition). How he did radiate bows and smiles and *Handküsse* on the way out! Really, though, he felt terrible at leaving us; all during the composition class he trembled so that I thought he'd collapse any minute, and when the final bell rang he gave vent to an inexpressibly poignant "oh!" However, he was much perked up by our fine send-off, and said that he couldn't have been more satisfied with the work we'd done. I can just imagine how our gift will go to his heart! I turned over the money—nearly $3.50—to Stein this afternoon; he will pick out the gift some time this weekend. He has more or less decided on one of those fancy ashtray affairs [a chrome smoking-stand]with all the fixings, which I'm sure Uncle Arnold will greatly appreciate. Now if it only doesn't encourage him to smoke more and more and shorten his dear precious life!

June 5, 1939

I finished up nearly all of the Trio today, and copied most of what I'd written. I've pretty well decided to use this for first-year Composition, and to write a second movement to the piece for second-year Composition. As I have a good theme already in mind, this shouldn't be difficult, and I'll start on it tomorrow. Of course, Uncle Arnold *might* object to my doing an Adagio instead of a Rondo, but, as it's for a trio whereas the Rondo would have been for piano, the task, to my mind, makes up in difficulty for what it loses in length. At least, I hope he'll see it that way. When I take him the fugue this afternoon, I'll try to get his approval on the plan. As a matter of fact, I'd rather counted on seeing him today, for Stein had said that he might be going out to his home this afternoon to show him his Special Studies Rondo, and would take me along to show mine if he went, but nothing came of it. I felt too timid to go to all the trouble of getting an appointment with Schoenberg myself. Well, it can still be attended to, I hope.

Ping-pong

A vigorous game of tennis (ca. 1940)

Interlude I
Summer of '39

Now days are drawing over the world
Wafted from blue eternity,
In summer wind the time drifts by . . .
    Paul Hohenberg, Sommertage
        (set by Alban Berg)

It had been a good school year, I thought, as we travelled home from Los Angeles. I'd left Schoenberg in a good mood; the presentation of the smoking stand, just before our departure, had been a howling success! Now we took a leisurely trip back to Michigan, breaking our journey in San Francisco to enjoy the World's Fair on Treasure Island, Fisherman's Wharf, Chinatown, and other traditional delights.

The summer was a busy one. Taking a few final courses at Michigan State, I would receive my B.A. in French in August. Schoenberg was never far from my thoughts. On July 14, I learned that I would receive another thousand-dollar grant from Independent Aid for my studies. I hastened to write him so the next day, in my best German, noting in the diary:

> I simply let myself go with the German language, telling him how grateful I was for all he had done to help me get this heaven-sent favor, how I would strive to make myself worthy of it, and, stealing a leaf from his own book, how "all would be over, there would be nothing any more" if I could not come back and study with my *geliebter Meister*. The, as a climax to all this guff (it sounds marvelous in German, though), I sent him my evening-dress photograph, complete with inscription "in Erinnerung unserer Verbundenheit," in memory of the time when he told us about his students in Berlin giving him a book of their photographs and signatures for his birthday. On top of that, I asked him, wouldn't he please send me *his* photo? In justice to myself, I must state that Mamma aided me, abetted me, and egged me on; by myself, I probably wouldn't have had the nerve!

No answer came to this effusion. Schoenberg, I'd learn later, was absorbed in the completion of the Second *Kammersymphonie*, which he'd begun in 1906 (right after finishing the First) and which he was now preparing for performance by Fritz Stiedry and the New Friends of Music Orchestra.[1] On August 15, he completed his work on the first movement. Meanwhile, on July 23, some new Schoenbergian excitement promised to unfold:

> I read in the *New York Times* music section . . . an account of the disposal of the music library of Paul Bekker, the late German musicologist.[2] It seems that a

---

[1]Fritz Stiedry (1883-1968) gave many important Schoenberg performances, including the premières of *Die glückliche Hand* and of the Second *Kammersymphonie*. His wife, Erika Stiedry-Wagner, was among the most distinguished interpreters of *Pierrot Lunaire* (see Book III). The New Friends of Music, founded by the philanthropist Ira Hirschmann with his wife the pianist (a pupil of Artur Schnabel) Hortense Monath, presented the most prestigious series of chamber concerts in New York of the '30's and '40's.

[2]Not exactly a "musicologist," Paul Bekker was nonetheless an excellent writer on music whose books on *Gustav Mahlers Sinfonien* (1921) and *Die Sinfonie*

N.Y. rare book dealer, Pierre Berès, has acquired the collection and is selling it by individual items. Among these . . . are many scores and manuscripts by modern composers, including quite a few signed presentation copies—*and* one of the composers named is Schoenberg! Well, of course I had to send off a letter post-haste to Berès, asking for a complete list of their Schoenberg items . . . if there's anything I should dearly love to acquire, it would be such scores or manuscripts—now that really would be something!

Berès' answer came on July 27. I was elated:

Got a letter from Berès saying that they were sending along a first edition of *Harmonielehre* (price only $2.25; I'd heard that it cost much more), and giving a list of their other Schoenberg items. And what items! Three autograph letters to Bekker, one evidently a sort of personal confession of S.'s whole philosophy of life, for only ten dollars.[3] And all the rest of the material—three books about him, including the *Arnold Schönberg zum 50. Geburtstag*, and *Gurre-Lieder* in Berg's piano reduction, *Pelleas und Melisande*, two copies of *Erwartung*, one interleaved and annotated by Bekker himself,[4] *Die glückliche Hand, Herzgewächse*, Op. 11 . . . the *Vier Orchesterlieder, Pierrot Lunaire*, and the *Fünf Orchesterstücke*—all that

---

von Beethoven bis Mahler (1918) can still be read with profit today. As Gunilla Bergsten has pointed out in her fine study *Thomas Mann's Doctor Faustus: The Sources and Structure of the Novel* (tr. Krishna Winston, University of Chicago Press, 1969), Bekker's *Musikgeschichte als Geschichte der musikalischen Formwandlungen* (1926) was used by Mann as a prime source for the musical portions of *Doctor Faustus*. (See *The Final Decade*.)

[3]The letter, presumably transcribed from a copy kept by Schoenberg, is in Schoenberg, *Briefe*, ed. Erwin Stein (Mainz, B. Schott's Söhne, 1958), pp. 114-115 (*Letters*, tr. Eithne Wilkins and Ernst Kaiser, London, Faber & Faber, 1964, pp. 109-110). (Note: future references to *Letters* will be to English edition only.)

[4]This is the piano reduction which Bekker used and annotated in connection with *Erwartung*'s performance at Wiesbaden (January 22, 1928), where he was Intendant of the Prussian State Theatre at the time. The other copy is a full orchestral score.

for only fifteen dollars![5] I was so delighted with the prospect of having them all to gloat over that I promptly made Papa telegraph for the whole set. They'll probably come while I'm in Diamond Park, and I'm afraid to have them forwarded, but then I will have an arch-treat to look forward to when I come back. I can hardly wait to see them! *Harmonielehre* ought to come before we leave.

I was enjoying a new activity that summer: compiling a Schoenberg bibliography, the first of many I'd prepare. Many a hot summer afternoon was spent in the stacks of the Michigan State College library, poring over dusty old magazines and newspapers in search of some elusive Schoenberg news-item. The task was a purposeful one. On August 17, the bibliography was "an accomplished and admitted fact, now—and, one of these days, it's going to turn into a biography, never fear!" A cherished recollection is of the great musicologist, Curt Sachs, then with the New York Public Library's Music Division, taking time to help me track down more items for the bibliography. I was enjoying a first visit to New York under uniquely exciting circumstances. On August 20, cute, curly-headed Lorin Maazel—Bak's newest discovery, and a thoroughgoing little "operator" at the age of eight—conducted my *Cradle Song* with the Interlochen orchestra at the New York World's Fair. The novelty of an eight-year-old boy conducting a composition which had been written by an eight-year-old girl generated much publicity; some of it agreeable, some of it condescending. I didn't much care for one article which described me as an "earnest, sandy-haired youngster." Ouch! With one year of Hollywood behind me, I viewed myself in a more glamorous light! Lorin seemed to interpret my piece with special enjoyment, and the World's Fair concert was his first big step in what would be an international career.

Home from the New York triumph, I delved into the Bekker collection, which had arrived in my absence. I played *Gurre-Lieder*

---

[5]The 1912 Schoenberg commemorative volume was also in the collection. *Arnold Schönberg und seine Orchesterwerke*, a special issue of the periodical *Pult und Taktstock*, had been sold by the time my order was received, but I acquired it elsewhere later.

The larger part of the Bekker Collection surrounds me as I write today. It's amusing to speculate on the price which some future dealer may ask for it.

on the piano for hours, singing all the parts with gusto. It was all I'd hoped:

> ... from the very beginning I fell in love with it. To me, *Nun sag' ich dir zum ersten Mal, Du wunderliche Tove* and *Herrgott, weisst du, was du tatest* are things of the sublimest beauty. The discrepancies that exist between the true nature of a masterwork such as this and what the critics say about it (without benefit of previous knowledge, I trow) certainly shows me how much trust one should place in critics.

Composing, too, wasn't being neglected. In New York, a young violist named Milton Katims (later to gain reputation as a conductor also) had suggested I write some pieces for him. I had long been interested in the literature of the viola because of Bak's prowess on the instrument. So on August 23, I started a viola piece. "It's in a gloomy, romantic vein, but has no name as yet." Then, I had a wonderful idea for another viola piece: "it will be called *Hommage à Schoenberg* and will be a musical depiction of a few of the livelier moments in his classes. I think it has definite possibilities! The music will have . . . a Schoenbergian tinge . . ." (This masterpiece appears not to have survived the years. A pity!)

I studied the first edition of *Harmonielehre* enthusiastically, comparing it with the third edition which I had already come to know in California. Bekker's copy contained a bonus:

> ... a clipping from *Signale* [*für die musikalische Welt*] for May 29, 1912, which consists of an excoriating 4-page review of the book by Dr. Hugo Leichtentritt.[6] And how he does "biff in"! Schoenberg himself could not have done better. Of course his fundamental criticism, namely, that the book devotes too much time to "outmoded tradition"—a mere padded, overextended *Durchkauen* [rehashing] of what everybody knows (but do they, Herr Leichtentritt?)—and not enough to so-called "modern harmony" is absolutely wrong. As if he did not realize that, in order

---

[6]Hugo Leichtentritt (1874-1951), musicologist, teacher, critic and composer, who taught at Harvard from 1933 onwards. In his *Music, History and Ideas* (1938) he presents a curious analysis of Schoenberg's Op. 11 and 19 as if they were tonal compositions.

to understand this harmony of our present day, we *must* absorb the tradition of all that has gone before! He says of Schoenberg, "he himself does not seem to be very clear as to how he comes to his strange chords,"* but I imagine that is his own case rather than Schoenberg's, for Schoenberg *always knows where he is going and why*! However, in spite of this fundamental falsity of criticism, I think Leichentritt has made one or two points that are absolutely true. This for example: "All those 'great originals' who are obsessed with the idea of distilling the whole of world history out of their own small persons have certain faults in common. They have no proper 'distance' from things; they belabor long-ago proven or disproven propositions at length; they give undeserved emphasis to matters of secondary importance; they do not know which aspects of their investigations are significant and new to the experienced reader, for, to these innocent self-taught souls, *everything* that they concern themselves with intellectually is significant and new."*—To my mind, it was downright bad taste to put this in what is supposed to be an impersonal review, but, *à part* some exaggeration, it's all the truth! (You see I am willing to recognize the faults of the Master. I can readily understand how his sometimes devious mental processes, "cute" to me, might not seem "cute" to Dr. Leichtentritt.) Well, I appreciate what is wrong here. Leichtentritt, almost exactly the same age as Schoenberg (he was born in January, 1874), a "composer" of sorts himself (so says *Grove's Dictionary*), and a "doctor" to boot, which Schoenberg is not—is simply jealous of a man of eternal genius and unique originality, and wants to show his own petty erudition. At least, that is the way I analyze the situation . . .

As the summer drew to a close, threats of European war were in the background of our thoughts. On August 24, we visited friends in the evening: "stayed quite late, listening to the numerous broadcasts on the international situation. A bad business, that! Mamma does not think there will be war, but I do. In fact, we have a dollar bet on the matter!" Warlike tensions were rising during the next

*Author's translation from the German.

days as we made our leisurely train journey across the continent. The grave news pursued us down the West Coast: to Seattle, where we gorged ourselves at that temple of gastronomy (alas, no longer extant) *Maison Blanc*; to my birthplace, Portland, and nearby quaint Quaker Newberg; to San Francisco, where we revisited many of the spots we'd enjoyed in June. But, the closer I drew to Los Angeles, the more the war seemed to recede in importance. I was going to be reunited with Schoenberg; that was the important thing![7]

[7]Such an attitude was not mere adolescent self-centeredness, but was in keeping with American isolationism of those years. An often-heard phrase on the UCLA campus was, "The Yanks are not coming!"

Enjoying a floral tribute (ca. 1941)

Book II
September, 1939 – June, 1940

We need a system-master, a teacher of the objective
and organization, with enough genius to unite the
old-established, the archaic, with the revolutionary.
Thomas Mann, *Doctor Faustus*

September 11, 1939

Had to go over to the University today, to see whether my admission
had come through all right or not. . . Schoenberg is giving that new
course in harmonic construction, just as I had expected. He has
dropped Form and Analysis to make room for it, and has also
dropped Advanced Composition & Analysis; but he's teaching a
graduate course of the same name which meets 3 hours a week
instead of two, so that he's really teaching a heavier schedule this
year than he was last! That is a good thing for me, of course, from
the educational point of view; but, considering his health, he really
shouldn't do it.

There came an acknowledgement of our check, from Pierre Berès,
and the news that, on going over the Bekker collection again, they'd
discovered two more Schoenberg items that they hadn't come across
previously: an octavo of the 2nd string quartet, at $1.25 and the *6
Stücke für Männerchor*, at 75 cents. I'm certainly glad now that I

89

bought the 3rd string quartet in New York, instead of the 2nd! This score costs less than the miniature of the 3rd did, and will be much easier on my eyes.

September 12, 1939

I hadn't thought of staying around the University after I had completed my business this afternoon; in fact, I very much wanted to get home and see the new piano I'd rented. I was just passing Kerckhoff Hall on my way home when I suddenly caught sight of my classmate Peggy. I stopped and talked with her a few minutes, about nothing of any consequence—I didn't even notice the large roll of music she had under her arm, when all of a sudden she said, "Say, have you heard about this?" and unfolded the paper, which proved to be a choral work of Schoenberg's! "It's a surprise we're giving him for his birthday tomorrow," she explained. "We're going to sing this and some Bach chorales, too. We're having a rehearsal this afternoon; why don't you come along?"

Well, say, I surely did accept *fast*! . . . I wasn't quite sure of whom the "we" that Peggy had mentioned consisted—thought it might be just a group of the girls from Sigma Alpha Iota[1] but it turned out to be about twenty of Schoenberg's former and present students, most of them people I already knew from last year, directed by, of all people, Dr. Rubsamen![2] Mr. Moremen from the a cappella choir was there, too, and I understand that Messrs. Nelson and Allen will be along when the Big Event takes place tomorrow. This, incidentally, is scheduled for about five-fifteen in the after-

---

[1] International music fraternity for women, which I joined at UCLA. Schoenberg was a faculty adviser of our chapter.

[2] Walter Rubsamen (1911-1973) had joined the UCLA faculty in 1938. He became known for his research in opera and film music, among other subjects. His article "Schoenberg in America" (*Musical Quarterly*, October, 1951) drew the wrath of some Schoenberg friends for its stress on the composer's superstitions. Schoenberg satirized him and other musicologists (e.g., Hugo Riemann) in his "Text from the Third Millenium," a joke-biography of the composer as perceived in that future era by the joke-musicologist "Hugo Triebsamen" ("Hugo Pushy"). See H.H. Stuckenschmidt, *Arnold Schoenberg: His Life, World and Work*, tr. Humphrey Searle (New York, Schirmer Books, 1978), pp. 547-48.

noon; we'll meet at the University for a brief rehearsal at 4:30, then drive out to his house at five. Uncle Arnold himself will be utterly surprised, for he hasn't the slightest idea that any such celebration is planned in his honor; Rubsamen, though, has already "tipped off" Mrs. S., and he told us that she promised him that, if necessary, she would sit on *Le Maître* in order to keep him there till our arrival! And, remembering how overcome and touched he was when the classes gave him that chrome-plated ashtray, I know that he'll be overjoyed at our thinking of him on such a momentous occasion as his 65th birthday. Really, I feel all good inside about it! Whosever idea it was, it certainly was a lovely one!

We rehearsed, and will sing tomorrow, three pieces: Schoenberg's own *Schein uns, du liebe Sonne*[3] (a work of beautiful simplicity and clarity that conforms as little to the popular stereotype of his music as does the man himself to the idea that so many people have of him as the "forgotten man of music"), and two Bach chorales from the Christmas Oratorio, *How Can I Fitly Meet Thee* and *Break Forth, Thou Beauteous Heavenly Light.*[4] I have to laugh at the ultra-appropriateness of the words of the first one to the occasion on which they are being used!

September 13, 1939

Arnold Schoenberg zum fünfundsechzigsten Geburtstage
How can I fitly meet thee,
And give thee honor due?
The nations wait to greet thee,
And I would greet thee, too.

Oh Fount of Light, shine brightly
Upon my darkened heart,
That I may serve thee rightly
And know thee as thou art.

[3]Text from the *Ambraser Liederbuch*, 1582; melody by Antonio Scandelli, 1570. The polyphonic, *a cappella* setting by Schoenberg was first published in *Volksliederbuch für die Jugend* (C.F. Peters, 1930). The chorus is now available as a part of *Das Singwerk* series (Edition Peters Nr. 4863).

[4]Translations by J. Troutbeck (Schirmer edition).

Schein uns, du liebe Sonne,
Gib uns ein heller Schein!
Schein uns zweilieb zusammen,
Die gern beinander sein.

Dort fern auf jenem Berge
Leit sich ein kalter Schnee.
Der Schnee kann nicht zerschmelzen,
Denn Gotts Will muss ergehn.

Gotts Will der ist ergangen,
Zerschmelzen ist der Schnee.
Gott g'segn euch, Vater und Mutter,
Ich seh' euch nimmermehr!

Break forth, thou beauteous, heavenly light,
And usher in the morning!
Ye shepherds, shrink not with affright,
But heed the angel's warning.
This Child, now weak in infancy,
Our confidence and joy shall be,
The power of Satan breaking,
Our peace eternal making.

(I wish they could have heard that last line in Vienna!)

These are the verses of the three songs that we sang for Uncle Arnold. I wanted to write them down entire so that I'd never forget them. It's so annoying, many years after some particularly memorable event . . . , to try to remember all the infinitesimal little details associated with it, and to find that they just barely elude you, no matter how hard you try to recapture them! In spite of my good memory for detail, I've often had that experience.

Well, the Great Occasion went off just as we'd planned, and I must say that never in all my life have I been so perfectly contented and serene as I was during the forty-five minutes or so that we were at Schoenberg's. As I'd lain awake quite a while last night in vigorous anticipation of the event, it's certainly a good thing that it lived up to specifications! After the short period of rehearsal that we'd planned, interrupted by all that frantic last-minute rounding-up of latecomers that always takes place just when you want to get somewhere in a hurry, we all piled into our cars, and, after the manner of a funeral procession (perish the thought!), proceeded solemnly, expectantly and a little apprehensively out to Brentwood.

When we arrived, we found Mrs. Schoenberg waiting for us outside the garden gate. "Sh!" she cautioned us. "He's out in the back yard playing ping-pong, and doesn't have the slightest idea you're here. I'll go out there and keep him busy while you get ready." You should have seen the elaborate caution with which we tiptoed down the gravel walk, and the painstaking care with which we unfolded our music so that the rattle of it couldn't possibly reach his ear. We were worried for fear Roddie, the red setter,[5] might let out a welcoming bark, or Nuria (his daughter, seven-and-a-half years old—my previous guesses about her age were wrong, I see—and what a love she is!) might make some sort of a noise in her excitement, but nothing happened. Finally, after a good bit of shifting around, we got ourselves arranged in serried ranks on the lawn, and, on a signal from Rubsamen, began to sing *How Can I Fitly Meet Thee*. As you can imagine, it wasn't long before Uncle Arnold made his appearance; I suppose he had to come right out and see what that horrible noise was! When I saw him, followed at a respectful distance by his little retinue of friends and relatives, coming out from behind the trees—his face a little drawn, as it always is, but lighted up with that transfiguring beatitude that seems to be so integral a part of his character—my heart gave a rather terrific leap (and my clear, bell-like voice, I trow, a corresponding one!) I just stood there and bellowed for all I was worth . . . The result may not have been good music, but it certainly was good sentiment. Amen!

As for the Old Ruin himself, he was happy as only he knows how to be: "I want to thank every one of you," he told us after we'd sung all three pieces and were in the throes of getting our pictures taken by Mrs. Schoenberg and getting our copies of *Schein uns, du liebe Sonne* autographed by the author; "really, I was wonderfully surprised, really! For me this the greatest honor. I am happy about it, yes, but that is not what I want to say; it is something bigger yet,

[5]After Roderick Dhu, from Sir Walter Scott's romantic ballad *The Lady of the Lake*.

something greater—" And that was as far as he could get; he just stood there in front of us, quivering in every line of his body just as Tammy does when he's excited over a new rubber mouse, and passing his shirt-sleeve over his eyes without any camouflage at all. That simple gesture was worlds more effective than the greatest oratory would have been. Of course, he simply insisted that we should all come in for refreshments. On account of our numbers, we demurred a little, but, of course, ended up by flocking in. The house, as much as I saw of it, is a lovely one: a great long living-room with a fireplace, and full-length mullion windows looking out on both the front and back yards. The mantelpiece has a great many books on it, but I wasn't able to get close enough to see what they were. I assume that the greater part of his library is upstairs or in another room, anyway. There are several paintings on the walls, which looked as though they might be his, though I didn't get a chance to examine them at all; and on a corner bookcase stands—oh inimitable touch of the egotist!—a great black bust *à la* Julius Caesar, of *le maître* himself. He certainly makes a wonderful subject, with that towering bald dome! I did not see my little work of art anywhere, nor did I ask for it.

Well, our time passed away pleasantly and quickly . . . before we realized it, it was time for us to be on our way! Uncle Arnold thanked us again for our kindness, and accompanied us as far as the gate. As we drove off in one of those delicate pink-and-lavender sunsets, he was standing there waving and beaming at us, with his wife beside him and Nuria, Roddie and the little boy in the background. I was sorry to leave that place of contentment and peace, only to return to a more workaday world where petty annoyances are always in the way of the fulfillment of our greatest wishes. As happy as I'd been all the time I was there, I'd never been able to help thinking, "Where will we all be next year at this time?", and that thought occurred to me even more vividly as we left. . . . But no matter what happens in the future, I hope things will never be so dark that I can't derive consolation from looking back a few years and seeing again that scene in a lovely suburban garden in Brentwood: Schoenberg standing among the trees with his friends and loved ones around him, a look of joy and wonder on his face, and his twenty devoted disciples standing on the greensward shouting their throats sore in his honor . . .

Oh Fount of Light, shine brightly
Upon my darkened heart,
That I may serve thee rightly
And know thee as thou art.

September 15, 1939

Well, I got to see Uncle Arnold this afternoon, as I was scheduled to do . . . And, oh joy, he didn't once look at me like a fish and exclaim, "So! Who you are? You go 'way!", or make threatening gestures at me, or, in fact, do a thing but act most glad to see me. I didn't get any chance to engage him in private conversation—there were five or six of us there to see him about our courses, and we all went in at once—but I found out that it will be fine with him for me to take all his new courses, just as I'd planned, and audit Double Counterpoint again if I want. In connection with this last, he showed the clearest comprehension of the credit system that I've yet seen in him. When I explained to him that he'd told me last term to audit DC this year, he exclaimed, "But you had this course last year! You cannot take twice the same course for credit, no!" First time I ever realized he knew that! I was able to get it clear in his mind at last, however, that I didn't care a bit whether I got credit or not. At least, I think I was; you never can tell with Uncle Arnold. He isn't quite sure, as yet, whether or not he will give Special Studies this term; but, if he does, he will combine it with his graduate course, so as not to have to teach eleven hours a week. This is, I think, an excellent idea; I'm glad he's coming to his senses enough to see that he can't do an unlimited amount of work and still retain his health. He is looking much better than he did in June, although it would be impossible to say that he has the appearance of a man in perfect, or even good, health, by any means!

September 18, 1939

The hottest day in 25 years, so say the newspapers and radio—the temperature was up to 106° in Los Angeles. . . . The high point of the day: Uncle Arnold's classes, Advanced Form and Composition (the graduate one), and Harmonic Construction. Speaking strictly, I guess I should say three courses, for the Advanced Form and Composition is going to be combined with Special Studies, just as he'd told me a few days ago. . . . He didn't try to teach in Harmonic Construction—didn't have his proper material with him, for he hadn't realized that particular class was supposed to meet today. How like him, I thought to myself! However, I don't see how he could, or even should, have taught energetically in any case, for in the classroom the heat was constantly about 95° F, and that was nothing to the outdoor temperature. Anyway, he was able to tell us the music he wanted us to buy for that class: an assortment of Beethoven symphonies and quartets, Mozart quartets, Haydn quartets, Brahms quartets, etc. Of course very few of the students can afford to buy the complete sets of all of these things, but as long as I am now richly endowed (!) I might as well order them now as later. But when Uncle Arnold reproaches me, as he occasionally does, for not having this or that work in my collection, I can always reply that I couldn't afford it on account of having squandered my small fortune on The Works of Schoenberg!

As for the Advanced Composition and Analysis, that will be a class where we can write more or less "what we want," though of course with certain restrictions. What you might call the official "project" for the term will be the writing of the first movement of a sonata, for which he wants us to write a theme by next time, if we can; but that will not hinder us from writing other things along the way. One thing, however, I gather that we will not do. During the course of discussion, one student piped up: "Professor Schoenberg, would you care to discuss the harmonic significance of the 4th chord some time this term?" To which the Master replied, bridling like a Shetland pony, "N-n-n-NO! All I want is you write correct triads. Even seventh chords is too much!" (One sees he hasn't changed a bit.) We spent most of this class-time listening to two songs by Mr. E., a former student of Uncle Arnold's who has come back for this course. They were, on the whole, quite good, but did not lack faults (harmonic, as usual) which Uncle Arnold complacently exposed at great length. I think I shall bring in some of my 10 recitations next time, and get his opinion on those. He said to me at the beginning of class, "Well, Miss Newlin, did you write a few manuscripts this summer, yes?", the while waving his hands to indicate a pile of manuscripts about the height of the Empire State Building. Really, if he read my beautiful German letters (which I much doubt), he ought to know what I did this summer. But, anyway, I started to tell him about my three viola pieces and nine or ten recitations. Well, "recitations" had him stumped; he didn't seem to have the remotest idea what I was talking about, until, by dint of infinite patience, I had succeeded in explaining to him that I meant reading poetry to a musical accompaniment. Then, suddenly, his eyes lighted with a maniacal gleam of comprehension. "Oh!" he exclaimed. "Melodrama!" Of course, he had no way of knowing that melodrama in English means something quite different from what it does in German! We all had a good laugh over the confusion.

September 20, 1939

The weather continued as hot as ever, if not hotter . . . Poor Uncle Arnold was simply in misery with the heat, and his situation wasn't helped a bit by his complete inability to cope with the Venetian-blind situation in our classroom. Try as he would, he couldn't get the things fixed so that they would keep the blinding sun out and wouldn't rattle. Finally, after a good deal of pulling and tugging, one of the boys in the class managed to adjust the blinds to his liking. He was immeasurably delighted, even to the point of exclaiming, "Ah, you see what the study of physics does for one, yes?" I have never seen a man so overwhelmed in the face of the simplest contrivances as he seems to be, except possibly certain of those immortal Thurber men! I was in hopes that he might look over my sonata-theme in the advanced composition class—so much in hopes, in fact, that I also brought everything I'd written during the entire summer! —but he didn't do it. I guess he was just too worn-down to face the task of criticizing our compositions today. Instead, he lectured about the sonata-form, with a great many quips at the expense of the theorists who use the term "exposition" and "development." "If I were forced to it," he remarked, "but only if I were forced, I would rather call the first part development, because there is where the themes are really developed!!" I saw one girl meticulously writing down in her notebook, "There are 3 parts to a Sonata. A. Exposition—lousy term. B. Development—also lousy. C. Recapitulation—

this is O.K.!'' In Harmonic Construction, he analyzed briefly for us the salient points of the 1st movement of Beethoven's Op. 54, notably the striking rhythmical resemblance between the principal theme and the chief subordinate theme. All this was most profitable indeed, but I could plainly see that he was in no condition to be in school. Often, while he was speaking, he became confused and had to go back and start all over again—an infallible sign of illness with him, as his mental processes are, normally, beautifully clear and logical, even though their expression may not always be so. He said that the heat made him suffer greatly, and owned to feeling "disturbed" and "uneasy." All I can say is, I hope he doesn't collapse in a heat-stroke one of these days! On top of all his other troubles, he had a terrible, deep cut over his right temple. I don't know where he got it (Mamma says he's probably taken up playing horse-shoes now!) but it certainly looked bad.

The mail brought the two other Schoenberg scores from Berès— the 2nd Quartet and *6 Stücke für Männerchor*. I haven't looked over the music of the latter yet, but have read the poems, from which I deduce that Uncle Arnold is not one of The World's Ten Greatest Poets (though he very well might be all of The World's Ten Greatest Composers). Some of the verses do not seem to mean much of anything, and, when they do mean something, the rather vague something has a slightly maddening theosophical and mystical tinge. It is all very much in the vein of that famous line from *Die Jakobsleiter*, "Yes, yes, yes, yes—it is beautiful to live in the mud!" But when you speak of the 2nd Quartet, that's something else again! I fell in love with it when I heard part of it on records this spring for the first time, and I do not find that my opinion of it lessens on closer acquaintance. To me, the first ten measures or so of that glorious first movement are as near perfection as anything could possibly be. And I still feel that certain "Franckish" quality which I spoke of a few months ago in connection with *Verklärte Nacht*; the music is imbued with that same burning aspiration towards the sublime which is ever-present in Franck's writings. I have gone no farther than the first few bars of *Litanei* but am eagerly looking forward to going on with that and with *Entrückung* as soon as I can.

September 21, 1939

The temperature "dropped" to 105° . . . I played *Litanei* and about half of that supernally lovely *Entrückung*. The more I see of Schoenberg's music—and I am seeing more of it every day of my life —the more I realize the truth of one thing Toch said about it in an interview I've just read: it is so big, so rich and fertile, that at the first playing one only begins to perceive its possibilities. The more it rests in one's mind, the more it unfolds its infinite variety and strength; the wonderful themes grow in one's heart and brain like living organisms. I can testify to this myself . . .

September 22, 1939

I'd half expected that Uncle Arnold might stay home today on account of the heat (which is still no better), but I guess that I credited him with more common, or horse, sense than he really has. He came all right, and taught for four hours (from one to five) with only the briefest of intermissions for an occasional drink of water. In Advanced Form and Composition, right spang in the middle of a sentence on the sonata form, he stopped dead and yelled, "I must have a drink!" and forthwith hastily exited to get one, to the accompaniment of his usual hacking cough. The warm water from the drinking-fountain affords him little or no relief, though; what he really needs is a little iced pocket-flask! We were all afraid lest he might have a heatstroke at any moment; it was with the greatest difficulty that we persuaded him to take his coat off, and that not until he'd been sweltering a good three hours already. "Of course I would like to take it off," he replied to someone's sympathetic query, "but I really should not; after all, I do not want to be only professor who does these things!" You should have heard 16-odd students all trying to tell him at once that he was the only professor who did not do these things! It took a bit of time to convince him, but, once convinced, he skinned out of the unwanted garment with alacrity, and seemed considerably the happier for it.

It goes without saying that, in spite of his suffering from the weather, he "gave" as much as ever. In Advanced Form and Composition plus Special Studies, he lectured on the sonata form in greater detail, and in Double Counterpoint, on the use of all the manifold types of contrapuntal imitation. Also, he seemed to be in excellent humor, which is never to be marvelled at in him. I record here a pair of amusing incidents that occurred in the two classes, because they seem to me to be so beautifully typical of the man's nature. First, in the course of his remarks on sonata form, he happened to bring up the question of the relative proportions of the principal and subordinate themes. "These terms," said he, "have really nothing to do with length." We took the statement down. "But," he continued, "I would say that the relationship of the two is approximately two to one." Like so many dutiful sheep (sheep can't write, I know, but anyway, you get what I mean), we had our pens raised to take that down, too. But he hastily thrust out his right hand in a nervous gesture of protest. "No! No!" he yelled. "Do not put this down and do not dare tell anyone I said this, because THIS IS NOT TRUE!" This in itself isn't a bad story, but the counterpart of it, which occurred during the next class, makes it even more important and interesting from a psychological point of view. This time, he was discussing the differences between polyphonic and homophonic music, or, to be more accurate, he was about to discuss them. Once again we had our pens lifted to write down whatever he said; once again he interrupted us, but this time with a different admonition: "Please," he begged us, "if you tell these things to anyone, please say it is from me. Of course I do not have copyright, but this is mine, you know?" . . . I can't help wondering at the way in which the two incidents dovetail into each other. I know it wasn't deliberate on his part.

September 25, 1939

Yesterday's rain and cold haven't affected Uncle Arnold adversely, as far as I can see. He was on the job as usual, talking about the elaboration section of a sonata form, and the structural functions of harmony, as spry as ever. One thing about his teaching thus far this term astonishes me a little; he seems to be putting off having us do any composing, or even any written analytical work, as long as possible. He gave us a little assignment in advanced composition: we're to find out from what elements (in the first section) the first theme in the elaboration of the Presto of Beethoven's Op. 10, no. 3 derives, but that's all. I would say that he must feel too worn-out to look at our stuff; at least, I can account for his state of mind in no other way, as it seems quite unlike him. Where are the days when, if I asked him, "Professor, shall I revise this Rondo for next time or write a new one?", he would reply, with a wilful toss of his head, "Both!"

He told us one lovely anecdote in Special Studies—particularly lovely because it's a shining example of the stuff biographies are made of. It's about a (mercifully) unnamed professor in the Vienna Conservatory, an old die-hard who was holding forth vigorously against Wagner at the time Uncle Arnold and his friends were young. He didn't say so, but I think it's the same man (described in *Harmonielehre*) who always told his pupils that the reason for the tediousness of the 1st act of *Tristan und Isolde* was the large number of diminished 7th chords![6] Well, anyway, Herr X always delighted in telling the younger generation how he had composed his great "Mess in G minor." (Sch. called it "mess" at first by analogy with the German *Messe*; when we informed him that it should be "mass," he beamed complacently and remarked, "Ah, but it was a mess!" To get back to Herr X: "First," he'd tell his pupils, pointing to the wonders in his score as he went along, "I wrote this theme; then, I wrote this; then, I had no more ideas, so I use now my double counterpoint!" Schoenberg's commentary: "Well, at least he was sincere, but he would have been more sincere if he had stopped composing. I never heard before of such a thing, that a composer did not just stop when he had no more ideas!" (Where does he think all the bad music comes from, in that case?)

September 27, 1939

A Sweet Thought For Today
"It sounds as if it were, but it is not; and even if it were, it would not be."

---

[6]Schoenberg, *Theory of Harmony*, p. 239.

Another One
"Psychologically, music must appeal to the Psych."

Not delirious ramblings these, but simply the latest gems of our immortal Uncle Arnold; the former in connection with a chord ambiguous of interpretation, the latter referring to the psychological effect of Beethoven's having deferred the appearance of the new tonic (in a definitive form) in the 2nd theme of the opening Allegro of Op. 2, no. 1. To fully appreciate the effect of the latter comment, you would have had to see him pointing happily to his yellow dome as he said "Psych," as though that were where the quality resided! But one can't get everything down on paper.

His character becomes more inexplicable every day: a curious mixture of the most childish impulses and the most sublimated intellectuality . . . Take, for example, his conduct in the Harmonic Construction class today. First of all, he assigned us a little written analysis to do for Monday. That works no hardship on us—it's to be just a page or so—and it's the first one he's given us this term. But he went all to pieces over it: "Oh, I am sorry I must do this," he cried, "I don't want to overwork you. I don't want to overwork Mr. Stein, but I must do it, I cannot help you. And please make it good. It is not for me, it is for you. All my classes always worked for me because they know it is for them I do this: I take so much pains to work this difficult thing out for you, I want you to do it so I will see you like to do these things for me . . . " and so on and so on. I realize he is a nervous person and has to have emotional jags of this kind to relieve the internal pressure. Everyone passes them off with tolerance and amusement. They really are funny sometimes, and yet terribly pathetic too, when one comes to think about it. But scarcely had he finished these meanderings and babblings, when he was off on a discussion—fascinating, enlightened, and marvelously logical—of the great psychological problem that has confronted composers of minor-key sonatas ever since Beethoven: the paradox of the too-sudden emotional change that is required by the traditional use of a major-key subordinate theme. When he was "very young and a leetle fresh," he had criticized Brahms's C-minor Quartet for turning too quickly from clouds to sunshine; but now he realized that the problem was, in truth, a difficult one. The change in his own nature, or at least in the outward manifestations of its different aspects, during the span of one hour was at least as startling as the one which he had criticized in Brahms. How to explain him? I don't know. I can merely do what I have been doing and will continue to: simply put down all the significant things he does and says, and let the facts arrange themselves into some semblance of a conclusion. He is far too difficult a problem for me to attempt to solve at one sitting!

September 29, 1939

I feel like singing, preferably hosannas of joy, but I'm afraid that, if I do any singing, "Over the Hill to the Poorhouse" would be most suitable for the gravity of the occasion. Uncle Arnold will let me take lessons of him (cheers! cheers!) at the slight cost of fifteen dollars per chop (muffled groans) . . . The expenses of this coming year make me stand aghast, but what can I do? I need the lessons, I want them, and that's that. After all, I am here on his account alone, and it would be abysmally foolish for me not to take advantage of every opportunity offered me, no matter what the cost. . . . I am terribly happy and excited about the thing.

S. was terribly tired today and had to dismiss the double counter-point class at 4:30. Four successive hours of lecturing is too much for him, that's all. He admits it himself, too.

October 2, 1939

Way back in June, I dashed off the first two movements of a Trio for violin, viola and piano, for the benefit of Uncle Arnold and of my final grades. Well, it looks as if the masterpiece is about to be dug up any day now and put on display, for "Nuncie" has recalled the scheme that I'd feared he might have forgotten, that of having a program of the best pieces written for final examinations by members of the first-year composition and double counterpoint classes. Rumor whispers that the affair will be in about two weeks. If Mr. Stein doesn't have copies of our pieces, we're supposed to get them to him as quickly as possible. So when I got home I started right in on that third movement (a Scherzo) which has been held so long in abeyance. Much to my delight, I didn't have to stew and fret over it; in no time at all, I had fallen on just what I wanted, a fine lilting theme that writes itself, like floating on foam. If it continues to come out in this style, I can easily have it done by Saturday, and will be able to have Uncle Arnold's advice on it in time for it to be included in performance if he so wills.

Nothing especially noteworthy happened in the classes. In composition, he continued to discuss the form of the first section of a sonata-movement, illustrating copiously with the most conspicuously non-conformist examples from Beethoven. "Beethoven," he remarked in introducing the most unusual first movement of Op. 22, "had all problem childs!" In Harmonic Construction, he gave us a brief review of the terms relating to the constructive functions of harmony that he coined last year for the form and analysis class (*functional, establishing, roving,* etc.)

🖉 *October 4, 1939*

Uncle Arnold looked at my dear old sonata theme today, and found it wanting. This is no humiliation, for he found everybody's wanting. His comments ranged all the way from the terse acidity of "I do not think we take time on this; this confused, very confused" (that was on my masterpiece) to the somewhat more fantastic whimsy of "Ah, I see the brains dried all up in the summer. And in the winter they will freeze, but there is still hope: in the spring they will toe [thaw] out, yes?" He has lost no strings from his last year's bow, judging by the tender virulence of these comments. And he still remembers that I leave out my accidentals! He was in the very act of telling another girl who had done so that she could borrow from my voluminous stores, when he suddenly stopped, fell to scratching his head, and remarked, "Well, I do not know 'bout that; maybe she lent them all out last year! Eh, Miss Newlin?" You could see him positively quivering with suppressed laughter as I blushed to the end of my nose and heartily wished that I were somewhere else, or at least invisible. Uncle Arnold can certainly bend the young resilient twig to his liking, and by the time the twig wakes up to what's going on it's too late to do anything about it. As if the lucky twig would want to! God knows, I don't. I prefer a barbed word from Uncle Arnold to a tender or a noble one from anyone else.

October 6, 1939

My little collection of Schoenberg material contains a new and unexpected item today. I guess I didn't mention before that, on Wednesday, S. didn't go home at four; said he had to see an interviewer. He gave no more particulars, and I thought no more about the matter, not even enough to remember to write it down. Well, this afternoon, while I was waiting for my medical examination in Royce Hall, I began to leaf through my Daily Bruin, and lo and behold, what should strike me right between the eyes but a whacking big photograph of the Master himself, complete with accompanying article and large headline? The article is just what you might expect a Bruin to write. It contains one marvelous sentence, "Schoenberg was at a loss to explain his compositions." Well, so would I be at a loss to explain mine to a student reporter! From it, I garnered one bit of information new to me, namely, that he's now working on his 2nd *Kammersymphonie*, which he started in Vienna in 1906. Funny, I'd just been wondering whether he was composing anything just now or not! The picture is a little blurred, but an excellent likeness.

I'd half hoped that he might glance over my new sonata theme today. He didn't, though; for, in the composition class, he took all the time to discuss the nature of transitions, and spared only about five minutes at the end for looking at the themes of those who hadn't shown him anything the last time. But he did look at my set of imitations in the double counterpoint class; admitted they were "not so bad," but couldn't let me go without the usual quota of sarcastic remarks. Best one, in reference to a spot where the two voices were almost rubbing noses: "So, so, I hope they do not have corns, because if they do, they will step on them and it will hurt, no?" At least, however, I did not relapse into the more flagrant sin of crossing-parts, which practically everyone else did. Every time he came to one of these passages, he would stick one hand over the other with a show of great effort, look sadly at the hands thus intertwined, wiggle his fingers ineffectually in a mock attempt to loose them, and finally remark, "Oh dear, oh dear, I will never get them uncrossed again, never!"; all this to the accompaniment of facial grimaces so pathetic that, unless you were gifted with the special sense of humor which you infallibly develop in a year spent with him, you would hardly know whether to cry with him or laugh at him. After he'd finished looking over our papers, he spent the rest of the two hours talking about and writing inversions, except for a short time at the close of the class when he showed us a few of the innumerable contrapuntal finesses of his *Drei Satiren*. He doesn't like them a bit less now than he did then, either; his face was all wrinkled up with childish glee as he pointed out to us one wonder after another. "But these," he called after us as we were leaving the room, "these not the best I ever wrote! There are better ones yet, finer ones. I will show you!"

I understand that there's been a bit of a dust-up in the first-year composition class. He has a tremendous class, for him—36—and wants to kick out about a dozen who he feels can't do the work; but it's too late for them to drop the course, the other section meets at a different time, and most of the prospective victims have conflicts at that hour. A neat little mess, but I don't think that any of the abovementioned considerations will keep him from doing what he wants. He's like that about always getting his way: the happy dictator, perhaps the only person now or ever living who could apply to himself, with absolute truthfulness, both the noun and the adjective.

The rain is coming down in buckets now, and there's a heavy wind—both unusual for this time of year. It has been pouring pretty steadily since about two-thirty. Uncle Arnold happened to be near the window when it started; he dropped his sentence like a hot-cake and exclaimed, in a voice replete with childish joy and wonderment, "Oh look! It rains! Is it not wonderful?" A typically Schoenbergian naiveté.

October 7, 1939

This is a great landmark in my life.

Today, at 1:50 p.m. I had my first lesson with Schoenberg. A wonderful experience, and, what's more, one that can never be repeated; for there will be, God willing, many more times, but there can never be but one first time! I was as excited beforehand as I used to be, many years ago, the night before Christmas; and, after it was all over, I felt a tremendous emotional letdown, a sort of vagueness and emptiness, so much so that I was in tears when I got home. I guess that it's only logical that, after any prolonged period of highly concentrated and alembicated happiness, a corresponding period of depression should occur. But, Heaven knows, this is no time to talk of such matters! I should, instead, be getting on with a circumstantial account of what happened.

Well, after the preliminary greetings and shows of *Gemütlichkeit*, he took me into what I assume to be his own special "inner sanctum": a cluttered little room, about the size of a telephone-booth, opening directly off the main entrance-hall, to the right, and separated from it by only a pair of portières. My God, what a room that is! One can hardly imagine anything more unbeautiful, but I have never seen any room that expressed more perfectly the personality and character of its occupant. The first impression one receives is of a veritable hurricane of papers, all kinds of them: music-manuscript, copied orchestral parts, sketch-books, letters to-and-from, magazines, bulletins strewn hither and yon over every one of the three or four tables and desks that have been somehow crammed into the tiny space. There is no pretense of order in any of it; but I wager he could lay his hand on anything he wanted in that farrago ... One whole side of the room is bookshelves, crammed brim-full of music of all shapes and sizes, up to the very ceiling. In one corner, next to the full-length mullion window that looks out on the gravel drive and front lawn, stands the piano: a dwarfed, battered upright, hopelessly out of tune. It, too, is loaded almost to the breaking-point with stuff; I especially noticed two glass jars filled with pencils, mostly stubs of the type that he has always chastised me for using.

(About the big window: it, like those in the parlor, has a yellow panel in the center, so that, when the sun strikes through it at the right angle, a rich gold light fills the room, and gleams with an especial halo-like brightness on the top of his bald head.)

The rest of the furniture is equally unconventional. Side by side with a tiny sofa vividly striped in black and white and a modern white-leather and chrome chair stands a nondescript-looking straight chair with an uncommonly low seat and an uncommonly high back, and another one, little higher than a footstool, with a round back whose top hits you, uncomfortably, right in the small of the back.

The rug is about the consistency and color of loose-woven burlap.

And his paintings! They are hanging all over the wall, some half-dozen big canvasses, mostly portraits of himself in what appear to be various stages of putrefaction. The two paintings that I saw previously in the living-room—staid, neat little affairs, as I remember them—must not be his at all, or else must come from a very different period. The faces are all stark, staring things, like creatures of a nightmare. There is a woman with a long, chalky face and bloody crescent splotches where the eyes should be; there is the head of a wild-eyed man, framed in tangled hair, barely visible in a dense grey mist. There is the best-known of his self-portraits, the one that is reproduced in Armitage's book, a work of strong, albeit distorted lines, which might seem to partake more of the flavor of real life if it were not all done in a cold and deadly ice blue like the color of the sky just before sharp winter dawns. All these, horrible as they are, have a sort of gruesome effectiveness all their own; but the one I liked better than all the rest does not resort to tortured lines and colors, akin to the stylistic writhings of the Gothic novelists, to convey a sense of power tremendous and crushing. The whole scene is shrouded in darkness; a lonely black street, walls dimly perceived on both sides, and his own resolute little figure in the middle, stalking towards the Unknown, south view going north. It is all done with a simplicity and naturalness that quite outweigh, in sheer emotional effect, the charnel-house atmosphere of the woman's portrait. And it could have been painted as an illustration for "Journey"![7] Atmosphere, scene, character, place—everything fits. Even if the picture does not specifically show you Death walking behind "with pace designed and overtaking tread," you can see it there without half trying. But how odd it seems to see, interspersed among these nightmares, charming little photographs of the *anmutig* Nuria and her little brother! That is just another symbol of the unresolvable contradictions in Schoenberg's character, which I have observed so many times.

But, my goodness, I'm not getting down to business at all here!

[7]A poem by my father's colleague, the Canadian poet A.J.M. Smith. I had set it to music as part of a cycle of recitations. (A.J.M. Smith, "Journey," *News of the Phoenix, and Other Poems*, Toronto, The Ryerson Press/New York, Coward-McCann, Inc., 1943, p. 12.)

Well, first he asked me if there was any particular thing I wanted to work on. Of course, that was my cue to pipe up and say I wanted to learn more about orchestration; and that was his cue to start the Inquisition. "Do you play any instrument? Do you play in the orchestra? Why not? You should play, you must play! Do you have records? So, you do not have them here! Why not? Well, you can run the machine at the University and use their records, no? Yes, you can do this. Now, have you piano reductions at home? Only of Beethoven Symphonies? Oyoyoyoyoy!" and so on. The point of the discussion is that he wants me to make a careful study each week of a few measures of the piano-score of an orchestral work, go and hear these measures on records, transcribe on paper what I think I heard (in orchestral terms, of course) and compare the resultant mess with the original score. He isn't going to start me on this work, which should be tremendously valuable and interesting, right away, however. For next week he is having me do what should be a reasonably simple task: the arranging of Schubert's *Sei mir gegrüsst* for string orchestra, two horns, and two clarinets. Most of the hour he spent showing me the various fine points of such a piece of work, except for a few minutes when he cursorily glanced through all the music I had brought with me, only to exclaim, "Oh, you cannot expect me to read this. Next time you must bring interpreter with you that I know what you do, yes? I, I never wrote like this; I always cared for these things." I do not think he exaggerates, either. The parts of the 2nd *Kammersymphonie* which he is working on are as clear as print, and even the rough sketches in his sketch-book hardly less so.

I am sorry to say that I don't think his trust in the fundamental integrity of human nature is all it might be. I always had a notion that his disposition was pretty suspicious, but I never really knew how far it went until now. A couple of little incidents which occurred this afternoon make my point clear. About half-past two, he suddenly jumped up in a great hurry and excused himself, to see somebody, he said, and left me quite alone in the little room. Naturally I took the opportunity to look around me a bit, to take in a bit more of the fuddled atmosphere of the place. I didn't get up from my chair at all, or walk around, nor—God forbid—did I touch any of his personal papers. Yet, he must have realized that I was uncommonly curious as to what was what, for, the instant he came back, he shot out at me, with the most disarming smile and the most cunning look in his eye, "So, I suppose you have been thinking over all the things I told you, yes?" And then he continued, still in the most innocent tone imaginable, "Have you to catch a special tram?" I told him I didn't, that they ran every forty minutes and it didn't matter if I missed one. "Oh, excuse me," says he, as cool as a cucumber, "I thought you were looking at your watch, but it must have been something else, yes?" He made this remark in so casual a manner, and drifted back so quickly into what he'd been talking about previously, that the true significance of his remark didn't dawn on me till much later. My God, perhaps he is right in his contention that he can read his disciples' minds like open books! The other incident is a little less savory to recount, especially for an ardent admirer. It seems that, instead of taking my money by the week, he wants "sixty dollars month" in advance! (Funereal note: what guarantee do I have that he will not die within said month? Very little, I should say.) The reason he gives for this policy is that he doesn't want to have to make so many trips to the bank; but personally I think he's just pulling my leg. What he's really afraid of is that the money won't come in quite as regularly as it ought! His attitude might seem a little petty to some, but when you come down to it I guess it's based on nothing less than good common sense. Believe me, I'm glad to see that he has at least some of that!

𝄞 *October 9, 1939*

This, roughly, is what happened to me in composition class today:

> Uncle Arnold (snorting disdainfully as he sees the length of my lucubrations): So, Miss Newlin, can you play this?
>
> I: Why, yes!
>
> Uncle Arnold: No, no, you had better not play it, I do not trust you! Here, Mr. Stein, you—
>
> Stein: Oh, no, let her do it—she knows her own work better than I do, after all.
>
> (Uncle Arnold sighs resignedly and lets Nature take its

course. I start to play, very badly because, in the first place, he has taken up 3/4 of the piano bench and has got himself schrooched all over the keyboard so that I can't reach the lower half of it, and, in the second place, every time I fumble a note he makes a series of exasperating deprecatory motions with his hands and head—it's a vicious circle! I am making out pretty well, though, and have just gotten into the swing of the thing when suddenly—)

Uncle Arnold: What are you playing—you play this again, no? I do not hear any theme—all I hear is nasty little accompaniment figures with nothing in. You play again! (I play again, a little worse than the first time.) I still do not hear a theme! You play me the theme with one finger, yes? I do not allow you more as one finger! (As I digest this, he continues) See, she does not even know what her theme is! HAW HAW HAW HAW HAW! (By this time, I have collected my wits and proceed to doughtily stamp out my theme, such as it is, with one finger, to the accompaniment of his hearty laughter.) Well, the first part has no connection with the second part, none whatever! See? What shall I write on to show you? Can one use this—oh, this is nothing anyway (he writes in indelible red pencil all over the back of my second theme, which he hasn't even looked at).

October 11, 1939

Our Beloved was the soul of *Gemütlichkeit* this afternoon, so very unusually so, in fact, that he actually gave me a lift partway home. That is a most unusual event; in fact, it happened only once before —in March or April, I think, when he stopped me on the road to give me that by-now-famous letter of recommendation. Nothing particular happened this time. I passed most of the time in pleasant conversation with little Nuria in the back seat, but the experience was a heartwarming one nevertheless; it left me feeling all "set-up" and elated . . .

Unfortunately, he didn't take advantage of this extravagantly good mood to look at our compositions. Too bad, for one never knows how long he'll be in that state of mind! Instead, he analyzed transitions in divers Beethoven sonatas for our benefit, and, in spite of our not having the music with us, one of Mozart. That was really funny! Before he goes into a detailed discussion of the particular point of form that he wishes to call to our attention, he has Mr. Stein play through the pertinent part of the piece in question, punctuating (or I should say accompanying) the performance with frequent queries about the salient constructive features. Now, on this particular occasion, we'd all had to gather close about the piano, for none of us had brought our Mozart, and it was necessary for us to see the music in order to get anything from his comments. All of a sudden, he shot out, "Well, where are we now?" meaning *where in the form*. But lo, a long lean hand reached forward from the back row, and officiously pointed out the *exact measure* "where we were" at that moment! Well, Uncle Arnold fairly quivered with laughter, his good kind face shot through with a million twisted little wrinkles and suffused with successive waves of pinkness, about the color of a boiled lobster. It must have taken him (and us, for that matter; his enthusiasm is notoriously contagious) a good five minutes to settle down.

He told us one interesting thing today, in which I scent scandal. Describing how he had kept his mind "always busy with music" for all the years of his life, he proceeded to say that it wasn't always his own music it was busy with. Often, he said, when Berg and Webern, to name but two among many, came for their lessons, he would tell them, "Ah! Now I have thought out a better continuation for your theme!" and put it down for them in full, right on the spot. Don't tell me that he wrote all their works for them, now! Apparently they used these "better continuations for their themes" just as he gave them. Anyway, whatever conclusions one might draw from it, it remains an interesting fact for the Future Biography.

October 13, 1939

Uncle Arnold was unusually informative today, both musically and autobiographically. In fact, he told us so many, many interesting things that I shall simply have to jot them down at length and let chronology and logic go to the winds, whether I like it or not.

Well, first he looked, seriously and fairly this time, at my finished first part of the sonata, and gave me some extremely valuable criticism of it. That it has its really good points he does not deny; he liked especially, for example, the transition between the first and second themes, but, as is only natural, it has its shortcomings, too. The first theme has not a definite enough character or form—more of an étude-like or impromptu-like character—and is too short; and the second theme is just trivial. If I can change these things, what I have is well worth continuing with, he thinks. . .

In Double Counterpoint, he simply let himself go in the autobiographical line, which is marvelous grist for the mill as far as I am concerned. During the first hour, he added a third part to a two-part combination for us, and then tried to add a fourth part to that, but couldn't finish it. He was terribly tired after two previous hours of lecturing, and, besides, the original combination of two voices had certain shortcomings which made the addition of other parts extremely difficult, not to say impossible. The time was by no means wasted, however, because it gave us a quickened insight into the problems relative to such a task, and also led him into a most fruitful discussion of the differences between Bach and Handel. As I said, the whole thing started from this business of adding parts; it was only natural that telling us how necessary perfection was in the original combination, so that the added parts would be smooth, should remind him of the experience he had in arranging Bach's E flat-major Prelude and Fugue and Handel's B flat major Concerto Grosso. In both cases he used a very full orchestration, so full, in fact, that most orchestras do not have the instruments he calls for, and these arrangements never get played.[8] He deplores this fact greatly, and, I think, rightly, for, if the Brahms transcription that I heard last December is any criterion, he is as inspired an arranger as a composer. He didn't want to resort to the all-too-common expedient of doubling parts *ad infinitum* in the organ-style, so he added parts of his own to give his big orchestra something to do. Now in Bach this was very easy, because of the perfection of the original

[8]Both were later recorded: the "St. Anne" Prelude and Fugue as part of Robert Craft's Schoenberg series for Columbia Records (Columbia M2L309), the Concerto Grosso Op. 6 no. 7 by the Manuel Compinsky Quartet with the Janssen Symphony Orchestra of Los Angeles (Columbia ML 4406).

counterpoint, and because it was constructed in double counterpoint of the 10th, 12th. etc. All S. had to do was to add these double counterpoints and the effect was magnificent! Not so in Handel. When S. set to examining *his* counterpoint, he found a fine melodic line, and a good bass line, but the inner parts were unbelievably poor, almost as barren of invention as the inner parts of a harmony exercise! This made the arranger's problem difficult; he solved it successfully, nevertheless; how, he did not say. The results of this work brought him to a neat and just formulation of the differences between Bach and Handel. Both, he says, begin with a fine, striking, emotionally expressive idea; but, whereas Bach carries his on to higher and finer developments—the longer his pieces are, the better they are—Handel allows his to become more and more barren, till finally the idea peters out in a meaningless flourish of empty figurations. The reasons for this? Of course, they lie mostly in fundamental differences in talent; but a point we should not lose sight of is that Bach is a symphonic composer of absolute music only, and Handel is a theatrical composer.[9] In absolute music, there is nothing for us but the notes that are there, nothing to fill out our impressions of them, to make us think they mean more than they really do, or to distract us from them. But, in theatrical music, it is only the first impression of mood that holds our attention. Let the first four to eight measures of the dramatic score pass—this span, the usual limit of Handel's greatest powers—and we are more interested in the meaning of the words, in the appearance of the actors and their gestures. (At this, you should have seen Uncle Arnold laying both hands on his heart and rolling his gummy orbs soulfully heavenwards!) Dramatic music serves only as a background to these more important matters, and its superficiality, painfully obvious when we look at the score in the cold light of day, does not bother us under these circumstances. So says Schoenberg: and I think every word is

[9]This statement is difficult for me to understand now, in view of the strongly theatrical elements in Bach's Passions and Cantatas and in the B minor Mass. Schoenberg's seemingly anti-theatrical stance in this discussion assorts ill with his own far-from-superficial dramatic music (cf. *Moses and Aaron*). But then, he was never obsessed with consistency.

as true as gold. Speaking further of Handel, he said that he thought Beethoven admired him very much (probably because he knew so little of Bach), but Mozart, considerably less so. This belief is based on his examination of Mozart's arrangement of some oratorio of H's, not the *Messiah*. [10] Mozart did some things that would seem odd in an admirer; he has cut out literally hundreds of sequences, and in one choral passage has consistently added, in the woodwind choir, a funny little passage that looks to Uncle Arnold like a satire of Handel's empty chord figures.

All this, however interesting, can hardly be regarded as the auto-biographical material I promised! But there is plenty of that, too. He spoke of the plan for an ideal music school which he drew up about 1910 and sent to the Mayor of Vienna, [11] and which that high-and-mighty functionary never even so much as acknowledged. Of course, he didn't tell us all the details, but he mentioned some of its more important features. One of these was that every student with the slightest degree of talent should, at the earliest oppor-tunity, be given a class of students two or three years younger than himself to teach. This would be invaluable experience, for in order to explain facts to his pupils he would have to understand them clearly himself. Another stipulation was that the composition of the classes should be constantly flexible, changing weekly if need be; the students who progressed most rapidly should be promoted into higher classes in accordance with their rate of advancement. This scheme would have a double advantage: it would enable the quicker students to forge ahead constantly, and would keep the slower ones from getting discouraged. "Von Webern was very slow, yet look what a great composer he has become!" He then launched into a discussion of the good old *Verein* for private performances of con-temporary works. (It's described in all the books about Schoenberg, but I don't think all the things he told us about it are in the books.)

---

[10] Schoenberg could have seen Mozart's "additional accompaniments" for *Acis and Galatea, Alexander's Feast*, or *Ode for St. Cecilia's Day*.

[11] Vienna's popular, notoriously anti-Semitic mayor Karl Lueger—called "der schöne Karl" because of his flashy good looks—died on October 3, 1910.

People like Kolisch,[12] Steuermann,[13] Webern and Berg were always as cooperative as they could be, but others were not. Take the treasurer,[14] for example: one of the all-too-common breed of petty administrative officials who wind everything up in red tape so that their presence to unwind it is absolutely necessary. Time after time, Uncle Arnold asked to see the man's books, and as often he demurred. Finally, however, Schoenberg did see them, and what a mess they were! The most complicated figurings you could imagine, at least "triple or quadruple bookkeeping!" "Well!", exclaimed Uncle Arnold, having examined this farrago at some length, "why do you not buy a rubber stamp and make a list of the members [there were between 250 and 350 of them at the time], and when a man pays, put the stamp before his name?" The upshot was, of course, that the accounts were thereafter kept in that manner, and the whereabouts of every cent was always known! So it was in everything; S. always tried to make all the arrangements as simple as possible, "and when I said a thing must be done, it was done!" "But you were a benevolent despot, weren't you?" queried one of the students. "Oh yes, yes, yes!" hastily put in the Master, "This I was, this I was! I always listened to good suggestions!" (If there is anybody living who has seen him listening quietly and appreciatively to a suggestion, I would like to meet that man. I have a sneaking suspicion that I never shall.)

And now he fell to talking of the hard days of the inflation after World War I, and of the sufferings that he and his colleagues had gone through at that time. He and Webern lived in Mödling then,

---

[12]Rudolf Kolisch (1896-1978), brother of Trude Schoenberg; leader of the Kolisch Quartet (first known as the *Neues Wiener Streichquartett*, later the Pro Arte Quartet). Their performances and recordings of Schoenberg's string quartets, of which they premiered the Third and Fourth, were exemplary.

[13]Eduard Steuermann (1892-1964), pioneer in performing and recording Schoenberg's piano music (the first to perform his Piano Concerto). His second wife, Clara Silvers Steuermann, who studied with Schoenberg at UCLA after my departure, is presently archivist of the Arnold Schoenberg Institute. For more on Steuermann's career, and on the cultural life of Hollywood's German/Austrian emigré community in the '30s and '40s, cf. Salka Viertel, *The Kindness of Strangers* (New York, Holt, Rinehart and Winston, 1969).

[14]Dr. Artur Prager.

about 10 miles from Vienna, and taught in the central part of Vienna afternoons. Train-service was very poor from Mödling to Vienna so, in order to be in Vienna at about two in the afternoon, they had to leave Mödling after an extremely early (and, one surmises, equally light) lunch. By the time he and Webern reached the Vienna station, they were so hungry that they would have to go into the nearest bakery and buy, at a cost higher than that of the train-ticket, a thin cake made of ground-up beetles! To such straits they were reduced! In spite of their weakness, they had to work steadily twelve hours a day. "And these things will be again in Vienna," he said, his eyes almost filling with tears as he spoke. "This war is so sad . . . so sad!" There was really nothing any of us could say to him. We know, all of us, what he must be going through, with his wife's relatives and friends (and his own too, I imagine) in such danger as they are now. The best we could do was to tactfully switch the subject back to the *Verein* as soon as we could. He'd barely gotten warmed up on that again when the bell rang and he had to take his leave. "But I will tell you more next time!" he cried back at us as he waved us good-bye at the door. And I hope he does!

October 14, 1939

Well, I had my first real lesson with Uncle Arnold this afternoon, and I'm glad to say that it really went quite well. I'd brought with me two of my viola pieces and the newly-completed third movement of the Trio. But he looked only at the first of the viola pieces, which he discussed in greatest detail, and heard me play the latest one through once. He probably would have covered more ground if he hadn't spent a good half of the time correcting my omissions of accidentals! He has a theory that since I play what I *really wrote* and not what is erroneously recorded on paper when I'm playing my own compositions, I must also not play what is written when I'm performing the works of other composers! I tried to talk him out of the absurd notion, but to no avail. All he would say was, "You cannot prove it, you cannot prove it. I know what I say, believe me!" What can one do in such a case? . . .

Mamma, much against her will, went into the house with me today, and sat in the front room during my lesson. She was very nervous about it, but needn't have been, as he was utterly gracious to her. The little boy, a cherubic tiny creature, with lovely curly hair, who is the very image of his father, even to his supercilious, slightly bored, diminutive pout, couldn't quite make her out. He kept running in to steal a peek at her, and then would run back to his own mother, shouting loudly the while, "Mamma! Is that the girl's mother in there?" Once he even wandered into the Inner Sanctum, to Uncle Arnold's great amusement and pride, for the little fellow is as much the apple of his eye as Nuria is. Roddie, the Irish setter, remembered me very well from last time; at least, he remembered my biscuit. The instant I came into the parlor, he sat down before me, fixed me with his liquid eyes, stuck his great furry nose almost into my face, and then, with infinite tenderness, placed his left paw in my lap, gazing at me the while with an expression that would have melted hearts of stone. I noticed today that there is a gray cat attached to the *ménage*, too; but I didn't make its acquaintance.

🖂 *October 16, 1939*

Alas, poor Uncle Arnold is sick today. He was at school, all right (though he'd no business to be), but I never saw anybody greener about the gills! He could hardly speak for the hoarseness in his throat. In composition class, he made Mr. Stein do all the analysis, confining his own activity to sitting with his head in his hands, coughing painfully from time to time, and looking utterly miserable. When he did lecture, in Harmonic Construction, you could see that he was straining himself as far as he could. Really, it was pitiful to watch him! Naturally, under the circumstances, there wasn't much he could do. He didn't even try to look over our compositions, but spent the time analyzing transitions of Mozart sonatas, or, rather, priming Mr. Stein to do it. In the midst of his misery, however, he let fall one autobiographical gem which I thought interesting. Speaking of how we should always strive to have some motivic connection between first theme, transition, second theme, etc., he commented, "And then, when I say so-and-so is not good, you can say to me, 'But this comes from this!' " As we laughed in what was meant to be a disbelieving manner (recognizing in our hearts, nevertheless, how true to life the remark was), he continued, "But, you know, I was so myself, when I was young man!" He went on to tell us how, when he was 18 or 19, he used to take his compositions to the music critic of Vienna's first newspaper,[15] whose work he greatly admired. One day the critic wanted to know what a certain rather dubious passage signified, and Uncle Arnold, as was his wont, glibly replied that it was derived, in an obscure and erudite way from so-and-so. The critic said nothing; but when, a few bars later, he came upon a similar bit of misguided ingenuity, he queried calmly, "So? Another one of your enigmas, isn't it?" And the young Schoenberg stood corrected. I quote this excerpt because it is so utterly typical of what later critics, less benevolent and less admirable, said about his subsequent work and are still saying.[16]

October 18, 1939

Poor Schoenberg didn't show up at all this afternoon—wise of him, for he simply must rest in bed and take care of himself. It's nothing serious, I guess; he's just recovering from his cold, and is expected to be back to normal by Friday. But then, any illness is a grave matter with a man as old and feeble as he is. Well, I do hope he regains his strength soon, at least by Saturday!

There's at least one ray of sunshine: tomorrow night, at Leopold Stokowski's benefit concert for the Polish refugees, Rose Bampton is going to sing the *Lied der Waldtaube* from the *Gurre-Lieder*. I don't know whether or not I'll be able to go, though . . .

October 19, 1939

We didn't go . . . the house had been completely sold out for a week! I can only hope, as Uncle Arnold does, that, if Stokowski becomes

[15]Can Schoenberg have meant the dread Eduard Hanslick (1825-1904), Brahms-loving and Wagner-hating, critic of the *Neue freie Presse*? The dates are right, for Hanslick was still going strong in 1892-93 (on December 23, 1893, his celebrated review of Bruckner's Eighth Symphony and its "traumverwirrten Katzen-jammerstil" [phantasmagoric hangover style] was published by the NFP). Nonetheless, the mind boggles at the notion of Schoenberg and Hanslick having a cozy chat about thematic relationships.

[16]In the 1970s, this "intellectual" component of Schoenberg's work was seen as a merit. Indeed, some writers (cf. *Perspectives of New Music, passim*) emphasized it at the expense of the music's emotional and spiritual content. Schoenberg would not have liked this; he believed in heart *and* brain in music! (Cf. his essay of that title in *Style and Idea*.)

the permanent conductor here (it is rumored he may, since Klemperer is in so bad a state), he may present the *Gurre-Lieder* in its entirety, and other works of Schoenberg, too! May it be so!

Wonder if Uncle Arnold was there tonight, in spite of his illness? It would have given him great pleasure, I know, to bow and smile at a wildly applauding audience. But, for the sake of his health, he really should have stayed at home . . . Well, I shall know tomorrow.

October 20, 1939

Uncle Arnold was back with us today, in a good mood, but not in the best physical condition. His cough was noticeably worse—he had several terrible hacking spasms—and his condition was not helped at all by his lecturing four hours in succession, with hardly a break. I thought all along he should have stayed home last night, instead of dragging himself out into the fog and cold! (He was there, all right; the review in the *Times* said he acknowledged the applause from his box.)

He has now decided to arrange the thrice-a-week composition or special studies class in such a way that he will lecture to us on Mondays and Fridays, and look at our compositions on Wednesdays. This, he thinks, will be less of a strain on him. Nevertheless, today he disrupted his well-made plan by looking over our sonata-themes. In the Double Counterpoint class, he lectured at some length about the chorale prelude, especially about the making of cadences. . . . I do not remember having heard him state his theory about the reasons for the fermatas before. In a manner which one could characterize only as "typically Schoenbergian," he based it on the difference in the speed of light and that of sound; it seems that the portion of the congregation in the back of the church would see the organist put his hands to the keys before they heard the notes he played, and that, whether they made their notes coincide with *sight* or *sound*, they would never be entirely together. Hence the fermatas, to enable them to make frequent fresh starts together—and also to give them a chance to get back on key. That this last was very necessary indeed is amply demonstrated by his story of the famous Viennese choral society which sang several choruses of Brahms, each strophe one key lower than the preceding! All this might be true; I don't know. I admit I find it a little hard to believe that the relation of the speed of light to the speed of sound has anything to do with it!

He tells us that with every succeeding day his accent gets "verse und verse." He made a perfectly lovely mistake today, one of the best in a long time. (I'm not forgetting "suppertonic" and "more smoozier" [smoother] nor "disconvenient" either!) Speaking of the rule that the chorale prelude should bring the chorale melody in its middle voice, he remarked, "Of course, one *could* do it otherwise, but it has no sense for us to—to—how you call it" (here throwing his hands up and down as if juggling a ball or two). "Juggle!" several of us provided the correct word at once. "Ach so, to *JUNGLE* with the voices!" He's etymologically correct, but the results are no less funny. The charm of his mispronunciations is of a piece with the charm of this exclamation, as he mopped his brow with a large and slightly soiled linen handkerchief: "Oh dear, I have only brought with me two handkerchiefs (waving them like limp flags of battle), and see, they are all wet through, *all* wet! Oh dear! If I had only known it was so warm!" How can you resist anyone who does unexpected childlike things like that in the very midst of discussing the most abstruse contrapuntal questions?

October 21, 1939

My lesson with Uncle Arnold went off uncommonly well today, in spite of the fact that he was still weak from his terrible spasms of coughing. In fact, when I gave him my telephone number just before I left, he remarked that, had he had it before, he would certainly have called me up for a postponement, he felt that tired and sick! ... He looked over my orchestration of the Schubert song *Sei mir gegrüsst* and found it all right for the most part, but, in general, a little mechanical and systematic. That is not really surprising, for I could hardly be inspired by a work which I consider in such atrociously bad taste: just one great long hiccup! For the next time, he wants me to make three arrangements of the brief Scherzo from Beethoven's Violin Sonata, Op. 24: one for ten wind instruments (including 2 horns), one for string orchestra alone, and the third for eight woodwinds and string orchestra. He thinks that this should prove a valuable study. Some time in the near future, though not just yet, he will have me make an arrangement of Bach's C-minor Fantasy and Fugue for organ; and, besides all these, he still has in mind his notion about the piano reductions which I described in full two weeks ago—wants me to find out just exactly which ones are in the library, and also if they have the Beethoven Septet there. He doesn't think the use of the Beethoven Symphonies will be too profitable, for I am too familiar with the original scores already. If that is the criterion, I think the piano score of *Gurre-Lieder*, the orchestral version of which I have never seen or heard, should be ideal! But, of course, it would be well-nigh impossible even to approximate the complicated original. The same goes for *Erwartung*. . .

October 22, 1939

I read in today's *Times* that Pro Musica[17] is to present, two weeks from today at the Women's Athletic Club, a concert consisting of *Verklärte Nacht* (as a sextet), Toch's[18] Piano Quintet, and five short piano pieces by Achron. The performers will be the Kaufman Quartet, Lillian Steuber, and Toch himself. I should love to hear this, but do not know whether it is open to the public.

I started my latest revision of the first viola piece this afternoon; once again got as far as the second theme, and find the new changes a great improvement. Mamma says that if Uncle Arnold marks up *this* clean copy with pencils in assorted shades of crimson, blue, magenta, and green, as he has done all the others, she will kill him with her own hands! I would not advise it.

October 23, 1939

Uncle Arnold was at school today, still coughing a little, but otherwise seemingly on the mend and in the best of spirits. He lectured

[17]A concert-sponsoring chamber music society in Los Angeles.

[18]Ernst Toch (1887-1964), Austrian composer and writer on music, was composing Hollywood film scores at this time, e.g., *The Cat and the Canary* (1939). Later, he wrote *The Shaping Forces of Music* (New York, Criterion Music 1948, repr. Dover, 1977). For his view of Schoenberg, see above, p. 99.

in both of his classes: in Structural Functions on the different types of half-cadence (he is taking us right back to the elements of harmony, but that can't hurt any of us), and in Composition on the character of subordinate themes, illustrated by examples from the Beethoven Sonatas, Brahms Trios, Schubert Quintets, and others. I think it was while going through the coda to the first section of Beethoven's Op. 2, no. 3, 1st movement, that he suddenly exclaimed at seeing a new theme make its appearance in an unexpected place, "Oh look! He wave his hand, and here comes little island!" just as a child might call on its mother to drop everything and come see the beautiful caterpillars. The analysis of the Brahms works—in which he was at some pains to point out to us the epic-like character of the principal themes, a feature upon which he lays great emphasis—reminded him that, only the other day, he had suddenly realized the superficial resemblance of the principal theme of his new 2nd *Kammersymphonie* with the second theme of the first movement of the Brahms Double Concerto. "But," he hastened to assure us, "it is carried out quite differently by me, quite!" I believe him, and anyway, what difference does it make whether the two themes are alike or not? As long as they are both good, I'm sure nobody minds; but the fact is interesting to note, nevertheless.

October 25, 1939

Uncle Arnold was in one of his kinder moods this afternoon—went through our compositions with plenty of constructive criticism and very few cutting remarks . . . (though he *was* stirred to mild sarcasm by the circumstance that every one of us had chosen to write in C minor, except for two who had gotten into F minor by mistake). [He] was somewhat less gentle in the next hour when, discussing whether we should buy the Beethoven String Quartets as a group through an agent for a 10% reduction (he thinks we should have at least 30%), he fell into a tirade against the excessive profits of the dealers. Of course, his grievance there is a very personal one; for example, for each sale of the eight-dollar set of *Verklärte Nacht* records he gets a 16-cent return! It simply goes to show that one can never make one's living by composing alone, a fact which I'd already divined! He lashed himself up into quite a fury over all of this, only to get into another one when he discovered that the music department library has only 3 copies of the Beethoven symphonies, instead of 5 as he'd thought. "But we *must* have five!" he shouted at the harassed Mr. Stein, who was trying to calm him down as much as he could. "I bought five, I know! You go talk to Dr. Rubsamen! He must have them! Someone must have taken these! This terrible! I will see Mr. Allen 'bout this!" (That's always his ultimate threat in case of trouble. Poor Mr. Allen!) All his ranting, however, could not produce the extra copies, so he had to quiet down and content himself with passing out among us the three existing copies of the Beethoven Quartets with stern injunctions to take very good care of them, as they were expensive. Every time one of us turned a page with ever so slight a rustle, you could see his eyes grow beady with alarm! With these divers matters settled, we settled down to an hour of analysis of the first movement of Op. 18, no. 4. This time, I came in for my share of ridicule. Perambulating the floor while Mr. Stein played the music on the piano, he suddenly stopped in front of me like the Ancient Mariner, said in a pointed manner, "Miss Newlin, you should be able to play scores like this!", and proceeded on his weary way, without even so much as giving me a chance to say, "But I can!" Then, when he began asking us questions and I would start to blurt out some kind of an answer whenever I could, he would hold up his hand and exclaim, "Take it easy, take it easy—I am *sure* it will be wrong!" He was at great pains to inform us that he had heard the expression "take it easy" on the radio program *Information Please.* [19] Every time he listens to the radio or reads a book, he has to let us know about it as though it were some tremendous phenomenon.

October 27, 1939

Uncle Arnold was in one of his more whimsical moods today, inclined to stray on a moment's notice into fields far distant from what he was nominally supposed to be talking about. In the five-minute intermission which he gave us between the two hours of double counterpoint, he leaped lightly from complaints about the

[19] The most famous of the radio quiz programs of the period (see above, p. 31).

architecture of our University buildings to a dogmatic statement that it's absolutely wrong to speak about landing on water, because land and water are two different things! His suggested alternative would be the use of two verbs: "landing" when you meant coming down on land, and "watering" when you meant coming down on water. When some of us tried gently to intimate to him that "watering" meant something quite different, he retorted, "Yes, but so many words have other, even contradictory meanings, why not this?" Quite right, but then why shouldn't "land" mean more than one thing? He is stubborn on this point, however and considers the existing usage just another example of current carelessness in language, which he heartily deplores. He gave himself over to a tirade against the language of the advertisers and newspaper-writers, one of his pet grievances, I take it. He said he was always distressed about it in Germany, too, and he certainly talks about it a lot now![20]

He seemed somewhat easily distractible today. When a formation of airplanes roared overhead, he rushed to the window and thrust his head out to look; every time he heard an automobile horn blowing on the road outside, he cocked his head to one side to see if it was for him, though he knew full well it wasn't. But he put on the funniest demonstration of all when, on entering the classroom for composition class, he saw among the notes left on the blackboard from the previous class the somewhat cryptic notation: $16 + 53 = 69$. Well, that simple sum stirred him up no end! He looked at it from one side and then another; he carefully read through all the names and dates on the board to see if it had anything to do with any of them and kept mumbling to himself, "This must mean something. but what can it mean?" Finally he asked who taught the class preceding his, and, on being informed that it was Mr. Nelson, replied happily, "Ha! I am glad to know it! Now I can ask him what this should mean, for it must mean something, it must!" With this weighty problem disposed of, he began a discussion of the loose

[20] For discussion of such style-problems, see also the writings of Vienna's super-satirist Karl Kraus (1874-1936), who was equally fussy about language and often expressed such concerns in his periodical *Die Fackel* (The Torch). Schoenberg, like many other serious thinkers in twentieth-century Vienna, was strongly influenced by Kraus. A useful English version of some representative Kraus essays is *No Compromise* (New York, Ungar, 1977).

form of the subordinate theme. I would have thought that the name of Hugo Leichtentritt, which appeared, for some unaccountable reason, in the midst of a spate of names of 18th-century Italian composers, might have produced more emotional effect on him,[21] but apparently he didn't notice it.

In double counterpoint, he devoted the first hour to an analysis of some fifteen of the chorale-prelude cadences on his mimeographed sheet. "I analyze these," he told us, "not to defend them, but to help you." He did a good bit of defending on the side, and was by no means unwilling to point out some of the clever contrapuntal *trücks* (as he pronounced it) that he had used in solving his difficulties, not always with equal success. During the second hour, he started to write a chorale-prelude for us.

October 28, 1939

Uncle Arnold's health seems to be failing again. He seemed to have quite a nasty cold today, as, in fact, did all of his family. He told me that the boy has been troubled with a sore throat these past few days. I would say that none of the clan were too sturdy! Of course the extremes of temperature we've been having lately—steamingly hot days and bitter cold nights—are not conducive to good health. . .

He didn't touch my "voly" [viola] pieces this time; I've a hunch he's getting a little tired of "voly," and to tell the truth, so am I. Instead, he spent the whole time on my orchestration. My three arrangements of the Beethoven scherzo he found all right but in large part thick and colorless, too schematic and too conventional. For example, at the beginning of the arrangement for eight woodwinds and two horns, I'd used a combination of two bassoons and two clarinets. It was not at all incorrect, and might even sound well in spite of a little weakness in the clarinet register; but, when he asked me why I'd used it, I was bound to hem and haw a little bit and admit I really didn't know why! Thereupon he told me that, whenever he saw that kind of writing in the work of his pupils, he always advised them that they should not use such things just because they'd seen them in the classics, but should, instead, listen carefully

---

[21] For the reason, see above, p. 85.

for the effect they wanted, and ask themselves if, say, that alto instrument was really a second clarinet, or something else? He sketched several other possible arrangements of the passage; none of them was necessarily better than what I had originally written, but they all illustrated this one principle on which he lays so much emphasis. I find that it is not so much the merit of individual cases that concerns him as it is the recognition of basic problems which should be discussed at the first opportunity; and this, I think, is an utterly right and good attitude.

For next time he wants me to arrange the Adagio of Beethoven's Trio, Op. 8, for one flute, one oboe, one clarinet, one bassoon, one horn, and string orchestra. In preparation for this, he spent the last half-hour analyzing the orchestral writing of the slow movements of Beethoven's Second and Fourth Symphonies with me. This, of course, is tremendously advantageous; though I have studied scores a great deal by myself, I always find that a few of his useful suggestions make me see twice as much in them. I was amused by some of his strictures on Beethoven's orchestral writing. "Of this," said he of the famous arpeggiated passage for the strings in the Fourth,[22] "I am not very fond, not really—" but that was mild compared to what followed. At one spot in the Adagio of the Second Symphony,[23] there is a melody played by one flute in the upper octave and by the second violins in the lower. He pointed this out as an example of the advantages of using pure string color in one voice and pure wind color in another, as contrasted with the disadvantages of, say, doubling flute and first violin on one voice and oboe and second violin on the other—a procedure too often resorted to by amateur orchestrators. "And yet," he continued, "I myself could have done this better—wait one moment—ah! now I have it!" Then and there, before my astonished eyes, he proceeded to rip off an up-to-date version of what Beethoven *should* have done! When he had finished, he gazed at his handiwork with self-satisfaction, and remarked complacently, "Yes, this good—this really fine—but, after all, Beethoven already good 'nuff."

You should have seen him rush off in consternation when he heard Ronnie and Nuria having a knock-down fight in the back room! I

[22]The string parts in measures 26-27, second movement.

[23]Measures 226-29.

don't know what it was about; from all I heard, it seems that Ronnie had been building something, and Nuria had either tried to help him a little too efficiently with it or had knocked it down. Those little ones are certainly the apple of his eye! He seemed scared to death for fear Ronnie was getting hurt! As a matter of fact, Ronnie was all in one piece when his loving parent got there, but no one would have thought so from the lusty yells he gave! All was soon patched up, however, for Uncle Arnold came back almost at once with the proudest of smiles upon his face, and the boy stopped squalling.

October 30. 1939

Sound the fanfares! Beat the drums! Why? Because I actually have in my hands at this very moment a book belonging to the Master!

He'd told me to orchestrate the Adagio of Beethoven's Serenade Trio for two weeks from Saturday. In order to carry out this task, Trios were of the essence! I half hoped they'd be in the library, but they weren't ... What to do? I lay in wait at the classroom door, after Structural Functions, and, as soon as he appeared, popped out at him. "Professor SCHOENberg!" I burbled. "Iwasjustatthelibrary antheyhavengottatriosyaknowyawannametadoth'triosfornexttime'n uhcanngettumsowhattagonnado?" not *quite* as fast as that, maybe, but pretty nearly! The secret of making a complete statement to him is to say it so quickly that he hasn't time to interrupt you. All the time I was talking, he was retreating down the hall backwards at a rate of speed that would have done credit to a much younger man. At first I was afraid that he would continue to do so until he was safely locked in his office and quite out of my reach; but, surprisingly enough, he weakened sufficiently to stop. "Well," he said, slowly and thoughtfully, "for this once I let you have my own copy. But, of course, you realize that I cannot do this always." A reasonable enough statement, to which I squeaked my ready assent. "Mr. Stein!" he bellowed, and the docile Stein came up ready for action. "You give Miss Newlin the Beethoven Trios, and you make note that *she have book from my private library*! So, good-bye!" and he was off like a shot, before I should have time to ask him for anything else.

Nothing especially noteworthy happened in the classes today. In composition, he continued to analyze the second themes of Beethoven sonatas, with more regard for their definable form—or lack of it —than for their connection with other motives. This does not worry him so much now, he said. He wants us, for the time being, to write instinctively, and then if our instinct turns out to have been uncommonly illogical he will tell us about it afterwards! In Structural Functions, he went further with his discussion of half-cadences in all their varieties, considering those to the upper and lower mediant this time. I notice that, in some of his explanations, he uses terms and methods somewhat different from, though not inconsistent with, those of the *Harmonielehre*. He does so, he says, because he feels that, in some cases, a slightly different explanation will make things clearer for those who do not have the background of "his" harmony, without at the same time filling their minds with oversimplified, wrong ideas which they will have to get rid of later.

October 31, 1939

We had a rollicking good time at the Hallowe'en party where we were all supposed to come dressed as songs. I was *Die Glückliche Hand*. I wore a bright scarlet skirt and a white sweater with a red belt, neckband, and necklace, and a scarlet beret and short jacket (to suggest the Austrian colors of red-white-red; I thought that might at least give my friends a tip as to the identity of the author!) Across the breast of the sweater I had tied a white ribbon, on which was pinned a royal flush in hearts, and I carried another royal flush in diamonds. (The Lucky *Hand*!) No one guessed my "song"! Then the title had to be acted out in charades; you should have seen the wild antics of *Handküsse*! Finally I had to tell the group what I was. There was a prize for the best costume, which I did not get . . .

November 1, 1939

Schoenberg was replete with good spirits and loving himself as much as ever. I don't know how the subject of mathematics came up, but it did, and elicited from him this comment: "I am not really mathematician; my mind is more geometrical. I think more in blocks and forms. They say the twelve-tone scale is mathematical, but I do not think the number twelve represent *such* high mathematics, no? No, I am *not* mathematician; but then, I was not bad in mathematics. In many, many subjects at school I was really rather good!" You should have seen the rash of knowing smiles that broke out all over the room! I even laughed, but softly. Of course, I do not doubt the truth of the statement in the slightest.

I got the little end in composition class. He glanced at my piece only enough to tell me that "second theme has nothing in" and "you get other one." However little time he has, he always has time to say that! Mr. Carr, though in the same boat as I was, was not inclined to let himself be put off. When Uncle Arnold asked him if he'd looked at his piece last time, C. replied, "Yes, but you made me rewrite it!" "Mr. Carr!" cried the Master, completely and purposefully ignoring the true intent of the remark, "I make everybody rewrite, yes?"

Advanced Analysis was sort of a mess, what with his eternal arguing back and forth as to whether he should order Beethoven Opus Eighteen for the whole class or shouldn't! He is simply dying to make us an assignment in them. After talking pro and con, he finally sent Mr. Stein off to order 12 copies, only to change his mind five minutes later, when he learned that we couldn't get them for 2 weeks and that the price might be higher than listed. So he sent Mr. Stein off again to cancel the order. Now nothing will do but that he write a letter to Mr. Kalmus,[24] with whom he's had dealings about the publication of his own works, telling him that if he wants to do the poor students a favor and give them a 30% reduction, he, the great Schoenberg, will order twelve (12) copies from him. Now wouldn't that touching little episode melt even a heart of stone? If encouraged, I think he would even send Mr. Kalmus pictures of us, showing how undernourished we are!

Once he got off this subject, everything was lovely as usual. He led the class in a fruitful discussion of the derivation of the themes of Op. 18 no. 4 from a basic motive. Our assignment for next time is to study the basic motive and other themes of the 1st movement of Op. 14 no. 1 in a similar manner. He was able to get humor even into as serious a subject as that. He asked, in a very matter-of-fact

[24]Edwin F. Kalmus, a major publisher of inexpensive reprints of musical classics.

way, [here I transcribe his accent] "Now, vat vood you say vass ze preenceepal *seeng* [thing] in zees movement?" Naturally, we all thought he had said *seme*, or *theme*, for that was the word we expected him to use; so we all started to think about the problem on that basis. After a few minutes of silence, he asked us, "Deed you see sompsinks onusual een vat I jost said?" More dead silence. "Vell, vat deed I say? Vat vood you say vass ze preenceepal—" "Theme!" we all chorussed, perfectly sure of ourselves. "Naw! naw! *naw*! I deed not say *seme*, I said *seeng*!" And I'll swear you couldn't hear a penny's worth of difference between his pronunciation of the two words! The reason for the distinction came out later; it was simply that the word *theme* was a little too definite for what he meant.

I was amused by his definition of the function of a teacher. Once, when he was in his early twenties (and already teaching six to eight hours a day), he happened to get into conversation at a party, with a man who was one of the old die-hards of the Vienna Conservatory; a good pedantic contrapuntalist and all that sort of thing, but utterly uninspired, and much scorned by Brahms. (For the sake of convenience, I'll call him Mr. G.) Uncle Arnold told him that his teaching tired him out so that he could hardly compose any more at all. But Mr. G. simply laughed, and replied, "Oh, why, I teach as much as that, and I never get tired at all! After all, all you have to do is just teach what you know!" "At first," Nuncie recounted, "I was much offended by this; but later I laugh to myself, and I say 'yes, all he must do is teach what he knows; this easy! What I do, I teach the student what *he* must know; and this hard!'"

November 3, 1939

My hand is tired . . . for I've already written out dozens of half-cadences to the 5th degree (for Structural Functions) and several chorale cadences (for Double Counterpoint). I'd rather be outdoors watching the tail-end of the Homecoming bonfire . . . but so much of great interest still remains to be recorded. I've long ago discovered that the only conceivable way of bringing coherence to an account of the many disparate subjects that pass through a conversation with Uncle Arnold is to set everything down in chronological order without any attempt to organize it otherwise.

Well, first of all there was composition class, in which he analyzed in brief the first sections of several Schubert sonatas. How he adores Schubert! "Many people say," he remarked, "that Schubert is too long. He is long—yes—but for me he is always too short!" Such was not the opinion, however, of Mr. E., who, when Uncle Arnold asked the class, after Mr. Stein's rendition of the 1st movement of the D-major Sonata, how they liked it, replied, "Well, it seems to me an awful lot of spinning out of not much!" "So?" queried *le maître*. "You think? Mr. Stein! PLAY IT AGAIN!" Talk about the rebuff royal! All during this performance he happily bobbed his head from side to side and danced about in a most outlandish manner, obviously enjoying himself tremendously. Then, at the end, he inquired, "Now did you find this very pleasant?" This time everyone assented, even the stubborn E., who, however, was not squelched even by this demonstration. Shortly afterwards, when S. was telling how, in contrast to Schubert's love of repeating his motives and rhythms, his ideal has always been, at least since the first *Kammersymphonie*, to say as much as possible in the least possible room, E. was heard distinctly to mutter in the background, "Not in *Gurre-Lieder!*"

In Double Counterpoint, he started out with the brave intention of writing at least two verses of a chorale prelude. He fetched his old easel and, in the process, got caught behind the piano, dropped the easel on his foot, stepped on a piece of chewing-gum, and dirtied his hands. Then, he spent the whole first hour writing cadences and showing how we should treat the two outer voices when the chorale-melody makes a cadence. When I returned to the classroom after stepping out into the hall for a few minutes during intermission, he was discussing a weighty problem: what causes him to have a little fever and "warm breath" twenty-four hours before it rains! He doesn't think it can be the moisture, because as soon as it gets to really raining he is all right again. Actually, in all seriousness, he propounds the theory that, previous to a rainstorm, the air must be full of little microbes or death-rays which get right into his delicate tubes! "Cal Tech must once look into this!" he pronounced soberly.

From this fascinating topic, which I fear Cal Tech will never get around to, it was easy enough for him to transfer to the next one: the question of whether or not climate has any influence on art. He contended that it does not and told a most amusing anecdote: when he was in Barcelona, one of his former pupils who lived there told De Falla that he had come, whereupon De Falla wrote him a little

note of welcome, saying that he hoped to see what the influence of
the Spanish climate would be on his composition, or some such
inanity as that. "Of course," continued Uncle Arnold, "this was only
a *maleece* [malice] . He hoped I would come to write like this!"
(Here he rushed over to the piano and biffed out a very creditable
parody of the *Fire Dance*.) "But I thought to myself, now if what
he say really happen, it will be too bad!" That ended the climate
question once and for all.

Just how he came to talk about architecture next, I don't know,
but he did. Naturally enough, he couldn't discuss architecture long
without bringing up the work of his very dear friend, Adolf Loos,[25]
whom he considers the greatest Austrian of his time, and one of the
greatest modern architects, if not the greatest. His houses are conceived of in three dimensions from the beginning, instead of being
thought of in terms of a series of planes fronted by a facade. They
are so constructed that, with the use of only a few occasional steps,
one can proceed from the first floor to the second without being
conscious of the change. Uncle Arnold compares them to sculptures
made of glass, in which one can see all the angles at once. He was
never able to understand sculpture, he wrote in an article for Loos'
60th birthday, until he saw L.'s houses. Loos once said that the
architect is never an artist, and to this view Uncle Arnold subscribes
in full, for he believes that nothing done for a purpose can be art.
What, then, about Chartres Cathedral, and, if you are going to
exclude everything that was done with a so-called ulterior motive in
mind, what about *pièces d'occasion* and portraits? In either case, he
has a ready, too ready, answer. He claims that painting and music
can always be separated from their ulterior motives; portraits depict
the artist more truly than the model, and one would never know,
from listening to a piece of occasional music, for what occasion it
was written; but architecture, never. Besides, he says that you can
never appreciate a building all at once, because you can never see

[25]Loos (1870-1933) was a true pioneer in modern architecture, a firm believer
in functionalism and the elimination of unnecessary ornament. His "House
Without Eyebrows" (i.e., without unnecessary trim above the windows) on
Vienna's *Michaelerplatz* was, to the conservative Viennese, as scandalous as
Schoenberg's music. For a good study of Loos translated into English, see
Ludwig Münz and Gustav Künstler, *Adolf Loos, Pioneer of Modern Architecture*,
tr. Harold Meek, New York, Praeger, 1966.

both outside and inside, back and front, at the same time. The only way you can appreciate the full intent of the architect is by looking at the blueprint, which is not the building. But one can see a painting all at once, and the whole of a piece of music is inherent in one measure of it, just as the taste of an apple is inherent in a single bite. To me, setting architecture apart from all other arts in this manner is an absurdity; but I've vowed to record all his opinions and I'll continue to do so, though I can't resist sticking in my own views here and there. Who could?

He was on firmer ground when he spoke of how nonsensical it was to call Bach a "harmonic" composer. Then, he proceeded to castigate those great admirers of Bach and Beethoven, who hear the beginning and the end of their favorite pieces and dream happily through the middle. They prefer Bach and Beethoven to other composers, because this music disturbs their reveries least. "And then," he added, "there are those who love Bach, call themselves conservatives, and say, 'Now will I hear nothing else as Bach.' Such should not be allowed to become admirers of Bach!" To go back to the problem of their absorption in their own emotions when they should be listening to the music, he says that anyone with a truly cultivated musical ear should be most receptive, when he listens to music, to a special set of musical emotions. Next year he wants to give a course on the production of these musical emotions through form, called *Esthetics in Music As Expressed Through the Technique.* ("Probably," he remarked sardonically, "in the catalogue they will put it *Music Esthetics and Technique!*") He has another one in mind, on *Text and Music*, about oratorios, songs, operas, melodramas, and maybe even monodramas! Both should be most rewarding, I think. He asked us what we thought of them, and everyone in the class expressed most enthusiastic approval.

Comment on Bach: "There was only *one* Bach, but then, there were—ahem!—many *Bachs!*" Well-marked distinction between Bach the composer and Bach the progenitor. He says Bach had an "infinite knowledge of the biology of tone"—rather nicely put, I think. He has real talent for aphorisms which are both trim and truthful.

November 4, 1939

Well, it begins to look as though that famous First Viola Piece, if it ever gets played at all, will have to be announced as "Piece by Newlin-Schoenberg!" Just when I was happily thinking that this revision would probably be the last one and I'd be ready to rush the music to Katims, Uncle Arnold told me that every bit of my harmony is illogical and will have to be completely rewritten! Some of my "interesting harmonies" really "teared his ears," he said. But I can see how much better the first page, which he has caused to look like the Wreck of the Hesperus with all his assorted curlicues and crosshatchings, is than the other three which he hasn't got around to yet. Still, one begins to ask oneself, "How long, oh Lord, how long?" Cheerfully he told me that "whole thing will have to be rewritten this way; we must postpone looking at other one and try to make this one really good. Of course, maybe we will not succeed, but in any case you will have learned something!" Laudable doctrine, but all I can say is, I hope Viola Piece No. 1 will be out of the trenches by Christmas! The piano part steps all over the corns of the viola part, too, which doesn't help a bit.

Looking for a piece of my own music, I chanced to handle some of his manuscripts on the piano. He cried out, "No! no! This *my* music! You not take this; I need this myself!" Playing one spot over on the piano, he fussed very much over how poor it was, until I called his attention to the fact that he was playing it wrong. "Ah, so!" he said brightly. "Then it even worse!"

November 6, 1939

Uncle Arnold lectured in both of his classes today: in composition, on the harmony of the elaboration section of the sonata form, and in Structural Functions on the way we should do our mid-term assignment for next Monday. It's really quite simple, as I should know because I've just finished doing it. You simply take a key (any key except C major; "I," he says, "would consider it degrading to know only one key!"), start with its tonic, and then proceed, in five different examples, to the regions of the dominant, subdominant, mediant, submediant, and second degree, respectively. Then you continue to the region contrasting to that which you have just left, and make a final cadence to a degree selected by him. In the most difficult of the examples, a Phrygian cadence to VI is reached after the example has gone through the region of II and, in contrast to that, the tonic region.

He grows no less perverse (though sweetly so, at least in my estimation) with the passage of time. As I already said, some time ago he decided that, in the composition class, he would look at our work on Wednesdays and lecture on Tuesdays and Fridays. Well, what should he do on this day, a bright little Monday if ever there was one, but inquire who had some compositions for him this afternoon? I think he probably did it just for the pleasure of catching us without our pieces; we'd all written them, but of course most of us hadn't thought to bring them, knowing this was to be an off-day. Be that as it may, but when Mr. E., the only one who had his work with him, started to show it, all Uncle Arnold could say was, "Is it really important? You know I must speak much from the elaboration today. Is it urgent?" "Well, yes," E. replied, "for I don't understand what to do with my second theme." "Oh, write according to your feeling!" exclaimed the Master, waving his arms in a series of fine careless gestures. "Write according to your feeling, and I will correct it later!" Then, without further ado, he went on to lecture about elaborations, and not a word was said about our compositions for the remainder of the hour. I think he rather enjoys giving us the come-on this way, just for the pleasure of slapping us down when we rise to the bait. It was the same in Structural Functions; after explaining our assignment to us, he practically worked himself up into a divine frenzy trying to get us to ask questions about it. Then, when poor C. asked him a question about something-or-other, he responded, "Oh, this not really important. You should ask 'bout other things as this!" The rebuff may seem a little rude, but then C. was already in the doghouse for having thought Nuncie had said we should write in major when, in reality, he'd said *measure* (metre). He pronounces the two words so nearly the same that, unless you were paying close attention, you could hardly tell the difference.

He told an odd thing in composition class—when he was orchestrating the Handel *Concerto Grosso* he found a modulation in one of the elaborations that he didn't like for some reason or other, so he simply remodelled it on the scheme of modulation customarily used in similar cases by Bach. He didn't remember which movement, for he did it in 1932.[26]

[26]Actually, he worked on it from May 20-August 16, 1933. Cf. Josef Rufer, *The Works of Arnold Schoenberg*, tr. Newlin (New York, The Free Press, London, Faber & Faber, 1962), p. 89.

Uncle Arnold could talk of nothing else but *Die Walküre* today.[27]
I'd had an idea he might be there last night, and sure enough he was.
He was very well pleased with the performance on the whole, though
he was no fonder of the "Wagnerian" style of acting than I am; as
to the conduct of the actors in the interludes, he takes the prudent
viewpoint that "the less they do, the better it will be!" Of course,
these long interludes are not the best part of Wagner's operatic style.
S. had more than one thing to say about that. He is not too fond of
the interminable dialogues between two or three characters, and
would prefer an admixture of choruses, duos, trios, quartets, etc.,
as in Italian opera, only not in such a conventional manner. (He
thinks Verdi is a great composer. I do not concur.) He thinks Wagner's idea of making the music-drama as true to life as possible—an
idea of which this making the characters speak one at a time is only
one of the aspects—is true only up to a point. After all, he says, if
two characters are speaking one to the other, it's natural for them
to talk one at a time, but if they are addressing the audience, why
shouldn't they speak together? For the same reason, he doesn't
understand why the monologue has been eliminated from modern
drama. He does not hold at all to the doctrine of those who think
that art should imitate life. "Art," he says, "is not as life; art is truer
as life. For life has no conditions; it just happens. But art has them!"
I think this is a bit of his conservative streak coming out. I know it
seems odd to use that word in speaking of a Schoenberg, but the
trait is there and he even commented on it himself today, in composition class. Somebody had brought a sonata theme in 7/8; he disapproved, for, he said, such a meter required that one should draw
consequences from it which demanded great skill and knowledge.
Then he told of what befell him in writing the 2nd quartet. He
originally conceived this passage [first violin part, opening of Trio
section, second movement] as a real 5/8 measure: later, he altered
it to 2/4, because he didn't quite dare to write it as he really felt it.

[27]The San Francisco Opera was presenting its annual fall season at the Shrine
Auditorium.

"You know," he added, "I was always rather conservative. I did not want to write the way I did, but it is as if someone made me!" I imagine this is a pretty true statement of the real conflict of his life; but I wager it would astonish a great many people, from the most rabid Schoenbergians to the most disapproving conservatives! Especially the latter.

November 10, 1939

Uncle Arnold seemed quite tired today, especially towards five o'clock. But he performed valiantly nonetheless, discussing elaborations further in composition class, and, in double counterpoint, writing a large number of beginnings for his chorale prelude. It was in this class that he was much taken aback at our failure to get the point of one of the most putrid puns I have ever heard. One of his chorale beginnings didn't quite suit him, because, he said, "there are too many E's in it. It is too eee-zy!" Why we didn't understand this at first blush I don't know; in any case, nothing followed but one of those silences that you can cut with a knife. He stood and watched us expectantly for a while. Finally, he could stand the suspense no longer, and exclaimed, "But I made a joke! Why do you not laugh? There were too many E's, I said, it is too eee-zy. Do you not understand?" By this time we were all rocking with laughter, not so much at the joke as at his incredible naiveté. I think he understood this, too, for he said, "Oh, it is very kind of you to laugh. This was really very poor joke, yes?" And, with that, the interlude ended.

November 11, 1939

Well, today I have made one most important discovery: if you want Uncle Arnold to give you an hour and a half lesson for the price of an hour, just let him know that somebody has come for you and is anxiously awaiting your emergence! When I told Ruth Lamb a few days ago that I wouldn't be able to get to her bridal shower till nearly four, she kindly offered to send a friend for me at ten-of-three, *chez* the Master. Uncle Arnold was just about through with my orchestration of the trio—the only thing I'd brought with me—and was finding himself at a loss to fill up the rest of my time, when suddenly the maid appeared and announced, "Miss Lamb's friend has come to get her!" "What? What is this?" queried Nuncie, mystified. I clarified the matter at once by explaining, "It's for me." "Ach. so!" he muttered, and a bright, cunning light crept into his eyes. You should have seen his manner change abruptly from that very moment! He rushed over to the bookcase, fetched down his copy of the Mozart symphonies, and started to talk at length about their orchestration. No point was too small to spend at least five minutes on: why the viola appeared above the second violin (I think he found at least three good reasons for this, and gave a full justification of each one of them!), or why two horns, instead of one, were used in such-and-such a place. Everything he could possibly talk about, in short, he talked about. When he ran out of subjects for commentary, he began to sing, ostensibly to demonstrate the wonderful character of Mozart's melodies! The funniest thing about all this is that I didn't "smell a mice." I simply took all this extra attention as a sign of unusual interest, when what he really wanted was for me to be nervous and distracted because he was preventing me from getting away and keeping my car waiting! Of course, my complete calmness was just ruining his fun. I know he expected the added little fillip of seeing me approach a nervous breakdown; but I guess he failed to count on my being so far gone in my devotion! As the minutes wore on and I showed no signs of anything except the most absorbing interest, his schemes became even more elaborate. Now he was officiously rushing out into the back room and cutting sheets of his own orchestra paper for me to use; now he was making specious offers of getting scores more cheaply for me from Germany through some of his still-devoted friends. All this time I was thinking of nothing but how terrifically sweet and thoughtful he was being today. It wasn't till I was riding down the street with Ruth's friend that it suddenly dawned on me what he'd been up to all this time! No doubt about it, it's utterly in keeping with his capricious, contrary nature; and what proves it is that once, while he was leafing through a Mozart score to find a particular example of the concentration of instrumentation at the cadence, he quickly turned and asked me pointedly, "Are you reading this with me?" I was, as I always do; but the sole reason for the question was that he expected me to be glancing out of the window anxiously, instead. Oh Lord! What a man!

November 12, 1939

The big event of today was the Pro Musica concert, but Uncle Arnold wasn't there! I am really surprised at his not being there, under the circumstances. Maybe he's taken sick since I saw him yesterday; or maybe he thinks E. Toch and J. Achron are getting a little more attention than they ought. No, that could hardly be, for they are his friends and admirers. All this, however, has nothing to do with the concert! *Verklärte Nacht* was beautifully played. I hadn't heard it as a sextet for a long time, but I certainly agree with its honored composer that it is much "nobler and purer" in that version, and certainly as rich. As many times as I've heard that wonderful climax where it forces its way up through D-flat major to D major, it still gives me tingles up my spine. I thought they played the inner parts a little too loud in that section, giving it a kind of "skating-on-ice" sound which it was certainly not meant to have; but that is a minor criticism. Every now and then, never in the noisy parts but always in the beautiful soft lyrical sections, an ambulance siren would come wailing down Flower Street. I really couldn't help thinking of the "einige grosse eiserne Ketten"[28] every time that happened! . . .

November 13, 1939

Contrary to my fears, Uncle Arnold was at work, and well, today. But did he say one word about last night? He did not! . . . In composition, he went on talking about the elaboration section, and then analyzing Beethoven elaborations to demonstrate how wrong everything he had told us about the form was. Now he has injected a bit of spice, romance, or what you will, into his definition of the elaboration. He calls it "the section in which all the themes go on adventures;" or, more metaphysically, "that section where the destinies of the themes are fulfilled." It was in this class that he expressed his conception of the duties of a composer as follows: "The composer should not write to please the audience, he should write to please himself; and he should like what he writes so much that, even if audience do not like it, they will respect and admire it." He has certainly practised what he preaches. In Structural Functions, he continued discussing "balancing of the regions."

November 14, 1939

Papa's latest letter mentioned a new article about Schoenberg in the

---

[28]The "several large iron chains" clanked by the restless spirits of Waldemar and his vassals (*Gurre-Lieder*, Part III).

November *Coronet*, so we bought it. The article was entertaining and clever enough, and fairly impartial, but simply a rehash of all the old stuff. Now why couldn't I do an article on a subject that's never been really treated before, "Schoenberg as Teacher?" I do seriously think of it, and Mamma likes the idea. She and Papa and I could all get together on it in the Christmas holidays, and if it were good I might even make $100 on it. Well, we'll see. Of course it would have to be signed "Anonymous!"

November 17, 1939

Anybody who thinks that "from the sublime to the ridiculous" is just a trite phrase should once see it represented in actuality in Uncle Arnold's classes; for there, if anywhere, it is exemplified in its full meaning. How a man can rise to the heights in discussing the most subtle elaborations and complications of the contrapuntal technique of chorale preludes one minute, and fall into the most atrocious punning on the subject of those "horrible beasties," flies, the next (examples: "Next year, I will especially order some baseball players to catch the flies;" "What we need is not a flute player, but a Flit player!") without being self-contradictory or ridiculous, is beyond me. But he is constantly going from one extreme to the other and, as long as we are under the spell of his tongue, we never perceive the discrepancy. Described to outsiders, I know this particular heaven of ours must sound like some strange surrealistic Cloud-Cuckoo-Land, but, from experience, I know very well that, once these outsiders had wandered into it, it would seem as natural to them as it does to us!

God knows how he got onto the subject—as I recall he arrived there by way of the use of nails in the piano to simulate the sound of a harpsichord in our production of *Le bourgeois gentilhomme*; the virtues of Moór's[29] modern double-keyboard piano; the obsolete-ness of octave-doublings; Verdi's occasional use of six *fortes* (in

[29]Emanuel Moór (1863-1931), prolific Hungarian composer, is best known for his invention of the "Duplex Coupler Grand Pianoforte." Schoenberg, while admiring the instrument's potential, seems never to have written for it. Full information on it is in Herbert A. Shead, *The History of the Emanual Moór Double Keyboard Piano*, published by the Emanual Moór Double Keyboard Piano Trust in 1978.

Otello) merely for the psychological effect on the player; Schumann's putting at the head of a piece "as fast as possible" and then following it up a little later with "Faster!"; his own habit of writing tempo indications a little faster than he really means them (because the tendency is to play too slowly)—but all of a sudden, he was going into the most elaborate detail concerning the different tempos of marching in Germany, Austria, France, England, and America, complete with demonstrations, which usually involved his tripping over my toes! No point seemed too small for him to go into: whether the length of the marching step was really seventy-five centimeters or sixty centimeters; whether marching in earlier times was, as he had been told, as slow as sixty steps a minute (it is 126 here, I believe, and was 118 in Austria when he was in the army), or whether, as Philipp Emanuel Bach seems to imply in his *Versuch*, the tempo was nearer the pulse-beat; whether, on account of people's eating more in the eighteenth century, said pulse-beat would be faster or slower than the present normal rate of about eighty; we began to think there was no aspect of the matter that he would not investigate! Then, suddenly brought back to earth by the reappearance of the fly (it was at this point that he exclaimed, naïvely enough, "Oh, the *horrible* beastie! What can he be finding on me?"), he asked, "Now how did we get to this?" And, although we'd all been listening spellbound, wondering what he was going to start talking about next, not one of us could recall to him exactly the route which had led him to this far-distant point! I think I've got it right here, but I dare say that if everyone in the class were to write an account of what happened, the stories would look very different from one another . . .

It was in composition class, while we were analyzing elaborations of Beethoven sonatas, that he fell back—justifiably enough, in this case—on what we erudite medievalists call "ye olde Henry Adams dodge." (You know: "Ooh, Dr. Brush, don't you think this is too, *too* sincere for translation?") Well, in this case, it wasn't too sincere for translation, but too tough for explanation, as the "it" in question was that devilish little elaboration of the first movement of Op. 7. He'd just been talking about the extremely abrupt reappearance of the tonic at the recapitulation without any preparation whatsoever, when E. asked, "Why is this so?" Peeking out coyly from behind one of his beatific smiles, Schoenberg replied, "One should not explain this. This one must feel!" And that was that, though he did at once proceed to give some possible reasons for the truly unique phenomenon (*not* explanations, as he carefully specified).

✍ November 20, 1939

In composition class Schoenberg came out with one of the most perfect examples of evasion that I have ever heard, even from him. He was discussing a sequence in one of the Beethoven sonatas and brought out the point that, beginning in the fourth measure, it differed materially from the model. "But," questioned a student, "doesn't it already begin to vary before the fourth measure?" "No, no," spluttered the Master, "this not important! As much as I see it, it is just the same till measure 4, and anyway we do not speak about what happens before, we speak about the fourth measure! Besides, you cannot expect that I should know every note in every one of these sonatas; would be a life work, no? But as much as I know, it is just the same, and anyway, is not important!" As a final sop to his own injured feelings, he gave us the assignment of carrying out the sequence the way it would be if it were strict! He does not like to be taken up in error, even if it is done legitimately.

✍ November 22, 1939

My sixteenth birthday—and the most wonderful birthday I've had in a long time. The finest present of all was Uncle Arnold. The dear man didn't exactly behave like a prize package today, though. He put my piece (sonata theme) off till last for the umpteenth time, and corrected it only by slicing out three measures in a very offhand way, then said "No!" every time I tried to answer a question about the Scherzo [of Beethoven's Op. 18. No. 4]. Mamma says I should contrive to slip little anonymous notes into his coat-pocket, or any other accessible cache, reading like this:
"Do you know Dika Newlin?"
"Dika Newlin thinks you are the cat's whiskers."
"Dika Newlin considers you the ideal man."
and so forth and so on, eventually leading up to the grand climax, "Dika Newlin is out of money!" Not a bad idea, though I fear he might begin to realize the provenance of the communications!
Celebrated at a double feature, *Jamaica Inn* and the Marx Brothers

in *A Day at the Circus*. One wonderful line from the Marx picture:
"You may be detestable, but you are also cute." Doesn't that apply
perfectly to Uncle Arnold? It should be cut out and framed, or,
better yet, carved over his office door.

🖋 *November 25, 1939*

Alas, alas, Uncle Arnold doesn't love me any more! At least, if one
measures the strength of his love by the amount of "overtime" he
gives me on Saturdays, for I didn't get one minute of it today. What's
more, I'm afraid I won't have any after this, for B. arrived just as
my time was up, and I fear that his lesson may have been put at that
hour. . . . Oddly enough, I ran into B. again later when I was buying
music paper at Kelley's. He told me that he is working on a viola
sonata! Now don't tell me we're going to have a bit of rivalry here?
I guess that was why Uncle Arnold asked me about my viola piece
just as I was leaving.

He looked only at my new orchestration of the Trio this time,
and found it correct enough, but a bit lacking in imaginativeness in
the creation of new parts for the added instruments. For next time
he wants me to do the first movement of Beethoven's Op. 18, no. 5,
and as much of the Minuet as I can. He would like to see me be a
little more daring in my orchestration, and not so afraid of doing
something wrong. He wants to see what I'm capable of doing when
I let myself go, and, I suspect, so that he can find more mistakes to
tussle with! Of course, the more mistakes I make, the more he
comments, and the more I learn.

Poor Mrs. Schoenberg was all in a flurry over having to take little
Ronnie down to the Village to have his curls cut. He's a very devil
to take out on the street, it seems; gets away from her whenever he
can, and the only way for her to get him back is to pretend she
doesn't want him. If he thinks she's worried about him, he runs
about so that she can never catch him at all. It's no use for her to
put a baby-harness on him, for then he simply lies down and won't
budge an inch. It looks as though he must have more than a dash of
Caledonian blood in him.[30] "Really," she told Mamma, "he'll have

---

[30]I.e., he behaved like my stubborn Scottie Tammy.

to be a conductor when he grows up, he wants so much attention all the time!" Of her two children, she seems to prefer Nuria, and is always talking about how dependable, quiet, polite, etc., she is. I think N. has a soupçon of her father's attention-getting desires, too, but is apparently submerged by her more ebullient brother ... I guess she is more like her mother in disposition. Poor Mrs. S. certainly has her hands full with the two of them, and the dog, and the cat, and, last but not least, the great man.

November 27, 1939

We had a jolly little four-hand session this afternoon in composition class. Mr. Stein and I were the occupants of the "hot seat", and the unfortunate victim was the first movement of Beethoven's Op. 18, No. 6. It really wasn't half bad, and Uncle Arnold was surprisingly decent about the whole thing. Of course, he stood over us and breathed hotly down the backs of our necks, and kept spurring us on to play faster and faster, but at least he didn't try to make a bear-baiting episode out of the performance! In fact, he even went so far as to compliment us. About five minutes before the end of the hour, when he suddenly took a notion to have us do the first movement of no. 5, he asked us if we thought we could play that as well as what we had done before. Naturally enough, we both replied that we could. "Well then," said he, "if you do as well as that, is all right, yes!" That means a lot, coming from him!

His cutest remark of the day was made in Structural Functions (where we analyzed Mozart's C-minor Fantasia), in reply to a student who told him that the reason all the people of last year's analysis class didn't have Mozart sonatas was that he'd told half the class to buy Mozart and half Schubert. "Yes. Quite so!" the Master replied. "One half of each student buys Mozart and the other half buys Schubert. This what I meant!"

November 29, 1939

In Structural Functions, he discussed the contrapuntal devices used in the Scherzo of Beethoven's Op. 18, No. 4, showing that they were not carried out in nearly as strict a manner as they easily could have been, because this is, after all, a homophonic piece and not a contrapuntal one. Trying to get us to make a judgment of our own upon this question without his aid—a thing he likes to do as often as he can, so as to train our minds thoroughly in independent logical thinking—he asked us, "Now, supposing you were a music critic—a music critic who could read score—what would you say about this question? No, don't laugh, why should not a music critic be able to read score? It could happen, no?"

One very good joke I heard of his making in first-year composition class: it seems that while Mr. T.'s piece was being played, S. suddenly started to gallop up and down the room yelling, "Hiyo, Silver!" to indicate what it sounded like. Isn't that terrible?

🖉 *December 1, 1939*

It makes me sick to think that I could have gotten Uncle Arnold to look at my new sonata if I'd only had it with me! Not having anything else to do in composition class today, he spent about half of the time looking at the pieces of those who had been smart enough to bring them along, and the rest showing us Beethoven's sketches, particularly those for Op. 2 no. 1 and the Adagio of the Ninth Symphony. He listened to the UCLA football game last night until about nine-thirty when he decided it was time for him to go beddy-bye. Well, I never would have expected the dear old man to be as Americanized as all that. It's true, though, that he does pride himself on his "modernity" and loves to work in a bit of the latest slang whenever he can. Just another inexplicable element in a strange character! As poor Mrs. Schoenberg said of her youngest, "He is unpredictable!"

That fly (the one from two weeks ago that gave rise to the remark about the Flit player) is back in Double Counterpoint again, as persistent as ever. "Oh, this beast must want to visit my classes!" exclaimed Nuncie, "or perhaps he is my enemy because I wish to exclude him from fugues!" (He doesn't believe at all that *fugue* comes from *fugere*, to fly, so that's the source of the rather recondite pun.) He kept on with his own chorale prelude, in spite of the interference of the winged demon; didn't look at ours, as I had thought he might.

December 2, 1939

Sigma Alpha Iota initiation was nice . . . but I'm sorry to say that it prevented me from spending a whole afternoon with Uncle Arnold when he was in one of the sweetest moods I've seen him in for a long time! When I went into the house, my ears were assailed by a terrific blast of sound, which turned out to be *Die Meistersinger* (the Metropolitan broadcast), and my eyes, by the funniest sight I've seen in a long time, a perfectly gorgeous example of Viennese *Gemütlichkeit.* To the accompaniment of the *Dance of the Apprentices* turned on full blast, Ronnie and Nuria were scampering about the floor shrieking and yelling, Nuncie dancing his wife all over the room with the greatest abandon and singing all the choral parts with much gusto, and I don't know what Roddie was doing, but it must have been something! Before I knew what I was doing, I had the score in my hands and was trying desperately to follow it, considerably impeded by Uncle Arnold's constant gesticulations right under my nose (by this time he'd stopped dancing and was busily pointing out to me all the high points of the orchestration, still singing all the chorus parts in the thickest German). Such an infernal racket you never did hear, and I would have had quite a hard enough time following the score without his help, but he kept on imparting gems of useful knowledge between verses of the chorus, and asked me from time to time, "You can hear the instruments, yes?" I could hardly hear anything except a general confused noise, but I nodded my head in vigorous assent anyway, and he continued with his program notes. We were having a high old time when suddenly it occurred to him to ask me if I could stay for the whole opera and take my lesson afterwards. Isn't it the limit? Any other time I would have been able to do it and would have had the time of my life, but I had to tell him that people were coming after me at three. I was really heartbroken over it, and he was disappointed too, for he thought it would have been a fine thing for me to be able to follow the score as I listened. Thank goodness he wasn't angry about it! In fact, he was sweeter than sugar . . . all afternoon; actually admitted that the third movement of my trio could be very good if completely reworked. And what do you suppose? The League of Composers wrote to him a while back and asked him to recommend some promising young composer for their December program, and he gave them *my name.* Isn't that marvelous? Of course, I may not be able to get this trio on to the program; he wants it done over as a piano quintet, which will take time, and of course it must be perfect to be sent in with his recommendation. But, all the same, think of his having done such a thing for me! I was quite beside myself when he told me, so much so that he commented several times on my being so nervous. I guess he was right, because when I left at 3:10 I completely forgot my purse and hat until I was practically to the garden gate, and then had to come tearing back after them, to his great amusement.

December 3, 1939

Deems Taylor happened to say something slighting about Schoenberg in the intermission of the N.Y. Philharmonic broadcast. I will write him a letter about it!

December 4, 1939

The "Old Man" seemed in good mood today. He actually condescended to look at the first part of my sonata, and let it go by without too much criticism. Well, he did say it was "*Mooch* Brahms," and he did say it was awfully long, or was that just because I played it too slowly? But those things are just in the day's work. He will let me continue with it and "we will correct it later"—that old game again. His chief preoccupation was with his newest brain-child, a students' foundation for the establishment of a music lending library. He certainly is fired up with enthusiasm over the idea, and rightly, for I think it is a good one. The whole thing is to be on a voluntary basis, at least in theory; in practise, he'll assign the students thus-and-so for their homework in such a way that they'll either have to be members of the library foundation at a cost of a nickel a week, or buy the books themselves! He estimated that, with some two hundred people paying that amount, we should be able to buy 800 volumes a year, not counting donations, etc. He can get books free from Universal and Peters, and, said he with unexampled generosity, he would even maybe buy us a few himself! Of course, before all these fine plans can go into effect the interest of the students must be aroused—and that's where I come in. He wants to have two committees to work the whole business out: a big one composed of representatives from each of the music classes and each of the music organizations, whose duty it will be to announce the project in their classes and organizations and collect the names of all who are interested; and a little one, which will tell the big one what to do! My duty is to talk the thing up big to my SAI sisters. Nuncie cautioned all of us not to make our announcements too dry: to lay great stress on the noble ideals of this wonderful thing we are doing, etc. etc. Of course, a few brave souls must take our final plans to Provost Hedrick so that he may give his approval for the collection of money in class. One reason Uncle Arnold wanted to have the movement emanating from the students was so that there would be as little red tape and "officiality" as possible about the arrangements . . . Nelson and Rubsamen were in on the discussion this afternoon and seemed to be highly in favor of his plan.

Tomorrow morning I will attend, in my official capacity, the first regular meeting of the SFFS Organizing Committee: Nuncie's name for the new white elephant—Students' Foundation For Students.

December 6, 1939

Oh, what a day, what a day, what a day—or should I rather say, what a night? All this excitement is because of our great Schoenberg's lecture this evening.[31] Just as I'd expected, the affair was absolutely a three-ring circus.

First of all, we were lucky enough to get perfectly splendid seats, right up in the front row on the center aisle. This was one of those long narrow rooms with terrible acoustics, in which a Stentor would have difficulty making himself heard, let alone poor Nuncie with his husky voice. A microphone on the speaker's table was supposed to obviate this difficulty; but Uncle Arnold seemed to think that placing his hand on the stem, or stalk, of the instrument would, in some way, cause it to magnify his voice. Of course most of the time he simply forgot that the thing existed; he walked happily up and down the platform just as he does in class, contentedly absorbed in his subject, having a wonderful time, deliciously titillating his friends and relations in the first four rows, and not being heard by a single

[31]At the Los Angeles Public Library.

soul in the back. Poor Mrs. Schoenberg kept frantically motioning to him in the direction of the microphone; three-quarters of the time he didn't notice what she was doing, but when he did he would favor her and the rest of the audience with the broadest of smiles, happily bounce over to the microphone, firmly grasp it with one knotty hand, hug it affectionately to his "buzzum," and continue to talk into space at a point usually a good arm's length from the mike. The only time he ever really got the idea of how the thing was to be used was when some long-suffering listener in the back row frantically yelled out "Louder!" "So!" shouted back the Master, beaming cherubically, and yelling right into the mike in such a way as to make it produce a most horrible grating noise. "This better, no?" For about five minutes thereafter he talked into it most dutifully; then he completely "disremembered" and began the perfectly goofy behavior which I've just been describing. None of this, as you can imagine, was helping the audience to understand him any too clearly, and still less helpful were his stutterings and stammerings and hemmings and hawings over the insoluble problems of the English language. Usually he was able to muddle through with some kind of word or other—sometimes *very* other, as when he talked for a good five or ten minutes about the techniques of operatic music in what he called "controversialal" passages. But every now and then he stopped dead, completely at a loss for grammatical utterance; you never saw anyone quite so stymied. Be it to his eternal credit that he was perfectly frank and open about these occurrences. With a look at the same time pitiful, trusting, and desperate, he would turn to Dr. Rubsamen in the front row, hop up and down like a jumping bean and cry out, "Word, word, word! Help me, *help* me!" It didn't take first-rate acoustics to enable the audience to appreciate that! From the first row to the last, everyone was rocking with laughter.

All this sounds terrific enough, but it is as nothing compared with the strange and wonderful things that occurred during the musical interludes. He had the lecture arranged in such a way that, after each discussion of a special function of operatic music (e.g., to cover up the noises made by the audience. He had a lovely story for this one, of how, while the Kolisch Quartet was playing Beethoven during the intermission of a performance of *Pierrot* in Spain, the people in the boxes folded up their programs in the shape of little

airplanes and sailed them from one box to the next. He may consider himself damned lucky that they didn't launch the flotillas
during *Pierrot*!)—well, after each of these discussions, Mr. Stein
would play, or a record would be played of, an operatic passage
illustrative of the point in question. The way Nuncie acted during
the music was something that cannot be properly described on
paper but had to be seen. He swung and he swayed; he tapped his
feet on the floor and flung his hands around in the most elaborate
conductorial gestures you ever saw, and he could even be observed
to sing very quietly and happily to himself, once in a while
completely forgetting where he was and bursting forth into magnificent sound-effects (notably in the "tunderstorm" of the *Barber of
Seville*). This may all sound like affectation when written down, but
it wasn't. I valiantly tried to keep my eyes level with his own the
whole time, so as not to miss one of his marvelous facial expressions,
but he was so sublimely comical during these little interludes that
several times I had to look very hard at the floor and hold my
breath, just to keep from breaking out in uncontrollable laughter at
the most inappropriate places. As I was sitting right up in one of the
most prominent spots in the room, it didn't take him long to perceive the devastating effect he was having on me. All during the duo
from the *Magic Flute*, he kept me on the verge of hysterics with his
clownish antics. The minute he had my eye, he would smile at me
very broadly and pinkly, with the most malicious twinkle in his eye,
and I, not wishing to be outdone in sweetness, would smile back a
little sheepishly. This would be repeated an indefinite number of
times, with him happily weaving his head back and forth all the
while and singing so softly that he couldn't be heard by anyone
beyond the front row, I'm sure! I got redder and redder with each
succeeding minute, and finally had to avert my eyes completely,
just to hold myself in one piece! Oh Lord, what fun! On top of being
all the other marvelous things he is, the man is a consummate clown
and a glorious mountebank, there is no doubt about it.

Right in the middle of discussing some very weighty problem—it
was after he'd had one of those unfortunate mishaps with the microphone—he suddenly exclaimed, "Oh, this reminds me good story!"
and rushed into the most charming little anecdote about Alban Berg.
In 1904 or thereabouts, when Berg, then young and very shy ("but
very nice," added Nuncie parenthetically), was studying with him,

high, stiff, fence-like collars and cuffs were all the fashion. In Viennese polite society one sat on the edge of one's chair to show deference to elders. Behold poor Berg, then, as perfectly reincarnated by his master, perched most uncomfortably on the edge of a very hard-looking chair, unable to turn his head in the direction of the great man's peregrinations (he walked while teaching then just as much as he does now) because of the confining wing collar, and reduced to turning his body stiffly and regularly to right and to left! A taking and pathetic picture, to my mind. I should very much like to have known Berg . . .

December 8, 1939
[written at Mt. Wilson where
I'd gone for a mini-vacation]

Dear Uncle Arnold seems terrifically far away now. I'll wager the poor old man is wondering right now why I wasn't in double counterpoint class! He was in one of his conversational moods today, just talked about one thing after another in the most fascinating way. He started out with a remark to the effect that if you habitually compose at the piano you should try composing away from it and vice versa, and then . . . got onto Sibelius. We'd just been talking of Horowitz, how wonderful he was (Nuncie'd heard him for the first time at some party of Berlin newspapermen when he was utterly unknown, and had gone home and told his wife, "Well, I heard a very remarkable pianist today!") Naturally enough, that led to the subject of Liszt. Somebody asked him what he thought of Liszt as a composer, and he replied that he'd never admired him very highly, that you have to be a follower of such a composer in your "very youth" to like him at all later. (Of course, he was a Brahmsian during his "very youth.") Then he proceeded to say that Liszt belonged in the same class with Berlioz, Mendelssohn, Bruckner, and Sibelius. Strange bedfellows, if you ask me! The Liszt-Berlioz part of it is all right, but I really can't see what any of the others have in common, especially not Liszt and Sibelius! He says that all these composers are "tone-poets" rather than symphonists, that is, they write episodically and without great care for closely-knit form. Take Sibelius, for example: he starts out with a very interesting idea, but pretty soon he begins to go astray. Then he stops, and then he gets a new idea, also very good, and repeats the same process, without any apparent reason for the stops or the starts. This method is characteristic of all five composers, as is also a tendency to be longwinded. That they are all great personalities, he recognizes; but he would certainly never put them in the first rank.

Then he got to talking about Toscanini's interpretation of the Ninth Symphony last Saturday [on the NBC Symphony broadcast]. He didn't like it one little bit! Of course, some things were good; the Adagio, for example, was taken at just the right tempo, and Toscanini's faculty of making two or three voices stand out with crystal clarity against all the others was still as strong as ever. But the Scherzo went much too fast, and in the first movement there were many illogical tempo changes, in contrast to T.'s usual metronomic regularity. In this connection, Nuncie has a very interesting idea on *accelerando* and *ritardando*. He believes . . . that these changes should not be sudden, as most performers make them, but should be so gradual as to deceive the hearer's sense of rhythm; and he thinks that this effect should be produced by "making the size of the measure slightly irregular"—to wit, by broadening the weak beats first in *ritardando*, and by shortening the strong beats first in *accelerando*.

December 9, 1939
[returned from Mt. Wilson]

Uncle Arnold was glad to see me for my lesson, but had apparently never noticed that I was gone part of yesterday. Had to wait for him a little while, as the family was still having lunch. Enjoyed watching the antics of little Nuria and little Ronnie, who came in to keep us entertained until the Master was ready. Nuria was having great fun batting a big yellow balloon about the room, busily describing her visit to Santa Claus this morning. Ronnie had asked him for a choo-choo train, but all she wanted was a "surprise," which she will surely get if I can do anything about it. Ronnie, in crimson boots and blue shorties, mostly unbuttoned and practically falling off, was deep in thought, rehearsing the little song he was to sing at a birthday party this afternoon.

Nuncie spent all the time on the third movement of the piano quintet. He thinks I've improved it a good bit, but much remains to be done and he finds new things to correct each time. One place had him absolutely stumped; he knew the harmony was weak, but couldn't for the life of him see why, or what to do about it. "Oh, this so queer!" he kept saying; "Oh, this mess!" Finally he found a satisfactory way out of the dilemma, but not without pointing a moral: "When you see in such a place the harmony is weak, you had better not try to correct it, but build something entirely new. You see, it took me one hour to correct this place; now, how long would it take you?" I hear no more about the League of Composers performance . . . He now talks of arranging a performance of it at school for me.

December 11, 1939

Uncle Arnold is in one of his pesky moods this week, I fear, at least as far as I am concerned. He didn't like me a bit today! When I offered the use of my apartment for the meetings of the composers and players club that he's trying to encourage (he even wants to offer dinners and entertainment, now, to induce interest!) he replied, "Oh, but your living-room is not big enough, no?" He's never seen my living-room in his life, but that doesn't seem to bother him any. I think the ideal place for these get-togethers would be the home of Arnold Schoenberg . . . Diffidently producing my copy of *Pierrot Lunaire*, I said, "You said you'd analyze the piano style of your *Pierrot* this time." "*Did* I?" he asked, with surprise and annoyance. This was not what I had expected at all, for he's usually only too glad to show us his works. However, we all urged him on, and, once he warmed to his work, he seemed to enjoy pointing out how nice this was and how well this sounded and how "smoozie" that was . . . I hadn't known before that he actually wrote it on commission for Albertine Zehme. He spoke rather sharply of her, said that it probably wasn't at all what she wanted, she would have preferred something with a crash here and a beep there and a few little trills in the middle. But she was "very nice" about the results of his labors, and, in fact, really enthusiastic about them. And here's another interesting fact: Ravel once told S. that he had received a letter in which Stravinsky quite frankly confessed his indebtedness to *Pierrot* for the idea of *The Story of A Soldier*. I wonder if the letter is still extant?[32]

Oh, he was all excited in Structural Functions about Fantasias. (This came up *in re* the Mozart C-minor *Fantasia*.) It's just occurred to him to wonder why their logic, or lack of logic, should be different from that of other works of art; why all works of art should not have to be equally and similarly logical. The only explanation that comes to him just now is that their logic is like that of the pictures in a dream, which are not logically connected but are connected just the same. But he couldn't say why it's right that this should be so. (Side-note: he dreams very often of flying when his foot gets out from under the covers at night.) Now, he wants to compare all the Fantasias he can, to find out just what their system of logic is, and what justifies their existence. The same problem, he says, exists with regard to recitatives, something I'd never thought of before.[33] His brain is incredibly fertile: every day a new idea, or five, or ten. If they do not all bear fruit at once, who cares?

Plans for the Library are blossoming cheerily. We even have a constitution drawn up now. All we need is official sanction to forge right ahead. Won't Nuncie be delighted? He was quite late to class today on account of a lengthy discussion of the business with Mr. Allen, I suppose.

December 13, 1939

We've had the last class of the year with Uncle Arnold this afternoon, and I really am going to miss him through the vacation. Not

[32]Stravinsky attended the dress rehearsal of *Pierrot Lunaire* on October 9, 1912. He was deeply impressed, and discussed the work with Ravel when they were both staying in Clarens, Switzerland, early in 1913. The fruits of this discussion were Ravel's Mallarmé songs and Stravinsky's Japanese songs. Later that year, Ravel wanted to present these works on a concert in Paris, together with *Pierrot Lunaire* (he called this "an admirable plan for a concert to stir up a row"). This was not done until fifty years later, by Pierre Boulez. (H.H. Stuckenschmidt, *Maurice Ravel: Variations on His Life and Work*, Philadelphia, Chilton, 1968, pp. 130-131.)

[33]Cf. Schoenberg, *Structural Functions of Harmony* (New York, W.W. Norton, 1954, rev. 1969), Chapter XI (section on the so-called "Free Forms").

that I won't be seeing him on Saturdays, but an hour once a week is different from two or three hours four times a week! I really am afraid that I may get cut out of one lesson during the vacation, too. As I suspected, he is going away at some time, I don't know when. To Kansas City, this time, [for the Music Teachers' National Association convention] to deliver two speeches, one on how a music student can earn a living, the other on composition as ear-training.[34] He's going to have records made of them, too, which will be played at one of the meetings of the Phi Mu Alpha (men's professional music fraternity) Convention here at the end of the month. That means I might be able to hear them, because SAI is invited *en masse* to one of the convention dinners, on the 29th.

Heard the rest of Part I, and Part II of *Gurre-Lieder* this afternoon. It is glorious, but I was surprised at the tempo of Part II, as fast as a quick military march. Is this right, I wonder?

I did write that letter to Deems Taylor *re* Schoenberg today, and posted it this afternoon. I hope it may have the desired effect. The original text (later somewhat revised) follows. Doesn't it sound just like a high-school oration?

> Dear Mr. Taylor,
>
> In your broadcast of December 3, commenting upon modern trends in composition, you made the remark that Arnold Schoenberg, after writing two works so representative of post-Wagnerian Romanticism as *Verklärte Nacht* and *Gurre-Lieder*, suddenly turned his back on all that had gone before, and deliberately set about to construct a carefully calculated, mathematical system of which the basis is the twelve-tone scale.
>
> *Verklärte Nacht* was completed in 1899, *Gurre-Lieder* in 1901; the first of the twelve-tone compositions (Op. 23) did not appear until 1923. Do not these dates in themselves postulate a slow, gradual and natural development, rather than a sudden, deliberately calculated and self-contradictory change? Schoenberg himself has said that, far from the iconoclastic radical that he has often

[34]"Eartraining Through Composing" was given at the MTNA convention on December 30, 1939. Reprinted in *Style and Idea* (London, Faber & Faber, 1975), pp. 377-81. (Note: all page references to *Style and Idea* will be to the 1975 edition unless otherwise indicated.)

been accused of being, he was always rather conservative. Even as late as the time of the second string quartet, he was constantly trying to restrain the impulses that drove him onward irresistibly towards the acme of concentrated logic. "I did not want to do these things," he says, "it is as if someone made me!" And, while that statement may contain some grain of exaggeration, is it not more logical to take the word of the composer himself concerning the development of his own genius than to believe in a hypothesis which implies that his mental habits are entirely alien to those of the true artist? The great innovators of all time did not institute their epoch-making changes in cold blood; they followed the irrevocable dictates of their artistic natures sincerely and courageously, against all opposition. Why should the mental processes of a Schoenberg be considered to be different from those of a Bach or a Beethoven?

As to the "mathematical" character of Schoenberg's latest compositions, I could not do better than quote his own recent remark on the subject: "They say I am mathematically minded because I write in the twelve-tone scale; but I do not think twelve is such high mathematics, do you?" This, of course, is pure sarcasm—but when I think about the matter, I myself begin to wonder why that scale of twelve should be considered so much more complicated than the scale of seven. Schoenberg himself has so often reiterated that his system is not destructive of the classical system, but is simply a natural extension of it, that I hardly need to say it again; but how many people seem to think that composing in the twelve-tone system is like resolving a complex problem in calculus, and involves little more inspiration than that! As a matter of fact—and again I am citing Schoenberg—compositions in the twelve-tone system are written as much according to the feeling and inspiration of the composer as are any others; which is to say that they are entirely so written, for the truly great composer dares to follow his imagination, knowing that it must lead him in the right direction. In the white heat of inspiration, one writes fast and fluently, and Schoenberg wrote his third and fourth string quartets, two of the most frightening of his works to the uninitiated, in six weeks each!

Bach, whose music is perhaps the most sublimated expression of human emotion ever written, wrote marvelous fugue-themes in double and triple counterpoint as naturally as he breathed. But do we mock his "arid mathematics" because he happened to be the greatest contrapuntist that ever lived? Why, then, should Schoenberg be reviled for his perfectly sincere attempt to extend that technique to its logical conclusion? Whether we believe that attempt to be successful or not, we must respect it, and, above all, recognize it for what it is!

December 22, 1939

Mrs. E. has offered to take us to the Schoenberg concerts of the Fourth Sunday Evenings on the Roof (January 28 and 30) at which Radiana Pazmor is singing.[35] I've known about the concert for some time, but have been afraid I wouldn't be able to go. Won't it be a treat if it works out? I *hope* Schoenberg will be there.

December 23, 1939

This was our day to wish Uncle Arnold a Merry Christmas in a most tangible fashion: for him, a box of candied walnuts, made by Mamma's own hands and cracked by mine, and A. A. Milne's *The House at Pooh Corner* and *Winnie-the-Pooh*, sumptuously wrapped by the clerks at Campbell's, for Ronnie and Nuria respectively. I'd planned to present them all to him with a bit of pomp and ceremony, but it just didn't work out that way. You see, not knowing what his reaction to the little gifts might be, during my lesson I'd carefully kept them out of sight, in a very flimsy brown paper bag in the corner. Such precaution may be very laudable, but in this case, it caused me to forget all about my mission until the very moment when I was making ready to leave his little room. "Oh!" I exclaimed, suddenly remembering the *raison d'être* of the brown-paper parcel.

[35]Evenings on the Roof, at that time Los Angeles' most distinguished chamber-music series, with emphasis on contemporary works, took place at 1735 Micheltorena Street, near Silver Lake. They were organized by Peter Yates and his wife, the pianist Frances Mullen.

"I almost forgot, I have something for you!" And, running back to the corner, I picked up the bag—only to have the bottom tear out, and see all the packages cascading to the floor in a perfect torrent of silver ribbon, Christmas seals, and wrapping-paper! Uncle Arnold practically burst himself laughing at me. I blushed a scarlet red, retrieved my parcels a little shamefacedly, and shoved them into his arms with a sheepishly muttered "Merry Christmas!" Well, he was tickled to death—fairly burbled over with "Oh, thank you! You are so nice, this so good of you, oh thank you!"—and kept wringing my hands in gratitude until I was quite afraid he'd make me miss the 3:30 Castellamare bus! When I saw his enthusiasm, I began regretting that I hadn't given the things to him before the lesson instead of after, for, as it happened, he'd been peculiarly dissatisfied with everything I'd done with the Quintet for this time . . . He wants to give me my next lesson on the first Thursday morning in January. All right; but I can't help feeling that said lesson will be the "first lesson in munce" in January, and that the hypothetical "5th lesson in munce" will go the way of all good things! I hope not, though . . . He delivered quite a little curtain-lecture on the great necessity of artistic morals, telling how all his great pupils had always been so sincere and straightforward and idealistic (i.e., perfectly devoted and loyal to him). "Of course," he remarked, "this I cannot teach; oh, there are some things I can do to help, but one must be born with this!" It was with great glee that he spoke of how he knew so well "what was good for young people": which ones to encourage and praise, which ones to discourage, in order to bring out the best they had in them. I'm afraid he sometimes thinks I belong in the latter category; not that he didn't pass out a few good words for me. He said that I'd made progress, there was no doubt (well, I should *hope* there was none!), that I worked hard, and that he wished me every success—this last after I'd given him his presents. By the way, today he made the first remark I've ever heard him make about musical talent in his family. He thinks his must have just happened, for the only musician in his family was his mother's uncle,[36] who was only a singer at that. His father sang a little too,

[36]Perhaps he was thinking of his mother's brother Fritz (Friedrich), who strongly influenced his intellectual development. Fritz' son Hans became a highly successful tenor and "created" the role of Waldemar in *Gurre-Lieder*. See below, p. 273, and Stuckenschmidt, *Arnold Schoenberg: His Life, World and Work*, pp. 16-18.

but only in an amateurish sort of way for his own amusement. He says Nuria has shown no signs of musical ability as yet, which is what I thought.

Nuria and Ronnie were lovely today! As soon as they heard my characteristic "ring-bell" they came into the parlor to show off their literary accomplishments: Nuria proudly reading three poems of Milne's *When We Were Very Young*, and Ronnie, in obvious imitation of her, busying himself with a story about an organ-grinder and a monkey. When the maid came to call him for his nap, he protested vigorously.

December 29, 1939

[I whiled away the time by writing a Schoenbergian parody of *The Ancient Mariner*. Its protagonist hurls himself into the ocean at the thought of studying with Schoenberg:

> But winged spirits rescued him,
> And bore him to the skies,
> Where angels all day long on harps
> Played Schoenberg lullabies.
>
> In great dismay he ran away.
> And straight to Hell went down;
> There they were playing Sibelius;
> Ah, what a lovely sound!
>
> But as he revelled in these strains,
> He heard a voice to say,
> "No! No! Zey can*not* practise here!
> Please make zem go avay!"[37]

[37]On that topic, I am indebted to Prof. J. Bennet Olson of the Department of Biological Sciences, Purdue University, for the following charming anecdote:

> I knew an undergrad named F. who was taking beginning piano at UCLA for the hell of it. He really was a physics major, or something like that. One noon as he was practicing in a little hallway practice room in the Education Building, there was a knock on the door. F. turned around, surprised to see Professor Schoenberg opening the door.
>
> "Please . . . You can't play," said Schoenberg.

And when he looked to see what 'twas,
He saw a little man,
Whose face was of the saffron hue,
His legs a dirty tan.

He paddled on a fleecy cloud
Across the sky so blue;
The halo on his sallow head
Was just a bit askew.

etc. etc.]

🖋 *December 31, 1939*

[Drawing up New Year's resolutions, I didn't forget to include this one: "To be unabatedly loyal to the interests, works and person of 'a man named A. Schoenberg.' "]

🖋 *January 3, 1940*

Just as I'd feared. All this recent cold and fog have made poor Uncle Arnold sick! He met his classes today, but he would have done better to stay home. He was constantly sneezing and coughing, and looked terribly worn and haggard. He actually admitted that he was "not very well" and proposed to take to his bed the minute he got home. When he admits he's sick, he must be *very* sick! I felt guilty about reminding him of his promise to give me a lesson tomorrow, but I did so anyway. He says it's all right for me to come, as far as he knows now. However, he wants me to call him up first thing in the morning, so that if he's much worse then or any unexpected business comes up he can put the affair off. Of course he will recover in a short time, but it is the greatest sorrow to me to have to see him in this condition. I suppose he got tired out at the convention

---

"I know I can't. That's why I'm practising," replied young F.
"You don't understand," said A.S., shaking his head. "You can't play because I have a lecture in the next room."
(personal communication from Prof. Olson, July 14, 1977)

in Kansas City. I understand that there were terrible blizzards there during the vacation, and one can just imagine the effect of such a change of climate on his delicate lungs! In spite of his illness, he taught with his customary vigor, and seemed to be as *gemütlich*—and as sharp-tongued when the mood struck him—as ever. . . In Advanced Analysis (where we worked on the elaboration of the first movement of Beethoven's D-Major Quartet, Op. 18 no. 3) he told us a rather odd thing. Once when the *Verein* was presenting a chamber-orchestra arrangement of some work—he didn't say what—it was discovered that in one place tympani, or the effect of tympani, were absolutely necessary. No tympani to be had, apparently—so our great man thumped on the strings of the piano, thus producing a sound which, by a great stretch of the imagination, could be considered to resemble that of the tympani. "And it sounded very well, too!" he reminisced, as he happily thumped the strings of this rattle-trap old instrument to demonstrate. He didn't discuss what effect such treatment might have on the nervous system of a piano!

Incidentally, I heard the third part of *Gurre-Lieder* this afternoon during the listening hour. I've actually gotten so I can run the electric phonograph by myself now. It's a good thing, too, because nobody seems to listen but me. Maybe I've got everyone discouraged by playing Schoenberg all the time. *GL* still remains, in my estimation, utterly magnificent cosmic music, even to the very iron chains. Of course Klaus-Narr's part is not done right at all on these records; it is partly spoken, whereas it should be all sung, and strictly sung. But the orchestra sounds wonderful! [38]

January 4, 1940

That lesson with Uncle Arnold didn't come off after all. When I called up this morning, Mrs. Schoenberg told me that he was still in bed very sick. She doesn't know whether he'll be well enough to teach on Saturday or not; I'm to call up then for further news. I certainly don't think that the present rainy weather can be very conducive to his getting well in a hurry. It did clear up this after-

[38]This was Stokowski's recording. In spite of its flaws, it is still a landmark in Schoenberg performance.

noon, but the air is still damp and I suspect it will be raining again tomorrow. What a shame that he had to start the New Year off this way! I only hope that his illness won't turn to anything more serious.

January 6, 1940

The news about Uncle Arnold is not good. When I called Mrs. Schoenberg this morning, she was just about ready to burst into tears, poor woman! She said he'd had a perfectly terrible night, had tossed constantly and not slept a bit. I imagine he must have quite a high fever. Under the circumstances, it was out of the question for me to go there this afternoon; but, feeling I had to do something for him, I had a potted pink hyacinth sent him from Naomi's flower shop when I went to the Village to do our errands. I hope he'll like it!

January 10, 1940

Thank God, Uncle Arnold's back! He isn't quite well yet; he looks pale and worn, and says he still coughs a lot in the morning and at night, but at least he's with us again, and we can once more enjoy his matchless wit and charm. This was ostensibly the day for him to look at our sonatas, but in fact he did very little of that. Instead, he talked all the time, which was more amusing to us and, I suppose, to him as well. I think his illness, conjoined with his previous over-exertions, has left him exhausted, both physically and mentally. The subjects of his conversation were, as usual, manifold; he has a way of starting with a topic very close to the matter of the moment and tracing ever-wider concentric circles around it, or else shooting suddenly off at a tangent into the most distant territory. This time he started out by showing us a great many examples of double counterpoint and skillful working-together of the motives in the opening movement of Brahms' First Symphony. These combinations don't come out as a rule in performance, he complains, for most conductors of the present generation have not been brought up in the Brahms tradition; rather, they were raised in the Wagnerian and modernistic tradition which was more anti-Brahms than anything

else. The only conductors who are really good in Brahms interpretation are Zemlinsky, von Webern, Jalowetz,[39] and Karl Rankl.[40] The
problem is somewhat less pressing in chamber music, for, at the
time the present generation of string players was being trained,
there was no chamber music of Wagner, Bruckner,[41] or Strauss, but
only Brahms (among the "moderns" of that day, that is). But for all
that—and here is the second of his concentric circles—the interpretation, good or bad, is much less important than the music! Music
need not be performed any more than books need be read aloud,
for its logic is perfectly represented on the printed page; and the
performer, for all his intolerable arrogance, is totally unnecessary
except as his interpretations make the music understandable to an
audience unfortunate enough not to be able to read it in print.
"Now do not tell anyone I said this!" he added; "for there are those
that would stone me for it!" They would, too; but there's absolutely
no doubt that he's right in the matter. He complained vigorously
about the fate of the second-rate composer, who is greatly over-
rated during his lifetime and completely neglected by later genera-
tions, even though he may have been a good solid musician; he cited
as examples Franz and Grieg . . . He's surely right when he says the
class of composers is higher than the class of performers, which is
exactly what I've thought ever since I was old enough to hold any
opinions at all about such things.

January 11, 1940

The library committee had its first meeting since vacation at noon
today, in Uncle Arnold's office. Our latest scheme is to issue cards

[39]Heinrich Jalowetz (1882-1946), conductor and composer, an early disciple
of Schoenberg. He contributed important essays to Schoenberg *Festschriften*.

[40]Karl Rankl (1898-1968), conductor and composer, a pupil of Schoenberg in
the 1920's. At the time of this diary entry, he had recently moved to England.
He became the music director of Covent Garden, and, later, conductor of the
Scottish National Orchestra. One of Schoenberg's last letters was to Rankl,
imploring him to finish the scoring of *Die Jakobsleiter* (a task later to be
completed by Winfried Zillig).

[41]There was, of course, Bruckner's *String Quintet*. Schoenberg does not seem
to have been acquainted with this work.

at 50 cents and a dollar, each one bearing a number of punches; every punch represents the issuance of one book for one week. The fifty-cent cards are good for ten punches, and the dollar ones for twenty-five; thus, there's an advantage of five weeks for the purchasers of the more expensive cards, which should be an inducement to buy them. This sounds very factual and practical, doesn't it? Well, as a matter of fact, all our plans are still in the extremely speculative stage; but it won't be long now until they materialize if things go through as there's every indication they will do. Mr. Tanner and Mr. Stein said that Uncle Arnold renewed his promise to give or lend the library a large amount of music, and furthermore, promised that if they wanted to give a musicale to get the thing off to a bang-up start, his house will be at their disposal. Isn't that elegant? Of course, the whole business was his idea in the first place; and one of his better ones, too, if you ask me!

January 12, 1940

Uncle Arnold was just as sweet as an angel to me this afternoon. What did he do but simply *leap* at me as soon as he saw me sitting in the front row of composition class, and exclaim with countenance of bursting joy, "Oh, Miss Newlin! Why did you not telephone me this week, hmmm? I could have seen you on Tuesday, yes?" This sort of reception, especially in public, would be enough to bowl anyone over; but, marvelous to relate, he followed it up by insisting on looking at my sonata first, and, even more marvelous, by actually admitting it was good! (Of course, I have to write it all over again for next time, but it's still good.) He even allowed me to make criticisms of Miss S.'s piece! Most of his cute remarks today were at her expense. When he was asking us all for criticisms of her work, and someone remarked that the piano style was very effective, he promptly retorted, "Yes, and it would be more so if she played it better!" That's the sort of thing he usually says to me! Not that I didn't get one lash of the acidulous tongue. Some of the sheets of my music were in the back of my folder, where they should not have been at all, and it was necessary for me to explain their presence and significance with profuse apologies. To which he bowed ironically and remarked, "For this one needs guide to the movie stars, yes?"

January 13, 1940

Things do not look so good in the Schoenberg ménage today. Roddie's lost—has been gone for the last twenty-four hours. Mrs. Schoenberg thinks someone must have stolen him; otherwise there'd be no excuse for his not having been returned, for he wears a collar with his license tag, name, address, telephone number, everything on it. She says that the last time he was lost, the finder demanded a reward of twenty-five dollars! . . . We told her of our experience with Haggis (alias Charlie)[42] last week; she promptly begged us to tell Uncle Arnold of it, for, she says, he is now insisting that they must give Roddie away; he won't have a dog that is so disloyal. If he only realized that other people's dogs ran away too, maybe he wouldn't feel that way about it!

The great man himself is not in very fine fettle, for that matter; there was every indication that he was catching another cold . . . It's no wonder he got sick, going to Kansas City! Mrs. Schoenberg said that she went with him, all right; in fact, he insisted that he wouldn't go if she didn't. But they sat up in coach all the way there and back, because he discovered at the last minute that the University would only pay his fare one way, and he didn't want to pay for a compartment. It was no use for him to get a berth because his terrible asthma makes it impossible for him to sleep in one. But what a senseless thing for a man of his age to do! It's a wonder it didn't kill him. Here's another gem, which accounts for his avid tennis-playing. [Mrs. S.] used to be a champion tennis-player, but when he married her he wanted her to give it up. She wouldn't. The solution? get him interested in the game. She did. Now she doesn't like to play any more, but he does it to exhaustion, even when his lungs and heart are all but broken. What to do? There seems to be no way of stopping him.

January 15, 1940

Today's principal news is that Roddie has returned to the fold. Mrs. Schoenberg told me that they'd brought him home from the pound yesterday. I'll be glad to see him tomorrow; for I have made definite

---

[42]A runaway Scottie who had visited us.

arrangements with Uncle Arnold to come tomorrow at eleven-fifteen or so. (Just in time for lunch, ha, ha!) The old man didn't look at my sonata this time, but he was all sweetness and smiles to me and to everyone. I guess he's got that incipient cold licked, for there was never a sign of it on him. He did get off one rather catty little remark at the expense of those of his "little apple trees" who insist on not using braces, so that it's impossible to tell which two lines [staves] go together. "I suppose you omit this to be original!" said he. "Well, let me tell you, I would rather that you would be not original at all than in this way!" He began a rather detailed discussion of roving harmony in Structural Functions class, using the elaboration of the first movement of Schubert's E-flat-major Piano Trio as an example. He's decided that we shall prepare for our final examination by studying the six elaborations of the first movements in Beethoven's Op. 18. He could have given us one whole quartet to study, but everyone preferred the former plan; he did, too.

January 16, 1940

Uncle Arnold *did* give me my extra lesson this morning, and a whole hour of it, too! But I have a sneaking suspicion that his mind wasn't on his business every minute, because here's the funny thing that happened. Everything was going on just as usual: he was looking over the first movement of my quintet making suggestions; Ronnie in the other room was prattling away at the top of his voice to Mamma, when, all of a sudden, S. burst into a fit of the most side-splitting laughter I've ever heard! I naturally assumed that there was something excruciatingly funny about my piece at that point, but I couldn't imagine what it could possibly be. Then he solved the enigma for me. "Oh, listen to Ronnie!" he burbled. "Oh, how he mixes his German and English! Is it not funny?" And just thinking about it sent him into new gales of laughter. Of course, he should have been studying my piece and not trying to hear Ronnie's latest cute sayings, but I guess you can excuse paternal pride, especially when the son's as adorable as Ronnie is. Just as Ronnie had settled down to a nice cozy chat with Mamma, the maid came to take him to the bathroom. Of course, he protested vigorously, but was going out anyway, when Uncle Arnold suddenly popped out from behind the study curtains. "Marie!" he bellowed at the unfortunate maid. "Warum entnimmst du ihn?" Of course the poor girl could hardly have broadcast the purpose for which she was removing the boy, so contented herself with replying, "Ich kehr' ihn gleich zurück!" which she did. (Finally, Mamma and Ronnie went out in the garden.)

January 17, 1940

Alas, Uncle Arnold took the blue pencil to my sonata again today: struck out two-and-half pages with one stroke, much to my horror and to the amusement of the others. (I revised the whole thing again with this cut and other cuts and changes he'd made. At first, it seems to have a queer truncated sound, but I guess I'll get used to it.) Today he had definitely *not* "the face that a child would climb to kiss," but rather "the face that launched a thousand quips," and nasty ones, too. Poor C., who, after the verbal lashing he got last time, took great pains to write out in his neatest handwriting the whole first section of a sonata based on all the wrong features of an easily perceptible Beethoven model, fared no better this time: "Here, you did not even *copy* correctly!" Uncle Arnold shouted at him, though he was the recipient of some sympathy from his colleagues. Then there was M., who, as so often happens, hadn't done anything for this time. "Oh, of course I understand perfectly," said the Master in the sweetest mock-sympathetic tone you can imagine, "you look so overworked, you are just a shadow of yourself!" We all howled at that, for M., overworked or not, is about the size of two barrels. But Uncle Arnold hadn't shot his last bolt yet:

"At least," he continued, "you will not lose your shadow, or at least you have not!" And then, as always, there was me. When, in one place that he couldn't make out at all, I showed him that two measures which I'd sketched out on a rather dirty piece of scratch paper were to be inserted, he remarked complacently, "One would never know it!" And then there was the worst moment of all, when he discovered a distinctly audible reminiscence of the Second Quartet in one of my best passages. "What you mean by this?" he demanded, in mock anger. "Oh, it was just an accident!" I faltered. "Well, you take out insurance against this sort of accidents!" was his prompt response. He is never at a loss for the retort discourteous!

✍ January 20, 1940

My lesson with Uncle Arnold went beautifully today . . . He took a last look at the Scherzo of the Quintet, which he approves now as it stands; he's most anxious for me to copy the parts as soon as I can, so that I can have it performed. He's planning to have a party for his students and the music faculty either the first or second Sunday after school re-opens, at which the students' music is to be played. I guess this is when my masterpiece is to take its maiden voyage. He mentioned this affair to me today so that I'd remember to tell the students of it in case it slipped his mind. My only fear is that, having told someone of his plan, he'll think it already accomplished, as is so often his wont. He looked at what I'd done of the first movement, up to and including part of the second theme, embracing his last week's corrections and suggestions. The main fault now seems to be that I make too much of an "Irish stew," or a "noodle" as he puts it, out of one motive and rhythm, a mistake which he says is characteristic of most American composers. Just why that should be, I don't know, but, as he's had a good bit of experience with the budding American composer, I wouldn't dream of doubting his word. He prefers constant, or frequent, juxtaposition of new themes as is so beautifully exemplified in Brahms. He has been showing me many examples from the F-minor Piano Quintet and the G-major String Quintet. He finds that my theme reminds him very much of that of the latter work (first movement); strange, for I never studied that particular quintet very much.

✍ January 23, 1940

My, my, Uncle Arnold was so sweet to me at my lesson this morning, and you'll never guess why: it's because he's just found a new use for me! I'd scarcely gotten off my wet clothes (we came to his house in a driving rain, which did not completely stop until about six o'clock this evening) when he popped at me the news that he expected me to come to his first-year composition examination tomorrow morning, to help the students from eight till twelve!

"Well, I'd love to do it for you," I replied, "but I'm afraid I could only stay till nine, because I have to catch a bus then to go to my lesson with Mr. Hilsberg!" "Oh, that all right," he cheerily replied,

"Mr. Hilsberg will surely be able to change your lesson to other time. And then you will come and help, no? I will point out to you the weaker students, and you will look over their papers and correct the harmony for them, and improvise on the piano. Understand, yes?" All I could do was utter a meek and mild "yes." . . . So that is absolutely that! . . . Of course I feel glad that I can be with him all the morning, and honored that he thinks me worthy to help him with his work. (I called up Hilsberg and he postponed my piano lesson till 2:30 on Friday, so that's all right.) But, when one thinks about the matter, all sorts of troublesome complications spring to the mind. What, for example, if I start improvising on the piano for the young budding geniuses and the Great Man comes posting in from the next room yelling, "No! No! They cannot practise here! Please make them go away!" Or, what if he looks over their papers previously corrected by me and finds a thousand things wrong? Well, I could imagine things of this sort till doomsday, but I guess the better thing for me to do is to simply follow his directions and let my results speak for themselves.

Where was I? Oh yes, I'd said he was so sweet to me because he could use me; having recounted the use, let me now recount that pleasanter thing, the sweetness. It consisted of his giving me another batch of paper: sliced-up orchestra paper with "Zur Instrumenta-tionslehre" and "Zur Formenlehre" written on it in red ink, and the odd pages numbered, and a very queer musical sketch of his in the middle (the whole thing is stitched together with heavy twine or rope); also, hunting up for me an advertisement of Longmans Green's new "arrow edition" [43] of the chamber music of Beethoven and of Brahms, three dollars apiece, in which he thought I might be interested. You bet I am! The total time consumed in these *Gemütlichkeiten* was about ten minutes, or four dollars' worth. Mamma's query is whether *Gemütlichkeit* is worth that much? To me, yes. As for what I learned: the main fault of the quintet now is that there aren't enough ideas in the first section—five at most, when there should appear, as is the case in Brahms, at least seven or eight prin-

[43] An edition with arrows pointing to the important themes, a device originally patented by Albert E. Wier for the Harcourt, Brace edition of Beethoven's nine symphonies. Schoenberg encouraged us to buy these editions because they were economical, but poked fun at their often inaccurate thematic analyses.

cipal ones, not counting subordinate material! This I'm to remedy by inserting at least two or three more codettas with very distinctive themes. I don't think he cared much for the elaboration, for a variety of reasons; he made no special correction of it, though, but told me rather to go ahead and make my sketches for the continuation so that he can better advise me as to what to do with it. That is often his way, and seems wise.

He got to talking about that first unpublished quartet of his (the one in C major that Wellesz mentions), written when he was 21 or so. [He] says it was so rich that he had to cut out loads and loads of it, and use many more ideas in a subordinate manner. I asked him if it had ever been performed publicly, and he replied it had, though never published. "At least, not *yet!*" he added meaningfully. "Oh, I must once find this manuscript!" he continued, rather plaintively. [44] Now he wouldn't be having something in mind, would he? After hearing that he's going on with the second *Kammersymphonie* begun in Vienna in 1906, I wonder!

January 24, 1940

Well, my first day's experience—and, I hope, not my last—in the gentle art of being an assistant went off wonderfully, but it certainly was hard work! I was at school from eight till one-thirty, without any lunch at all. When I got home I had to practise as soon as I was through eating, and right after practising I started to make a good copy of my sonata, which I just now (10:45) finished doing. I can't remember having worked so much all at once in a long time! But then, it's good for me.

Funny incident when Uncle Arnold first came into the classroom —the same room that's been used for the examination in this class for ages—and found every seat full. "Oh," he remarked querulously to Stein, "is not this room much smaller as the one we used to have

[44]The *D* major quartet, which he may have meant here, was discovered after Schoenberg's death in his legacy to the Library of Congress. It was published by Faber Music, London. Cf. my article "Schoenberg's Quartet in D Major (1897)," *Faber Music News*, Autumn 1966, pp. 21-23.

for this class?" Stein: "No, Mr. Schoenberg, the class is larger."

As will have been deduced from the fact that I finished making the fair copy of my sonata this evening, Uncle Arnold gave a final look at it this morning and pronounced it good. This is more than I feel like saying for it, but if he's satisfied, I should be! And now I do hope that the work I did for him will be pleasing to him.

January 27, 1940

I had a lovely treat today, one which I'd never expected! Just as we were making final preparations to leave for Uncle Arnold's—it must have been about 12:30 or so—our buzzer rang. I ran downstairs at once to answer it. Yes, it was Uncle Arnold. He wanted me to come later in the afternoon, say about four o'clock. Of course I said that I'd be glad to come any time he wanted, but that he'd have to drive us back as far as Wilshire, as there was no other way we could get home otherwise. A quick consultation with Mrs. Schoenberg and I was assured that this could be managed. So far, so good.

But, when it came time for us to leave their house, at five-thirty— the loveliest part of the evening—what should they do but take us for a delightful long ride along the ocean-front, as far up as Castellamare and beyond, and then drive us all the way back home to boot? I was in seventh heaven! Unfortunately, we just missed the sunset, but we saw the short twilight, and were able to get a refreshing whiff of the sea air. That's something in itself, and how much more enjoyable in such company as his! The funny thing was that all day long we'd been thinking how nice it would be if we could go to the beach, the weather was so perfect; but we just didn't see how we could manage it. Then this happens! We were uncommonly happy about the whole thing. There was much evidence of flooding along the road; one could see where great quantities of dirt and rock, and even houses, had been entirely washed away by the beating waves.

This sort of incident certainly seems to prove that I am out of the Schoenbergian doghouse, if, indeed, I was ever in it. And this wasn't the only evidence of his being well-disposed, either. Oh, he still thinks there aren't enough "semes" in the quintet: "It must be pleasure to you to write these themes," he says, "why then you not put more of them here?"; and he was inclined to be just a bit recalcitrant about writing me a letter of recommendation for the University Fellowship, but he almost kissed my hand when we said our good-byes at the car door. Not quite, but almost. I have proof positive, too, that he'd noticed my new red hat on the last occasion that I wore it for his benefit. Today, commenting on a modulation I'd made which was quite proper up to a certain point and then suddenly turned in the wrong direction, he said, "It is as if one would say, 'Oh dear, I have left my red hat in the other room, I must go and get it!' " So you see! Alas, though, I'm afraid that doesn't make up for the ignominy of one insult that cuts me right to the core—me, the daughter of a Harvard Ph.D. in English! You do remember the big party he's going to throw in honor of his beloved disciples, first Sunday after the new term 'gins to ope its eyes? Well, he's started making invitations for it by hand, with maps of how to get to Ye Olde Manse 'n' everything: the most elegant concoctions you ever saw, as carefully done as copperplate. Naturally enough, he wanted to get the English approved before he made any more of them. Mrs. S. had told him not to do any until he'd shown the text to somebody, but he was that excited about the idea he simply couldn't wait. So, he started to ask me to do them: "Do you know something of English?" he queried, and then, before I had gotten over my first few indignant splutters at the idea of anyone's asking me a silly question like that, he interrupted, "No, no, I think I better have your mother do it, hmm?" Oh, I could have gladly throttled him! Nonetheless, he went in and started asking Mamma's advice. She looked the thing over, and, while admiring the artistry greatly, could not gainsay the regrettable facts that the word "which" is not spelled "wich" and that it simply does not mean "whom." Obviously, that wasn't what the Great Man wanted at all. "Oh, but this do not matter!" he responded blithely. "Everyone will know what this mean, no?" Mamma was obliged to concur that they would, so I guess those invitations will go out with their "wiches" intact. It doesn't matter, anyway; in fact, I think it's cute. He thinks so, too!

They have the loveliest new big photographs of the children, which were taken at school. Ronnie's is a speaking likeness, though his expression is slightly posed; and one of Nuria's, where she is smiling her sweetest and the sunlight falls full on her face, is just about the most beautiful bit of photography I have ever seen! Mrs. Schoenberg prefers the other, in which N. is very seriously poring over her books; but I do not think it quite so flattering. Uncle Arnold is quite ravished with them, and wants smaller prints made as soon as possible so that he can "always have them with him." Ronnie was quite determined that Mamma should have one of Nuria's pictures. Each time that she'd put it back on the organ beside the old man's bust he'd gleefully fetch it down again and shove it into her hands. He was determined that I shouldn't have one, though, and when Mrs. Schoenberg asked him to go and get me some fruit drops his only answer was a categorical "Nein!" However, when I began talking German to him in my most persuasive tones, he unbent enough to go and get me half-a-dozen orange hard candies, which he laid in my hand with as much ceremony as though they were so many rubies and topazes. He comes by his character naturally, all right! He's the old man all over again. The reason for the change of time, incidentally, was that Mrs. had to go shopping for some shoes, and both Ronnie and Uncle Arnold insisted on going with her. The old man hates shopping, but he refuses to let her go anywhere without him; and the same with Ronnie. "It is not fair that I should have to take both of them!" she cried to Mamma in a moment of despair, and I quite see her point of view. Nuria, poor thing, is confined to bed with a cold, but I don't believe it is anything serious.

January 28, 1940

Oh, I've had more joy today than has ever come my way before in my life! . . . It seemed as if everything went together to make this "Evening on the Roof" a perfect one . . . The site is quite off the beaten track, six blocks east of where Santa Monica Boulevard cuts Sunset, and three blocks above Sunset on a steep hill. The "Roof" is simply an attic studio . . . with great windows stretching across the back of the room and affording the most glorious view of the city lights: an altogether delightful place . . . The Great Man was there and as merry as a cricket; well he might be, for in my opinion his music was magnificently done . . . In particular, Frances Mullen's performance of Ops. 19 and 25 was remarkable in its technique, emotional content, and understanding; and as for Radiana Pazmor, she is truly a marvel! I never heard a singer intone so perfectly; and consider what difficult music *Das Buch der hängenden Gärten* is for the voice! I was quite beside myself with love of it; it is so gloriously rich, at times tender and at times ferocious, almost frightening. I wish we could have heard the songs in a larger hall; P's voice has great power, and, when she raised it, the beating on your eardrums was almost intolerable! . . . After the program I spoke to Uncle Arnold. I'm tongue-tied on these occasions, but all he had to do was look at me to see how deeply moved I had been by the performance, and it pleased him greatly. "So, do you some day want to compose like this?" he queried, his eyes twinkling ever so gaily. "Oh, maybe in ten years I can do it!" I answered, in the same vein; "*or* twenty, *or* thirty, *or* forty!" Mamma piped up . . . "You can do this in five, six years, maybe!" he then said; "but do you not *dare* it before, not *one hour* before!"

January 31, 1940

Merciful Heavens, what a day I've had! Everything seems to have gotten itself unscrewed in the most amazing manner. Uncle Arnold's examination days are always most hectic, but this was a little messier than usual . . . He had promised the advanced composition class that all we'd have to do would be to bring and play our sonatas, we wouldn't have to write anything. But, when I got there, he was busily passing out themes for three-part song forms, the ones the first-year composition class had used. The idea was for us to make them as marvelous as possible, so the beginners could see what they should have done! Well, I spent an hour and a half writing two of the things (about twenty measures each), by which time it was eleven-thirty. Aha, thought I, I'll dump the papers on *le maître* and have time to pop out for lunch before twelve! But such was not to be. When I approached Uncle Arnold and asked him would he please take the papers now because I want to go out and eat, I saw that certain light creep into his eye, and knew my doom even before he spoke. "Oh, but do not you want to play this over on the piano?" he luxuriated. "Well, I don't really think I—" "But yes! You better play this! This important this time, this important!" As usual, I gave up and bowed to his will. By the time I'd finished playing the masterpieces, it was noon; and I knew what would happen to me if

I were to come late to my Structural Functions examination for so crass a reason as mealtime! So, to coin a phrase, "little elephant no eatie hay."[45]

Everything happened in Structural Functions class just as I'd known it would. Sure, it's supposed to be a two-hour examination, but each of us got twelve lovely questions, each of which was to be answered in the fewest possible number of words and the largest possible number of nasty little diagrams. Everyone had to analyze the elaboration of a different Beethoven quartet; my Christmas gift was Op. 18, no. 2. Now I love Beethoven, and I adore analysis, but I am also fond of the pleasures of my tummy; and the harder I thought and the more fluently I wrote, the hungrier I got! Nothing to be done about it, though. I thought I was going to get a minute off when Mr. Stein came and told me that Uncle Arnold would look at my sonata in about ten minutes; but, when the ten minutes were up, all Uncle Arnold would say was, "Are you finished? No? Then go, and come back when you are!" Well, finished or no, at two-thirty I knew I'd have to leave to do something about my French examination. So, telling Stein I'd be right back and hoping to heaven that U.A. wouldn't see me go, I threw on my coat and tore pell-mell over to Royce Hall in the heaviest rain . . . was able to arrange to take that French exam tomorrow at 10 . . .

Now it's impossible to believe that this tale of woe could become any sadder, but it just gets "vorse und vorse." After finally having put the finishing touches on my Structural Functions paper, I handed it to Stein and sallied forth to Uncle Arnold's lair with my two sonatas; by this time prepared to expect almost anything, but still with enough starch in me to be as proud as a peacock of that egg I'd laid yesterday. When I stuck my head in the door of his classroom, he looked as if he'd never seen me before in his life. "You looking for piano?" he inquired, with utmost blandness, "or did you want to see me 'bout something?" "Why, I came to show you my sonata!" I replied, more than a little surprised at this reception, for, after all, he'd distinctly told me to bring the sonata as soon as I was through with my examination. "But," he queried, "did I not

[45]My gloss (as a four-year-old) on Debussy's "Jumbo's Lullaby" from *Children's Corner*.

see already your sonata?" Here was the perfect opening for me to play my trump card. "Well," I answered, "you have seen one of them, but I wrote another one—a new one—yesterday!" His response was absolutely monumental. He looked at me with a quizzical, somewhat childlike smile, and simply asked, "Why?" I felt like two cents! "Well," I stammered, with all the nonchalance I could muster, "naturally I wanted to get practice—" "So," was his retort, "Yes, it is good that you have the practice, but I do not want to look at this now. I am so tired; I have already had five hours from music today, and I think this enough, no? Still," he conceded, "I might look at it a little bit," and, taking the manuscript from me, gave a cursory glance at the top page. "Hah!" he exclaimed almost immediately, pointing a dirty and accusing finger at one inoffensive-looking measure, *"Death und Configuration!"* "I do not like this," he remarked plaintively a moment later; and then, returning the piece, "Well, it is good that you had the practice, but I do not need this for examination. No, no, no, no, no!" This last flood of No's was all because he saw I was trying to tell him something, which I finally succeeded in doing: namely, that I had the parts of the Piano Quintet (Scherzo) and wanted to ask him to whom I should give them. "But what is this with parts and Scherzos?" he answered, still with that air of childlike innocence. "I know not from what you speak!" "Why, surely you know," I remonstrated. "You told me to hurry up and copy those parts so I could have the piece played at your party, and now—" "Oh, that!" he laughed carelessly. "But now we cannot do this till next semester. Why did you not tell me of this before? I did know nothing of this! There will be no one here in vacation, you know—hahahahaha!" And with that, he gave me my *congé.*

February 3, 1940

The rain poured down so that I was afraid for a while I wasn't going to be able to get to Uncle Arnold. But I got there all right, though I had to go and come in a taxi, and that cost 80 cents each way! I brought him new extensions of the first part of the Quintet (1st movement) and a small beginning of the elaboration. He showed me a great deal from his first and second string quartets this time, chiefly with the view of giving me some idea of the marvelous contrapuntal combinations of themes that he has used, which he would like me to emulate, at least in some degree. Strangely, and, I think, contrary to popular supposition, the first quartet is by far the most complicated of the four in this regard. The second is much simpler, and one need but glance at the fourth (with which I'm not familiar, but today he was showing me a bit of the score) to see a much larger proportion of sincere homophony. He says the reason for his simplification was that he soon perceived that the contrapuntal finesses looked very fine on paper, but that they did not come out. I think this tendency is right in line with his trend towards increasing simplification since *Kammersymphonie I.*

February 10, 1940

S. took a very sane attitude about the contrapuntal horrors of my elaboration. He said that the dissonances I used might have some meaning in a real atonal style, but were out of place in diatonic writing, except in so far as I might consider my motives as one of those conventional formulae by virtue of which certain dissonances are allowable. Though there is much that needs to be done: for example, I must later construct an introduction to this elaboration —he wants me to go right ahead, and make the alterations later. He suggested that I first improvise the whole section through on the piano two or three times, then start making many sketches. Of course, I have written some of those already, but this time he wants more extended or developed ones.

A charming bit of byplay occurred just as I was leaving. I went to pick up my manuscripts, whereat he hastily yelled, "Be careful that you do not get my works!" I checked through my packet to be sure I hadn't, and announced, "Well, that's all right." He, taking me up on my unintentional ambiguity: "Perhaps it is all right with you when you get my works, but is not all right with me!" I replied, "These are all mine—I've got to be sure all of my stuff is here. You know, one time I left a sheet of my orchestration here—" "And what happened?" he queried. "Nothing, I just found it here the next time I came, and brought it back home with me." "Oh! This relief! I was afraid you would say I stole this for mine own!" "No, no, it wasn't worth stealing." "So! Are you sure of that?" and with that, the little episode ended, by which time he was very sweetly accompanying me and Mamma to the garden gate, followed at a respectful distance by Ronnie, Trude, Roddie and Nuria.

February 12, 1940

Had to execute that long complicated trek out to Uncle Arnold's after registration. He'd told me on Saturday that all the students in the composition class were to come today for last-minute check-ups of their sonatas; though I'd explained to him about registration, he insisted I should make my appearance as soon as I could. So! I arrived at his house at four, tired and sweating, and what greeting does he give me but, "Oh, you are *terribly* late! You should have been here at three o'clock, no?" I faltered that I couldn't help it, which seemed not to impress him. G. and F. were still there, so he finished looking at their sonatas before he got around to me. When it came my turn, he gazed at me sweetly and said, "It is not necessary that I look at yours, no? I am a little tired now, you know!" It was on the tip of my tongue to ask him what he thought *I* was, after standing in line two hours at registration, but I only said, "Well, you seem to have thought it necessary, seeing you told me to come out here!" That stopped him a minute, but even so he wouldn't look at more than a few measures of the piece. I'd hoped to try it through on his grand piano (Ibach) but no such luck! Oh well, such is life. And I still love him, anyway . . .

February 14, 1940

Well, Uncle Arnold is getting wuss and wuss. All he can think of now is party, party, party! (I can just imagine the kind of lesson I'll get on Saturday!) As an example of his state of mind: he spent the entire hour in our composition class arranging and re-arranging the order of the program according to the keys the pieces are in! Can you imagine anything goofier? He spent what seemed like hours carefully studying all the permutations and combinations of our seven sonatas, weighing all the difficult esthetic problems which their order on the program involved. We could hardly keep from laughing out loud. We'd look one at the other, and try pitifully to hold our mirth in, but it was no use, the whole thing was too funny! Finally he got an arrangement that pleased him ("Now this fine!" he cried, and we practically burst), but he suddenly noticed that the last place on the program was vacant. He looked and looked, and scratched his head, but couldn't figure out whose was missing. Well, you might have known, it was mine, and I didn't hesitate to tell him so. "Oh well," he remarked blithely, as he wrote my name down at the bitter end, "Miss Newlin is the youngest, she can wait." Did you ever hear of such? Two to one, I won't get to play my piece at all, or, if I do, everybody will have left during the intermission. Oh yes, I forgot, that's another of his brilliant ideas: to have a first part of four sonatas, then an intermission of an hour during which the hundred-odd guests are supposed to consume a leetle refreshment, and then three sonatas. Wouldn't you count on him to cook up a crazy scheme like that? He was very much disturbed as to whether he should put the best pieces last or not, because, while they would leave the most satisfactory final impression, all the audience might have left by that time! "Well, lock the door!" someone suggested. "Oh, this would not help," he answered, "because those who do not like the music will be stronger as door!" "Give a small prize at the end of the program!" I tooted. "Yes, but who will provide the prize?" he inquired. "Oh well, it does not matter. I hope only the guests will not become annoyed!" ... It certainly will be a cross between a circus and the maddest kind of madhouse!

H., who is auditing first year composition this term, told me of the terrific slam that Uncle Arnold took at me in that class. "Well," he told them, "all of you made very good examinations, except those whose frequent use of the Neapolitan sixth shows influence of Miss Newlin!" According to H., everybody simply howled their heads off, and I'm betting H. was one of the chief howlers ...

February 16, 1940

Dress rehearsal went off pretty well. We discovered that, all together, the seven sonatas (only seven, for Mr. Stein will not play his after all) take only about 50 minutes. "If this true," says Uncle Arnold, "this wonderful! But I am so afraid this will take much, much longer!" If one crazy thing doesn't pop into his head, another does. What do you suppose he did before class but pass out pieces of paper for us to list facts of our lives and musical backgrounds, so that he can give program notes between the numbers? Program notes for regular concerts are bad enough, but program notes on the works of students are simply absurd! After all, what can we have done worth lucubrating about? I filled my paper with lists of my performances, which I imagine he'll either ignore or comment on in a nasty manner. Of course, I expect he'll tell my age. I imagine that the whole procedure will be quite ghastly.

I had to leave double counterpoint for about a half hour to go to the meeting of the dance group to which, I learned yesterday, he's recommended me as composer. Don't know whether the project will come to anything or not. The only one of the suggested dances that interested me was one in abstract architectural forms, which should have contrapuntal possibilities. I discovered that Uncle Arnold had also recommended four other students for the job, but none of them were there. I'm to come back again on Monday afternoon, for further discussion.

February 17, 1940

I went to Uncle Arnold's this afternoon, but, just as I'd expected, he was too busy and too excited to give me much time. Altogether, Mamma and I stayed only about a half hour. When we saw how things were with him, we offered to go away at once, but he wouldn't hear of my having made the trip for nothing, looked over the new portion of the elaboration, and made some very pregnant suggestions. His chief criticism is still that I don't stick long enough with my ideas. The next time I come he's going to show me some more examples from his First Quartet, with special emphasis on the combination of two or more themes that are carried out at great length. I have been using combinations of this kind, but not developing them sufficiently; that's why he wants to show me the difference.

Preparations for the party are in full swing already. When I got there, all the furniture was moved around, the rug rolled up, and chairs stacked against the walls . . . As for Uncle Arnold, his chief task seems to have been writing the program notes. He's just gotten down to my introduction, he says. He wants me to get there by a quarter of three tomorrow. Mrs. S. especially wants me there early; she doesn't remember people's names too well, so she wants me to stand behind her and prompt her with their names as they come. Then she can greet them as if she really knew who they were.

February 18, 1940

What a super red-letter day this has been! . . . In my opinion, I played my sonata pretty well; if I'd had no other advantage over my colleagues and co-performers, at least I was not scared half to death as the others most assuredly were. Mamma says that from where she sat in the front row you could see their hands shaking as they played! Temple came just before me on the program. When he got to her, he announced that the next two numbers would be by two young ladies "which could be called ex-infant prodigies." . . . Then he proceeded to make some rather nasty remarks about child prodigies, apparently meant more for me than for her; expatiated quite a while on her numerous accomplishments, and finally concluded by saying that he "think we would like this." She then played her sonata from memory . . . Now it was my turn; he looked around an awfully long time for his program notes about me, but finally found them . . . Of course he told my age and all of that, and carefully explained that his remarks about child prodigies had not been aimed at me, a statement which failed to entirely convince. No sarcastic remarks, though, unless you count what he said about my "premature works having been played in many important places!" But it was the finish that was really a scream . . . "Well," he said, "I guess I do not need to say anything more, but I will let Miss Newlin's piece speak for itself—for I am sure you will like it almost as well as Miss Temple's!" All his previous program notes during the course of the concert had been so sublimely inane and so exquisitely embarrassing that everybody in the performers' room had been exchanging amused glances with me, and even speculating as to what he might say about me; but we hadn't expected anything quite as goofy as that! He was surely proud of us all, and said so, even if his introductions lacked a little in tact . . . he made up for them by his subsequent treatment of us. He insisted on making every one of us take two or three bows . . . and what's more, he put his arm around each of the performers, male as well as female, as they left the piano. Yes . . . he even put his arm around me, and patted my shoulder to boot! He did the same, too, when I came up to him as I was leaving, to tender my *adieux* and thanks. I've never seen him quite that affectionate or demonstrative before. I guess the excitement of the occasion must have gone to his head . . . Every one of the girls got a lovely corsage of purple violets and a yellow rose, bound with silver ribbon, from no less than the Great Man himself!

The minute the program was over, everybody bolted to the dining room for that most important item, food. I would have helped pass things around, but Mrs. Schoenberg wouldn't hear of my doing a thing but stuffing myself as full as I liked and having a good time. Before the concert began, I had been helping her, introducing people she didn't know, and escorting them upstairs to take off their coats so that she wouldn't have to bother with that. She wouldn't let me go upstairs more than once or twice, because she was so afraid that I would get tired out for my playing. Can you imagine a more kind-hearted, thoughtful woman? She always goes out of her way to be nice to me. There was a splendiferous layout on that table: canapés, and cakes, and cookies, and dozens of coffee-rolls, and plates upon plates of candy and salted nuts, and all the coffee you wanted. After we'd had our fill, we moseyed back into the living room and circulated around a while among the guests before leaving . . . I met some new people—Adolph Weiss[46] was there, and so was Joseph Achron with his wife. We had quite a long talk with that couple; they were the first intermediaries between Bak and Uncle Arnold.[47]

So here we are, tired, but happy and home.

February 19, 1940

Uncle Arnold was right down to business today; apparently not at all tired, and bright and smiling as you please. The very first thing

---

[46]The bassoonist and composer (1891-1971), one of Schoenberg's Berlin pupils. He wrote, among other things, *American Life*, a jazzy overture which Nicolas Slonimsky characterized as "paradodecaphonic."

[47]Cf. above, p. 14.

he wanted to know was how we felt on this "morning-after," and if we'd all taken our Alka-Seltzer like good little children? Of course, there was a bit of post-mortem about his remarks, and about the general atmosphere—whether you like it or not, the morning after the day before is always a letdown—but, all in all, he was very pleased with us, and already eagerly planning a "next time." The next time, he'll let us know longer in advance, so we can practise more: "For sometimes," he said, "one really could not tell what it was all about!" The general impression, even though most of the pieces were much too long, was very good; proof of that was that each of us found at least three or four people to say that ours was the best. "But if I had thought of it," he remarked, "I would have told the audience not to think of whose was the best, or who had the most talent, but simply to listen for the general impression!"

Now for next term in composition class he wants all of us to do some kind of chamber music work, and much more than last term. My choice (one he'd dictated to me previously) was a violin sonata. We're to start on our pieces as soon as possible. Next class meeting he's going to analyze piano trios and Beethoven's Rasumovsky Quartets. He got to talking about orchestration this time. He never teaches orchestration at all in the sense of "this color business;" says that if you get the proper combination of parts, you can orchestrate them (or better, think them orchestrally) for any combination of instruments at all, and the result will sound fine. Everybody knows how wonderful his orchestral writing and Berg's and Webern's is! Webern, he says, had and has a perfectly wonderful ear for the orchestra. Berg was a little less natural, but still very fine.

I'll definitely compose the "architectural abstract" dance with its contrapuntal possibilities. Roddie is in hospital with distemper. Tough luck!

February 20, 1940

Went to Uncle Arnold's this morning for the lesson I didn't get last Saturday. He was as sweet as pudding-strings, even though he pretty largely disliked what I brought him of the elaboration. One place he said was "feelthy" and then actually asked me if that was the right word! He showed me lots and lots of examples of the introductions to elaborations in Brahms Quartets, Quintets, etc., and in his own First Quartet, whose contrapuntal combinations he shows me each time with renewed delight. The elaboration of that is based on the form of the elaboration in the first movement of Beethoven's *Eroica*. His chief concern now is to give me an idea of the form; he doesn't care whether I finish the piece or not, or whether it turns out well, so long as I get that! Of course I hope it turns out a good piece besides, and so does he.

Mamma's talks with Mrs. S. always yield fresh material to whet my curiosity and interest. Two good items today. She says he is terribly stingy, has a tremendous sense of property; hoards things, even lead pencils (ample evidence of that, you can see in his study!) and won't give anything to anyone, not even a nickel to a beggar. That doesn't entirely tally with some things I've seen him do, but of course his public and private characters are so different it's really hard to tell. The other story furnishes some interesting leads to the past. She told that one time he promised one of his sons (first I've heard of these; they must have been by the first wife, Mathilde) [48] a motorcycle if he passed a certain examination. "But of course," she added, "he never passed it."

February 21, 1940

Uncle Arnold was pretty chipper ... In composition class he analyzed the treatment of the instruments in Beethoven's Violin Sonatas, especially the Kreutzer. Mr. Stein and I played examples, I taking the violin part (on the piano!) In advanced analysis, we started in bravely on the first Rasumovsky Quartet, and didn't get beyond the first four measures. Nice going! He had me and five others diagram the first theme on the board. The minute he saw me putting down a couple of words, he screamed, "No! No! I will not have melodram! Take it away! I will not look at it. I will close my eyes, see?" I took the words away, and then everything was once more rosy.

[48]This was Georg, Schoenberg's only son by Mathilde (Alexander von Zemlinsky's sister).

Uncle Arnold was very sweet today, actually lent me a piece of his music! He never lends, you know, and his own pieces least of all, especially since he has so few copies of them and can't get them from Germany any more. But he wanted to make a special exception for me so that I could study at my leisure his piano septet (the Suite for piccolo-clarinet, clarinet, bass clarinet, violin, viola, 'cello, and piano) which I do not own, have never heard, and don't know at all except by name. Pretty nice of him to let me have it, especially considering the way I keep my own music! He thought of that, too. "Now listen," he said, shaking a half-affectionate and half-admonitory finger at me as he placed the *summum bonum* in my hands, "do not forget, this is not your Beethoven!" And, what's more, he saw that I tucked it very securely indeed into the manila envelope which I always use for my manuscripts. When, on the way out through the garden, he saw me casually hand the parcel to Mamma to carry, I thought he'd die; so I hastily pulled out his piece and shouted at her, waving it in her face, "Now, Mamma, you aren't allowed to carry that upside down, 'cause look what's inside!" That restored his confidence, or at least I hope it did. He wants me to study the piece very carefully and then bring it to class and analyze it there! The very thought of that horrified me, and I told him as much: "Oh, I wouldn't dare to do that!" "Why not?" was his calm retort. I could think of lots of good reasons why not, but prudently refrained from expressing them.

Alas, I hadn't much to show him, just a new introduction to the elaboration, but it was plenty for him to go into, and he gave it a thorough reworking, which pleased me very much. The general form is all right, but replete with my usual faults; I still do too much mere alternation of the piano and strings, which is not really the style. In one place, I had something a little like a bugle call; he perked up his ears and asked, "What this, the mailman coming?"[49] Just to give me a bare idea of the possibilities I was neglecting, he named all the possible combinations of the five instruments, and asked me to write them down and count them. I did so, and discovered there were thirty. Add to that the different combinations

[49] I.e., the German posthorn.

of melody and accompaniment within those instrumental combinations, and you have over one hundred! He thinks it a good idea to list combinations in this way and thus have a better conception of your variety of resources. That is what he did for the instrumentation of *Pierrot Lunaire* and as a result in all the twenty-one pieces there is only one duplication of combination.[50]

February 25, 1940

Played the first movement (overture) of the Schoenberg suite. A difficult piece of sight-reading, that! Of course playing it will never be enough; I'll have to sit down and study it away from the piano for hours. It's hard enough to assimilate the page with your eyes, let alone your fingers. My favorite part of this movement is the witty, lilting waltz-like section, which Mamma disrespectfully dubs the "Dance of the One-Legged Crickets." I am terribly anxious to go on with the other movements, but was too tired by night to play any more than one. Anyway, I think I'll comprehend it better if I take it in small sections.

February 26, 1940

I outwitted Uncle Arnold just a bit this afternoon. During composition class, he had occasion to use the Beethoven piano trios and sent Stein out to get them. While waiting for S. to return, he sat down at the piano and began absently to strum chords, as is his wont when he's in a reflective mood. All of a sudden, without any warning, he turned to the class and demanded, "What was that chord?" The class named the tones correctly, but I said not a word ... This had the unfortunate effect of attracting his attention to me. "So, Miss Newlin, did you not know it?" he inquired blandly. "Of course I knew it," I replied, somewhat nettled by his tone; "I have absolute pitch!" It takes a confident remark like that to bring out the devil in him. "Oh, you have?" he exclaimed truculently;

[50]In *Heimfahrt* (no. 20) and *O alter Duft* (no. 21).

"well, then, what is this?" And he smashed out on the piano the nastiest dissonance he could think of. Of course I named it correctly and without hesitation. "That," he said, "is fine. And now, Miss Newlin, will you please resolve this on the blackboard?" "What!" I ejaculated; "resolve that?" "Why, yes!" he replied. Well, I waltzed up to the blackboard and wrote the first resolution that came into my head, fully expecting to be blackballed out of existence. And what do you suppose? My solution was good! I'd felt it was the right thing, but couldn't have explained why it was right if he'd asked me. He carefully explained to the class that the resolution was good because I used all the dissonant tones like leading-tones. I felt very proud because I had unconsciously utilized one of the precepts of *Harmonielehre*, one whose wording I had forgotten, but whose principle had made an impression on my mind, sufficient that I could employ it without even thinking about it.

I never knew before that he thought the organ should be played by more than one man, but it seems he does. This question came up in Structural Functions, in connection with the impending performance of Ravel's *Concerto for the Left Hand*, which he considers nonsense. Way back in 1904,[51] when a new concert hall was built in Vienna, he came out with an article saying that, when they got a new organ for this hall, it should be one with three or four manuals so that three or four men could play it at once, thereby bringing out the fullest possibilities of the instrument. He thinks that such an innovation would make it much more interesting to composers to write for organ.

He made an interesting characterization of Strauss' use of motives. Strauss treats them like cambiatas: consonances at the beginning and end, and dissonances in the middle, with occasional consonances occurring by hazard. I must remember to listen for this the next time I hear Strauss; I had never thought of his themes in quite that way before. That is always Schoenberg's way, to give you, unintentionally or intentionally, a new light on everything in your life.

---

[51]Cf. entry "The Future of the Organ," no. 1 under heading "C. ARTICLES, ESSAYS," in Rufer, *op. cit.*, p. 156.

✑ February 28, 1940

I find myself very much prejudiced against Coates[52] because of his sentimentalism and his condescending attitude towards the [Los Angeles Philharmonic] orchestra . . . he has what Levant[53] would call the "goodfellow" or "just call me Al" approach . . . Uncle Arnold, of course, dismissed the 3 o'clock class, so I was with him only for composition class. His best bits were: 1) a long tirade to the effect that you shouldn't use the term *obbligato*, because it means obligatory and now we write nothing that isn't obligatory (no power could explain to him that *obbligato* parts are, if anything, non-obligatory); 2) the deathless remark about cheap glissando effects on the violin, "It turns me the stomach over!" 3) in reference to the clear distinction between *staccato* and *spiccato* in his scores, "This why my music so transparent—which has only the effect to make it difficult!"

✑ March 1, 1940

Uncle Arnold is sick again; he has the flu, and a bad case of it too, if one can judge by his appearance. "I took six aspirins and three table-spoonsful of my cough medicine so I could come to class today," he confided to the advanced composition class, "and still I feel terrible!" Of course he should have stayed home, but you know how he is about that: thinks we "need him," even when he is too sick to put one foot before the other. As for my having my lesson tomorrow, that seems to be out of the question. When I walked downstairs with him after double counterpoint, he told me that I should call him up in the morning to find out for sure whether I can come or not. But he's expecting to go to bed as soon as he gets home, and stay there all week-end, which is sensible enough.

[52]Albert Coates (1882-1953), Anglo-Russian conductor and composer, specialist in Russian music. His compositions, including the opera *Pickwick*, have been largely forgotten.

[53]Oscar Levant (1906-1972), pianist, composer and movie actor, author of three witty books of reminiscences. The "just-call-me-Al" characterization comes from the first of these, *A Smattering of Ignorance* (New York, Double-day, Doran, 1940), pp. 10-11.

He wasn't too sick to have a few good laughs at my expense. The worst was in double counterpoint, where he looked at our 3-voice fugues. Stein started to play my canon, and what should pop up in the very first measure but a completely unexplained dissonance which I'd absolutely missed in checking the thing over? "Well," inquired Uncle Arnold truculently, "what is the meaning of this?" "Why," I finally stammered, "it must just have been a mistake—I can't understand how it happened!" At that, he started laughing so hard, loud and long that you never in the world would have known he was sick. "Oh, this a new species of counterpoint: counterpoint by mistake!" he bellowed between chuckles. "Five species: correct counterpoint; sixth species: counterpoint by mistake! Oh, this wonderful joke!" I thought, really, that he'd never get over laughing at that.

Went to Raya Garbousova's [54] concert tonight . . . asked her afterwards if she was familiar with Uncle Arnold's 'Cello Concerto. She is indeed, and considers it a beautiful work, though not comfortable for the instrument.

March 4, 1940

Uncle Arnold seemed quite well again today; well enough, in fact, to vigorously reject my violin-sonata theme on the grounds that, though correct, it's too classical. Besides, it's in minor, a circumstance which irks him peculiarly. When he commented on that, I replied somewhat acridly, "Well, the last time I brought you one in major and you didn't like it." "Well," he retorted promptly, "next time bring one in major which I will like!" "Yes, that's very easy to do," I heard Stein mutter sardonically under his breath; but I don't think the old man heard him, for he continued as blithely as ever, "You know, now I criticize your ideas rather than your form, and this for you a progress; you should be proud that I do this!"

The real three-ring circus came when he looked at E.'s two songs (settings of two *sehr warm* poems by James Joyce). In the first place, he was determined that someone should sing them, and no one would or could. We ended up by executing a ghastly sort of whistling chorus to the first song. We were never together, S. kept forgetting to turn the pages for E., and E. kept getting lost in his

---

[54]Garbousova (1905-   ) was a popular concert 'cellist at this time. Born in Tiflis, Russia, she settled in the United States in 1927. She was a soloist with major American orchestras.

accompaniment, which added to the fun. I don't know how long this would have gone on if someone hadn't conceived the brilliant idea of having C. play the voice part of the second song on the violin. Uncle Arnold helped out this time by standing squarely between C. and the music, waving his arms about imperially, and yelling, "One! Two! Three!" on the wrong beats. The result was something which you would have to have heard to have believed it.

March 5, 1940

I did go to Uncle Arnold's this morning from ten to eleven or thereabouts. On the whole, he was pretty well satisfied with my elaboration now; he thinks I can make a very short end of it in ten minutes or so. If that's true, I'm really on the home stretch, because the recapitulation is nothing to do. Alas, the greater part of our time was devoted to a "nice frank talk about counterpoint." He still doesn't think my counterpoint has gone ahead as it should, and can't understand why, because his infallible method works on everybody else. Personally, I think this is just a bad case of stubbornness on his part, but that is the last thing in the world I would tell him. I shall go ahead quietly working on my fugues, etc., as usual, and maybe he will drop the idea pretty soon. He lent me another piece of music. This time it was Felix Greissle's [55] 4-hand version of *Kammersymphonie*, which he wants me to play in composition class with Mr. Stein tomorrow. "Of course, you know," he muttered as he lugged out his only copy of the arrangement for me (he had one other, but Klemperer borrowed it and he doubts he'll ever get it back), "I never borrow [*sic*: lend] music, and you must understand I could not let you have everything!" Recalling that I had his piano septet at home, he remarked, "You must not forget to return this, for if you did, I would become very mean!" I can imagine that he would, nor would I really blame him. I can't get over how nice he has been about loaning me things of his which I would never have had a chance to study otherwise.

[55] The husband of Schoenberg's oldest daughter Gertrud (1902-1947). Born in Vienna in 1899, he studied with Schoenberg, Berg, and Guido Adler. His article, "Die Formalen Grundlagen des Bläserquintetts von Arnold Schönberg" (*Musikblätter des Anbruch*, January, 1925, pp. 63-68) was one of the earliest articles about the twelve-tone method, along with Erwin Stein's "Neue Formprinzipien" (Arnold Schönberg zum 50. Geburtstag, September, 1924). In later years, Greissle worked for G. Schirmer, Schoenberg's American publisher.

Mrs. Schoenberg's sister[56] was there visiting while I was around;
I didn't see her. Mamma says she is much like Trude only better-
looking. Family affairs do not seem so good, for Ronnie, Mrs. S.,
and her mother were all breathing out germs like fire-eating dragons,
in spite of their protestations of feeling better. Ronnie coughed
accidentally all over Mamma, much to her horror. And as for Roddie,
he is dead. I suppose it happened at the beginning of the week,
because he was still living on Saturday. T. thinks the vet must have
put a peaceable end to him; I wouldn't be surprised, either, for there
would be nothing much else to do with a big dog that couldn't even
get up off the floor. Uncle Arnold is anxious to have another dog at
once. She isn't in such a hurry, for she is really very grief-stricken at
the loss of this one; but they've been shopping around for a new
one, nevertheless. They've considered a collie, an English boxer, and
a Scottie. I hope they decide on a collie; the estate really demands a
big dog, and the collie's disposition would be ideal for the children.

Ronnie now has it in his head that he wants to be a violinist; I
suppose he caught that idea from Nuria. Well, maybe he won't be a
great violinist, but with his character he certainly will be a great
something, even if it is only Two-Gun Schoenberg, Public Enemy
No. 1. Mrs. S. says he always steals things when they go to the dime
store, so he may end as P.E. 1 at that!

March 6, 1940

We didn't play *Kammersymphonie* in class after all. Stein and I
rehearsed it once through after school, and Stein took the music to
put in Uncle Arnold's office. We'll probably rehearse it a couple
more times and then play it in class some time next week. I am glad
it worked out this way, for now we will do it much better. Instead
of hearing this, Uncle Arnold played the records of his beloved First
Quartet for us; he didn't get quite all the way through them, but will
finish them on Friday. Oh, that is a glorious work! I could sit and
listen to it all day long, especially the sublime Adagio. Today he
offered a tantalizing new sidelight on the work, one that I'd give

---

[56]Marie (Mitzi) Seligmann, a most congenial member of the Schoenberg family
circle.

anything to know more about. He said that some of the extravagances of the form were because the piece was really a sort of "symphonic poem," and, when Stein pressed him as to whether there was a definite program to it or not, he replied promptly, "Oh yes, very definite—but private!" After that he whispered a few words to Stein, and while I didn't catch all he said, I understood him to reproach Stein for having asked such a question, and to say, "One does not tell such things any more!" So I guess the great secret will remain forever unrevealed. I tried to prod Stein about it, but his ignorance seems to be as complete as my own.

A student quartet played the first movement of Beethoven's Op. 59, no. 1 in analysis class today. They broke down in two or three spots, but on the whole did very well considering the short time they have had for rehearsals. Uncle Arnold was really tickled with their performance and told them so. He is going to set us hard to work at analyzing that movement now. He has given each four of us a section of it to study, and in a week we must all report our findings in class. Now he has a notion that some of the harmonic peculiarities in the first movement, especially at the beginning, might be due to Russian folk-influence (shades of Rasumovsky!). Might be; certainly such things occur in the last movement. He can't explain the phenomena in any other way.

March 8, 1940

Uncle Arnold was the picture of happiness throughout the advanced composition class, for this time he finished playing the records of the First Quartet. All the time the music was playing, he strolled up and down the room, perfect contentment mirrored in his face; for which I cannot blame him, as this music is nothing short of celestial. This is the first time I have ever heard the work all the way through. In some ways, the lovely tranquil coda is the best of all. But the height of his delight was reached when Mr. Stein put on the very last record, which consists of a speech in German by the Master himself, a speech by Alfred Newman[57] (who was responsible for

[57] The film composer (1901-70), longtime music director of Twentieth Century-Fox. His musical memorabilia are housed on the University of Southern California campus, not far from the Arnold Schoenberg Institute.

the making of the records), speeches by all of the Kolisches (these in German, except for K.'s own, in which he says that he is indeed happy to listen to this work, which had always been one of his "dears"), and finally a speech by the sound engineer. I thought that S. would burst with pride on hearing all those wonderful words about his great art! He says the speeches were his idea; there is one side of them for the recording of each of the four Quartets; a very nice idea, too. But I don't know why so much German is spoken, except for sentimental reasons perhaps.

After about the first hour, double counterpoint class usually turns into a clearing-house for all the old man's pet ideas, which may or may not have anything to do with double counterpoint. So it was today. The prize idea of the lot is his plan for a class in modern counterpoint: the counterpoint of Wagner, Brahms, Mahler, Debussy, Reger and Schoenberg. He makes a great distinction between this kind of counterpoint and that of older composers; says that modern contrapuntal art consists of combining two or more themes together in as many ways as possible, and is thematic, whereas the older counterpoint makes a point of deriving all the free counterpoint as much as possible from the given strict motive, and so is motival. Very neatly put. Such a course would, I think, be tremendously valuable for composers.

The next best idea is that a law ought to be passed compelling American symphony orchestras to devote 50% of their programs to American music. He says such a law obtains at present in Italy. I suppose the other half would be Schoenberg, Berg, von Webern, and Mahler!

🖉 *March 9, 1940*

Bad foggy weather, but no rain. We were thankful for that, as I had to go out to Uncle Arnold's this afternoon, and when it rains the trip is exceptionally difficult. When we got there, he was listening to the Metropolitan broadcast (*Figaro*) with score in hand; so I got to follow the score with him, which was very nice. He'd like it if I could come early every Saturday so as to be able to follow the operas with scores. I think he has all the most-played ones. Of course, I could not get in at the very beginning, but if I could come about

one o'clock that would be good. We didn't make any final arrangements about this, though. I'll be pleased if it works out; we don't
usually listen to the operas at home, because they come at an incon-
venient time, and I have no scores. But if I could listen with a score
and at U.A.'s side, that would be something else again!

March 11, 1940

The theme for variations will be all right, Uncle Arnold says, if I
simplify the harmony and accompaniment to a great extent. My too
elaborate inner voices he characterized as "little worms which wind
about." How fertile in strange creatures is his imagination! Well, I'll
give the patient some worm medicine tomorrow and hope that it
cures rather than kills. He is still talking about last Saturday's performance of *Figaro* which I was so lucky as to listen to (in part) by
his side. He says he wishes every one of us had heard it, not so much
for the execution (which was poor) as for the marvelous qualities of
the music. Its most especial merit, according to him, is its explosive
character, which makes it so dramatic. This is produced by the
juxtaposition, within one fairly large section, of a great many small
ideas which contrast violently with one another. He mentioned this
particular quality because he would like us to get some of it into
our sonata themes.

March 13, 1940

Schoenbergs have their new dog; have had him for three days, but
the first I'd seen or heard of him was today, when I stepped out to
speak to Mrs. Schoenberg in the car on my way home. He's a brown
and white collie, four months old, as friendly and sweet as can be,
and lovely for the children. Nuria and Ronnie, who were sitting in
the back with him, looked proud enough of their new acquisition to
burst! (Especially Nuria, who had the signal honor of holding the
end of his leash.) His name is "Snowy." Mrs. S. seemed quite
delighted with him. Today, she looked better than I've seen her in
some time; I think that being busy with selecting and taking care of
a new dog has been psychologically good for her in taking her mind

off Roddie's death. Well, I'll probably be seeing a lot of Snowy, for she intends to take him around in the car as much as possible to get him used to riding.

Uncle Arnold, contrary to my fears, was not a bit sick today, but as fair and blooming as a rose, and as sweet as peaches and cream. I think he's tickled with the new acquisition to the family, too. I showed him my "wormed" theme, and he approved it pretty nearly *in toto*. One spot in the harmony he would like to have changed, but otherwise it's all right and I can forge right ahead with it now. It didn't take him quite the whole hour to look at our compositions, so what do you suppose we spent the last ten minutes doing? If you please, we were all trying to figure out, in the midst of the most uproarious hilarity, questions to send in to Mr. Levant for *Information Please!*

March 15, 1940

Uncle Arnold presented to us a compendious discussion of the 4-voice fugue, interwoven with a goodly number of juicy reminiscences. This counterpoint class is the best place of all to pick up reminiscences, inasmuch as by four o'clock or so, having already lectured three hours, the old man is worn out and feels like doing anything but getting down to business. "You know," he told us, "I am so tired now after four hours, and in former times I would teach six and seven and eight hours a day, and not feel it at all. I cannot understand this! And also I taught as much to my students then as now—I was not lazy, no; but what has happened to me?" He seems to have no idea that old age is catching up with him; naturally, no one dares tell him.

Back in the days when he lived with Zemlinsky, life was no bed of roses. He never used the piano for composing, or hardly ever; but Zemlinsky was pounding away at it all the time, till the noise practically drove Uncle Arnold crazy! He never could, and still cannot, compose effectively when other music is going on about him. This was bad enough, but, to make matters worse yet, the house where they lived[58] was within earshot of a church. They lived on the fifth

[58]Upon Schoenberg's return to Vienna from Berlin in late summer, 1903, he and his family moved into a three-room apartment in Liechtensteinstrasse No. 68/70, where the Zemlinskys already lived. Schoenberg met Mahler about this time. (Stuckenschmidt, *op. cit.*, p. 78.)

or sixth story of this building, and it and the church tower were the only tall structures in that quarter of Vienna, so there was nothing to cut off the sound of church bells. Daily, from one to six, the organ and the bells would keep up a ceaseless din. Uncle Arnold was telling Mahler of all these troubles one day; Mahler, however, replied rather grandiosely, "Oh, don't let that bother you. Why, you can incorporate the bells into your next symphony!" U.A. was a bit irked by this, but kept his own counsel. Soon he had his revenge. Mahler couldn't stand noise, either, while he was composing, so he had a special one-room house built for himself on a high mountain-top, and did most of his work there. All went well for a time, but soon Mahler became dissatisfied, and told U.A. so: the birds disturbed him terribly while he was at work. "Oh, don't worry," said U.A., "you can put their songs into your next symphony!"[59]

His prize boner of the day: "Now in the model for your sequence, do not artificial-dominantate too much." Typical Germanism.

Rehearsed *Kammersymphonie* with Stein this morning. From now on we will be working on it every day, as Nelson would like to have us do it for his Collegium Musicum program in a couple of weeks or so, and of course we want to "do it up brown." I took the score home to practise. I'm getting on quite well with it, and I think that between us we'll do our Beloved Old Man justice. I hope so!

I was out at Uncle Arnold's nearly two hours this afternoon; the extra time was on account of an interruption by two men who are going to completely rebuild "his" wing of the house. He wants extra shelves put in, new entrances built, a sliding door put in the entrance to his study for greater privacy, and such things. This was the only time the builders could come with their plans, and of course the working-out of them takes time, as he wants everything just right. I didn't mind—I got my full hour of teaching, so I should worry—but poor Mamma was completely exhausted when she left. Imagine, at her age, crawling around for two solid hours on her hands and knees, playing cat-show with Ronnie and Nuria, who are active and lively enough to wreck six of her! Snowy, too, claimed a good bit of her attention. Instead of being a collie and male, she is a Saint Bernard, but without the little keg of brandy.

---

[59] For earlier confrontations between Mahler and the birds, see Natalie Bauer-Lechner, *Recollections of Gustav Mahler* (ed. and tr. Newlin and Franklin, London, Faber & Faber, 1980).

March 18, 1940

I'm much surprised to learn that Uncle Arnold actually thought
there was some good in the Roy Harris symphony![60] When he
came bouncing into advanced composition class—twenty minutes
late, as usual—the first thing he asked was whether anyone had heard
the piece. I was the only one that had, so he asked me what my
impression was. "Well, I definitely didn't like it . . . There weren't
any ideas, and the form wasn't clear, and the harmony didn't have
any structural meaning. Besides, the whole last part was stolen right
out of *Petrouchka*!" "Oh well, this does not really matter," he
remarked carelessly, and then proceeded to say that, in spite of the
work's many faults, the last part really did contain some genuine
musical expression, even if overstylized. (He seems to believe R.H.
is a sincere artist.) The orchestration, too, was not bad, he thought.
The latter section made a better impression on him than the first,
perhaps, he conceded, because he didn't know just what to expect
at the beginning. "But anyway," he concluded, "this made more
favorable impression on me than *Johnny Goes to Town*!" (Usually
known as *When Johnny Comes Marching Home*, as we all hastened
to tell him; at that, he simply laughed and said, "Oh well, this all
the same!") As I said, I did not expect him to have a good word for
the symphony at all. The one previous time he'd spoken of R.H.,
he'd pilloried him as a horrible example of what studying with
Boulanger does to people.[61] Well, maybe it is true what he says,
that he always tries to find the good things in a new work rather
than the bad. Which may come as a surprise to some!

I actually thought that Stein and I were going to play *Kammersymphonie* in class, and indeed U.A. intended for us to do it, but he
got to reminiscing about the fourth-chords and, before we knew it,
the hour was up. We will do it on Wednesday now, he says. Probably
we'll get no further than the first page: his annotations take so
much time, you never cover any ground at all, but it's worth it. We'll
play it for *Collegium Musicum* in about a month.

---

[60]Harris (1898-1979) was at this time a major proponent of "Americanism" in
music. His popularity later faded.

[61]Schoenberg was still complaining about "la Boulanger's" influence nine years
later. Cf. letter to Rudolf Kolisch, April 12, 1949 (*Letters*, p. 270). He satirized
her in his "Text from the Third Millenium" (cf. above, p. 90) as "Budia Nalan-
ger."

We played *Kammersymphonie* (the major part of it) in advanced composition class this afternoon, and it went wonderfully, because Uncle Arnold wasn't there! No, he isn't sick in bed, it's just that he was out at a very "reetzy" faculty luncheon in Bel-Air (The Sycamores) and didn't get back till nearly three o'clock. We told him what we'd done, and he seemed quite pleased. I imagine, though, that he was in a condition to be pleased about anything and everything. The food was no doubt good, and from the unusual pinkness of his cheeks and brightness of his eyes one might deduce that alcoholic beverages had been offered to him and he had not refused! "Of course," he said, "it is too bad that I missed my classes, but I could not stay away from this. I wanted too much to go!" He toyed with the idea of keeping the class two hours on Friday to make up for his nonfeasance, but Stein judiciously pointed out to him that he couldn't on account of the double counterpoint class. So he had to give up that little plan, much to his disappointment . . .

U.A. and I had a beautiful fight in Structural Functions—just a play one, of course, but pretty hot nevertheless. It all came up over the first section in the first Rasumovsky Quartet. This section ends with a series of codettas, and then turns back through a retransition to what sounds like a recapitulation. When he asked me to describe the codettas and retransition, I did so in this way: "The retransition begins in measure 98." That didn't seem to satisfy him; he asked several others for the answer, but didn't seem to be satisfied with theirs, either. Finally, he asked, "Do you not know why I am not content with what you say?" We didn't, and said so. "Why," he ejaculated, "do you not see that the codettas end in measure 97 and not in measure 98?" "But that's what Miss Newlin said!" shouted Abraham. This was where the real tangle began. "But you did not say this!" U.A. fairly bellowed, turning full on me. "You said that the codettas end in measure 98!" "I did not!" I retorted, getting blue in the face. "I said the retransition began in 98! Of course the codettas end in the measure before!" "Mr. Stein," U.A. now inquired, taking a different tack, "did I misunderstand her? Did she say this? Now, don't become embarrassed; tell me frankly if she said it, for I might have misunderstood her!" "Well," muttered Stein, "all I heard was 98." (He has to keep his job, you know!) "Mr. Abraham," yelled U.A., getting desperate, "did she say it? Swear to tell the truth, the whole truth, and nothing but the truth!" "Well—er—" "Say yes or no!" "YES!" (chorus of assent from whole class) "And I still say she did not say it!" That was that. DRAW!

March 22, 1940

Went over at noon to practise *Kammersymphonie* with Stein and he wasn't there! Mixup about rehearsal time . . . Uncle Arnold didn't look at my outline and beginning of a 4-voice fugue, but he did see my sketches for new variations; pronounced most of them useful and one even "good," which is going strong for him. His chief criticism is that they are too homophonic, not contrapuntal enough; and some of them have "nothing in." Well, even if none of them were useful, the practise of writing them would have been good for me anyway. I was interested to hear what he had to say about Mrs. Warren's [62] *Passing of King Arthur*, which I hadn't heard, though I'd already heard conflicting reports about its performance last night. He said that his impression was partly not bad; the orchestration seemed fair, though often too thick and muddy (which may have been the fault of Coates' vague conducting), but the work on the whole lacked structure and form.

As I said, he didn't look at our fugues; instead, started to write a four-voice fugue as example for us. This year, he's starting us on four-voice fugues with only one subject and a two-part canon. He spoke much about his philosophy of rules. To him, a rule is like a law of nature, and admits of absolutely no exceptions. Hence, he gives us but few rules for our counterpoint, but much advice. This latter is not meant to be followed slavishly, but rather to develop our ear so that we can use our own judgement. Such, for him, is the meaning of our entire contrapuntal training. He sees no sense in teaching us to write fugues in the "ancient style" or the "Palestrina style," because our place in music history has already been taken by what he picturesquely calls "great mens!" I don't know whether I've told this idea of his before, but he expressed it so concisely and well today that I wanted to put it down anyway.

[62] Elinor Remick Warren (b. 1905), composer also of *The Harp Weaver* for baritone solo, women's chorus, harp and orchestra, and of many songs. She was a prominent figure in Los Angeles.

Annette couldn't play her sonata in class because she'd broken her glasses—so what should he do but produce, seemingly from thin air, a reading-glass for her to use? He has to have one all the time now because he's hurting his eyes writing on too small paper.

March 23, 1940

At long last I have the Schoenberg birthday pictures. Mrs. S. gave them to Mamma this afternoon. For group pictures, they are really quite good. I don't look a bit like myself—quite snooty and smug; but then, I never do look myself in a photograph. Everyone but me is showing at least six rows of teeth. Uncle Arnold himself looks utterly insane, but very happy withal.

I had expected they would be listening to *Tristan* when we arrived (we heard the first of it before we left home) but they weren't . . . U.A. looked over my new sketches and two variations, and analyzed examples with me: his own variations in *Serenade* and in the Suite which I just finished studying, and examples from Beethoven quartets. I tried to persuade him to analyze his Variations for Orchestra, too, but he wouldn't, as he says they are too difficult even for *him* to imitate! Now he wants me to have four or five variations and a coda; he picked out those of my sketches which he thought would be most useful for this. Then, I will make a movement of variations for my piano quintet, but on a much simpler theme, perhaps on a folk-song or a theme from one of the Bach 'cello sonatas. The chief trouble with the set I'm composing now is that the theme is too "entangled," or "feelthy," as he puts it. I think "entangled" sounds better.

March 25, 1940

In Structural Functions, Uncle Arnold was muttering a good bit under his breath about next week's Music Educators' Convention. He's scheduled to speak, but doesn't think he will be honored sufficiently or have a big enough audience to make the occasion worthy of him. "Now in Kansas City," he said, "I was treated in the manner to which I am accustomed!" This sounds a bit pompous, but I think his attitude is really quite right.

Once a friend asked him if he remembered the telephone number of a certain man. "Oh, of course I know it," he replied, "I know all telephone numbers." "All telephone numbers?" inquired the friend incredulously. "Yes, all telephone numbers—but I do not know to whom they belong!"

March 27, 1940

Uncle Arnold is in fine trim, merry as a grig and disposed to be nice to everyone. He looked at my two new variations; one of them he wants me to discard because it hasn't sufficient character, but the other one (not quite finished) is the right thing. When I've written another to replace the one he threw out, and finished the good one, I'll have finished the whole movement except for the coda. I don't know yet how that should be done, but he has promised to discuss it on Friday for my benefit. I guess it's a good thing that I decided not to go out of town after all! . . .

He told one thumping good story in the composition class, about the first performance of his *Pelleas und Melisande* under his direction in Prague. As usual, he remarked with obvious delight in the recollection, there were riots of all descriptions, and a veritable torrent of hissing broke out at the end of the piece. He tried to come back and take his bows as a conductor should, but it was no use; the public opposition was too much for him, and he finally had to retire. Sporadic hissing continued during the first part of the intermission (which *Pelleas* immediately preceded), but bit by bit the audience calmed down. After the intermission, Pablo Casals was supposed to play the Haydn D major 'Cello Concerto. As he stepped out on the stage expecting his usual cordial reception, the audience began to hiss, because they thought he was Schoenberg! However, as soon as they realized who he was, they applauded as usual. I never would have thought C. and S. looked that much alike, but maybe they do to a Schoenberg-enraged audience!

March 29, 1940

Uncle Arnold . . . talked about the coda of a set of variations, which he likens aptly enough to the coda of a rondo, with the difference

that the codettas or cadences are represented by reduced variations.
. . . In the double counterpoint class, he talked about double counterpoint! Yes, I know that sounds funny, but he never does introduce
double counterpoint till near the end of the year. Though he looked
at fugues (4-voice), I didn't show him mine because I want to make
a clean copy of it before he sees it.

Year-after-next he wants to put in graduate courses with enough
credits so that there can be a whole College of Composition: a laudable ambition! He would use all of his own best students as readers
and assistants . . . I doubt his taking me except as a last resort, for I
know that, despite his fondness for young ladies, he doesn't want
them for helpers. He believes woman's place is in the home, quite
after the fashion of the old country.

March 30, 1940

The highlight of my lesson with Uncle Arnold this afternoon was
his analysis (harmonic and contrapuntal) of the *Suite in Ancient
Style*, a work which I'm always happy to renew acquaintance with.
(He analyzed it once in class last year, and I heard it when the New
York Philharmonic did it years ago, but I don't remember it so well.)
He pointed out its finesses with greatest pride and at greatest length,
and finally said, "Now just to see how fine all these voices are
written, one should blindfold oneself and stick in the finger!" I
accepted this as a bit of harmless bravado and thought nothing
more of it, but what was my surprise when he turned on me and
exclaimed, "Do it!" I did it, too; but it was just my luck to "stick
in the finger" on the first violin, which wouldn't really prove U.A.'s
point at all! (His idea was to show the independence and cleanness
of the inner voices.) But I must say that I *don't* think he should
spend valuable lesson-time playing games with me! Or with Ronnie
either, for that matter. He gave R. about three dollars' worth of
hugs, pats, kisses, and general loving; called him in from the hall,
where he was passing by to go out into the yard and play, and made
him come a-running all the way to the far end of the living-room so
he could see him, show him to me, and make a fuss over him. The
love he bears the little fellow is truly touching! It makes you feel
good to see how happy the old man is when he's stroking Ronnie's
curly head, or holding him on his lap.

We had to work in the living-room today, because his rooms are being rebuilt. It's a relief to play on a piano that is in tune!

April 1, 1940

. . . Uncle Arnold talked and talked in composition class; didn't look at our pieces at all, since only four people showed up (because of the Music Educators' Convention) and I guess he felt in a talkative mood anyway. The point of departure was the contention that school music programs should contain more modern music. He believes this only if the school program of music is expanded in general, because too large a proportion of modern music might have a bad effect on young people who had not yet developed a sense of balance. Of course, he is firmly convinced that more modern music ought to be played by major symphony orchestras and outstanding performers, for obvious reasons! If he were musical dictator of this country, he would pass a law requiring all performers to devote at least 10% of their programs to the work of contemporaries. If they couldn't do it on their regular series, then let them devote some of their excessive profits to playing special programs of modern music. From an experience of his own, he realizes that performers are sometimes prevented from doing such things by concert managers, etc. The time the Flonzaley Quartet played his First Quartet ("they told me they had rehearsed it fifty-two times," he reminisced fondly, "and then I know they are fine people") he took them and the concert manager to dinner afterwards and then to the railroad station, for they had to leave at once. In his very presence, while they were at dinner, the concert manager addressed the Flonzaleys as follows: "Well, if you insist on playing that kind of music, I can't give you any engagements in Germany, but if you stick to the classics I'll see that you have concerts in every important city!" What a nerve! "And I told him what I thought of him, all right!" exclaimed U.A., his voice still hot with anger at the memory . . . He spoke bitterly of the lack of protection for composers. "Copyright," says he, "is the right to steal after fifty-two years!" He has had much hard experience with such things . . . Ended his remarks on this subject with this gem: "Like other crimes, music does not pay!"

April 3, 1940

No Uncle Arnold this afternoon. He was out at the Convention giving a speech on "Learning Through Teaching."

My classmate H. tells this story: that good flutist of L.A., by way of Vienna and Cincinnati, Ary van Leeuwen, played in the Vienna Philharmonic when they first gave *Kammersymphonie*. Schoenberg was originally supposed to conduct, but he was so confusing that they pushed him out diplomatically (don't ask me how!) and put Mahler in instead. The change was apparently for the better.[63]

April 6, 1940

I thought U.A. seemed rather nervous and overwrought this afternoon. No wonder, for poor Nuria is sick in bed with a cold again, and Ronnie is not very well either. U.A. has been busy clearing out his rooms and answering scads and scads of back letters which he doesn't want to bother with, but has to . . . I'm sure from the way that he acted with me that he must have been upset. It isn't that he was angry with me . . . but a lot of little things came up. For example, in one of the variations I had wanted to construct a strict canon between the two violins, but had been unable to because I couldn't fit it to the changing harmony. I explained this to him and his only comment was, "But why did you have this difficulty?" "Why, that's just what I've been trying to tell you. I couldn't make the canon fit the harmony!" "Yes, I know, this you just said, but why could you not do it?" I thought and thought, but I couldn't see what he was driving at, so I shut up and just looked at him in a helpless goggle-eyed sort of way which was meant to indicate complete ignorance on my part and to elicit a helpful suggestion from him. This, however, seemed only to bring out the animal in him. "Well," he shouted in throaty exasperation after a few minutes of this sticky silence, "you must either know or not know. You cannot sit there and look at me like that!" Isn't that the worst ever?

---

[63] Mahler did not conduct the première of the *Kammersymphonie* on February 8, 1907. He was in the audience, vigorously defending Schoenberg's music against hostile listeners.

I wasn't surprised by it, though, for he's super-sensitive to the way people look at him, and always has been.

April 7, 1940

This evening, Hal and I went to the record-concert at the Religious Conference building. As I'd heard someone call up Uncle Arnold yesterday and ask him to come as an honored guest because they were going to play *Verklärte Nacht*, I certainly had no intention of missing it! Well, he didn't come; the student who was in charge of it announced that both he and Levant had planned to appear, but that L. had to go back to N.Y., and U.A. was detained by illness in the family. (That would be Ronnie and Nuria; I do hope they're no worse!) However, *Verklärte Nacht* was played, and a long program besides ... We had brought along my score to follow while the records were being played, but it turned out that we had to listen by firelight, and dim firelight at that! This, for the benefit of the "spooners" with whom the gathering was infested. Nevertheless, we made a valiant effort to read the music; we lay down on our stomachs right in front of the fire, thus getting completely covered with soot and smudge, and all but burned up to boot. We certainly felt right in tune with the *sehr warm* passages! Anyway, we dug our noses right down into the score. By the time the piece was over, we were terribly stiff and sore from being in such an uncomfortable position, but it was worth it! U.A. would have been impressed by our devotion.

April 8, 1940

The most interesting piece of news today was something that C. told U.A., which received the old man's unqualified approval and enthusiasm. It seems that a full orchestra of the very best studio musicians is being organized to play only modern works, and that various prominent composers about town have been approached and asked if they would be interested in having their works performed. In U.A.'s case, this would involve his conducting, too. They could have as many rehearsals as they wanted, the orchestra could be expanded to any desired size, and in case of need singers could be obtained (e.g., for *Vier Orchesterlieder*). You can imagine how U.A. was delighted with this plan! He thinks *Kammersymphonie I* would be the best work to start out with; *Kammersymphonie II* would be good, too, but he has promised its first performance to the New Friends of Music in N.Y. Well, I hope that the affair amounts to something, for I've heard so much about Uncle Arnold's fabulous conducting that I can't wait to see it. As far as that goes, the organization will be a good thing for the players, too; for it's a shame that the talents of so many really fine musicians are wasted on worthless music. U.A. doesn't think that music for the movies can ever be good. This is no condemnation of his *Begleitungsmusik zu einer Filmszene*. That was not really for the movies, but only symbolically. At the time the talkies first appeared, some publisher[64] in Magdeburg was putting out a jubilee series in honor of the occasion, and invited U.A. to write this music, which he did. "I don't think," he says, "they would ever have played it!" And after looking at the score—which I saw today for the first time—I concur. It has never been played at all, I believe; at least, he never conducted it. [65]

April 10, 1940

Uncle Arnold very much upset today because he's been asked to dismiss his first year composition class Friday for a program by Phi Beta (national dramatic and music sorority) and doesn't think the program is worth it. He was particularly incensed about the presence of an Arensky Trio on the program. That's his idea, I guess, of the ultimate in triviality. It just happened that he was analyzing the themes (note, please: themes, not melodies) of a lot of Brahms chamber works for us in advanced composition class, and naturally a number of trios came under consideration. Every time he came to one of these, he'd point triumphantly to the title and cry out,

[64]Heinrichshofen Verlag, F. Charles Adler, later famed for his early LP recordings of Mahler, had commissioned this series.

[65]Klemperer premièred it with the Berlin State Opera Orchestra on November 6, 1930; Slonimsky presented it in a Hollywood Bowl concert on July 23, 1933. It has been used as background for several films; I have seen only Jean-Marie Straub's, in which a narrative of anti-Jewish atrocities is imposed on it.

"Oh, see this wonderful theme by Arensky!" The effect was devastating.

We pretty nearly had an embarrassing moment in connection with *Kammersymphonie*. In this same class Stein and I have been practising from the copy of the Greissle 4-hand version which U.A. lent me. Well, we've been practising it so much, turning the pages so often and so vigorously, that it is just about in the battered condition of my Beethoven sonata volume now, only more so! So, when U.A. lugged out the orchestral arrangement of KS to analyze its theme for us and asked us if we wouldn't like to play, please, we were considerably alarmed for fear he'd see the state our copy was in and take us to task for it. Thus, we were in a state of jumpy jitters all the time he was pointing out the music's innumerable marvels. We needn't have worried, for he never did get around to asking us to play. Got wound up in an involved explanation of why he writes horns, clarinets, etc., as non-transposing instruments, during which he made the deathless remark, "Others conserve bad things. I am conservative, too—but I, I conserve the progress!" However, the worst was yet to come. During his disquisition, I'd laid our *Kammersymphonie* down on the back of the piano, and bit by bit conveniently forgotten about it. Imagine my shock when I suddenly realized, after the bell had rung and the old man had left the room, that he'd carried it away with him! "Good heavens!" I yelled at Stein; "we've got to have that music back. How can we ever work without it?" Stein concurred that we had, indeed, to have it, and immediately left the room, in hot pursuit, or so I supposed. But when he came back for Structural Functions (analysis today—we examined the Fugato in the first Rasumovsky Quartet) he didn't have the music with him, and I was in a state of nervous prostration during the entire class, for fear U.A. had refused to yield up the music to Stein because he was angry at the condition to which we'd reduced it! I needn't, however, have worried. It turned out that Stein had simply forgotten to ask the old man about it! When I finally caught up with U.A., after a mad chase (he'd a big black briefcase under his arm, which I feared contained what we were after, and I was alarmed for fear he'd get to the car and ride off with it before I could catch him), he was perfectly willing for me to have it back. He'd simply thought we didn't need it any more, and so had stored it in his office. Apparently he'd never even noticed the damage. What an anticlimax!

April 13, 1940

Miserable today because of the extreme heat (96° I believe). Cooler in Brentwood, but still hot enough. The old man was in a pretty bad way himself and not too anxious to teach. He looked over my partly finished coda to the variations and decided that I needn't bother to complete it; I'll learn more by starting on the Bach variations. My edition of that Sarabande was all wrong, so I had to copy the original from his music. I was afraid that would make us miss the bus, but it didn't.

Vignette of life at the Schoenbergs': Ronnie busily practising a song for Nuria's approaching birthday, "Happy birthday to you, happy birthday to you, happy birthday, dear Nuria, happy birthday to you, you heel!" The comic effect of this was increased by the fact that he was running around without any clothes but what God gave him. He had a pair of pants on when we came, but soon discarded those.

April 15, 1940

Not very much news from the Schoenberg front today. As the cumulative mass of our immortal works is getting to be a bit too much for him to handle in the class, he wants to take some of the manuscripts "to home" to look over. I suppose mine will not be included in that group, as he would see it at my lesson in any case. Besides, I really haven't time to make a good copy of it, and I would have to do so if I were to give it to him. (The "it" is the first draft of an arrangement of the Bach theme.)

In Structural Functions, he is busy putting us through a course of harmonic insertions. We take I-V, V-I, II-V, V-II, and so on through all possible harmonic combinations of two; first insert one harmony between these two, then two, then three, and then four at last. When we've gone through all this, we should know everything about the Schoenbergian (or *Harmonielehre*) system of harmony, with its firm basis of the ascending-descending progressions theory.

After school, Stein and I practised on *Kammersymphonie* for an hour or so. We'll have to work more on it from now on, for I learned today that the *Collegium Musicum* performance is due in only two weeks.

April 17, 1940

U.A. questioned us as to whether we thought we were deriving advantage from his newest harmonic exercises for us, and got a whole flock of unquestioning affirmatives in reply. Vouchsafed us some interesting ideas *re* his teaching of harmony. Doesn't believe in teaching harmony and composition concurrently, because the compositions you'd write while just learning would be Czerny exercises harmonically, and what would be the meaning of that? Besides, there's no time to work on the two together. One of his most talented pupils[66] learned harmony with him in five months; but he took two lessons a week, worked literally day and night at it, and did practically nothing else. But what about U.A.'s own harmonic and contrapuntal training? As far as taking lessons goes, it was practically nil. He had five or six (free) lessons in harmony from the assistant to a famous organist in Vienna,[67] and perhaps an equal number in counterpoint from another man.[68] But other than that, all he knows, he learned himself through writing.

April 19, 1940

Uncle Arnold is going to play the records of his second, third and fourth quartets at his home next Tuesday afternoon (beginning at 4 o'clock and lasting God knows how long) and we're all invited! . . . This is one chance in a million and I'm determined to take advantage of it. I can probably persuade Stein to drive me out so I won't have to bother with Castellamare bus.

As the old man was in a humoristic mood this time, we had loads of fun with him. Most amusing was the act he put on when he saw my piano reduction of *Erwartung* (the one with Bekker's notes, diagrams, and interleavings) lying on the piano. "Whose is this?" he cried out; "yours, Mr. Stein?" "No," I hastily retorted, "it's mine!" "You got it from the library, I suppose?" "No, I bought it." "Oh, so! (seeing the interleavings) I think it is second-hand, yes?" (He knows perfectly well that I bought the Bekker library, but I patiently repeated this to him.) "So, how much you paid for it?" "Three

66Karl Rankl (see above, p. 164).

67Probably the blind composer and organist Josef Labor (1842-1924).

68Most of Schoenberg's instruction in such subjects came from Zemlinsky.

dollars." "This enough!" This is what happens when you try to put on swank by bringing copies of his works to class. Funny in a different vein was the conniption-fit he put on when he heard some money drop out of his billfold onto the floor. He crawled all over the place looking for it, and set the whole double counterpoint class looking for it too. Finally one of the students found the coin, and what do you suppose it was? One penny!

U.A. complaining vigorously because his Schirmer publications do not sell. Last year the Suite in Ancient Style sold two copies. At least Universal gave him enough publicity so he had sales, if few performances, but now he has neither.

April 22, 1940

Today he got to talking again about his composition of *Erwartung*. He wrote it in fourteen days, you know. Wellesz says "almost in a condition of trance,"[69] but from the old man's own account, I doubt that. He began writing it about the first of September , while he and his wife were on their vacation. When he was about halfway through, he found something in the text that didn't seem to fit the rest, so lost a whole day correcting that. He had to write to Marie P.[70] about it and wait for her answer. Then the last day of the allotted time (his birthday, I believe, for he said that they left for home again immediately after his birthday) he had to spend packing. In all, then, he spent but 12 days on the actual writing. Considering the length of the piece (it lasts at least a half-hour on the stage), that must establish some sort of a record!

Tomorrow's arrangements are going to be a little complicated, I discovered when talking to Stein while we worked on *Kammersymphonie*. His folks want the car at that time, so he'll have to take

---

[69] Egon Wellesz, *Arnold Schönberg*, tr. W.H.Kerridge, London, Dent/New York, E.P. Dutton. 1925, repr. New York, Da Capo Press, 1969, p. 130.

[70] Marie Pappenheim-Frischauf (1882-1966), dermatologist, poet and dramatist. Contrary to the statements of many writers, she, and not Schoenberg, conceived the idea for the text of the monodrama *Erwartung*.

The dates on Schoenberg's short score (*Particell*) of *Erwartung* are: beginning, 27./8.1909; ending, 12./9. 1909. One surmises that he hurried to finish it before the fateful 13th. A typical performance (Helga Pilarczyk's with Robert Craft for the Columbia Records Schoenberg Series) lasts 26'50".

the streetcar out there and can't drive me. Besides, he has to go two hours before the set time, to help Uncle Arnold with some secretarial work. The old man is going to be so busy that he probably won't be able to hear us play *Kammersymphonie* through before the program, but Stein is going to bring it along with him, just the same. I guess he thinks he can persuade U.A. to hear it after the others have left. I don't know how I'll get home, but I trust it'll be all right.

April 23, 1940 (8:30 p.m.)

Well, I've just gotten home from having the time of my life out at Uncle Arnold's. Stein and I and another man stayed long after the others left, and didn't break away from the old man till nearly seven-forty-five. The other man was a young violinist (unfortunately I didn't catch his name)[71] who has been working on the Schoenberg violin concerto with Stein. Not the one who is going to play it on the Roof next Sunday night. Seems he has worked out a new system of "back-handed" fingering (playing with the fourth finger underneath the third, for example) which makes some of the hardest spots in the Concerto much easier, and wanted Schoenberg's approval on this. The old man was quite "het-up" over the idea, so much so that he wants this violinist to send Schirmer's his fingering and notes on the technique and ask them to publish that material. He (the violinist) has sent an article on the same subject to *The Stradivarius*, an English publication for string players, in reply to one by André Mangeot which just appeared in that magazine.[72]

S. didn't hear Stein and me do the *Kammersymphonie* this time, but promised he would on Saturday. In the meantime, he gave us some pregnant suggestions that have set us all a-dither; the most pregnant and dithery one being that we both cut off our feet so's not to use the pedal! And here I've been working my right foot more than my hands! Well, we shall see what we shall see.

Now about the Quartets. When I arrived (at four o'clock) they'd just put on the Fourth. Unfortunately, I had no score of that, so

[71]Sol Babitz, later famous for his individualistic views on baroque violin-playing.

[72]Cf. *The Strad*, April, 1940.

couldn't follow it entirely, but what I understood I enjoyed very much. After this was over, we had our refreshments in the dining-room: coffee and big slices of that delicious dry coffee-cake that seems to be the specialty of the house. Then, we went back to the living-room to hear, first, the last movement of the Second Quartet (played, by itself, for the benefit of some people from the University of Southern California who had to leave almost at once but wanted to hear that one thing before they went), and, finally, the entire Quartet. Oh, I love that work! The first movement is so warm, and I can't imagine anything more other-worldly than the last. But still I stubbornly cling to my preference for the First among all the Quartets.

I had my score of the Second there—the one I'd bought in the Bekker collection—and Uncle Arnold was much excited over it. It is a real first edition and only a few copies of it exist now. It is lent added value by the fact that it's taken from his own handwriting. Well, I'd an idea that I had something rather rare and special there, but I didn't know it was that rare! Today I told him for the first time exactly how many of his works I'd gotten for the $27 by buying that collection, and he was really astounded; said he envied me! I did not mention having the three letters.

After the music was over, the old man got to reminiscing about the gorgeous riots which used to attend the performances of his works, and of which he seems so proud. The one at the Second Quartet was a real prize. During the entire first half, the audience was in gales of laughter, and, though they quieted down during the last two movements (sung by Marie Gutheil-Schoder) they started hissing again as soon as it was over. [73] It was during this performance that Berg and von Webern went around smiting the recalcitrant members of the audience and getting smitten in return, I take it. What fun! At the first performance of the First Quartet, [74] poor little Mahler almost had a fit backstage on account of one man in

[73]This scandalous première took place on December 21, 1908. Wellesz remembered that audience misbehavior continued throughout the last two movements (Wellesz, *op. cit.*, pp. 25-26). For reviews of the concert, see Willi Reich, *Schoenberg, A Critical Biography* (New York, Praeger Publishers, 1971), pp. 35-36.

[74]By the Rosé Quartet in Vienna, February 5, 1907. Paul Stefan and Alma Mahler give similar accounts.

the front row who insisted on hissing at the top of his voice. Finally Mahler came out and demanded, "Why don't you go to the back if you have to do that?" The oppositionist retorted, "Maybe you can give orders at the Opera, but you can't give orders to me here. I'll do as I damn please, and, what's more, the next time they play one of your symphonies I'll be right out in front hissing!" Mahler fairly shook with rage, and would probably have struck the man if his brother[75] hadn't come out just then, and forced him to go backstage and calm himself. If there had been a public fight, Mahler would have lost his job! At *Verklärte Nacht*, U.A.'s brother was very useful;[76] he's a big man, about six feet tall, and I guess he just lugged the offenders out bodily. And then at *Pierrot Lunaire* in Turin, there was the man who, after it was all over, stood up and yelled, "Not a single triad!"[77] Uncle Arnold later found out he was a professor at the Turin Conservatory, and said, "He hears enough triads all day at the Conservatory. Why does he have to come to *Pierrot Lunaire* to hear them?"

April 24, 1940

Today's biggest news is that the performance of *Kammersymphonie* has been postponed exactly a week, probably because not all the other performers on the program were prepared. I certainly am glad, because now we will have that week to practise putting into effect the things he'll tell us on Saturday. He's promised to hear it right after my lesson. Well, he'll probably wipe up the floor with us, maybe not let us play at all. I understand that he's been questioning Stein as to my ability to play it; Stein has, of course, given him

[75]Mahler's brother-in-law Arnold Rosé (Rosenblum) 1863-1946), leader of the Quartet and concertmaster of the Vienna Philharmonic.

[76]Heinrich, Schoenberg's younger brother, was an opera singer (for a time at the German Opera House in Prague under Zemlinsky's direction). He was killed by the Nazis during World War II.

[77]On April 6, 1924, as part of Schoenberg's Italian *Pierrot* tour with his select ensemble.

favorable answers, but apparently he's received them with skepticism. On the other hand, he may be as sweet as peaches and tell us we play wonderfully. Only time will tell, I fear; meanwhile, we are both worried.

Nothing special happened in either of the classes . . . In analysis, he started us analyzing Beethoven's Op. 95, that first movement in which nothing is usual and everything is unexplainable (as so often happens in Beethoven). He did not speak about any of his personal opinions, except to give vent to his usual vigorous diatribe against conductors who cut repeats in classical works. Case in point: the performance of the *Jupiter* last Saturday. He said it made him want to cut a piece out of Toscanini!

April 27, 1940

Well, you could knock me down with a feather even as I write it, but it's true: Uncle Arnold heard Stein and me play *Kammersymphonie* this afternoon after my lesson, and not only are we both still alive, but he actually said it was good! Yes, when we left him he wrung our hands, and slobbered all over us like a happy St. Bernard, and thanked us again and again—and here I'd been expecting to be kicked out on my ear with a good half-dozen broken ribs! All morning long, especially while practising over at school with Stein, I'd been in a state of near nervous prostration, and that was nothing to the way I felt during my lesson, even though the old man was very sweet during that time and hardly said a thing against my Rondo. But when the dread moment finally arrived and there proved to be nothing to dread about it at all, what a relief! Of course, he had some criticisms to make: chiefly that neither of us played sufficiently legato (not having yet become accustomed to playing without the pedal) and that my loud bass sounded like an omnibus coming uphill (his own expression, and very picturesque, I think). Sometimes we weren't rhythmical enough to suit him and he would conduct at us till we were all in knots and beat two great slabs of wood together till our ears fairly popped! But then, those were really minor matters. In general, he was completely satisfied.

Uncle Arnold was not cross today, but he was terribly tired; wasn't able to come to advanced composition till nearly half-past two. ("Of course, he had a hard week-end," says Stein in his inimitable way. "He had to hear us play *Kammersymphonie!*") He looked all pale and puffy; and, to make matters worse, his hair was newly cut so close as to make him resemble an escaped convict, so that he didn't have any of his usual *anmutig* appearance. I don't know what is the matter with him, but when he looks like that I know something is! He didn't look at my composition, but he did have me play part of Brahms' G-major Violin Sonata with Stein; I played the violin part on a second piano. And, with demonic foresight, he made me write on the blackboard in Structural Functions, so that my good black dress was completely covered with chalk-dust in preparation for the following party. I sometimes think the man must be psychic!

News today is none too good. To be brief about it: Uncle Arnold has found out about the concert tomorrow on which I was to play my Waltz and Intermezzo and has summarily forbidden me to play them—or anything else of mine which he has not approved, unless I make a specific announcement to the effect that such pieces were written before I studied with him and that he should not be considered responsible for them (and, if there is a printed program, such a statement must appear on it). Well, as far as tomorrow goes, that doesn't really matter, because I'll simply play the first movement of the sonata that I wrote last term under his direct supervision; but what, what about the Dance Recital music? A week before performance is too late to show it to him. If I did, the whole dance would have to be cancelled, because I couldn't possibly rewrite it in time in accordance with his dictates. But, on the other hand, if he attends a performance with my name on the program as composer, and realizes that I have disobeyed his orders (though I didn't mean to do so, as I knew he'd recommended me for the job, and hence assumed it was all right to go ahead without bothering him further about it), his fury would know no bounds! I know that's true, from simple observation of the scene he made today in class. Well, I went over tonight to see Miss Deane [78] and talk the whole thing over with her. We decided that the best thing to do would be for me to appear under my own name as performer only on the program, and use a pen-name for the composition. As no newspaper article has yet used my name, this will protect me, unless he knows already that I have done it. And, even so, I don't see how he could protest against my having it performed under an assumed name, because, as no one would know that I'd written it, his reputation would in no way be damaged. Oh dear, it's an awful mess, and I do hope it disentangles itself with as little strain as possible. I love, adore, and am devoted to U.A., but if only he were a little more like other people!

May 2, 1940

The Phi Mu Alpha program went off without mishap as far as I was concerned. I played the first movement of the Sonata instead of the two forbidden pieces, and did it well, considering that I hadn't practised the music for nearly a month. Everyone wanted me to play an encore (preferably *Intermezzo*, for which there were several loud requests from the audience), but of course under the circumstances I couldn't. Gr-r-r! My public life is certainly getting curtailed with a vengeance; no doubt said curtailment is very salutary and all that, but it wounds one's pride a good bit. However, a Schoenbergian can't afford to be self-proud, I guess; he must completely submerge himself in devotion and respect for The Great Yellow Father. All right, I'll do just that. I've had my last fling at "freedom"!

As for the matter of the "alias," I'll use Uncle Zander's name. [79] That way, if U.A. questions me at all about the music, I can say that I arranged this piece of my uncle's for the use of the dancers, and that I only mixed into the affair at all because I knew that

[78]Martha Deane was director of the dance group.

[79]My uncle, Alexander Hull (1887-1953), was a composer as well as author of the popular novel *Shep of the Painted Hills* (New York, Frederick A. Stokes, 1930). It was filmed (*The Painted Hills*, 1951) as a vehicle for the celebrated collie Lassie; the amphitheatrical score was by Daniele Amfitheatrof.

Schoenberg had recommended me. I hate like thunder to lie to him, but, with him in the mood he's in now, to do anything else would be as much as my life was worth!

May 3, 1940

Thank goodness I passed through Uncle Arnold's hands today without mishap, but that was just good luck. For he is in a foul humor at everybody and everything—especially angry with his first-year composition class because their work is getting worse and worse, or so he says. He has threatened to flunk them all if they don't snap out of it. This mood he's in leads him to wistful reflections on how far behind we all are in our musical careers, considering that our average age is over 20 (I should hope he excludes me from this mass condemnation on account of my tender—?—age, but you never can tell with him), and on how much better they did these things in Germany, and to cheerful remarks such as this one to Mr. Nelson: "This is the advanced composition class—that is, if they have advanced with their compositions!" All this produces a comfortable feeling in the breast of the truly devoted disciple, somewhat akin to that induced by sitting in the same room with a time-bomb! That comparison is more apt than it sounds, for really, during this past week or so, I've been afraid to come near the old man for fear he'd explode right in my face. I've seen him bad before, but never this bad and never for this long!

He now has a new idea (well, not so new for him, since he used to tell it to his pupils in Vienna, but, so far as I know, new in the annals of piano pedagogy!) on how to become a good pianist: Don't practise individual sections over and over again, but instead read the music over until you know it absolutely by heart and have a feeling of the sound, then go to the piano and play it perfectly. No fuss, no muss, no practising; but what about technique? Ah, that's the perquisite of such low rabble as the Hofmanns, the Horowitzes and the Rachmaninoffs! (Stein and I practised *Kammer.* this p.m.—and I do mean practised!)

☙ May 4, 1940
(1135 State Street, Balboa Beach)

... A word on Schoenberg. He treated me all right this morning—nothing to say about that—but I think he'd just been quarreling with Trude. She was telling Mamma that he's getting worse and worse every day and she is nothing but a slave now. This is in harmony with what I've been noticing at school. Once, right in the middle of the lesson, he saw her and Mamma talking. A strange fixed expression came into his eyes and he muttered, "She is mad! This German roughness! Bosh!" He wouldn't be going loopy, would he?

☙ May 6, 1940

"Oh frabjous day! Calloo! Callay!" ... Which may sound a little silly, but I know of no other way to describe the inexpressible elation which pervades me ... after such a tremendously successful event as our performance of *Kammersymphonie* this afternoon was. In the first place, we played it splendidly, to my mind. Stein skipped a few beats, but not so that you'd notice it. Of course, coming at the end of a rather badly played program, our brilliant execution stood out all the more by contrast. And even if we had played all the rest of it terribly, that glorious smash ending—one of the most exciting musical moments I know of!—would redeem everything. We had an enormous and enthusiastic audience—all chairs and all standing room taken; of course, I can't say how many of them came just to hear us, but I'm betting that many of them did! ... But, best of all, the old man was utterly delighted with us. He insisted on pushing us to the front and making us bow with an arm around each of us, and told me that I had "wonderful temperament—and such mastery of the music and the instrument!", and kept wringing my hands and patting my arm, all of which was very touching and lovely. He had seemed to be quite nervous before the performance, though out of last week's bad humor. He was rather pale and agitated when he gave his little introductory speech, but all that vanished completely as soon as he got going.

Well, at this rate I could keep on for hours, floating the while on a beautiful pink cloud just the color of spun-sugar floss candy; but I think I'll go to bed instead to prepare for the coming difficult week.

May 7, 1940

This is Nuria's eighth birthday. I sent her a little card and pink-flowered handkerchief yesterday; hope it reaches her in time. She is giving a dinner-party for twelve little girls tonight.

May 9, 1940

Our maiden performance [of Dance Recital] went very well this afternoon, I thought . . . In the evening, I heard the tail-end of the Standard Symphony Hour. Their programs get worse and worse: movie music, *Darling Nellie Gray* and such trash, with the only good music usually the Strauss waltz which Svedrofski[80] always conducts at the end, a nice tribute to his Viennese provenance.

May 10, 1940

The whole lot of us . . . even poor "Hull"—really saw Dance Recital tonight, and everyone of us was much better impressed by the full performance than we had been by the bits of rehearsal we'd seen previously. My dance, according to the rest of the folks out front, was very effective and the best of its group. Of course, that the oh-so-anonymous music was the best goes without saying! And the playing—oh my! . . .

His *bon mot* on the Svedrofski rendering of the *Eroica* which I'd missed last night: "I never heard anyone less interested in the *Eroica*!" Someone asked him if he'd heard the *Rebecca* music and he replied, his voice pregnant with meaning, "I started to!" No more was said by anyone.[81]

---

[80]Henry Svedrofski regularly conducted this popular series.

[81]A concert adaptation of the score by Franz Waxman (1906-67) for Alfred Hitchcock's *Rebecca* (1940).

🖋 May 11, 1940

Uncle Arnold was remarkably nice to me this morning . . . he again praised the quartet in high terms, and, as for the quintet, he said "Good" to it FIVE times! I make a special point of all this praise for a reason which will appear at once. Mrs. Schoenberg, a naturally solicitous woman, has been good-naturedly fussing about my underweight for some time past, but today she went further: she actually thought I looked sick, and told Mamma so. Mamma threw this off with some noncommittal remark about my being pretty tired because I'd been so busy of late. Now, all the time this charming badinage was going on in the garden, Uncle Arnold was busy showing me how to carry a voice out more melodically in one place where I'd muffed the part-leading a little. "When you write so, it is this style!" he shouted, and started pounding *Chopsticks* on the piano with one finger to demonstrate what style he meant, to the vast amusement of both of us—and to the alarm of Mrs. Schoenberg. Rushing to the window and banging on the screen, she screamed, "Dika is over six!" "But I am just trying to show her that she is not!" retorted the old man, laughing even louder. Not having heard the previous conversation in the garden, I didn't quite understand her irruption, but laughed it off as just one of those things which so often occur in the Schoenberg family. However, when Mrs. Schoenberg came tearing into the living-room a moment later, frantically appealed to her Arnold to come and speak with her at once, pulled him into his study (which we never use any more for lessons since the new doors were put on it; I wonder why?) and closed the door after them, I was frankly surprised! About five minutes later he returned by himself, with an odd sheepish expression on his face. "So!" he muttered, and went on to a further examination of the muzzy part-leading he'd mentioned before. Well, when I say "further examination" I exaggerate a bit, for what he did was simply to glance at the spot again and say, "Well, you can correct this later, but we need not bother now!" That surprised me a little, too. However, I thought no more of the incident till, after the usual affectionate *adieux*, Mamma and I were on our way home. Then I thought to ask her what Mrs. Schoenberg had been up to, anyway—and she told me. As soon as Trude had heard him pounding on the piano, she'd begun to be alarmed for fear the old man was heckling me when I wasn't feeling well, and she'd further imagined she saw tears in my eyes. I don't know what gave her that idea, but there it is. Hence the window-banging incident—and, when that didn't strike to his heart, she took him aside for the simple purpose of telling him that I was not well today and that he shouldn't be so hard on me! To which touching plea, it seems, he replied that he'd already noticed that I was looking sick, and that he would do as she said—if, indeed, he hadn't been doing so already.

The funny part about this story is that I did not, and do not, feel in the slightest degree sick, nor do I look so, to the best of my knowledge. I might look a little tired on account of all my late rehearsals, but that's all. However, if the Schoenbergs want to show maternal and paternal solicitude, respectively, over the state of my innards, I don't mind. In fact, I think it quite nice.

May 15, 1940

Since I'd been out of school for three days (I had the flu after all!), after supper I decided that I'd better call up Uncle Arnold to tell him that I was planning to take my lesson tomorrow as previously arranged. (He wants it off Saturdays, which suits me now.) I'd just taken the requisite nickel in hand and was about to go downstairs, when the phone rang, a moment later our buzzer rang, and who should be on the line but Mrs. Schoenberg? She said to Mamma that the old man had told her to call up and find out how I was, as my two days' absence had convinced him that I was sick and he was quite worried about it. Now wasn't it nice of him to think about me at all, let alone to that extent! That ought to silence anyone who accuses him of being heartless or inconsiderate. We left it that I would come to him tomorrow morning unless I got worse, in which case I would let him know.

May 16, 1940

My lesson this morning went off very well—of course, I had not written much new on account of being sick, but he had understood that in advance and was not angry about it. He was glad to see me better, but not at all sure that I was well enough to be up, and particularly alarmed at the idea that I might communicate a microbe to his honored self. "You should not come with fever to me," he remonstrated gently, "because then I will get it and it will be very heavy!" I assured him that I was past the sneezing and coughing stage and hence strictly sanitary, but I don't know whether or not I entirely allayed his misgivings. Anyway, if he does catch cold, it will not be my fault, because while Mamma and I were waiting on the corner for the bus to take us home we saw him whizzing by on his way to a luncheon date in an open sports car and an even more open sports shirt, and absolutely nothing on his gleaming bald head! Well, if he insists upon taking part in such shenanigans at his age he doesn't need to blame me for his colds. But I don't suppose that will stop him from it, and if he does, I might as well commit suicide right this minute!

Young Ronnie is in prime condition; spent the morning pretending to be a blackbird, and being restrained with great difficulty from swallowing worms and pebbles. As it was, he consumed at least half a box of chocolates in the time we were there, so I fear he has quite an outsized young tummyache to his credit at present writing. Young Snowy is getting a bit out of hand; she means no harm with her rough play, but she's so awkwardly big that one flick of her tail or one touch of her paw can do incalculable damage to silk stockings and delicate female flesh. She's just the type of St. Bernard that would take a fiendish joy in golloping down a tourist and washing down the pieces with that little keg of brandy![82]

May 17, 1940

I went to Uncle Arnold's composition class from two to three in the afternoon, but left for home after that at the old man's own express request. You never saw anyone quite so determined that I should go home and to bed! In spite of my protestations that I was much better now and all my fever gone, he insisted that I still didn't look at all well and that I had better take very good care of myself, as

[82]She would occasionally knock down the children. Trude would look calmly on and say, "I think she likes to see them fall."

colds are always latently dangerous. His new phase of tender solicitude for my welfare is really amusing! Of course I appreciate his
kindness and sympathy, but I definitely do not want him popping
up on Sunday night and insisting that I am not able to endure an
evening of *Gurre-Lieder*! However, I may look more like a normal
human being by then; I admit I don't, yet.

May 19, 1940 (11 p.m.)

Mamma and I have just gotten home from having the time of our
lives over at the Religious Conference Building . . . If you can think
of a pleasanter way to spend an evening than to listen to those gorgeous, sublime, immortal *Gurre-Lieder* in their entirety, seated by
the composer's side and enjoying the inestimable privilege of having
him point out to you every nicety of the score as it flowed along
(especially when, after placing his hand on or near yours to point to
something in the score which you were holding, he sometimes forgot
to withdraw it or else did so very slowly indeed), I would just like
to know what it is! (Well, I would settle for the four String Quartets
—especially the First—performed in similar company, but I can
imagine no other suitable substitutes.) But the nicest thing of all I
haven't even mentioned yet, and that is that I now have a lovely
autograph from him in my handsomely bound copy of Berg's piano
reduction! After the last record was played, while everyone was
crowding around the old man to tell him how wonderful they
thought the music was, I came to his side with the score and a
borrowed fountain pen, and, as soon as there was an opening, shyly
asked him if he would mind writing in my book. He complied without the slightest hesitation—"What do you want me to write?", he
asked, taking the pen in his thin warm hand and smiling at me with
that certain quizzical-sweet smile which always makes me blush to
the roots of my hair. But I didn't give him any advice on that subject; and a good thing, too, because had I done so I should never
have been favored with this imaginative masterpiece:

> To Miss Dika Newlin, but not as a model;
> or: royalties!
>   Arnold Schoenberg

Which, being translated into plain English, simply means that if I
steal, I'll have to pay! I shan't mind, either.

He said that the first 9 songs of the cycle were composed for piano and voice for a song-cycle contest; he finished them half a week too late for the contest and this decided the fate of the work! Would be interesting to compare original piano version with Berg's piano score.

He told an anecdote about his own conducting of GL in Amsterdam and Vienna. Twice at rehearsals in both places he was forced to stop the orchestra for corrections just at the great climax (high B for the soprano) of Tove's song "Du sendest mir einen Liebesblick." Both times, the orchestra were so enthusiastic that they played right on through the glorious interlude that follows, and up to the next song, before they stopped! That is certainly a marvelous tribute to the drive of the music.

May 20, 1940

Uncle Arnold saw my string quartet this afternoon—all finished now, save for a few measures of the elaboration which still need to be carried out—and pronounced it *good*. Its main fault is that it relies too exclusively, in its development, on the "noodling" (Boulanger) method instead of on the "blooming" (Schoenberg) method. Elucidation: instead of creating new motive-forms from old ones, it elaborates and re-elaborates the same forms incessantly till nothing is left. However, this is nothing that need be changed now, though if I ever looked the work over again with a view to use sometime in the future I might consider it. Besides, there are places where it "blooms," which he characterizes as "very nice" and "good;" and believe me, when he praises you in those terms, he is outdoing himself! I am certainly immeasurably encouraged by his present attitude. He says he is terribly tired now, and hence perhaps a little irritable, but he hasn't been a bit irritable lately where I was concerned. I don't know quite why, but I had feared he might be hard on me today—you know, a sort of reaction, half-unconscious maybe, against his being so nice to me last night; he's the sort who might figure I'd get a little uppity when treated too well, and change his tune accordingly. But, thank God, he didn't!

Stein and I polished up our ammunition after Structural Functions class. Yes, we actually got to work and pounded out dear old *Kammersymphonie* once more, and it sounded as good as two weeks ago though we haven't touched it in the interim. We want to brush it up a bit so that we can really go to town when we make our recording (which we'll do in the next two weeks).

May 22, 1940

Today had an extra fillip to it by reason of an additional hour spent with Uncle Arnold this morning from nine to ten. He was lecturing in the music history class which Hal takes, and of course H., knowing only too well my Schoenbergian propensities, had taken pains to see that I was informed of the coming event as soon as he knew about it himself. So at nine o'clock sharp, there I was, plunked down in an ideal seat right in the middle of the third row, where I might gaze into the dear speaker's dancing eyes (by the way, has that question of whether they do dance or not ever been satisfactorily settled?) to my heart's content. Well, the old man showed up as per schedule, and scintillated to everyone's delight; he got a tremendous ovation at both beginning and end of his speech. His wittiest remarks were at the expense of one poor soul who was convinced that the twelve-tone system must be a mechanical contrivance incapable of expressing romantic feelings (have you ever tried flirting among the tone-rows, brother?) simply because Uncle Arnold had chosen to diagram a typical row on the blackboard by using numbers. "But I need not have used numbers!" thundered the Master at his still unconvinced and somewhat terrified auditor. "I could have used letters, or notes, or I could have made faces!" Which he then proceeded to do in his most excruciating manner. If he hadn't become the world's greatest composer, he was destined for the stage, I'll swear it! Then, there was his lovely reply to the young lady who demurely asked if it was true that Paramount[83] had once asked him to write music for one of their films. (This started out, you see, to

---

[83]Boris Morros invited Schoenberg to score *Souls at Sea*, with Ralph Rainger (his pupil, composer of "Thanks for the Melody" and other popular standards) as backup composer. (Roy M. Prendergast, *A Neglected Art: A Critical Study of Music in Films*, New York, New York University Press, 1977, pp. 46-47.) Nothing came of this. The film was released in 1937 with a score by one Roland Anderson. The story of Irving Thalberg's attempt to get Schoenberg to compose *The Good Earth* is well known; *that* score was eventually composed by Herbert Stothart (of *Wizard of Oz* fame).

be a very solemn lecture on the twelve-tone scale, but soon digressed to lighter topics, mostly because of the old man's indisposition to concentrate on such abstruse matters in the early morning.) "Yes, it is true," he answered in his best manner, "and I replied to them that if I must commit artistic suicide, I must live by it!" That was a bit too subtle for some of the thicker skulls, but most of us got it.

. . . The afternoon, of course, was again occupied with the Great Man, who seemed to have been pickled in an excellent humor by the morning's adulation, and said not a cross word to anyone. He spent most of the time in composition class analyzing the finesses of the piano style in Brahms' Violin Sonatas, especially the many varieties of figuration. Ended up by bringing out a work of his which I had never previously seen . . . the *Zwei Balladen*, consisting of *Jane Grey* and *Der verlorene Haufen*. I just got the barest of glances at poor Jane; Stein played through the piano part of *Der verlorene Haufen*, there being no one present who could sing it. It seems a marvelously effective work, powerful in its expression of the emotion it portrays.

In this class, incidentally, he let fall for the first time his reasons for never having learned to play the piano. In the first place, he never had a piano till he was twenty-one, by which time he thought himself too old to learn; and, in the second place, he was unfortunate enough to be born into that particular generation of young composers who scorned the gentle art of piano-playing because Wagner had not been adept at it. Such, he grieved, is the influence of biographical facts. Perhaps some day there will be a generation who will remember that Schoenberg couldn't play the piano!

After school, bought Ronnie's birthday present: a diminutive train of four cars, and a little gold bag of that chocolate candy done up to look like money . . . In the toy-shop there was an elegant little cash-register, complete with money, which would have made a perfect gift for the lad (and for his father too, for that matter!), but it cost a dollar and a quarter, and I couldn't blow that much on a mere birthday present!

May 23, 1940

. . . the old man was on the whole well pleased with what I brought to my lesson, but would have me make an entirely different use of it than what I'd intended. ("It" is the beginning of the trio-elaboration of my rondo for piano quintet.) He wants me to use the first seventeen measures or so of the elaboration as the model (this contains several different elements from the first section, and a number of sequences), and then build, instead of a sequence of it, a free kind of repetition in which the order of the several elements is changed and some of them receive a much further development, and in which the harmony is constantly roving. This is the structure in the *Eroica* and also in that other work so closely modelled upon it, Schoenberg's own First Quartet. He spent most of the time analyzing the elaboration of this with me (he's done that several times before, but each time he shows it from a different viewpoint) and also pointing out many examples of fine "contrapuntal" writing in his second and third quartets. (Especially the passage ca. mm. 220-40 in the second movement of the second Quartet, which he thinks one of the finest things he ever wrote, and of which he is justly proud.) I put "contrapuntal" in quotation marks for good reason; he makes a definite distinction between real counterpoint, as in a fugue, and semi-contrapuntal circumscription of homophony, as in the best string quartet writing (his own, for example). "Now do not tell me that another could tell you this!" he twitted me, after having explained the difference brilliantly. He doesn't need to worry, for I realize that he is perhaps the only person in the world who understands the distinction and its importance.

I delivered Ronnie's presents to the family. They were vastly tickled, especially the little fellow himself, who couldn't help seeing me give his mother the paper bags in which they were. "Thank you very much!" he burbled at me as I ran to the gate. (The old man had just been thanking me effusively and R. instinctively imitates everything he does.)

✏ May 24, 1940

Uncle Arnold seemed in high good spirits during the scant hour I saw him this afternoon (double counterpoint class, except me, never did show up; I wonder why not? The old man must have gone home at 3.) He got a glance at the copy I was making of the string quartet and pronounced it very good indeed, thus causing all the others in the class who haven't had time to finish their pieces, let alone copy them, to turn vividly green with envy. He certainly is a changed man, as far as I am concerned, since *Kammersymphonie*! Julius Toldi visited the class today. He's a devoted disciple of fifteen years ago, author of a fairy opera (*Sleeping Beauty*, I think) and I suppose of other things too. A funny-looking little man with darting brown eyes and a great brown pompadour; might be in his forties.[84]

May 27, 1940

There was no composition class on account of Adolph Weiss' lecture on modern music. Music he played included the fifth movement, *Tanzscene*, of the Master's own *Serenade*, quite new to me. It's a wholly winning and delightful work, full of Viennese spirit, though not quite à la Strauss . . . Uncle Arnold devoted most of the following Structural Functions class to expanding on some of the points Weiss had made—notably the matter of thematic recognizability, recognizability of retrograde inversions and similar developments, etc.—and thereby came to some interesting points *re Verklärte Nacht*. It seems that the wonderful passage in D-flat major near the end, by which he returns to the theme in D major,[85] is the structural counterpart of the long introduction which ends in E-flat minor and is followed by the same theme (coming at it from above and below, you see!); and that the D-flat major—D minor or major relation is adumbrated in the main theme itself.[86] Of course, none of this was done, or could have been done, consciously ("This did the man behind me," he says); nor is it realized by the listener except inasmuch as he feels the inner compulsive logic of the whole without knowing what causes it. S. himself only knew it many years later, when he conducted *Verklärte Nacht* in Barcelona.

[84]Toldi, Hungarian composer, had recently settled in California. Later, his series of broadcasts on the *Music of Today* (radio station KFWB) would be praised by Virgil Thomson as "one of the very few distinguished modern music programs available on the American air." Schoenberg, too, would praise Toldi's series of four broadcasts devoted to his works on the occasion of his 75th birthday: "I am convinced that should my work still be appreciated later on, this deed will never be forgotten." (Quoted in Toldi's memoirs, *American Kaleidoscope*, New York, Philosophical Library, 1960, p. 366.) Though forgotten today as a composer, Toldi should be appreciatively remembered for such contributions as this.

[85]Measures 320-336.

[86]Cf. the D—C sharp (enharmonic D flat) clash in measure 16.

May 30, 1940

Had my lesson with Uncle Arnold this morning at eleven, or rather eleven-twenty, as some changes in the street-car schedule which I hadn't known about made me that much late. Characteristically, at twelve on the dot the old man began to perk up his ears, and asked hopefully, "Are you perhaps already tired?" I negatived vigorously, and thus succeeded in getting my full time . . . He found the general outline of what I had written for the quintet fairly good, though some of it is a little superficial on account of insufficient imitations, combinations of motives, etc. These things, together with the fine carrying-out of individual parts, are what he has especially emphasized in my case all year long, rather than the broader aspects of form. Perhaps, he says, we overdid such combinations a little bit, but that is better than underdoing them! He looked at the latest extension in the coda of my string quartet, too; found it too long, now, and made suitable cuts, which I hope will fit together better than those in the piano sonata did. I will show him the revision tomorrow afternoon when he comes to school.

He wants me to write the other three movements of my Sonata, and the other three of the String Quartet, and finish the Piano Quintet—all during this summer. He frequently interspersed these golden words with remarks that I must also take "three or four weeks" (!) off to "rest" and "play a good game!" How long does he think a summer is, anyway—that's doing in three months more than I did in my nine months here! Of course, I will not have him cutting off two measures for every one I write, which will speed up the work considerably, but will also make the results pretty lousy, I fear.

May 31, 1940

. . . When I got to school at two-thirty, Uncle Arnold was very busy indeed with the first-year composition students, and unable to look at my newest revision of the coda of the string quartet; not that it matters, for I know it is just as he wanted it. I waited around till three o'clock in hopes that he might be able to slip me in somewhere, but no such luck—he had to leave at three o'clock himself! He was leaving about half the students uncared-for, but that didn't faze him a bit; in fa¢t, he bountifully offered them my services as well as Mr. Stein's. Well, I would have been glad to help, because I really enjoy it, but my Old French exam was calling me and there wasn't a thing I could do about it. U.A. seemed rather inclined to grumble about my defection, but wasn't really angry, for he realized that it wasn't my fault. Everyone to whom I spoke says he was terribly cross all afternoon (probably because Mr. Stein had forgotten to telephone him to remind him to come at one), but I didn't see him so.

June 4, 1940

Was at school from 11 to 4, helping Uncle Arnold's first-year composition students with their final examinations. I hadn't gone there for that purpose—all I intended to do was to ask Mr. Stein when we could make the *Kammersymphonie* record, and to get from Uncle Arnold a piece of his special paper which I need to finish the last page of my quartet; but, to tell the truth, I'd rather expected the old man to ask me when he saw me, so I had come well prepared. Which is to say, I had eaten lunch before going! Well, I hadn't said three words to him before he asked me if I couldn't please stay and help the class, so my hunch was right! Of course, the work is hard. I am not allowed to write any of my corrections down, and it's difficult to convey the idea simply through improvisation to people who mostly don't have absolute pitch. But it is fun all the same, especially if the students are so grateful for your help that they insist on taking you out afterwards and treating you to ice-cream sodas and candy bars! Uncle Arnold was very grateful; he squeezed my hand very prettily before I left and said, "Now, you worked very hard, no?" But he didn't do anything about it.

June 6, 1940

Was at school from ten till five-thirty working for the old man. Though I did get to go out for lunch, that was all the free time I had. As it turned out, I needn't have come till one-thirty, for he didn't get around to looking at our compositions till that time.

Ostensibly, he was ensconced in his office grading the rondos of the first-year composition class, but I heard rumors that he was enjoying a cozy little chat with Mr. Stein most of the time. Even then, he never once looked at my string quartet, on the grounds that he'd seen practically all of it before, and that he needed more to look at the other students' pieces. Well, I understand his reasons all right, but then it's a shame that I had to lose so much time for nothing. Of course, I got to work on my quintet, and to help the double counterpoint class a little bit into the bargain, but I could have worked to much better advantage at home.

I think I was about the only one to finish the Structural Functions examination. Contrary to his usual custom, he let us work on it only two hours, from three till five. For a given section from the elaboration of the first movement of Beethoven's Op. 59/1, we had to describe the motival content, relate it to the previous section, tell where the harmony was establishing and where roving, describe the way of the harmony in terms of keys and degrees, and, finally, find a point or points from which we could modulate to G minor, F major, and C minor, and carry out such modulations, using Beethoven's motives if possible. Those of us who did this last question all made the task too hard for ourselves by composing new material, when, had we known it, there was one single point from which we could have effected all three modulations by simply transposing! However, he will not penalize us for this error, for he knows who his good students are anyway and in all probability he will not bother with these papers at all.

June 7, 1940

Had my very last lesson with Uncle Arnold this afternoon . . . he was full of helpful recommendations for the summer, not the least of these being that I must get the newly-finished string quartet played at the earliest opportunity. Really, he makes me laugh; although he's been unable to arrange any performances of my chamber music here, he grandiosely offered to write to any of the important musicians in Detroit and see that they played it. "I do not know them," he remarked, "but they know me, oh yes!" He even had dreams of getting it done in Chicago, and when I patiently explained to him that most people would probably be away in the summer, he exclaimed brightly, "Oh no! the men which run the trams will be there, and those in the restaurants will be there, and the gangsters—oh yes!" . . . I carried the matter no further. He still wants me to get in a two- or three-weeks' rest at the beginning of the summer, and told Mamma to watch me and have Papa watch me to see that I didn't take pen in hand during that time! Oh, and I mustn't forget the best of all—"*Please* write to me—I will not answer, for I am too busy!" That sort of remark is rather discouraging; however, I will write to him, and to Mrs. and the children too. I'll see him again tomorrow at his lecture, but this is probably the last I'll see of the others till fall.

Ronnie, the little angel, insisted on giving Mamma his favorite red ball when she left; she tried to make him keep it, but he would have none of it. Mrs. S. says that he claims Mamma is "all his friend" and he won't let Nuria have any of her. Isn't that precious?

June 8, 1940

By all odds I should be very sad tonight, for this day I saw my last of Uncle Arnold for three long months. But my spirits are up rather than down, for that marvelous man did the most unbelievable thing you ever heard of! After his lecture in EB 320, I ran right up to tell him my last fond goodbyes, and, much more important, to deliver to him the check for fifteen dollars which I'd forgotten to give him yesterday. After having told him how much I'd enjoyed the talk (very true, for he'd played a perfectly wonderful program of his own records—"Nun sag' ich dir zum ersten Mal" and the final chorus from *Gurre-Lieder*, the Adagio of the First Quartet and the Finale of the Second, and the third movement of the Fourth), I came to what I considered the really important point, simply by pressing the check in his hand. To my surprise, instead of taking it he looked at me wonderingly and inquired, "What is this?" "Why, it's your check for yesterday!" I exclaimed. "Oh, no,no,no,no,no!" he chortled, shoving it back into my hand with one hand and squeezing it (my hand) with the other (his hand). "No, you keep this! I *invited* you to this lesson!" I got very red in the face then, and so did he. Hal, who was standing nearby, swears that we were both on the verge of tears. All I know is that I suddenly felt very small indeed, but at the same time I felt very happy too. We talked a few seconds longer, and then I made as if to leave, but he stopped me long enough to say to me, with his sweetest smile, "Goodbye now—and do not stay away too long!" And with that I left him.

I got to see Mrs. Schoenberg and Nuria again, too. For Nuria, this was a very special occasion—the first time she'd ever heard "her daddy" give a public address! She was dressed all in white, with a white ribbon bound about her dark hair, and looked very pretty indeed.

June 10, 1940
(just out of El Paso)

I keep thinking about the funny story Uncle Arnold told at his lecture to illustrate that he was by no means vain. When they went to live in Barcelona in '31 after his severe illness, they took a house which was high on a hill. It commanded a magnificent view but was quite inaccessible except by foot, for neither horse nor cab would attempt the road. Thus, when the old man returned from town he always had to walk up, and this was most tiring to him. One day on this road he observed a donkey—"monkey" he insisted on calling it, in spite of his wife's frantic corrections from third row back—ascending the hill in a most peculiar manner. Instead of walking straight up the hill, it was systematically zigzagging from side to side of the road. At first he merely laughed at this strange natural phenomenon, but the more he thought, the more the donkey's idea looked good to him. So finally he tried it out—and it worked, for it materially reduced his fatigue by reducing the steepness of the slope. "This," he concluded, "first time I ever learned something from an ASS!"[87]

[86]Hanns Eisler, a controversial Schoenberg pupil who later became a major figure in East German music and politics, noted this story also. Bertolt Brecht based a cantata text ("Ich habe von einem Esel gelernt") on the anecdote; Eisler set it to music. Unfortunately, the work appears to be lost. Cf. Hans Bunge, *Fragen Sie mehr über Brecht: Hanns Eisler im Gespräch* (Munich, Rogner & Bernhard, 1970), pp. 173-74. A good selection of Eisler's writings (on Schoenberg and other topics) translated into English is *A Rebel in Music* (ed. Manfred Grabs, tr. Marjorie Meyer. New York, International Publishers, 1978).

Interlude II
Summer of '40

Oh fragrance old of fabled days!
Albert Giraud, *Pierrot Lunaire*

This would be a great summer of chamber music: playing it, writing it, listening to it. Feeling the need, as a composer, to improve my knowledge of the violin, I threw myself into learning to play it better; first with young Eddie Simons, later with Francis Aranyi, the ebullient Hungarian who was now professor of violin at Michigan State, and would in the future organize an outstanding youth orchestra in Seattle.

"Rany" (pronounced *Ronnie*), as I dubbed him in my diary, proved to have a special value for me: he was a walking repository of the most delightful Schoenberg anecdotes (some, as I was later to learn, inaccurate). One evening, he was full of reminiscences of the rehearsals for the première of *Gurre-Lieder*, in which he'd played.[1]

---

[1]In the *Tonkünstler-Orchester* under Franz Schreker, the then-famous opera composer (1878-1934), on February 23, 1913.

235

I hurried home to write it all down:

Rany said that this première absolutely changed his life, and, judging by some of the anecdotes, I don't wonder that it did! Things started to go wrong immediately. The second violins were supposed to begin in second position, and in 1913 that was absolutely preposterous! First position, surely; third position—well, all right, if you didn't have to go up too often; but no self-respecting second violinist of an orchestra, in 1913, even knew what the second position *was*! So, instead of that beautiful, endless flowing and rippling of serene sound that you get when you put the Philadelphia record on the turntable, that first rehearsal began with a charivarian, calliopeian mess of unrelated sounds. Schoenberg, sitting down below the orchestra with his nose buried in the enormous score, suddenly raised his head in dismay. 'But there *can't* be such a misprint in my score!' he expostulated. "That's no misprint!" retorted Schreker, "that's just my second violinists playing badly!" And there were hours of patient rehearsal on those first few measures that seem so sweet and effortless to us as we hear them.

Then there was the strange case of the first horn-player, Weiss. He was a fine player, as were the other members of the section; but, try as they might, they just couldn't get the hang of the supremely difficult horn-parts in the *Melodram*. One day, things seemed to be going worse than usual; Weiss was tootling his damned best, but the harder he tried the worse he got. And then, all of a sudden, something snapped —and Weiss stopped dead in the middle of a note, leaped up, and, defiantly facing the other horn-players, shouted, "Well, if you won't help me kill him, I'll go down there and do it myself!" And, before anyone could stop him, he made a flying leap at Schoenberg (who, as usual, was completely unaware of what was going on beyond the pages of his elephantine score) and would probably have succeeded in bludgeoning him to death with his horn—he had no other weapon on him—if some of Schoenberg's pupils nearby had not seized and overpowered him. Apparently the whole auditorium was one blessed free-for-all until Weiss was finally calmed down sufficiently to be taken home.

Well, Weiss came to rehearsal the next day again, broke down again, and finally stood up to Schreker and said that he couldn't, wouldn't play this mad and murderous stuff. "Get out, then!" thundered Schreker; "you are here to play and obey orders, not to judge!" Weiss got out. He went home.

For four days he shut himself up in his room and played that terrific horn part until his very bones were saturated with it.

Suddenly, he recognized how beautiful it really was, and what a terrible thing he'd done. He hurried to Schoenberg's house to apologize for his stupid and well-nigh fatal mistake. "In these moments," says Rany laconically, "Schoenberg is not very nice." To Weiss' heartfelt pleas for pardon, he simply turned an impassive, stony back and let that misguided soul stew in his own juices.

Finally, after innumerable trials like these, the great day of the performance arrived. It was an overwhelming success —the first Schoenberg had ever had. When the glorious music of the sunrise finally came, the audience rose as one man and just stood there till the end—when an utter pandemonium of whistling and cheering and stomping broke out. "Schoenberg! Schoenberg!" they yelled and shrieked till their throats hurt, those crazy Viennese, but no Schoenberg came. An emissary sent out to get him at all costs finally found him huddled in the most distant and darkest corner of the auditorium, his hands folded and a quiet, quizzical sort of smile on his face. They dragged him down to the platform by force, Schreker pushed him up onto the podium—and then he did the strangest thing that a man in front of that kind of a hysterical, worshipping mob has ever done: he turned his back to them, just as he had to Weiss, refused to recognize their unprecedented ovation; bowed slightly to the orchestra in token of his heartfelt appreciation, and then made a quiet, unobtrusive exit. And that was all.

"Why, the crazy fellow!" "What's the matter with him, anyway?" Queries like these were on many lips that night, during those interminable discussions in the sidewalk cafés and in the streets after it was all over; discussions lasting till two or three o'clock in the morning. Think what an atmosphere there must have been in Vienna that night!

Schoenberg answered those burning questions later, when his wondering friends put them to him. "For twenty-five years," he said simply, "I have been a composer, and these people never knew it, never recognized me. Why should I recognize them tonight?"

Later Rany recalled a time, right after Schoenberg's first marriage, when the composer "was so poor that the family had to live in one single attic room, divided into two parts by a curtain. On one side they lived, ate, slept, etc.; on the other side Schoenberg composed."

Then,

> there was a heartwarming little tale about the first, or Arnold
> Rosé, performance of *Verklärte Nacht*.[2] The audience, as
> you might expect, received it terribly, with much blowing of
> whistles, heaving of rotten eggs, etc. But Rosé took it like a
> rock. He led his sextet through faultlessly, and, after the
> music was all over—just as the worst hell broke loose—he
> smiled and bowed to the seething hall just as if he were
> receiving the most tumultuous ovation! Schoenberg was not
> present at this historic occasion; had he been, be sure the
> story would have had a few more interesting quirks.

I was steadily enriching my knowledge of Schoenberg's music
and texts, playing through my scores from the Bekker Collection.
For example, on July 10, Papa's 49th birthday, I was peacefully
reading the librettos of *Die Jakobsleiter* and *Erwartung*, in the midst
of domestic turmoil: linoleum-laying and furniture-moving. (Papa
said that this was the happiest birthday he'd had since July 10,
1918, the day the Germans broke through the English defenses in
France!) Nine days later, domestic order having been restored, I was
able to sit down at my piano for a one-person rendition of *Erwartung*.

> Played and sang through the entire *Erwartung* tonight,
> trying to follow the orchestra score and piano reduction
> simultaneously. Now I certainly do understand why it has
> received only three performances! There are very few singers
> that I can imagine in the part . . . though I think Radiana
> Pazmor might do it justice. What a gruesome thing it is, and
> how terrifying! it seems to carry you right into another world,
> yet it lies at the root of our own life as well. The effect of
> that final crushing chromatic passage for the horns is magni-
> ficent. It is impossible for me to conceive perfectly how it
> would sound in the orchestra—it is too novel, too different
> from the things one is accustomed to hear—but such an idea
> as I can form is of something ineffably grand and powerful,
> yet tender and beautiful in its way as well . . .

As we packed for California, I tried my hand and voice at *Pierrot*

[2]The Rosé Quartet with two additional players performed the work in Vienna
on March 15, 1902. Schoenberg was living in Berlin at the time.

Lunaire. My great "party piece" of the summer had been the *Sechs kleine Klavierstücke*. I cheerily played them to all who would listen.

Of course, there was correspondence with the old man during these months. (A very onesided one, to be sure; when I'd left in June he had said cheerfully, "*Please* write to me. I will not answer." He had kept his word!) In default of letters from him to me, I summarized one from him to Bekker who,

> it seemed, had sent Schoenberg . . . an invitation to the performance of *Erwartung* in Wiesbaden. The invitation arrived just the day before the performance, and of course Schoenberg couldn't go! This letter is his explanation of his action. He hopes that B. won't be angry with him for refusing, but under the circumstances it was unavoidable. Besides, he doesn't want people to look upon him as just another one of those composers who spend all their time going around taking bows—if he'd been able to attend rehearsals and influence the performance, it would be another matter, but as it is, he didn't consider it dignified to come. (This is all pure Schoenberg!) He follows this with a warm recommendation to one Herr Cortolezzi [his spelling: actually, Fritz Cortolezis] for a conductor's post at Wiesbaden. C. had created a marvelous performance of *Die glückliche Hand* out of poor material— had actually made the performers like and understand the piece—so he must be good, says A.S.![3]

If Schoenberg wasn't writing me, other Californian friends were. On August 20, Leonard Stein wrote me enthusiastically of a newly formed UCLA Composers' Workshop which had already presented two concerts of the students' works. The idea had, of course,

---

[3]Schoenberg is speaking of a performance of *Die Glückliche Hand* in Breslau on March 24, 1928; its first performance since the première under Stiedry in the Vienna *Volksoper* on October 14, 1924. In a letter to Intendant Josef Turnau on March 29, 1928, he specifically mentions Cortolezis in his lavish praise for all involved in the production. (*Letters*, p. 130.)

Here is the third (previously unpublished) letter from Schoenberg to Bekker, in my translation:

16.III.1924

Please don't be angry because I haven't yet written you about your Wagner book. I had much to do and have had many experiences (mostly, as usual, annoying ones!) I hope I'll soon have some peace and quiet again. Then you'll hear from me!

Meanwhile, best wishes and hearty Christmas greetings, also to your wife.

Schoenberg's enthusiastic endorsement. There were plans (not to be fulfilled) for us to record our four-handed performance of the *Kammersymphonie*: other plans (most happily fulfilled) to play the work in many places. But the most exciting news was this:

> ... Schoenberg and Co. (Kolisch, Steuermann, Bloch and Linden) are rehearsing—guess what!!
> You're right! They plan to make a recording of it for Columbia with Erika Wagner, whom Schoenberg says has a beautiful speaking voice. I hope, too, that they will consider a performance. Now don't delay to read the score as I have been doing for the past few weeks. But to *hear* it! The most fantastic and amazing thing you can imagine! About "PL" there is too much to say, so I shall not try; but you must hurry here to attend the rehearsals, tout de suite.
> Der Meister has, except for one short coughing spell, been feeling ganz gut, considering his 66 years (and his birthday is on Friday, the 13th, this year!) As a matter of fact, he still plays tennis as miserably as ever (but don't tell him I said so).

On August 26, a piece of really BIG news hit town!

> Herr Doktor Professor Arnold *von* Schoenberg . . . IS GOING TO HAVE A BABY! And it's just as much of a surprise to me as it is to you! . . . The funniest thing about all this, though, is that not a week ago, without any reason at all, I thought (or dreamed, I forget which) about Trude's having a baby! Explanation, please![4]

Three days later, we started back to California. I did not know that it would be my last journey there till 1949. My last, and most difficult, year with Schoenberg was about to begin.

---

[4]This would not be my last strange dream-experience concerning the Schoenberg family. See *July 13-14, 1951.*

Book III
September, 1940 - June, 1941

You have not suffered enough.
You must suffer.
                 Arnold Schoenberg to
                 Dika Newlin
I apologize to all those whom I
have forgotten to insult.
                 Johannes Brahms

September 4, 1940

This was a great day indeed, for today I saw Uncle Arnold for the first time since June! We went to the house about four o'clock, armed with a box of candy for each of the children, not expecting to stay more than a half-hour or an hour at the very most. But before you could say "Komposition mit zwölf Tönen" we were being served with coffee and overwhelmingly rich apfelstrudel and little buns spread with meat paste or avocado or anchovy paste; the upshot of that was that we didn't get home till nearly seven o'clock! Trude was, of course, not in any condition to help much with the serving; she looks quite worn out, and, what's more, I have a sneaking suspicion that the third little Schoenberg may be arriving sooner than we thought! But the old man more than made up for her debility by his fluttery solicitude for our comfort. Why, he even went scurrying out to the kitchen to fetch a pair of sugar tongs for us to put sugar in our coffee with (we don't use sugar in our coffee) just because he thought we might be offended at the lack of them! (We don't even *own* a pair of sugar tongs.)

He doesn't look too well. She says he was terribly tired and nervous all summer, but I guess he has been taking a much-needed rest. What do you suppose he's spent the summer doing? Arranging and cataloging all his books, manuscripts (both musical and literary), so that when Hitler comes he will know what he is getting! ... I was very, very much surprised to learn that he seriously considers accepting the East Lansing lecture offer; in fact, he talked to Papa about it for a long time. He wouldn't think of talking about the usually requested subject of "Modern Music," because, he says, he doesn't know the works of his contemporaries, but only *a few* works of Bach, Beethoven and other classical composers. "I am not really interested in my contemporaries; it would be better were they interested in me!" But, as it happens, he's been selected to give the annual research lecture during this year's Charter Week, and has been working very hard over a little number on twelve-tone composition. He thinks that, if he talks at Michigan State College, he'd like to repeat that one instead of preparing a fresh one. Of course, he also has several already-written lectures in German which he might translate for the occasion, notably one on Brahms which he delivered over a Frankfurt radio station in '33, Brahms' 100th anniversary. It was the last public speech he made in Germany before the blow fell.[1] "And now," he continued in a very quiet but very meaning way, "they tell me that the English have completely destroyed Frankfurt, and Hamburg, and Essen—" A very uncomfortable silence ensued, during which I heartily wished that I were somewhere else, even in Frankfurt, Hamburg, or Essen. However, the cloud passed away quickly; but you could not forget at once that it had been there.

Mrs. Seligmann, Trude's sister, has moved to Los Angeles for good. She has taken a house on Bowling Green, just a few blocks from the Schoenberg house. Trude let fall the remark that they had thought of my living with her in case I came back here to live alone. ... I suppose that would be next best to living with the Schoenbergs themselves.

---

[1] This appeared in *Style and Idea* as "Brahms the Progressive."

Mr. Stein took me to a meeting of the putative Composers' Workshop tonight. The meeting itself (at Leon Kirchner's[2] house on Pickford Avenue) wasn't very exciting, being devoted mainly to discussion of policy, and plans for the program we're going to give on Sunday—for which, it seems, *Kammersymphonie* is going to be a featured number! (This means some practising between now and then, I think.) More interesting was the brief trial we made of the 4-hand version of the *Suite in Ancient Style*, which Stein is fixing up with Schoenberg's approval. But most interesting was all the dirt dished up about the recording of *Pierrot Lunaire*. To be brief about that, it has all the earmarks of a recording that will never be made. Schoenberg gets mad and won't direct rehearsals, leaving that to Kolisch; Kolisch gets mad, I don't know why; Linden leaves town for a few days, thus balling things up immeasurably, and he isn't a very good flute-player, anyway (everybody else wanted to have Ary van Leeuwen,[3] but Schoenberg wouldn't have him); Kalman Bloch has never tootled a bass-clarinet in his life; no parts are to be had, and the players are having to play from miniature scores until such time as parts can be copied (Stein and I are going to get to work at that right away); all the full-sized scores in the U.S. seem to be out of commission in one way or another (Steuermann's is back in N.Y., and can't be found; mine's still at the bindery in Lansing, etc. etc.); Schoenberg wants the recording made before school starts, and Erika Wagner'll be in town any day now, but it couldn't possibly be done before two weeks; then it would be too late because Kolisch and Steuermann will have gone back to N.Y. to participate in the performance under Klemperer! Schoenberg is mad about that because he doesn't think Klemperer sympathetic to his works; Schoenberg is mad at Kolisch because he gave Kolisch the choice of taking the cost of the recording or the royalties and K. chose cost (doubting, and I suppose rightly, that the royalties would be worth taking). Did you ever hear of such a mixup in your life?

To take the bad taste out of my mouth, I must end with this funny Schoenberg tale. The summer that the Schoenbergs were at

---

[2]Kirchner (1919-) was briefly a student of Schoenberg. He is known favorably for his chamber music, but his opera *Lily* (after Saul Bellow's *Henderson the Rain King*) was not well received. He has been professor of music at Harvard since 1962.

[3]See above, p. 205.

244   Schoenberg Remembered

Chautauqua,[4] there was a ping-pong tournament which Trude entered and, of course, won. The next day, the two of them were walking down the road together when a little boy loped up and asked, "Say, kin I have your autograph?" "Certainly!" beamed Schoenberg, and started to take out his pen; but the lad snorted scornfully, "Naw, not you. I want *hers*!"

September 5, 1940

Stein was supposed to come up here today and practise *Kammersymphonie* with me, but he didn't . . . What can he be thinking of? doesn't he know that we have to perform on Sunday? Anyway, I did my duty . . . I copied the flute part of *Pierrot* as far as the *Madonna*. I am supposed to finish this flute part by Monday, which is when Linden is returning.

September 6, 1940

At dinner with my friend Chaia, learned more about the relations between Schoenberg and Slonimsky.[5] It seems that Slonimsky was supposed to have begun the translation of *Harmonielehre* a good six months ago, and that Schoenberg had made extremely generous financial provisions for him; but, what with one thing and another (notably a summer-school job at the University of Colorado), he hadn't even begun the work! Well, came the day when he was supposed to go before Schoenberg (after not having seen him for God knows how many years) and break the bad news to him, you can imagine that Slonimsky felt pretty nervous. To top things off, C., whose duty it was to drive him out there, lost her way; and so the party showed up at dear old 116 exactly forty-five minutes late,

---

[4]Chautauqua, N.Y., the site of the famed Chautauqua summer institute which has been offering cultural and educational events since 1874. The Schoenbergs were there in the summer of 1934.

[5]Slonimsky's championship of Schoenberg's music (see above, p. 207, n. 65), as well as of other contemporary works, in his concerts at the Hollywood Bowl, had "created such consternation that his conducting career came to a jarring halt." (See his autobiographical article in *Baker's Biographical Dictionary of Musicians*, 6th ed. [1978], p. 1615.) Nonetheless he remained a Schoenberg admirer—but, perforce, one of *Harmonielehre*'s many non-translators.

only to be met at the gate by The Master with a stop-watch in his hand and a most stupendous frown on his forehead. C. most gallantly took the blame upon herself; she claims that she thwarted the old man's natural annoyance by proclaiming that she was my friend, but I strongly suspect that part of the story of being apocryphal. Be that as it may, I am quite sure that poor Slonimsky must have spent one of the stickier afternoons with his beloved friend. C. said that he came home looking "all flattened out"!

September 7, 1940

Mr. Stein showed up—at last!—to tell me that I won't need to copy *Pierrot* any more, as the parts have at last arrived from Associated Publishers. I had already finished about 3/4 of the flute part. Also I learned that they've gotten a new flutist, some Italian[6] from the studios, to replace Linden. I don't know anything more than that about him; neither does Stein.

September 8, 1940

The performance of *Kammersymphonie* that Stein and I gave tonight, at an open meeting of the composers' group . . . went very well and was quite popular, even though the measly little upright that we had to play on was by no means suited to our forces. The hostess looked very nervous for fear we might inflict some damage on the piano's beautiful rosewood case! As a matter of fact, we damaged much more than *our* beautiful rosewood cases; both of us thought for a while that we'd burst blood vessels in our fingers. The rest of the program consisted of two Schoenberg-ish songs by one of our number, Earl Kim;[7] my own rendition of the second movement of my piano sonata; and Hindemith's violin sonata Op. 11 . . .

Stein and I are going to practise KS again tomorrow in preparation for an engagement next Sunday night. Ernst Krenek is going to be present! Thrilling?

---

[6]Leonard Posella, who worked into the ensemble beautifully.

[7]Earl Kim (1920-) became a respected composer of chamber music and multimedia works. He has held professorships at Princeton and Harvard.

September 9, 1940

Stein came and worked with me this morning . . . suggested that we might go and play *Kammersymphonie* for Schoenberg on his birthday! He thinks he can get Radiana Pazmor to sing some parts of *Das Buch der hängenden Gärten*, and Helen Swaby and Frances Mullen to do the violin concerto. I'm supposed to get in touch with Mrs. Schoenberg as soon as possible to find out if this plan would be agreeable to the family. As a matter of fact, Trude had phoned this afternoon while we were out, but when I returned the call *she* was out and I had to talk to Nuria. She said, "Mamma wanted to know if you could come on Friday at four o'clock," and of course I was delighted to say I could. I'll get all the particulars from Trude tomorrow . . .

Stein called a little while ago to say that Kolisch is awfully anxious to get hold of my "big score" of *Pierrot*; so I dispatched an airmail letter to Wagenvoord's, asking them to rush it as fast as they possibly can . . .

September 10, 1940

Tried to phone Mrs. Schoenberg this morning, but got the old man instead, which for once was *not* what I wanted! He reiterated the invitation for Friday afternoon, making it clear that it applied to all three of us, and also said that I might come for my lesson tomorrow at two o'clock. To Stein, who showed up later in the morning to practise *Kammersymphonie* with me as well as to try through his just-completed four-hand arrangement of the first movement of the Suite in Ancient (!!!) Style, I entrusted the charge of getting in touch with Mrs. Schoenberg or at least Mrs. Seligmann before tomorrow if he possibly could, so that we may know if our plans for a "surprise" would be agreeable to the old man if carried out. Judging from our last year's experience, I'm sure they would be; in fact, as Stein rather shrewdly observed, he is probably *expecting* to be surprised!

I picked out his birthday present this afternoon . . . it's a blue leather, or at least fabrikoid, pencil-case, completely equipped with a flock of little pencils and even a six-inch ruler! He's been needing

Schoenberg's self-portrait "South going north"

"South going north" photographed by Harold Halma in front of Kerckhoff Hall, UCLA

Schoenberg near Kerckhoff Hall, UCLA, with his pupil, Harold Halma, late a well-known New York photographer

such an article ever since last year, when his old case wore out and left him with nothing to carry his ubiquitous pencils in but a large box which ruined the fit of his coats. The gift ought to please him greatly. I had it nicely wrapped up in much white tissue-paper and baby-blue cellophane ribbon, and bought a pink-and-blue card to go with it. The whole gift, card included, cost only 55 cents; an inexpensive way of distributing pleasure, no?

September 11, 1940

Stein called up this morning to let me know that he'd been at Schoenberg's last night, and had talked with the old man about our idea of a Schoenberg Society, which, needless to say, received A.S.'s hearty approval. Uncle Arnold had also told him something that he himself was not supposed to know, namely, that the Kolisch Quartet was going to surprise him on the afternoon of the 13th! This rather puts a crimp in our idea of doing *Kammersymphonie*, for I certainly wouldn't care to compete with the Kolisch Quartet! Mrs. S. thought it would probably boil down to whether there was time for us to play or not. Of course the party is beginning rather late; the Kolisches are supposed to play; then Nuria will play, and by that time it will probably be tea-time! She suggested that the best thing to do would be to have Mr. Stein bring the music along and just await developments. By the way, Uncle Arnold is scared to death over *Der Tag*'s falling on Friday the thirteenth! He has also been indulging in many lugubrious prophecies to the effect that his sixty-fifth year isn't over yet, and that we'll see something terrible happen to him before it *is* over, all because 65 is a multiple of 13. None of this, incidentally, is supposed to be funny. He really believes these things.

He was in a bit of a dither this afternoon on account of having to go downtown and see about joining the Musicians' Union because he is conducting *Pierrot* for Columbia. In fact, the Schoenbergs picked us up on Sunset Boulevard on their way there, while we were waiting for the bus . . . He showed me the manuscript of his second *Kammersymphonie*, pointing out the fine structure of its theme and combinations. I had never seen the work before, and found myself impressed with as much as I could read of it; but even here the element of humor was not lacking. On the first page, he had thoughtfully omitted the key-signature in the 'cello and bass parts, and apprised the world of that fact in a monumental footnote to that first page, reading: THIS FIVE FLATS BELONGS ON EVERY-THING. His English, as he himself remarks, has gone to pot during the summer, or German-speaking, months.

Mrs. Schoenberg told Mamma that Blue Bootees, or Pink Bootees as the case may be, are expected to make their appearance as early as December or January. Arnold got a letter from Aranyi this morning saying that the MSC lecture would probably be scheduled for early January. Most inopportune!

September 12, 1940

Mr. Stein came in close to noon to practise *Kammersymphonie*, and I told him what Mrs. Schoenberg had said about our chances of performing it tomorrow. He agreed with me that he was so glad to be present at the great occasion that he didn't much care whether we played or not! He said that he will drive us over there . . . As usual, we exchanged all our latest facts and fancies on the subject of Schoenberg and his friends. By chance, I put a question about Webern, and was amazed to learn that he is still in Vienna and, what's more, holding down a government position! And still loyal to Schoenberg! Can such things be? It seems, oddly enough, that when Schoenberg's works appeared very prominently at that famous exhibition of "degenerate" art and music in Vienna some years ago, Webern was very much put out because *his* works had not been condemned, and loudly demanded rectification! Incidentally, I don't think that Webern is the only one of Schoenberg's friends in a similarly anomalous position; I happen to know that up until quite recently Schoenberg was regularly receiving music from Universal-Edition through the influence of such fence-sitting friends. In fact, he mentioned this circumstance to me last year . . . but named no names at that time.

IX-13-40

FRIDAY, SEPTEMBER THIRTEENTH, 1940

What a stupendous day this has been!

. . . as far as I'm concerned, it started at 4 p.m., when we rolled up in front of 116 North Rockingham in Stein's car, and ended about eleven p.m., when we rolled away from there in the same conveyance. And I'll wager that I've rarely spent a more exciting seven hours in my life!

We marched in the front gate, all in our Sunday best. I wore my black crepe dress, with a plain gold necklace and gold bracelet with blue sets, my red hat, and red gloves to match. We were greeted by a super-effulgent Arnold, radiantly attired in white. How happy he was to receive my little package! It was just what he'd been needing all the time, as I'd thought; and he was delighted with my ingenuity in thinking of it. "You see?" he proclaimed to the room at large; "she has ideas! Now if you only had *musical* ideas . . ."

We were among the first to arrive, but soon the other guests began to make their appearance: Mrs. Seligmann and her son Mischa, the Kolisches (she's Rosanska, an excellent pianist especially famed for her renditions of Chopin, and, what's more, right attractive—and does Schoenberg know it!), the Kreneks, the Weisses, Klemperer and his daughter Lotte with his sister-in-law and her husband, Khuner (the violist of the Kolisch Quartet), Steuermann and Feuermann, Buhlig, and the usual faculty people: Nelsons, Rubsamens, McManuses, and Knudsens (dean of the Graduate School). Oh yes, and Mr. Schreiner, who was organist here two years ago; and Don Estep, the lone student with the exception of me and Mr. Stein; and Miss Fisher.[8] I think that's all who were there, though I must say they seemed like a lot more. Of course, Nuria and Ronnie, who were very much a part of the festivities, always seem like at least six children instead of only two. Well, anyway, in about half an hour or so after we arrived, the eating and drinking began. There was coffee with whipped cream (lots), and six or seven kinds of sandwiches made with cheese, liverwurst, and such good things: whole platefuls of rich little pastries, coffee-cake, chocolate raisin cake, peach cake, and orange cake. This, keep in mind, was just a little light afternoon

[8]Emanuel Feuermann, the 'cellist (1902-1942); Richard Buhlig, the pianist (1880-1952). Both were frequent performers of Schoenberg's music. George McManus was University organist; Alexander Schreiner was for many years Salt Lake City Mormon Tabernacle organist. Fisher was a member of the UCLA psychology department.

For a fascinating account of Feuermann's career and relationship to Schoenberg, see Seymour W. Itzkoff, *Emanuel Feuermann, Virtuoso* (University of Alabama Press, 1979).

tea. The real feast of the day, the birthday dinner, hadn't arrived yet, nor had the birthday drinks, of which more anon. After eating all these good things, we drifted out into the back yard, to watch a series of sizzling ping-pong games between Stein, Steuermann, Schoenberg, Mrs. Kolisch, Khuner and Feuermann . . . The afternoon drifted on this way; and, before we knew it, it was nearly six o'clock. "Time to go home," we were beginning to think; on the contrary, the real fun was only about to begin! Ever since Stein had found out, near the beginning of the party, that the entire Kolisch Quartet wasn't going to be present and that there would be no music unless something else was done, he'd been set on our doing *Kammer-symphonie*, which we'd prudently brought with us. Schoenberg was for it, too, but what with everyone's intense interest in the food and the ping-pong tables, the opportunity hadn't presented itself. At the moment of which I'm speaking, a few people had begun to wander back into the living room, so we judged that the time was ripe to strike. Without further ado, full to the gills of sweetmeats as we were, we strode into the nearly empty living-room, plunked ourselves down at the piano and began! The effect was really marvelous. At first no one seemed to be paying much attention, but little by little, as people began to realize what was going on, they came in to listen to us. Soon, we had a full-sized, eminently receptive audience. I think we never played it better. Kolisch was so pleased with the clarity of our performance that he promptly invited us to come and play it at his house some time after a rehearsal of *Pierrot*. Steuermann was most complimentary, and was able to give us many valuable suggestions, coupled with an impromptu performance of his most amazing two-hand arrangement of the work. And, as for Schoenberg, he was fairly bubbling over with enthusiasm. "I always said this was music of the future," he remarked, "and I am right. See, now even children can play this!" Well, I don't think we're quite such infants as he makes out, but consider the compliment a very nice one, nevertheless.

At this point, the strictly musical portion of the evening was interrupted by the advent of some more pastries, a bottle of Black and White whiskey (one of several such bottles which had been most appropriately brought to the old man in honor of the great day), and some glasses. I tried a little—a very little—of the whiskey, in spite of Uncle Arnold's merciless twitting. Then . . . supper was called! Into the dining room we scurried ... I waded through a platter of sweetened sauerkraut, frankfurters, baked potatoes, salami, shrimp salad, rye bread, anchovies, all washed down with plenty of red wine ... Then, the circlet of birthday candles was brought in and the old man most miraculously blew them all out with a single puff. After Nuria had played "Happy Birthday" on her violin, and Ronnie had sung same slightly off key, one more round of the wine was served so that we could all drink his health and exchange *Prosits* with him, and a large *Apfelstrudel* made its triumphant appearance.

Scarcely had we settled down after supper ... when Weiss asked me if I wouldn't play something? Nothing was further from my desires, but the few people within shouting distance of me urged me to it so vociferously that I couldn't get away without it. So, I staggered over to the piano and played the *Sechs kleine Klavierstücke*, hoping secretly that Schoenberg was upstairs or outside or somewhere out of hearing. Weiss asked me to play them again, so I did—and this time, Schoenberg came up with a bound, seized my hand warmly, and informed me that I'd delivered a wonderfully understanding and intelligent performance ... Not satisfied with this, he proclaimed in a loud tone, "Who else can play them like this?"—a very silly question with Steuermann in the room! Immediately following this, Steuermann ... performed the Op. 25 proving that nobody can play Schoenberg like Steuermann! The rhythm of the Gigue proved so catchy that, before we realized it, it had melted imperceptibly into an Apache dance, executed with vim and vigor by Schoenberg (complete with white carnation in buttonhole ... which we'd sent him along with a bouquet of red gladioli), Mrs. Kolisch, Weiss and Mrs. Weiss, and accompanied by Steuermann at the piano with Stein and me noisily clapping hands and emitting Apache yelps at appropriate intervals. Oh, what *der Wein, den man nicht mit Augen trinkt*,[9] does do for one! Spurred on to further enthusiasm by all this, Schoenberg fetched out Zemlinsky's four-hand arrangement of the Mahler symphonies, and he, Khuner, Steuermann and Stein had a wonderful time taking turns at a pony-express version of these. I turned pages. I was thrilled with this music, much of which I'd never heard before. The last movement of

[9]"The wine that eyes alone may drink" is the first line of *Pierrot Lunaire*. Wine at Schoenberg's parties was *not* drunk with the eyes alone!

the Sixth Symphony, in particular, is one of the most magnificent things I've ever heard! But, after all, I still must say

I wish Mahler

Had written some things that were smaller.

At last the Sixth Symphony came to an end, and Uncle Arnold hastened to "step out" with his own absolutely scorching version of that famous old song about Vienna,[10] which is definitely not the city of his dreams any more. He was dead set on getting out some more whiskey with which we might drink "to the doom of Vienna!" We would have, too, but by this time it was eleven o'clock, and we had to leave! So we said our fondest good-byes and sincerest "happy returns" to the old man, and he responded in kind. I have rarely seen him so warm-hearted and affectionate, not only to me but to everyone. I never had a better time in my life . . . I wish that Sept. 13 came twice a year—at least!

September 16, 1940

I always think that the first day of school is a lot of fun, but this one was more so than usual because of an unexpected thing that came up in the afternoon. Here's how it happened. I knew that there was supposed to be a Composers' Workshop meeting tonight, so after advanced composition . . . I asked Mr. Stein about it. And what should he come bursting out with but the news that Kolisch had invited us to the *Pierrot* rehearsal this afternoon so that we might play *Kammersymphonie* afterwords? Rehearsal was to begin at 3, but we couldn't get there till 5 because of classes . . . Kolisch lives right in Westwood (1254 Holmby Ave., 2 blocks south of Wilshire) so it didn't take me long to get there. When I arrived, the group, most vigorously directed by Schoenberg, was in the middle of the second section of *Pierrot*. Doing very well at it, too; of course, Steuermann and Kolisch are the most brilliant of the players, but the others are excellent as well, and Schoenberg is certainly a most decisive sort of conductor! Erika Wagner was there: a tall, big-boned, gray-haired woman, who must be about 50. She recited in only one

[10]"Wien, Wien, nur du allein" (*Vienna, City of My Dreams*) by Rudolf Sieczynski.

of the pieces—*Rote Messe*, I believe—so I did not get a chance to hear very much of her delivery . . . The rehearsal ended between six and seven. Kolisch wanted us to play *Kammersymphonie* afterwards, but Stein didn't feel like it after all, on account of having a cold. So, after a light snack of coffee, strudel and plums, we left with the Schoenbergs. And they drove me right to my door!

The Composers' Workshop has been postponed till Friday night (so Weiss can come, *maybe*).

September 20, 1940

I've just been having a very exciting evening indeed . . . When I slipped my newly-bound full score of *Pierrot* to Uncle Arnold this afternoon, he invited me to come to rehearsal this evening at seven o'clock . . . I arrived late, and what should I run into but a bang-up fight between Schoenberg and the 'cellist Stefan Auber? Auber had been playing a very difficult passage in the Serenade slightly out of tune, and made bold to reply to Schoenberg's repeated accusations by saying that he was doing the best he could. Well, raged Schoenberg, that's not good enough for him; bad intonation is bad intonation, and he is not going to put up with it any longer. His fury was brought to the boil by Auber's having dared to dash off a little scale during these last words, and out of the room he stomped!

Other than that, I had a wonderful time, complete with refreshments (coffee with whipped cream and cheesecake during the intermission). Aside from the performers, there were only Mrs. Seligmann and Mrs. Kolisch, Dr. Rubsamen, Fritz Stiedry, and Julius Toldi . . . Uncle Arnold, when he noticed my presence, was very sweet to me, even going so far as to pat me on the shoulder when he issued a standing invitation to me to come back to future rehearsals as often as I like. There is going to be another one tomorrow night, so I won't fail to take advantage of that invitation . . . On my way home with Auber, he told me about a tour he'd made in an orchestra under Hermann Scherchen in 1929-30, during which he participated in a performance of *Kammersymphonie* . . . I'd let Uncle Arnold take my big score of *Pierrot* just so Steuermann would have it to play from. Well, now he won't play from it because it's so beautifully bound he's afraid of damaging it when he turns the pages! "And anyway," he says, "from the miniature score I can play softer!"

✍ September 21, 1940

The Official Translator of *Pierrot*—that's my title at the moment! It
came about very suddenly at this evening's rehearsal. Intermission
time, it was; we were all very tired, and had just been quaffing red
wine and eating wienerwurst and rich sweet pastry . . . Uncle Arnold
was chatting away very glibly with Kolisch and Stiedry in lickety-
split German, when he suddenly became aware that I was taking in
every word they said. "Do you understand German?" he asked me,
for the umpteenth time in the years we've known each other, and as
usual I replied (in English) that I sure did. "Well, then," he continued,
"could you translate this?", pointing a finger at the Great Work. I
fairly turned myself inside out ejaculating that I would, could,
should, and would be oh, so happy to—during all of which Uncle
Arnold was explaining that he knew I could do it, because after all
I'd studied French for years, and now France was occupied by
Germany, *ergo* my knowledge of German must now be tremendous!
What a language sense the man has got! So I took my score home
for a change.

The recording will be made Tuesday—probably in the morning.
Hope I can be there to see it done.

✍ September 22, 1940

I never thought I could do it as quickly as this, but I have! The
translation of *Pierrot* into poetry which I don't think is too bad is
all written, and more than half typed. I spent most of the day doing
it, but it will be worth it if the old man approves it and I have the
pleasure of seeing it in print in the little pamphlet to accompany
the records.

✍ September 23, 1940

I brought Uncle Arnold the translation this afternoon, and it was a
treat to see how thrilled he was with it! He didn't have much time
to look at it—I just slipped it to him in his office between classes—
but from what he saw of it and what I told him about it, he could
tell that it was just what he'd been looking for. He asked if it were

possible to recite it with the music, and I told him that in general I'd kept the original metre strictly except where it absolutely had to be changed so that the verse might sound natural in English. That seemed to please him very much. I know that he was surprised at my having finished it so quickly, because when, a few minutes later, Mr. Stein and another student came into the office, the first thing he told them was that I'd finished it all, yes, *all*! "This fine," he kept exclaiming as he leafed through the pages, beaming from ear to ear. But alas, he's going to take it home and compare it with the German; perhaps, when the first delight of astonishment has worn off, he won't like it quite so well. Still and all, he went so far as to say that he was going to submit it to Columbia as soon as possible. It is all typed up very neatly, so they can use it at once. I asked him if it was true that the recording was going to be made tomorrow morning, but he said something evasive about "not having the time" to do it then. I believe that it will be made at that time, but that he thought outsiders shouldn't be present during the delicate operation, and hated to tell me point-blank that I couldn't come (though I hadn't asked to) after I'd done so much work. Oh yes, he asked how much time I'd spent on it, and I told him, "all day yesterday." That seemed to tickle him immensely, too. So you see that the atmosphere was *gemütlich*, not to say, SEHR WARM!

He was analyzing first movements of the earlier Beethoven sonatas in advanced composition. In answer to a question of his, I explained why I thought a certain twelve measures were a "condensed repetition" of a certain twenty. "Yes, this true," he conceded when I had finished, "but you know, when you say condensed I always think of steam!" It turned out that he wanted me to call it a "reduction" instead of a "condensed repetition"—a dainty distinction, but one not without basis . . .

September 25, 1940

When I went up to Uncle Arnold after class this p.m. with the intention of asking him, or reminding him rather, about my lesson tomorrow, he briskly volunteered the information that a good chunk of the recording of *Pierrot* was going to be done over at CBS tonight, and wouldn't I like to come? . . . No need to ask if I went! I've just gotten home from three hours of concentrated listening to take after take of the seven pieces of the second part. I'd had the quaint idea that the recording would be a very quick process indeed, but I learned that they'd worked all last night up till midnight on takes of the first part, and will be doing the third part and retakes of some of the others tomorrow morning, thus making it impossible for me to have my lesson till Friday or Saturday. I may go to the recording tomorrow on account of its being the last one (Frau Wagner is leaving for N.Y. that evening)—if I can get transportation, that is . . . The process is rather nerve-racking for listeners as well as performers. You should have seen poor Uncle Arnold shake and tremble when the man in the recording booth called out, "Ten seconds!" before each take. Frau Wagner got so exhausted that by the time the work was over she could scarcely talk. One very amusing incident occurred during an intermission between takes. Several of those present, including Uncle Arnold and Auber, had sent out for ham sandwiches. Auber was happily munching his sandwich in the extreme back of the studio when the voice in the booth bawled out, "Ten seconds!" "Great heavens, Auber," yelled U.A., "we're ready!" A. streaked down the aisle like greased lightening, still chewing his ham sandwich and calling out, "So, wunderbar!" "Aber wir warten auf Sie," screamed the old man, "das ist nicht so wunderbar!" even as A. slid into his chair and caught his first note right on the beat, still chewing his ham sandwich!

About my translation: U.A. himself has not read it yet, or at least not all of it, but all the others have, and think it's fine. Mrs. Schoenberg and Mrs. Seligmann were especially complimentary. There were some markings and corrections in the text, Mrs. Schoenberg's doing, I think; he told me to take my folder home and see if I wanted to make any such changes or alternate versions, and give it to him when next I see him. He is definitely going to send it to N.Y.

September 26, 1940

Couldn't go to the final recording session . . . Was disappointed; after all, the dear man did invite me to come, and I didn't refuse in so many words. But I'm sure he'll understand.

September 27, 1940

No Uncle Arnold today! He was at his morning class of double counterpoint, and spent all the time talking about the recording and his plans for the future, I heard. By the time I was supposed to be with him, he'd hopped off to CBS to hear all the completed takes played back to him and decide which he liked best. He doesn't know it, but I've got one of his books: the *Verein* copy, completely annotated in his own hand, of Mahler's Sixth as arranged for 4 hands by Zemlinsky. Stein fetched it over from the office to the Composers' Workshop meeting at three; we thought of trying it out, but there was no time after all, so he left the music here with the promise that he'd play it with me some time soon. I hope so, because I've been wild about it ever since hearing him and Steuermann play it on a certain memorable Friday 13!

I called up the old man tonight, arranged to come for my lesson tomorrow at ten. Besides the quartet, I'm going to bring the translations (both old and new versions in some cases). He sounded very happy over the phone so I think he must be pleased with the completion of the records. But I bet he's worn out!

September 30, 1940

Schoenberg is going to play the *Pierrot* records at school especially for his students, next Monday at four o'clock. I learned that he'd told the Structural Functions class all about it and had been greeted with a wave of spontaneous applause. Better yet, he had gone into ecstasies over my "wonderfully expert" translation, and had charged Stein with having a large number of mimeographed copies of it made so that they might be passed out on Monday . . .

October 2, 1940

Uncle Arnold certainly was extra-special nice to me today. Not only did he accept my newly written theme for the first movement of a string suite as being "useful," but he arranged that I should teach one of the three weekly quiz sections of Structural Functions, and

announced the fact in class. . . . To top things off, he invited me . . .
to come out to his house in the evening and hear the *Pierrot* records
. . . I found out that he still had two or three takes of each side of
the records and wanted some outsiders who were not quite as
familiar with the music as he is to help him pick out the best one of
each. Many of those invited couldn't come, so Estep, Stein and I
were the only outside people there . . . Otherwise, there were performers and family: Kolisch with wife, Auber, Posella, Khuner, and
Mrs. Seligmann . . . I vigorously participated in selecting the takes, a
rather ticklish job, since in many cases the differences were slight
yet important. After this main job of the evening was over, we fell
with a will to drinking sour red wine and eating frankfurters in rich
pastry, then amused ourselves with playing the records of *Gurre-
Lieder* until the phonograph broke down, after which we listened to
a record-program on the radio. During part of the time, Uncle Arnold
and Trude were looking over my translations . . . and found several
spots they wanted to change. He dreams of having this version
revised so that it fits the music perfectly enough to be used in performance and in an English edition, if there ever is one. This will
entail a little work, but it will also entail frequent conferences with
the Schoenberg family, which I shan't mind a bit!

Mr. Stein and I gave *Kammersymphonie* a run-through this afternoon after school. We are going to record it as soon as we can,
especially now that A.S. is in a recording mood, being so well satisfied with *Pierrot*.

October 3, 1940

Had my lesson with the old man this morning. I'd thought he might
be rather exhausted after last night's session, but he greeted me most
chirpily with an amused, "So, you got home ver' late last night, no?"
. . . I gave him the copy of the translation with all of last night's
corrections in it, and told him that I'd deliver the other copy to the
mimeograph office this afternoon as soon as I got Mr. Allen's requi-
sition. This satisfied him fully, and he again brought up the idea of
my making a new version of the translation which would fit the
music perfectly. If I do, he'll see that it is used in the English
edition, if one is ever made . . .

✍ October 7, 1940

First and foremost, *Pierrot*. The records were played at school this afternoon at 4, just as scheduled; they were received with favor and delight by students and faculty alike! Uncle Arnold stood up in front of the room all the time the music was being played, beaming from ear to ear and chortling audibly; occasionally exchanging a Significant Look with me at certain spots which had been of special difficulty at rehearsals or recording sessions. [These] had a special meaning for us, aside from the obvious pleasure which their correct performance on the records caused him, as in the case of some of Auber's famous *glissandos* ending in a harmonic. He did not give much explanation of the music beforehand, preferring rather to lambaste Vernon Steele of the *Pacific Coast Musician* for his recent proposal that "what this country needs" is a Society for Sanity in Music . . .; but at least everyone knew what the poetry was all about, thanks to the mimeographed copies of my translation which were distributed . . . Mrs. Schoenberg remarked, "We can't bear to listen to it any more since Ronnie has taken up the *Sprechgesang*!" That must be something to hear—if Ronnie is about when I'm there on Thursday, I shall certainly ask him to demonstrate.

In composition class, E. explained pompously what he felt like doing next in that string quartet of his: "I had thought of a soaring melody—" U.A. interrupted quickly: "You mean perhaps snoring?"

✍ October 9, 1940

Uncle Arnold didn't look at our compositions this afternoon, but spent the time analyzing the themes of Schubert's E-flat-major Piano Trio and the two Brahms String Quartets of Op. 51. Mr. Stein and I demonstrated very creditably on the two pianos . . . He was in his best vein when commenting on Stein's somewhat grandiloquent announcement of the Workshop program for Sunday night; it's to feature *Kammersymphonie* and the *Six Little P.P.'s*, and will be graced by the Schoenbergian presence if we have to drag same there by its back hair! Schoenberg remarked that he was "not guilty" about the *Kammersymphonie*, because Mr. Stein had just that minute told him that we intended to do it; but really, it wouldn't

hurt anyone to hear it! He went on the say that he was more interested in the students' hearing the "advanced music" of pupils like
me . . . "And," he continued, brightly beaming, "I hope that it will
inspire many of you so that perhaps another year your works could
be played!"

October 10, 1940

Had quite a lively session with Uncle Arnold this morning. As a
matter of fact, Mamma and I were there till well past one o'clock,
for after my lesson was over he wanted us to help him fill out his
second citizenship papers. We had a jolly time indeed trying to
extricate him from the hopeless confusion into which he had fallen
in regard to them. He would insist on putting the wrong bits of
information in the wrong blanks, and then would have to cross his
mistakes out and write over them in most illegible fashion, and then
would groan and moan that he simply knew they would make him
do the whole thing over again when he went to file it. "The trouble
with you," said Mrs. Schoenberg when he was in one of his more
"mizzled" [misled] moments, "is that you never learned to read!"
That didn't go down at all well, nor did her assertion, made while
we were all riding back to Westwood in their car (they had to go
downtown to file the papers, so dropped us off at our house on the
way) that he was as nervous and excited about the whole thing as if
he were a criminal! I don't know about that, but anyway some of
the questions and answers on his sheet were surely funny. One of
the questions is, "Have you ever been committed to an insane
asylum? If so, why?" (T. was heard to mutter under her breath, "If
not, why not?") Then there is the little spot where you have to put
the name of the ship or other conveyance on which you last entered
this country. He had written here, with quaint simplicity, "On foot
from Mexicali." And, for one of the witnesses whom he must bring
with him to his examination, he nonchalantly inscribed, "*Mr. and
Mrs.* Adolph Weiss," justifying his action by saying, "Well, if one
could not come, the other could!" More interesting than these divers
blunders, however, are the little biographical facts, so fascinating to
me, which keep cropping up throughout the whole. "I have four
children: Gertrud Greissle—born January 7, 1902, Berlin; Georg

Schönberg—born September 22, 1906, Vienna [and still, Heaven help us, living in Mödling!]; Dorothea Nuria, born May 7, 1932, Barcelona; Rudolf Ronald, born May 26, 1937, Los Angeles." (At this point Rudolf Ronald came running to the sofa to bury his sleepy head in his father's arms. All the way home with us, he slept soundly in the most grotesque of positions, standing on the floor of the car with his head resting on a pillow on the seat.) "The name of my wife is Gertrud Kolisch. She was born in Carlsbad, July 11, 1898. [Older than I thought!] We were married in Mödling, August 28, 1924."

As for what happened at the lesson, that is not quite as romantic as that list of dates and places which, even in the dry setting of a standardized government form, carry about them something of the illusory and fragrant vapor of the past which they represent. This lesson marked the end of the String Symphony. I've been expecting this for a long time, as Uncle Arnold's mysterious "sixth sense" always seems to tell him when I am going to enter a certain work in a contest, and to force him to put a stop to the further composition of that work. Not that this was the reason he gave; perhaps he is not even conscious of its existence. He said only that, as the quartet is doing quite nicely now and much of the quintet is finished, it is more important that I should finish these two better works by the end of the semester and drop the string symphony, which I have only now begun in earnest and which is not as good as the other works.

. . . A word about *Harmonielehre*. Mrs. Schoenberg says Slonimsky has indeed abandoned the project of translation, and that now they don't know what to do. McManus and several others are anxious to make a stab at it, but the Schoenbergs don't like to make a decision, because they are anxious to find someone who is a perfect master of German, can write elegant English, and has a complete knowledge of Schoenberg's theories. Sounds like there's an opening here for me! I'll talk to him about it as soon as I can.

October 11, 1940

Schoenberg was in the most exuberant good humor because of an incident, trivial but indicative, which had happened to him during his lunch hour at school. He and Hedrick were eating together in the cafeteria when suddenly a series of loud cries burst from one corner of the room: the students practising their football yells for tomorrow's game with Texas A & M. Schoenberg, thrilled but mystified by this performance, wanted to know what it was all about. So what does Hedrick do but jump up and start to harangue the yelling students, telling them all about how their great Schoenberg (of whom I suppose three quarters of them had never heard) was here, and how he was enjoying their rally! And, if you please, what does the whole cafeteria-full of students do but rise *en masse* and cheer Schoenberg as loud as it can cheer! He was so overjoyed by this demonstration that he had to come running back to his advanced composition class after he'd already gone out of the room wishing us a happy weekend, just to tell us about it. To top this off, there was a squib about Sunday night's performance of *Kammer-symphonie* on the front page of the *Bruin*, and a full-length article about Schoenberg himself on the back page, so you can imagine how he was feeling! As he walked downstairs after our last class to wait for Mrs. Schoenberg and the car, I caught up with him and began to talk to him about the possibility of my translating the *Harmonielehre*. His reaction was far beyond my brightest hopes. He said that he thought that it would be a fine thing for both him and me, if I have the time to do it without pressing myself too much. He would be delighted if he could give it to me; but both McManus and Schreiner want to do it too. He knows that he must make up his mind in the next few days, so I am to remind him the next time I see him (probably Sunday night), by which time his decision will most likely be made. This evening I prepared a translation of the *Vorwort* and will have Mamma type it tomorrow morning so that I can send it to him special-delivery at once. It might just tip the balance in my favor!

October 13, 1940

Went over to the Hollywood High School to hear that orchestra of studio players which Carfagno organized last spring take a workout under Stravinsky. I'd never seen him conduct before . . . he's quite a cute little bug, hardly bigger than Schoenberg, and almost as bald;

extremely graceful, and bursting out into the strangest little dance-steps and frisking leaps every other beat . . . When to these peculiar jumps were added divers wild yells of no particular meaning, the effect was that of some weird Cossack dance! None of this seemed to be affected at all; quite natural, on the other hand, and highly amusing, especially when he did it with the upper part of his torso modestly swathed in a bathtowel! The music played was Tschaikowsky's Second Symphony and Haydn's *Oxford*. Sol Babitz was supposed to have played Stravinsky's Violin Concerto, but the music never arrived. Schoenberg is going to direct the group on Nov. 10, or so Carfagno promises. He will do either the 2nd *Kammersymphonie* or the Brahms arrangement—probably the latter. We'll be there!

Later, called up Uncle Arnold about the translation of *Harmonielehre*. He couldn't have me bring my sample to the house this afternoon, as the whole family was going to the beach with some friends, but told me that I might come and see him on Tuesday if I liked, and to be sure to remind him of it tomorrow at school. He didn't come to the Workshop this evening, by the way, and here's what he told me about it: he thinks it looks ridiculous for him to go and bow every time a work of his is played. He never has done it, and he doesn't see why he should start doing it now! . . . He wasn't angry with me about it; it's just a recurrence of his old pride, in practically the same words as those he'd used to Bekker so many years ago.

October 14, 1940

The *Harmonielehre* business looks clinched . . . I contrived to slip the translation of the preface to the old man right after our class together. Much to my delight, he set himself to reading it at once . . . After having tried over a few of the crucial sentences on the tip of his tongue, much as a wine-taster tries a drop of vintage wine, he remarked that the whole thing seemed quite fluent and clear to him, though of course he couldn't vouch for the English and though he questioned certain special passages. More than that he didn't want to say at the moment, because after two hours of teaching he didn't feel fresh enough to go into the matter in detail; but I'm to come out to the house tomorrow at eleven and talk the whole thing over with him. As a matter of fact, I'll have even more to show him then, for I dictated about half the first chapter to Mamma this evening . . . it was pretty slow going, being one of the more confused philosophical chapters, but once I get into the music proper it will be much easier.

October 15, 1940

The Great Conference took place this morning at the scheduled hour . . . and it went even better than I had expected. Of course, one of Uncle Arnold's first questions was how long the job would take me if I were to do it. I gave him an extremely liberal estimate of a year, explaining that I preferred to give him too long a time and surprise him by finishing it sooner than to tell him a short time and disappoint him by taking longer. Both he and Trude agreed that, if I named a definite time, I was far more likely to finish it sooner than later (without giving up any of my other essential work, which he has no thought of my doing); also that—unlike some others!—if I said I'd do it, I'd really do it, instead of getting halfway through and then deciding I didn't like it any more. It would take Trude to come forth at this point with the cheerful statement that there was a curse on the work—*ein Fluch*—which would prevent its ever being finished, and that in my case this curse would take the form of my getting married in the middle of it all and so giving it up. You can imagine how quick I was to assure her of the contrary! These preliminaries established, I'd all but signed on the dotted line; all that needed to be done now was to send a telegram to Slonimsky, asking him to return the copy of the third edition which Schoenberg had given him. As for the financial question, I will enter on the same terms as Slonimsky did: a share of the royalties up to a certain amount, Uncle Arnold forgets what (or says he does). When all these matters had been discussed, we settled down to work in earnest, all three of us, carefully checking the translation against the original and making necessary or desirable changes. One amusing incident occurred in connection with the passage of the preface which begins "Unsere Zeit sucht vieles." Now, by an odd coincidence, this passage sounds a bit like certain tenets of Nazi doctrine; no sooner had we begun to work on it than Mrs. Schoenberg called her dear Arnold's attention to the fact. It didn't seem to bother him much, though;

he laughed heartily and said, "Now, you see they stole this idea from me! I thought of it already in 1911!"[11] When the work was finally done, we went in to lunch: liverwurst, braunschweiger with pistachio nuts, avocado slices, lettuce with French dressing, raw apples and grapes, rye bread, and coffee; the whole flavored with a delightful atmosphere more pleasant to the palate than the most exotic spices. Old Mrs. Kolisch was at table with us, and so was baby Ronnie, whose adorable prattle kept us in stitches all the time. Right in the middle of the meat course, what should he do but stand up on his chair and start pounding the table, yelling "We Want Woosevelt!" at the top of his voice! Such practises, Mrs. Schoenberg tells me, don't meet with Nuria's approval at all; she'll wear a Willkie button on one side and a Roosevelt button on the other till after the election! Snowy didn't come in the house while we were eating, but was very much of a silent partner in the proceedings. All the time I was eating, she stood outside, her nose pressed against the screen-door just behind me, and followed my every mouthful with dirty and reproachful eyes. It seems she thinks that, when a guest comes, she is being deprived of her rightful place in order to make room for the guest—and it hurts her feelings!

Had to leave at one o'clock to catch a bus to the violin-shop (Koodlach's). While there, I picked up an eighth-size peg for Ronnie's violin. One of his was broken, and the old man, knowing that I was going to Koodlach (in whom he has confidence because K. does all of Rudy Kolisch's work), charged me with getting a new one. It didn't cost me a cent, and I'm quite sure it will fit.

---

[11]"Our age seeks many things. What it has found, however, is above all: *comfort*. Comfort, with all its implications, intrudes even into the world of ideas and makes us far more content than we should ever be. We understand today better than ever how to make life pleasant. We solve problems to remove an unpleasantness. But, *how* do we solve them? And what presumption, even to think we have really solved them! Here we can see most distinctly what the prerequisite of comfort is: superficiality. It is thus easy to have a 'Weltanschauung,' a 'philosophy', if one contemplates only what is pleasant and gives no heed to the rest. The rest—which is just what matters most." *Theory of Harmony*, pp. 1-2.

Today, this passage scarcely seems to have a Nazi "taint." Most serious thinkers, of whatever political stripe, would doubtless accept Schoenberg's realistic world-view.

✍ October 17, 1940

Unexpected class visitor today: Lotte Klemperer.[12] I delivered
Ronnie's peg, and Uncle Arnold was quite delighted with my having
taken the trouble to get it; kept asking me how much it cost, and
seemed to think, when I told him it didn't cost anything, that I was
just trying to be "nice." Better yet, he told several of the students
that I had begun a "very successful" translation of *Harmonielehre*;
still better, he accepted (albeit not too enthusiastically) my latest
theme for a string-quartet scherzo. He was in such a good humor
that he didn't even get mad when, on account of not being able to
see the notes in the tiny score, I made a hopeless mess of one
measure of the Mozart D-minor Quartet which I was playing, two
pianos four hands, with Mr. Stein. He readily accepted my excuse
of extreme nearsightedness, though he did suggest that on such
occasions I should wear three kinds of glasses: one for the right
notes, one for the accidentals, and one for the rhythm! He said all
this, however, in the spirit of good clean fun, and not in a carping
way as he used sometimes to do with me. Even this light blow he
softened by urging me "not to get so nervous." All of this serves
only to confirm my impression that he has been, and still continues
to be, much, much sweeter to me this year than ever in any previous
year. I don't know why, but only hope he keeps it up.

✍ October 17, 1940

Says U.A., "This composing is a serious business. It does not matter
if what you write is not good—what matters is the *pain* you had in
writing it!" Our lesson today was good but not at all unusual. He is
now mostly satisfied with the slow movement of the quartet (all
finished now save some 10 or 15 measures) but has again decided
not to like my beginning of a Scherzo, so I'll have to start that over
once more. However, as he showed me some types of scherzo-
characters which are more interesting than the sort I've been working on, my next beginning should be far better. He expressed himself

---

[12]I had met her at Schoenberg's birthday party (see above, p. 266). She was a
great Schoenberg favorite.

extremely anxious to see the translation of *Pierrot* made to fit the music. So I polished that work off tonight and Mamma typed it for me so that I can give it to him tomorrow.

October 18, 1940

A day of scorching desert heat. Uncle Arnold in a good mood, but too roasted by the heat to do much but talk of this and that, and hear Mr. Stein and me play some more Mozart Quartets for demonstration purposes, I gave him the new *Pierrot* down at the car, and he seemed quite pleased to have it; he already had with him a big envelope addressed to "Mr. Smith" in New York, which, he told me, contained the first version. I am glad he's sending it. He talked a bit about the novel combinations of instruments in *Pierrot*, some of which he does not like any more—says this due to influence of Brahms, who was very much interested in such combinations.

Did the second chapter of *HL* tonight. It's much easier to follow than the metaphysical ramblings of the first!

October 21, 1940

When U.A. was showing Annette models for the characters of an *Andantino grazioso*, what models do you suppose he showed her? *Andantes* from the quartets and quintets of Brahms and the trios and quartets of Beethoven (wonderfully performed by me and Mr. Stein), and then, right on the heels of Brahms and Beethoven, he said, "And *Miss Newlin* has just finished a *very* good *Andantino grazioso*—yes, it is really very good. very fine, it must once be played here, yes?" Yessir, me, Brahms and Beethoven are ideal models for young composers, ain't we? I'm sorry to say that The Three Graces with Dirty Faces . . . snickered at each other most disrespectfully when Schoenberg uttered these golden words, and M. even went so far as to clap silently. He had a reason to be a bit up in the air, though, for Schoenie had just gotten off a scorching joke at his expense. M. had brought a couple of disconnected themes for a violin sonata, and S. was patiently explaining that that was not the way to compose; one should conceive the whole composition at once and add the themes afterwards as details, just as an apple-tree produces its fruit all at once and not part-at-a-time. "Or," he continued, his face lighting up fiendishly, "just as one draws a portrait—" and he promptly rushed to the blackboard and started to draw a portrait of M.! In nothing flat, he'd completed the most horse-faced, cross-eyed caricature of our ugly friend that you could imagine. Of course, the entire class was simply *howling*. M. looked as if all 6 feet of him would like either to sink through the floor for good and all, or to paste Schoenberg one! Uncle Arnold, of course, was having a wonderful time through all of this. I strongly suspect that he was showing off for Lotte's benefit. She was there again this afternoon, looking right pretty, and you may be sure that this didn't escape his notice. Hal told me that she came into the Structural Functions class a little late, while the old man had his back turned to the room and was writing on the board. When he turned around and saw she was there, he lit up all over as if he'd been turned on with a switch! *And* he was wearing a super-spruce new shirt and tie today . . .

October 21, 1940

. . . there seems to be some doubt as to whether Slonimsky is or is not working on the book and whether he did or did not sign a contract with the University before leaving L.A.: doubts which have caused me to hold off on the work for a little while, at least till something definite is learned. Uncle Arnold is still all enthusiastic about having me do it; Dr. Rubsamen was telling me (in front of the whole musicology class) how the old man had been talking the work up to him and Arlt [13] the other day, in glowing terms. I must have a good talk with him about it on Thursday . . .

October 23, 1940

A.S., bless his heart, got off one absolutely immortal remark in advanced composition today. He was talking about the contrast between principal and secondary themes in a sonata, and said that,

[13]Gustave O. Arlt, head of the German Department.

if we wanted to attain such contrasts in our own works, the most efficient way would be for us to give a definite name to the mood of each of the themes, in our own terminology or language, of course. "Now I always made this joke," said he, " that when I talk to myself I sometimes use very rough language—and you can do the same!" That really brought down the house. He was very funny in Structural Functions, too, trying to think of simple children's songs the harmony of which would exemplify his concept of "function-less" successions—and suddenly being helped out by a deep bass voice in the back row booming out *O, du lieber Augustin*! He's got those students analyzing Bach harmony now. That's unusual for him; his usual examples are Beethoven and Mozart.

After Structural Functions and my quiz section were over, Mr. Stein and I went home to practise *Kammersymphonie*. We're to play it at a party at the Yates' (the Roof) on Saturday night, rehearse it with Schoenberg Sunday p.m., and record next weekend with Lange.

Ah yes, Lotte was at school again this afternoon. She's getting to be quite a fixture with Schoenberg!

October 24, 1940

It looks as if the *Harmonielehre* job were drifting out of my sphere. I was talking about it to Uncle Arnold this morning at my lesson. He hasn't heard from Slonimsky, and has pretty much given up on him; what he would like is a translator who could get the job done by February, so that the book could be published by next fall. This, of course, I am not prepared to do. I told him quite sincerely that I hoped, for his own sake, he could find someone who would be able to devote his entire time to the work, but that, if he could not, I would always be glad to step in and do my part as I had pre-viously agreed. This seemed to satisfy him.

October 25, 1940

Slogged through driving rain to confront Uncle Arnold at two o'clock. Not that he needed much confronting, for he was in so good a humor that he even qualified my newest continuation of the string quartet Scherzo as "good." (Not bad, considering that his greeting to me when I came in yesterday was, "Well, it seems you cannot write a Scherzo! What is the matter?") In one place, though, I'd distributed a certain rather slight motive among all the instruments: the 'cello goes "pum" and then stops, the viola goes "pum pum" and then stops, and so on through. This he criticized for obvious reasons, and compared my procedure to something he'd done in a youthful work of his, also a string quartet. The thing he was proudest of in it was such a "distributed" theme. Well, when he'd finished it, he took it to a certain famous Viennese music critic for judgement, and what do you suppose the fellow said? That such technique reminded him of those Russian bands in which many of the instruments can play only one note, so that the melody must constantly shift from one instrument to the next. That cured Schoenberg of "distributed" melodies; forty-five years later, it has also cured me.[14]

The biggest piece of news *re* Schoenberg and myself, however, has nothing to do with the string quartet. Franz Werfel's[15] 50th anniversary is coming up shortly, and it seems there's a man in the music dept. at L.A.C.C. who is going to give a lecture honoring him on Nov. 13. Well, this man wrote to Schoenberg as follows: I am enclosing five of Werfel's simpler poems herewith. Now, of course I realize it would be too great an imposition to ask you to set some of these to be performed along with my lecture—though it would be wonderful if you could—but, perhaps, there are some of your advanced students . . . And that's where I come in. I have the copies of the poems that were sent to Schoenberg; some of the other fellows made hand-copies from mine, and will probably be working night and day to beat me to the punch. But I bet I'll have all five songs finished and ready to play in class on Monday!

---

[14]We had not yet learned to admire Webern's use of this style, or to call it, somewhat inaccurately, "pointillism." For a delightful example of Russian horn band notation, see Robert Ricks, "Russian Horn Bands," *Musical Quarterly*, July, 1969, pp. 364-71.

[15]Werfel (1890-1945) was a major Austrian-Jewish Expressionistic poet and dramatist; later, author of many popular novels (*The Forty Days of Musa Dagh, Embezzled Heaven, The Song of Bernadette*). He was Alma Mahler's third (last) husband.

October 26, 1940

To the Yates' with Mr. Stein. We had a pleasant evening sipping mulled cider, munching doughnuts, and playing *Kammersymphonie*, which, as a result of our whiz-bang rendition, is now definitely scheduled for the March 25 Schoenberg evening. They tell me that the New Friends broadcast *Verklärte Nacht* last Sunday, at a horribly slow tempo. Think that *Kammersymphonie II* will be broadcast at least in part. And Stein was describing to me a new publication of Mahler's complete letters, issued by the present Mrs. Werfel, who used to be Mahler's wife. It's full of grand stuff about Schoenberg, but will probably be inaccessible now on account of being a German book. It's reviewed in July's *Musical Quarterly*, he says. He hasn't seen the book—only this review.[16]

Wrote two and one half Werfel songs—*Der Wanderer, Ich habe eine gute Tat getan*, and half of *Unsterblichkeit*. All of which inspires the following:

> A mystical German named Werfel
> Writes "pomes" which are perfectly fearful.
> For Schoenberg I set them,
> But when he looked *at* them,
> He surely was not very cheerful!

October 27, 1940

Finished the last of the Werfels today: the rest of *Unsterblichkeit*, *Allelujah*, and *Gottesferne, Gottesnähe*, complete with translations by myself. They're good songs, I think. And won't Schoenberg be surprised (and I hope pleased) at my having them *all* done! That'll show 'em!

Stein and I had been going to play *KS* for Schoenberg this afternoon, but at the last moment arrangements fell through . . .

---

[16]Carl Engel, "Views and Reviews," *Musical Quarterly*, July, 1940, pp. 393-400. The review is enthusiastic: "The frankest, most outspoken account of a musician's grandeur and misery that we have seen . . . among the most remarkable documents of its kind."

✐ October 28, 1940

I presented the *Werfel-Lieder*, all but *Allelujah*, today with fear and trembling; but really, their fate wasn't such a terrible one. Oh, of course, I'd done a quite a few things wrong: written in a too-constantly high range for the voice; changed the character of the music in the middle of a song (*Ich habe eine gute Tat getan*) when there was no special justification for it in the words; accentuated words unnaturally in some cases, thereby violating S.'s fundamental principle that the melody of a song should be a mere elevation of the spoken melody of the words. But, in general, the old man's impression was very good, and so was everyone else's . . . The whole hour was taken up with a detailed study of these songs. Many amusing incidents occurred. U.A. claimed that the beginning of *Unsterblichkeit* sounded like grasshoppers, and proceeded to prove his point by drawing the front end of a grasshopper on the blackboard! But the funniest was when he was reading to himself my translation of this same *Unsterblichkeit*. The German is very complicated, and so is the English, so he was having some difficulty in puzzling out certain places. While he puzzled, I, patiently waiting to play the song, was twiddling a pencil in my hands. All of a sudden, just as he was thinking extra hard, pop! the pencil broke in two between my fingers. Of course everyone roared, and I turned red as a beet. Uncle Arnold snickered a little, and, turning towards me, inquired with monumental calm, "Does this help you?" This disrupted the class for at least five minutes.

✐ October 30, 1940

I showed Uncle Arnold . . . *Allelujah*. Rather to my surprise, he thought it one of the better ones of the lot. He thinks the first one I wrote, *Der Wanderer*, is the best; I think so, too, and so does everyone else who has heard it. He suggested a few changes, but they are not so radical. I was much interested to hear him say that he'd seriously considered writing a song on the *Gute Tat* just to show me what its true character should be; he'd found mine too "aggressive" in its gaiety. He hadn't, after all, had time. But imagine such a great composer being willing to consider writing a piece only for the special purpose of helping one of his students! It makes me feel very humble indeed, and very proud to have the privilege of being a friend and pupil of such a man.

We were talking about music contests and such. He volunteered the information that he'd only won one in his life, when he was 19. *Friede auf Erden* and *Zwei Balladen* were both entered in contests, but lost to inferior works. Oh yes, he had the Liszt fund scholarship in 1903—1000 marks a year for two years. Good going!

November 1, 1940

Uncle Arnold devoted about half the class today to hearing a dress rehearsal of Estep's songs . . . In general he thought both works and performance "nice." He ended the class by having Mr. Stein play the dramatic ballad *Jane Grey* . . . However, what interested me most of all was his statement that, out of all his family, he is just about the only one without a good singing voice. Both his brother and his sister[17] were operatic singers, and in respectable companies; anywhere from three to six (I never could get the exact number) of his cousins were tenors, and one at least of these, at the age of 22 or so, had so fine a voice that everyone thought he would be the tenor of the generation![18] At about that time, he sang the lead in the first performance of *Gurre-Lieder*, and immediately following this had offers for engagements with the opera houses in Berlin, Vienna and Dresden. He tried both Vienna and Berlin in succession, but, as he could not have the major parts that he wanted in either place, he resigned himself to singing in secondary musical centers where he could have the leads. Hence, he never enjoyed the reputation that he deserved and could have had.

November 3, 1940

Got to Uncle Arnold's about two-thirty (Mr. Stein came after three)

---

[17]Heinrich and Ottilie. Their careers are described in Stuckenschmidt, *op. cit.* See also Book II, p. 214, footnote 76.

[18]For Hans Nachod, see also my article "The Schoenberg-Nachod Collection: A Preliminary Report," *Musical Quarterly*, January, 1968, pp. 31-46. The complete collection of letters, post cards and compositions is reproduced in John A. Kimmey, Jr., *The Arnold Schoenberg-Hans Nachod Collection* (Detroit Studies in Music Bibliography, No. 41), Detroit. Information Coordinators, 1979.

and had some very serious discussion with the family on various topics, not the least of which was the ever-recurring *Harmonielehre* question. U.A. still hasn't written to Slonimsky, and still doesn't quite dare to take it away from him unless he knows it will save him time. Now his latest wrinkle is that if I want to do it I should drop out of school and give all my time to it and to composition. Of course I kept trying to explain to him that I had to have my degree ("Why?"), that my money might not be granted to me unless I stayed in school ("Why?"), but not one thing I said would make the slightest impression on him, even when Mrs. Schoenberg, bless her, bore me out in the reasonable tenor of my statements. He kept saying over and over again: "Frankly, I must say this. You can get your degree anywhere; you can get your piano anywhere; only *me* you cannot get anywhere—and you know and I know that I am the only one which really matters—and *me* you will still have!" This is tantamount to saying, "Give all your time to me—or else!" Of course the situation was a terribly delicate one, and all I could say was that he must at least give me time to think over such an amazing proposition. This, he readily consented to do. But it's at best a temporary postponement of a problem which I always knew would come up some day, in one form or another.

Luckily Mr. Stein's arrival saved me from further embarrassment . . . we fell right to work on *KS*, and stuck with it for about an hour or so, the old man all the time expressing his hearty approval of our rendition, to our great joy. Just as we were polishing off the last few pages, the Weisses came to call. As soon as we were through, we joined them in a cup of coffee with whipped cream, helped along with tea-cookies and strudel. Leave it to Uncle Arnold to fetch out his bottle of Haig & Haig Horse Liniment—it never fails! We all had a little glass of it straight . . .

Schoenberg to me, on contests: "The judges know so little that they will surely give the prize to someone like you—or to one who knows even less, if this is possible!" Mrs. S., covering up: "But of course we know it's possible!"

November 4, 1940

Uncle Arnold and I had some fun in class today. He'd brought along the early songs Op. 6 and had Mr. Stein play—and me sing!—

Verlassen, Lockung, and *Der Wanderer*. Really, the thing went off quite well, and I'm amazed to say the old man didn't get off any sour cracks at the expense of my voice (though he could have). I provided a running translation of each of the poems before we did the songs, at U.A.'s request and with results much to his delight. He's amazed that I can read German as well as I can, with the comparatively little experience in speaking it that I have had. All this is very nice; but, while U.A. is going through this "song period," what is happening to the real work of our class? Only yesterday he was wondering why he was so far behind with the work of all our classes; well, ask yourself, why?

November 6, 1940

I'd thought that the election of Uncle Arnold's favorite candidate [19] would put him in an extraordinarily good humor today, but I was wrong . . . I had prepared good copies of three of my songs (*Der Wanderer, Gottesferne, Allelujah*), the last two with slight revisions, and had brought them with me; for I knew that, if the performance was to come off on the 13th, today was none too soon for them to be sent over to LACC. Well, U.A. breezes in and announces to all and sundry that . . . the concert must be postponed "until the others will have finished works"—that is to say, at least until after the end of next week. "And besides," says he to me, "I have not seen yours in a definite form yet!" To which I replied by telling him of the three good copies, adding that I had not bothered with the other two because such radical changes would have been necessary. "Yes," he retorted, "you are quite right. The best way to revise these would be—" (here a good imitation of ripping a piece of paper in two). The rest of the class passed without special incident . . . until he got around to asking me what I was going to show. "Well," I answered, "I've these songs, and some more of the quartet—" but already he was off. "Don't talk so much, just show me what you have! That is the trouble with all of you—you have long explanations and little music! Yes, I know, with the words you can deceive me, but with your little music, never!" etc., etc. Finally, however, he was able to

[19] Franklin Delano Roosevelt had just been re-elected President.

settle down enough to hear me do the new version of *Gottesferne*. I'd changed it in only a few places, for last time he'd said it was very good. But this time! After I'd finished it, he played over the first two measures very sadly, and said, "I do not like this—no—what does this mean? I told you already last time I did not like this, yes?" "No, Mr. Schoenberg! Maybe no one else cares to remember this, but I do; you said it was very good, one of the best ones, except for this—and this—which I have now changed. So what's the matter?" But he wasn't convinced . . . Later I encountered him bustling downstairs and reminded him that I was coming for my lesson tomorrow. "Yes, yes," he beamed, "that is right! You come, yes—and bring the songs with you, yes?"

November 7, 1940

My lesson is postponed till Saturday—U.A. is busy making arrangements for a trip (alone!) to New York to begin on the 12th of this month and end—when? The two main reasons for the trip are the *Pierrot* performance and a scheduled lecture, apparently to be given in conjunction with it. From all I could gather, the minimum time of his absence would be two weeks, with three weeks more likely. Well, I'd known that this would be coming up at some time during the year, but I'd never expected it so soon nor at so unpropitious a time. I feel very sad about it . . .

November 8, 1940

Uncle Arnold in pretty good humor today. Didn't talk about the projected trip in my class, but I was told that he had spoken of it in his other classes and given a few specific details. In the first place, he is actually going to conduct *Pierrot* himself, and am I glad of it! What about Klemperer? Well, there's a story going the rounds about his having gotten himself into a peck of trouble in N.Y. by shooting his mouth off about the War, at one of his recent concerts. I don't know all the details, having heard the thing only indirectly. In the second place, the lecture is to be before the American Society of

Musicologists,[20] which is a laugh, considering what he thinks of musicologists! He is supposed to return on the 26th, exactly two weeks from the date of his departure.

November 9, 1940

Stayed practically the whole morning at Uncle Arnold's ... The lesson was frequently interrupted; for one thing, he had to take about 15 minutes to read all his important mail from N.Y., during which time I, at his request, sent a telegram to Aranyi telling that Schoenberg would be going to N.Y. next week and asking if it would be possible to schedule his lecture for some time between the 24th and 26th (also asking about the very weighty matter of "the small check"). Then, after my lesson proper was over, Mr. Stein came to get final instructions on how things should be managed during the old man's absence (I got in on this too). As the Schoenbergs had to drive into Westwood anyway to cash some checks, they took us both along. In spite of being much occupied with arrangements for the trip, U.A. was in very good humor. On the way home he was full of talk about the opera. He had gone with Nuria (and, I think, Lotte) to see *Figaro* last night, and had found it not badly performed on the whole but totally out of place in such a huge auditorium as the Shrine. He wishes that there were more smaller opera houses in this country of the type so common in Germany ...

November 11, 1940

This was the day of fond *adieux* to Uncle Arnold but not many were at school to bid them to him. It was a half-holiday and apparently all but about five of us had decided to take the other half-day off, too. Said he: "I think this armistice for them too, yes?" We had a very peaceful and uneventful class, with most of the time going to

[20]I.e., the American Musicological Society. Schoenberg gave his lecture, *Melody and Theme*, on November 23, 1940, before the Society's New York chapter, at Schirmer Hall. He repeated it at Michigan State College. Eventually, it became Chapter XI of *Fundamentals of Musical Composition*.

278 Schoenberg Remembered

my string quartet (Scherzo). He accepted the major part of it, and made not a single sarcastic comment! (This reminds me of a terribly funny thing that happened on Saturday which I quite forgot to note at the time. There was a little melodic section near the end of what I had written which resembled the second theme of *Kammersymphonie* a little too closely. So what does U.A. do but grab his pencil and write "quote, unquote" around the offending section!) After class, I spoke to him alone, and wished him the finest of trips; asked him where he wanted his mail sent, and he said in care of Schirmer's. At seven tonight, I called him up at his request; he told me that he'd just gotten a telegram from Underwood[21] at E.L., offering him $100 and the evening of Nov. 25 for his lecture. He's almost sure that this will be all right for him, and thanked me effusively for the trouble I'd taken to further the event. Oh yes, and he's taking my latest version of the *Pierrot* translation (the one suitable for recitation) to New York with him. He sent the other one to "Mr. Smith" some time ago but has had no answer. *Pierrot* will be broadcast from N.Y., at least in part, next Sunday . . .

November 14, 1940

Have just been writing letters to Uncle Arnold and to Uncle Rany, both being necessitated by a note from Papa this p.m. saying that U.A.'s telegram of acceptance (not yet sent when I last heard from him before he left) had indeed arrived, and that preparations were in order for his coming. He will stay with the Aranyis; I'd hoped he could stay at our house, but that really isn't practical so long as we aren't there to fix the place up a bit. I telephoned Mrs. Schoenberg right away, with the specific purpose of asking her what, if anything, she'd heard from the old man *en route*. He'd telegraphed her from Chicago that very day that he was all right; he'll arrive in N.Y. tomorrow morning. She told me that I really had better let him know about trains, etc. I lost no time in doing my duty!

November 18, 1940

Mr. Stein, Goldie and others had lots to say about the *Pierrot* broad-

---

[21]Roy Underwood was head of the Music Department at MSC.

The Arnold Schoenberg Institute, University of Southern California campus, Los Angeles

The Schoenberg children in their father's reconstructed studio at the Arnold Schoenberg Institute (l. to r., Larry, Nuria, Ronnie)

The opening concert audience, Arnold Schoenberg Institute, February, 1977

Dika Newlin, a recent photo

Marta Feuchtwanger, Herbert Zipper, and Rudolf Kolisch at opening concert, Arnold Schoenberg Institute, February, 1977

cast (which took place on November 17. Ironically, I had to miss it!) Everyone says that it was very fine indeed, better than that on the records in that the balance between voice and instruments was finer; and the flute passages were exceptionally well done. About the last five numbers were not broadcast out here, probably on account of a long and unexplained wait which took place between the Schubert octet and *Pierrot* . . .

November 19, 1940

Gave Mrs. Schoenberg a ring this morning to talk with her about the broadcast and other matters. She was as pleased with the success of the performance as everyone else was, and says that the latest letters she's received from dear Arnold express the liveliest pleasure at the way things went off. He's feeling fine, standing the cold better than she'd expected he would. "But that's just the trouble," she added; "when he thinks he's all right, that's when the trouble begins!" She's well enough, but of course dreadfully lonesome, though she has to admit that things are considerably more peaceful around the house these days!

November 20, 1940

Sunday's N.Y. Times article *re Pierrot* includes a perfectly horrible picture of Uncle Arnold. In fact, it makes him look like a very sad rabbi who'd been on a binge the night before—which he probably had!

> Schoenberg to Professor L.W. Allen and students of the Music Dept., UCLA, telegram, 7:09 p.m. November 21:
>
> I enjoyed your telegram the performance and my New York friends but most I will enjoy returning to my classes Greetings
>
> Schoenberg

November 22, 1940

A pretty elegant 17th birthday, this . . . Spent much of my birthday money at Schirmer's, Preeman Matthews', and such spots . . . For

75 cents at Schirmer's I bought the New Music publication of Uncle Arnold's Op. 33b, and for a dollar, the Schirmer collection of modern art-songs which contains Schoenberg's *Erhebung* . . . an exquisite thing . . . At Preeman's found something I'd been longing for, a score of The First Quartet for the price, reasonable considering its rarity, of $1.80. That's one purchase I didn't haggle over, believe me!

> Schoenberg to Claude Newlin, November 22: (addressed from Carl Engel's, 125 East 36th St., New York)

> Dear Professor Newlin:
> Thank you very much for your kind letter.

> To arrive at Lansing seems rather difficult. Unfortunately my ticket at present binds me to a train leaving at 9 AM in the morning, arriving at Detroit 9:30 PM, at Jackson 12:07 AM. There I should get a bus to Lansing.
> This is not very satisfactory and I consider taking a taxi at Detroit—or,—if there is, a bus. Would you advise against this? Is this too expensive?
> Probably I have also to take my whole luggage with me —another problem.

> I am glad, I will see you again, and I hope Mr. Aranyi, whom I telegraphed, will tell me the best way.
> Many hearty greetings.
> > Yours truly,
> > Arnold Schoenberg

November 24, 1940

Uncle Arnold supposedly arrived in Lansing this noon (12:30 or so, Lansing time). Trude called me early this morning to get Papa's address, for the old man had told her to wire him there today. She has not been too well—chiefly from worry about him—but told me she had received letters from him containing marvellous reviews of *Pierrot*, notably one by Downes.[22] She expects him back Thursday

---

[22]The review (*New York Times*, November 24, 1940) was especially enthusiastic about Schoenberg as conductor: " . . . he is one of the few composer-con-

morning on the Super-Chief; promises me he'll call me as soon as he gets home. But, thinks I, I'll beat him to it by meeting him at the train! Maybe I can even get her to take me . . .

Claude Newlin to Dorothy and Dika Newlin, November 25

Well, the Great Man got on the right train all right and is here . . . I was going down with Aranyi to get him. Well, Aranyi drove home from Chicago yesterday and got here so worn out that he couldn't make the trip to D. so *John Clark* [23] *and I went down last evening and got the old man.* We left here abt. 6:45 and got to the R.R. station at 9 and the train (due at 9:35) got in just before 10. S. was sure delighted to see somebody there at the station to meet him. He was in fine spirits and we really had a very nice ride home. Conversation went very easily . . . We stopped at Howell for a sandwich and glass of beer in one of the restaurants. S. asked for *whiskey*, but we explained that it couldn't be served on Sundays. He said he had some in his bag for use on the trip. We got him to Aranyi's house about 1 A.M. You should have heard A. greet him with an "Ah! MASTER!"

(I just got a telephone call from Underwood. He *asked me to introduce S.* at the lecture tonight and to come to the reception which he is holding for him afterwards).

The lecture is to be on "Melody and Theme." He sd. he gave it in N.Y. at Schirmer's and they want him to come back and give a lecture every year. He seems to have had a fine time in N.Y. . . .

S. is leaving here tomorrow to catch the Santa Fé "Super-Chief" which leaves Chicago at 7:15 in the evening. His train gets to Los Angeles at 9 A.M. Thursday.

He says D. is learning a lot. Seems to be *very well* satisfied with her work. Mrs. Aranyi sd. he had written to

---

ductors who are indispensable for the complete understanding of their music. If conductors of our great symphony orchestras have come no nearer Schoenberg's real intentions than they came at previous hearings in this city of *Pierrot lunaire*, then we have never heard the major Schoenberg scores." (For the complete review, see Irene Downes, ed., *Olin Downes on Music*, New York, Simon and Schuster, 1957, pp. 293-96.)

[23]John Abbot Clark, one of my father's colleagues in the English Department at MSC.

them about the excellence of her work. I asked him about
M.A. thesis and he sd. the work she is doing now—the
quartette or quintette or both could be her thesis! Sd.
also he would like to get a public performance of both of
them in L.A. (Don't tell him I told you this. He didn't
say keep it secret, but he may have meant it to be confi-
dential.)
     . . . Of course since we got home so late last night and
S. is leaving tomorrow and Underwood is giving reception
tonight after the lecture, there will be no chance for me
to do anything for him at the house. But it doesn't matter
since I had about 3 hours with him last night and am
going to introduce him and be at the reception tonight . . .

November 27. 1940

Wonderful, wonderful news about the East Lansing lecture, via
special delivery letter from Papa. It seems that it was a howling
success! About 200 people—as many, I think, as the music auditorium
will hold—were present. People had come from as far out of town as
Flint, Albion, Detroit and Ann Arbor to hear the speech; my old
counterpoint teacher, Otto Stahl from U. of M., was there. Of
course, not everyone understood the technical points that the old
man was trying to make, but they were fascinated and stimulated
by his words all the same. After the speech was over there was "prolonged and enthusiastic applause." Better yet, when Papa and Mr.
Underwood escorted him to the little artists' room across the hall
from the auditorium, he was simply mobbed by admirers and well-
wishers who wanted to say a few words to him or to see him close
to. Papa had to introduce most of them to him, as Underwood
hasn't been in E.L. long enough to know many people. Well, finally
they were able to tear him away from this group and take him to
the faculty room downstairs, where Underwood's little reception
for the music department in his honor was under way. It broke up
around eleven o'clock, so Papa bade his fond *adieux* to Schoenberg.
S. asked if there was any message for him to take back to us, and
Papa said yes, tell them that Tammy and I are fine! And so they
parted. The next morning, Aranyi drove him to Chicago; they started
off at nine in the morning, so I'm sure he caught his train all right.
And he'll be here at nine tomorrow morning! Just think of it!

November 28, 1940

Well, He is back! And I heard his voice over the telephone this noon with as cheerful and hearty a ring to it as I've heard there for a long, long time. He was full of good spirits (whether Haig & Haig or Black & White, I do not know); also, I suppose, he was much refreshed by having just taken a bath. (I had called up an hour earlier, only to be greeted by Nuria's flat statement, "Daddy Is In The Bathtub.") Everything, he said in response to my inquiries, had been nice, fine, wonderful and lovely. Papa had introduced his lecture in a "very nice way," and better yet, Papa "certainly is a very nice man—but I think he regrets that you are not there, no?" He said that everyone back in E.L. seemed to know me, and that he had told them "very many good things about me," "which also I probably should not have done. Don't worry—" this as I remained silent on the other end of the line—"this joke, yes?" We exchanged a few words about *Pierrot*, and then he fell to asking me how I'd been and what I'd done during his absence, not forgetting to add, "And you want now again to come to me, no?" "But yes, certainly!" "Well, we talk this over tomorrow, when I see you at school."

November 29, 1940

It's about 9:30 p.m. now, so I should write very briefly before going to bed. But how can I write briefly on the day of The Great Reunion? Yes, Uncle Arnold was at school this afternoon, all glowing with happiness. The minute I saw him, I rushed forward and grabbed his paw with a hearty "Welcome home! *So* glad you're back!" He was pretty glad to see me, too. Right there in the middle of the hall, in front of everyone, he announced that he brought me greetings of all kinds from home, and went on to say once more what a fine introductory speech Papa had made. "And he told this story that I am supposed to have said—" (here the tale of the six fingers required for the violin concerto, and the immortal answer, "I can wait")— "only, of course, he told it *much* better as I do!" Oh yes, and speaking of the violin concerto, it will be played by Krasner[24] with the Philadelphia Orchestra on the fifth of December. Maybe, *maybe* we'll be able to get the broadcast out here.

---

[24]Louis Krasner (1903-) gave the premières of the Berg and Schoenberg violin concertos. Berg's was written for him.

November 30, 1940

Had a very lovely lesson with Uncle Arnold this a.m., centering on the now-completed slow movement of my quintet. When I'd told him it was all finished he'd replied jocularly, "Well, now you will have the whole movement to rewrite!" But he was very well pleased with the work when I played it for him, and was impressed by the fact that I'd written certain especially good passages on my own. "This," he said, "is a progress!"

On returning home I found this screamingly funny letter from Helen Renwick;[25] its subject-matter, let alone the naive way in which it is told, is sufficient reason for keeping it. U.A., incidentally, told me about his and Aranyi's nightmare drive to Chicago. First it snowed, then the car broke down, then it rained and produced a silver thaw, then it snowed some more—and the four-hour trip took them seven and a half hours! Bet Mr. Aranyi got it in the neck!

Helen Renwick to Dika Newlin, November 27

... after the experience I have had I just can't keep still. That experience is that I have met your teacher Arnold Schoenberg. You know that I also live at Aranyi's and so of course since Mr. Schoenberg stayed with us I was so fortunate as to see a great deal of him. I count so far in my life three great experiences and this meeting is the fourth great experience. I am just in the clouds and I have been so excited I feel terribly sick. I was so afraid to meet Mr. Schoenberg because I didn't know what I could say to so great a man but when I met him I found it very easy to talk to him. He was so kind to us and so interested in everything. Imagine, he asked some questions about *my* studies—and who am I? I had a very funny meeting with him because early the first morning he was here, there was a telegram for him and the phone is in my room. Everyone was asleep and I jumped into my house-coat and ran upstairs and how I trembled at having to wake the Master early in the morning particularly since he had never seen me before. However he was already

---

[25] Renwick was a pupil of Aranyi's. I'd accompanied her in Bartók's *Rumanian Dances* at a MSC recital the previous summer.

awake but he just stared at me and didn't seem to understand but finally he did and went down to the phone. We were formally introduced at breakfast. But it was the farthest thought in my imagination that I should ever meet Schoenberg let alone see him for the first time in such an embarrassing way. This is to me the same as meeting Beethoven ... Some of them [the music students and faculty at MSC] were not the least impressed and they go on in their stupid self-satisfied way as though they are the top of the world. Of course you can't expect they are going to like Schoenberg's music because through no fault of theirs they don't have much chance to hear his music ... and they don't know what it's all about anyhow. I don't know any of his music either and I don't understand it but I know when I meet a man who is closer to God than any of us can hope to be and I am not indifferent to this ... His lecture was about melodies and themes—a chapter from the book he has been working on the last three years. It was very clear and easy to understand and it was illustrated with slides ... While he was here Mr. Schoenberg listened to a symphony and overture of Dr. Reed,[26] the theory teacher here, and to some compositions of a pupil of Mr. Krenek, who was his pupil. It seems he didn't like Mr. Erickson's[27] compositions very well. I believe they were full of mistakes and I know he said only to him that he used six tones too many. He had written his compositions with the twelve tone scale. He did not make much comment on Dr. Reed's compositions.

    ... I cannot forget Schoenberg, how he looked and talked and what an inspiration he is ... believe me that I have been deeply and tremendously impressed and overcome with the genius of your Maestro.

---

[26]Owen Reed (1910-), then an instructor at MSC, later chairman of the theory department; known for his theory textbooks and especially for his band music (*La Fiesta Mexicana* and others).

[27]Robert Erickson (1917-), presently on the faculty of the University of California at San Diego; author of *The Structure of Music* (New York, Noonday Press, 1955).

Schoenberg was *magnificent* today! I brought'him the completed
third movement of my quartet, half expecting it to be heaved out
the window. But, after Mr. Stein and I had achieved a rather rough-
and-ready interpretation of the work, what happened? Let the Great
Man's words speak for themselves. "This *very* good piece—how do
you like it? It is so full of spirit! And the string-quartet writing is
good—see, you have really learned something from this! Perhaps
there are few things which one might correct; but then, they are so
few, and when one is as far as you are, I would no longer want to
take the responsibility of your works away from you! Now see,
class, how she used the wonderful finesses I taught her—show here,
Miss Newlin, how you come back to the recapitulation in F minor
instead of A minor—this *fine*! And see how then she comes back to
the tonic—but little by little, not mechanically—this *fine*, really *fine*!
Now we must have this performed as soon as possible (here followed
a brief discussion on the assembling of a quartet)—and we can have
a performance at your *Sunday school* (this means the Composers'
Workshop)—and we can make the rehearsals at my house, so the
players will come to the rehearsals, yes?" By the time he'd finished,
I was about ready to fall on my knees and kiss his feet; for I've
never heard him praise the work of any of his students in such
unequivocal terms!

He talked a bit about *Pelleas*; said that he'd first planned it as an
opera, that a friend had tried to persuade him to do another play of
Maeterlinck's instead, and that he'd ended by doing the tone-poem
instead of either play. It was after hearing *Pelleas* that Strauss asked
him why he didn't write his own life in music; but this idea was not
new to him, for he'd already written his own life, at least in the
First Quartet (no! *Pelleas* came first!)—but probably in everything
he'd written up to the time of *Pelleas*. For how can you compose
without writing your own life? This was especially true in the
Romantic period when the composer was too much in the center of
his own work; and it was Schoenberg who first led away from that
trend, especially in the objective *Pierrot*. He does not feel insulted
at being called a romanticist, because after all Beethoven and Schubert were good romanticists too, but he wishes people would realize
that he isn't one any more.

December 4, 1940

Advanced composition was rather uneventful today, for Uncle Arnold came to class a half hour late, held up by some business or other; hence, there was not time for much to happen. He looked at C.'s new twelve-tone composition, and, surprisingly enough, accepted it in the main! also, analyzed the variation movement of his Septet a little. This was the first I knew that its theme is, believe it or not, an old folk-song. [28] Well, I don't think it would recognize itself in its elaborate Schoenbergian dress! In Structural Functions, he gave the students an assignment on sequences, to be written in class, so I had quite a bit of helping to do.

December 5, 1940

My lesson with U.A. went very smoothly. We worked over the part of the first movement of the quintet that I'd finished last year (about 188 measures). Mr. Carfagno dropped in about halfway through the lesson to pick up the first violin part of *Pelleas* (U.A. will conduct the studio orchestra in that work on Dec. 22), as well as to tell the old man that the Philadelphia broadcast would come from KHJ at 12:15 p.m. tomorrow. A phone call to the radio station informed us that the Violin Concerto will be the first composition broadcast. U.A. will have a portable radio in his office so that he can listen to it . . . I wish I could get back from my lessons in time to hear it with him, but I'll have to listen to it at Brodetzky's [29] instead. (I called up B. and he said I could.)

December 6, 1940

Uncle Arnold and all his friends had a bitter disappointment today. The violin concerto, in spite of all word to the contrary, was not

[28] *Ännchen von Tharau* by Friedrich Silcher (1789-1860).

[29] Julian Brodetzky, violinist and organizer of the Brodetzky Ensemble, which played chamber works in arrangements for full string orchestra. I was studying violin with him. See Leonard Wibberley's charming memoir *Ah, Julian!* (New York, Ives Washburn, 1963).

broadcast! The poor old man—he'd had a portable radio brought to his office, and Trude had come there at noon with a hamper of food and steaming hot coffee so that they could enjoy the première together. How low he must have felt! If he did, however, he showed no signs of it in advanced composition class. He didn't talk about the affair at all, and even when I privately expressed my condolences to him he said hardly a word. He got off one good joke at my expense, but it was a *gemütlich* one, not a mean one. He'd just asked me for the second time (apparently not having heard my first answer) what a certain passage in my introduction meant, and I replied, "Well, as I told you, it's—" a little abruptly, it may have been, for I'd had quite a tiff with Hilsberg in the morning and was really very much put out by that and by the falling-through of the violin concerto broadcast. "Ah," said he, bowing and smiling to me obsequiously, "excuse me for not knowing it! But then, perhaps, once I will read it in your biography!" The beauty of this remark is that he could really have half meant it!

A big article in the *Daily Bruin* referred to U.A. as "formerly connected with UCLA." Mr. Stein has written the paper a very clever "growl" in answer to this boner, and had the whole first year composition class sign it!

✐ *December 8, 1940*

Bridge party at Mrs. Seligmann's. Weiss brought with him a clipping from yesterday's *Hollywood Citizen* concerning the performance of the violin concerto. Apparently it was not too well received, at least by the critics and by a handful of old dowagers who saw fit to walk out. Weiss had talked to Schoenberg over the telephone this morning; S., though still burbling about his N.Y. success, seemed not too happy about this latest. A squib in the *L.A. Times* (repeated, in an abbreviated form, in the *Examiner*) says that Stoky rebuked the audience for their conduct. We wonder sometimes if he doesn't plant paid boo-ers around in the audience so's he'll have an excuse to make a speech!

✏ December 9, 1940

Uncle Arnold, so far from being downcast about the Philadelphia affair, as Weiss had implied he was, was really in topping good spirits about the whole thing. The front-page article on him (*sans* boners) in today's *Bruin* stated that he had received a telegram from Krasner congratulating him on the fine success of the work; and he confirmed this enthusiastically. After all, he said, it was only about 1% of the audience that walked out, and that was nothing compared to the 10% or 20% that used to fly off the handle in the "good old days!" As a matter of fact, it always used to worry him when the performance of a new work of his did not cause a scandal, for if everyone liked it he was afraid that there must be something superficial about it! Even in a city as musical as Vienna, he could never count on more than about 500 people who really liked and appreciated modern music. He says that one can count on about 800 in L.A., which is rather surprising considering how comparatively new our local music life is. As for what the critics say—well, they used to take dirty digs at him in Germany, too, and by some strange chance every time a critic wanted to say something especially malicious he would always make a stupid error in his article! For example, there was the sourpuss old lady in Vienna [30] who, about the time of his 50th birthday, wrote an article saying, "Schoenberg is not as much persecuted as one might think; as a matter of fact, he even had a little success at one time [this, to him, was the worst insult she could have concocted]; but the number of things he has written can be counted on the *12* fingers of his two hands!" (She must have been thinking about the 12-tone row!) This reminds me of the one who said that S. composes "with 12 tones instead of the usual 8." And then another joke, which loses some of its point in English, is concerned with the time when, by chance, the First Quartet, a group of songs, and the *Kammersymphonie* were all performed in

---

[30]Dr. Elsa Bienenfeld, who had taught music history as a colleague of Schoenberg's at the Schwarzwald School in Vienna. She was also a music critic for the *Neues Wiener Journal*.

Vienna within one month. This coincidence afforded a heaven-sent opportunity for one critic to vent his wrath. Wrote he, "If poor Hugo Wolf had only had such success, he would be alive now instead of having died in such misery and poverty. But, of course, in order to get performances these days, one must have a friend (Mahler, whom S. had known about a year) for director and a brother-in-law (Zemlinsky, at this time director of the *Volksoper*) for conductor!" The blunder here, which comes out much better in German, is that the indignant critic should have said, "a director as a friend and a conductor as brother-in-law." In this connection, I was interested to learn how S. had met Mahler for the first time: Mahler just wandered in on a rehearsal of *Verklärte Nacht* one day, completely unannounced and a stranger to Schoenberg. And thus it was that a friendship so fruitful to both began.

S. thinks the Second Chamber Symphony will be a great success —but he can't always tell. He made similar statements about the First Chamber Symphony and the Second String Quartet, and they were among the greatest scandals of his career!

December 11, 1940

U.A. a little peevish today. It was probably my fault. While practising in the morning I'd conceived a brilliant idea that Mr. Stein and I might give an impromptu performance of the 4-hand arrangement of *Pelleas* on Friday afternoon at 3, especially for those who might be going to hear it for the first time on the 22nd. I'd called U.A. to ask him if he'd let us have the music today for that purpose. Well, he would. As a matter of fact, he brought it to school, and we practised it together at home afterwards; the first reading went very well, too. But you could see he wasn't really enthusiastic about the idea. Though he didn't say anything, he showed his state of mind pretty clearly by subjecting me to quite a nice little blitzkrieg in composition class (*re* my Rondo). It's my theory that he was annoyed at my telephone call asking him for what he considered an unessential favor . . .

His comments on teaching the method of 12-tone composition— brought about by C.'s attempts to write a theme and variations using that method—were most enlightening. He says that he can't teach 12-tone writing at all. Of course, he can write that way, but he does it instinctively and not theoretically, and could not help himself if he made a mistake, let alone helping someone else. One should not attempt to write in this way unless one is at the peak of one's technique and is perfectly sure of being right the first time—and, in that case, why study with anyone at all? To all this, C. queried, "You mean there can't be any bad compositions in the 12-tone scale? And, Mr. Schoenberg, if you knew all this before, why did you have me simplify this piece last time instead of telling me right away I couldn't use it?" Schoenberg: "Well, I hoped I could help you, but now I see I cannot." S. says further that as far as teaching "fundamental harmony" as used by Brahms, Strauss and himself in his earlier period goes, he is unsurpassed. "This is not an arrogance of mine, this is fact"—especially as he has the rare good fortune of being the only living composer whose formative years were in Brahms's time and who is now a true modernist. I was glad indeed to hear him give this view of himself.

December 12, 1940

As I'd feared, half my lesson with Uncle Arnold was taken up with his demonstrations on the new Novachord[31] which he has on trial until Sunday. He doesn't like the instrument (for which who can blame him?), but that doesn't prevent him from playing on it, in all possible combinations of tone-colors and degrees of dynamics, until he drives poor Trude almost crazy! How glad she is that they're taking it away on Sunday! However, she suffers enough from his noise-making even when he's deprived of his Novachord; says that he likes to turn the radio on as loud as it will go in the evening, and then go to sleep in his chair, soothed by these horrible sounds!

December 13, 1940

Oh joy—Uncle Arnold invited me "und muzzer" to come and hear the *Kammersymphonie* broadcast on Sunday! Mr. Stein will have his car, so he can drive us over ... I had nothing to show the old man this time; alibied myself by saying that "unfortunately" I had

---

[31]A type of small electric organ which was being popularized for home use at this time.

forgotten to bring it. He replied, "Well, perhaps it was fortunate— this I could not say!" Stein and I played *Pelleas* after he left, for a small but quite appreciative audience. I'd brought my orchestral score so some listeners might look on during the performance.

Quite a spread on The Violin Concerto in *Time* today.[32] Horrible picture of the dear man!

✒ December 15, 1940

Laid up with a fever of 102° tonight—but didn't collapse soon enough to keep me from enjoying the thrill of hearing the *Kammersymphonie* broadcast with Uncle Arnold. I was sitting next to him, by his special request, and looking on the manuscript with him, so if my illness is contagious it will be just too bad! There was a fairly good-sized little gathering present—Stein, Estep and Meltzer, with a friend of theirs, Mr. Shriver;[33] Mr. Allen, Dr. Rubsamen, and Lotte. Nuria and Ronnie were out of the room during the broadcast, but came in later to help serve the refreshments: many kinds of rich canapés and pastries, coffee with whipped cream, and, later, rum with lime juice . . . The old man's reaction to the performance was very favorable. Though he found the first movement a little slow and stiff, he thought that the interpretation was in general good and that certain moods of the second movement were particularly well presented . . .

✒ December 20, 1940

Attended the Los Angeles Philharmonic directed by Bruno Walter.

---

[32]*Time*, December 16, 1940, pp. 53-54. The description of the composer was as unflattering as the photograph: "For 30 years, bald, parchment-faced . . . Composer Arnold Schönberg has written music so complicated that only he and a couple of other fellows understand what it is all about."

Time was equally snide a year later concerning Schoenberg's conducting of the "Rehearsal Symphony" (see Dec. 22 entry below). "The Symphony invites conductors, well and little known, to preside over its sessions. José Iturbi, Igor Stravinsky, Georg Szell, Arnold Schönberg were glad of the chance. . . . Favorite conductor so far has been Bruno Walter . . ." *Time*, December 29, 1941, p. 46.

[33]Henry Clay Shriver, who studied with Schoenberg for a while and commissioned a string quartet (never finished) from him. The Piano Concerto, Op. 42, is dedicated to him.

Of course the big (literally big, in all dimensions) feature of the program was the Mahler First, and how magnificent it was! I was deeply, deeply impressed by it—have heard it several times before, but was never so moved as this time. The performance, too, was fine. Audience gave Walter a terrific ovation, which he certainly deserved.

December 22, 1940

To Hollywood High School to hear Schoenberg conduct the studio rehearsal orchestra in *Pelleas*. It went very well; U.A. was in excellent humor, and the orchestra played wonderfully for a first reading —and the music was wonderful! U.A. was so pleased with the results that he wants to direct the orchestra again some time in January. I know they'll be glad to have him; all that I spoke to thought that he was a fine conductor.

December 24, 1940

Had planned to take the children's presents (a sailboat for Ronnie and a blue necklace for Nuria) over to Schoenberg's today . . . but when I phoned Trude told me he would be so busy throughout the day that he wouldn't be able to have me come even for a little while. So I agreed that I would bring the gifts a day late, when I went for my lesson on Thursday; and, in the meantime, remembered the rest of the family with the gift of a potted cyclamen sent up from Naomi's. I was sorry not to have been able to talk to Uncle Arnold himself over the phone, but he was in the shower-bath (of all places!) when I called, and couldn't possibly come to the phone.

December 26, 1940

Had my lesson with Uncle Arnold this morning; took Papa with me. U.A. seemed in quite good humor, though of course pretty tired. He was very glad to receive the children's presents, and also thanked me very sweetly for the flowers. After all the above sweetness and light, it seems almost a shame to have to record that he finally and definitively pitched out *Gottesferne*, and made me change *Allelujah* in one place so that the music would sound more like (I quote the text) transparent disc-like bodies. My God! "Mr. Werfel," says he, "is ver' sensitive 'bout these things. He would not like it if the music did not sound like transparent bodies!" . . . He is very much offended, now, because more of his students did not come to hear him conduct *Pelleas*; says he will never again tell them of his performances . . .

December 29, 1940

This noon we heard most of Zemlinsky's *Symphonietta* on the [N.Y.] Philharmonic concert. It seems a very fine work; solid, spirited, and often quite Schoenbergian. One sees where S. learned some of his cute tricks, all right! I'd gladly hear it again, but probably never will.

January 6, 1941

This first day of school got off to a quaint start with U.A.'s declaration that from now on he wants to analyze in class instead of looking at our pieces. "I cannot write your compositions for you three hours a week," fulminated he, "and if I must write for you I had better do it at home without your beer notes!"

January 8, 1941

Uncle Arnold lived up to his promise to analyze in class today. He stuck mostly to the elaboration of the *Eroica*, and especially to that so-called "false entrance" of the horn,[34] which, he claims, is a simple slip of the pen. Beethoven should have written "Bb Horn" over the passage, which would make things right with everybody.

---

[34]Schoenberg believed that the horn's famous entrance in E flat just before the recapitulation of the first movement was a mistake—it should have been in B flat!

Maybe. As he's finished writing the Research Lecture, I can have my lesson tomorrow morning. I asked him about Werfel and he said the *two* Werfels had visited them yesterday, so I guess that's all right. I give myself credit for bringing them together, for wasn't it I who told Mr. Krakowski[35] that S. had better hear from W. or else?

January 12, 1941

N.Y. Philharmonic played my dearest favorite of the moment, the Mahler First. You should have heard that audience *rave*! There was an even bigger demonstration than here; they clapped and yelled and stomped and shouted until I was quite beside myself with surprise and pleasure! Mahler, like Schoenberg, suddenly seems to be coming into his own . . .

January 13, 1941

Introduced Hope [the singer of my Werfel songs] to Uncle Arnold. He seemed extremely pleased to meet her, and even wanted to have her sing the songs then and there, but she had to leave too soon for that. I asked him again about Wednesday night; he still couldn't make any promises for sure, but wants me to remind him again on that day—so there is still hope. The baby, by the way, has not yet arrived.

January 15, 1941

Well, the Werfel affair went off all right, and was a great personal triumph for me . . . the two songs were a great success with the audience—as, indeed, with such a good performance, there was no reason why they should not have been. But then, when I plunked myself in front of Werfel with my prettily bound red-and-white booklet in my hand (the red matched the color of my dress) and shot off my "Es würde mir die grösste Freude machen, wenn diese

[35]Meyer Krakowski, who had arranged the Werfel celebration.

kleinen Lieder, die ich Ihnen nun präsentiere, nur ein bischen würdig Ihrer Dichtungen, die mir eine solche Anregung gaben, wären",[36] meanwhile shoving the book at him—well, that was the high point of the evening! I think he was touched by my presentation, and I *know* he liked the songs, for he told me so at the reception afterwards in no uncertain terms. He said he thought they showed a real temperament and understanding of the verse, and, best of all, laid his hand on his heart in a sincere gesture with the exclamation "I feeled it *here!*"—than which I can imagine no greater compliment from a poet as sensitive to music as he seems to be. I was really quite delighted with him. and with his wife, too (the former Frau Mahler, you know, and a woman with quite a history behind her). She's very different from what you might expect to see; quite excessively plump, with frizzly hair whose blondness seems to owe quite a bit to the beauty-shop. In fact, when she first came into the concert-room to sit down beside me, I thought, "Why, she looks like an ex-Follies queen!" But a few minutes of conversation with her utterly destroyed that impression; she is a charming person, and must have been lovely to look at in earlier years. I think they are leaving L.A. in a few days, which is a pity, as I should love to see them again and get to know them a little better.

Schoenberg didn't come, after all—which is probably just as well. He felt he couldn't leave Trude. I bet she felt differently!

January 17, 1941

Schoenberg owned up to feeling chipper. No baby yet. He says Trude expects it in eight days. Well, I should hope so! He has an amusing characterization of the Funeral March in the Mahler First; says it represents a "moral hangover," which I think quite an apt little phrase. He thought that last Sunday's performance of the symphony was an excellent one, except for certain too-great variations in the tempo.

[36]"It would give me the greatest pleasure if these little songs that I am now presenting to you were even slightly worthy of your poems which brought me such inspiration."

✍ *January 18, 1941*

The chief feature of the NBC program tonight was *Verklärte Nacht* beautifully played and preceded by a lovely intermission-talk entirely devoted to The Master himself. There was just one thing wrong with it, and that was the glowing account of how he was at present teaching at *USC*! Gr-r-r! I hope he heard it all; had thought of telephoning him to let him know of the performance if he didn't already, but decided it might annoy him.

✍ *January 22, 1941*

Telephoned Uncle Arnold this morning to ask if he still wanted me to come and help with the examinations tomorrow (he does) and also to inquire about Trude. As a matter of fact, I spoke to her as well; she's not so good, she says, but hopes that it will be all over soon. Well, I should think it might! The old man, it turned out, was quite well pleased with Saturday night's performance of *VN* . . . He seemed to be in a good humor and to be feeling pretty well (hope this lasts).

✍ *January 23, 1941*

Spent most of the day over at school with Uncle Arnold, helping with the first year composition examination. About the *Harmonie-lehre*, he says he hasn't heard a thing from Slonimsky since the first (and last!) 50 pages, so that job may still fall into my hands. But, whether it does or not, he has something more immediate for me to do, and that is the translation of all the lyrics of his early *Lieder*. We didn't get to talk very long about this, there being plenty of other business to attend to, but my understanding is that we are to work on it during the vacation. It shouldn't be hard work at all, and, as he will have to lend me the songs (I don't have any of the early ones except *Erhebung*), it will afford me a good excuse to renew my acquaintance with them. Of course, I am very happy that he has favored me with another such honor. Wonder if hearing about the great success of my songs with Werfel had anything to do with it?

Still no baby, and frankly I am getting a bit worried. When I left the old man in front of my door (Stein had to drive him home anyway so dropped me off on the way) I told him to give my best love and sympathy to T.—as though that would help her much! I reminded him that he wanted me to come on Saturday and he said yes, but not to come without telephoning as "they might not be at home." So maybe that will be *DER TAG!*

January 25, 1941

This was not *Der Tag,* or anything like it. In fact, things are going from bad to worse in the dear old loony bin, for Nuria and Ronnie have chosen this inauspicious time to catch colds. Ronnie came downstairs once while I was there, looking pretty and rosy-cheeked as usual, but his little voice sounded very miserable indeed! Thank goodness, the old man was in a good humor in spite of all his woes. He found some further changes to make in the last movement of the string quartet, but they were made in the spirit of wanting my work to be as good as possible, and not in the spirit of "ma*lee*ces." So I left him very happy, but believe me, tonight I am going to offer up prayers on poor Trude's behalf. I hope and pray that nothing happens to her or to the baby.

January 29, 1941

Oh, the biggest and most wonderful news today: Uncle Arnold's baby (a boy, as we'd hoped for) came on Monday night about ten o'clock, and is doing just fine, as is Trude. The old man was just radiant all over; before I left for my French exam at three o'clock he had to stop me and tell me, "Now be sure and tell your mother we got a boy, yes?" I'm so happy that it's all over with and that all is well. Of course, when I'm out there tomorrow I'll have more time to make inquiries; he was so occupied with his other students (examinations in 3 classes!) this afternoon that I really didn't have much time to talk with him about it. Well, I won't go near the place tomorrow without a present for the dear baby. Mamma is taking a box of linen-bound storybooks for Ronnie (consolation prize?). Now that my vacation is here, I hope that Mamma and I can go and visit Trude in the hospital.

January 30, 1941

Out to Uncle Arnold's today, equipped with a storybook for Ronnie and a prettily wrapped present for baby, and had the unexpected surprise of seeing both baby and Trude at home and in the best of trim! Baby, it seems, had arrived so quickly on Monday night, within an hour after T. felt her first pains, that there had been no time to reach a hospital, so the delivery had taken place at home under a doctor's care and with the greatest of ease. T. was delighted with my present, a blue and white checked oilcloth elephant; of course, baby wasn't old enough to be delighted yet! He is really awfully pretty for a babe that age; the spittin' image of his father, believe it or not, "beak" and all! He is going to be named after his father and his birthplace: Arnold Brentwood. And, if you can imagine it, the only reason they hadn't definitely decided on a name and sent out their announcements yet was because they wanted to consult us! They were afraid the name might be too pompous or "princely-sounding," but I was quick to assure them that it was beautiful, and that furthermore there was no reason why a child with such princely heritage should not have a princely name indeed! Of course they were immensely tickled by that, and the old man was even more thrilled when I told him that I knew A.B. was going to look just like him. He did say that it might be better if it looked like Trude, but there wasn't a bit of conviction in his tone. My, what a flood of congratulations they've been receiving from friends! The parlor was fairly crammed with flowers, everywhere they could be put, and Josephine, the maid, said that the telephone had literally been ringing every five minutes yesterday! Josephine also confided that if only the children didn't have their vacation now, and Mamma Kolisch weren't on the premises, everything would be just ducky!

February 5, 1941

Had a consultation with Dean Knudsen and learned to my annoyance that my string quartet will not be accepted as a master's thesis. I must write a dissertation. What, oh what will Uncle Arnold say to this? Bet he'll burn up!

February 6, 1941

Had the most wonderful extra-long lesson from Uncle Arnold this morning. Mamma, cynically enough, says he kept me longer than usual so that he might have more of a respite from family troubles; for the children are a bit irritable these days, and that crazy maid, Josephine, is inclined to be quarrelsome. Both Trude and the baby are well, however; in fact, she's already been up and around several times, though she was in bed when we brought her the holly, which she and Arnie appreciated very much. Baby looks fine, except for a little puffiness about the eyes, which is probably quite insignificant. But what have they done to him? They've changed his name—without consulting me—to Lawrence Adam! I didn't know this when I was with them in the morning; but in the afternoon the following very quaint announcement, bearing all the earmarks of having been composed by The Master himself, arrived in the mail, "January 27, 1941, at 10:02 p.m., a son has been born to the very happy Arnold Schoenberg family. We will call him Lawrence Adam." . . .

U.A. wasn't one bit annoyed by my announcement of Dean Knudsen's dictum. Frankly, he says, he doesn't think the degree should be awarded for a composition, because if a composer is really a composer, he has to compose, degree or no degree; so he should be made to do something extra—that is, the dissertation—for a degree, instead of doing what he would have to do anyway. So now he will help me select a subject for a dissertation . . .

February 12, 1941

Uncle Arnold talked about the master's theses in composition class this afternoon. I suggested to him my idea of tracing his string quartet style through his four quartets, but he thought that too difficult, large, and vague a subject, as no doubt it is. He wants us to take very limited, technical questions and really do them up brown, which is quite sensible.

I spoke to him about having the Op. 6 from the L.A. Public Library and he said all right, go ahead and translate them; so I did tentative translations of five of them tonight. Most of them aren't too difficult to fit to the music, but I had a bit of trouble with *Alles*. My favorites are *Traumleben* and *Ghasel*, with which I'm most familiar.

🌿 *February 13, 1941*

Found out quite a few interesting things at my lesson with U.A. this morning, besides that the quartet-finale needs some more retouching and that I can or should start on the Serenade now. For one thing, Arlt called up while I was there, to find out what's being done about *Harmonielehre*. When the old man told him that Slonimsky was out, Arlt promptly offered to do the job himself, even though U.A. had already named Schreiner, McManus, and me. U.A. found this idea very pleasing; he wants me to go and talk to Arlt and offer to help him with the work. He'll send Mr. Stein to A. tomorrow with the book; I'm to leave a note in his University mailbox this afternoon reminding him so to do, as I can't be there myself tomorrow on account of having a free ticket to Stravinsky's concert. (I had to break it to him that I wouldn't be with him, but told him that Hilsberg had put my lesson later, for that one day. I didn't dare mention Stravinsky.)

Trude is up now, looking terrible. What do you suppose she had to say about not naming the baby Arnold? It seems an *astrologer* friend of theirs[37] told them that Arnold would be a horribly unlucky name, and that Brentwood would be terrible because it had a B in it! So they named him Lawrence because they'd half thought of doing so already; and, as for Adam, it was the first name in the dictionary, and numerologically all right, so why go further? Maybe this dependence on astrology explains some of the old man's other queer actions!

The old man and I decided on a thesis subject: The Problem of the Key-Relationship in the Recapitulation of the Classic Sonata Form. Sounds like good stuff? I'll start right in on it.

🌿 *February 14, 1941*

Lord, how the rain did pour today! I suppose it was God's revenge on me for cutting Uncle Arnold's class to go and hear Stravinsky!

[37]Charlotte Dieterle, wife of the film director William Dieterle. Both were ardent believers in astrology.

... the pianist extracted as much from the rattly old Capriccio as could be extracted from it. I didn't like it, or the *Jeux de Cartes* (most of which I was hearing for the first time), or the Symphony (except just the very end), which leaves the *Fire-Bird* and the intermission as the two best parts of the program. Stravinsky didn't "yoomp around" quite as much as in rehearsals, but he did to a certain extent. He's cute to watch, but I'd never call him a first-rate conductor.

February 17, 1941

Uncle Arnold in good trim today. Stein and I played the Brahms Piano Quartets in G minor and A major, and the Piano Trio in C major, in class. I got to take the piano part, at the old man's special request; but I had to play it on the bad piano, which is always rather sad. His most notable statement of the day was a diatribe against the use of opus numbers instead of keys in the indexing of the Longmans chamber music volumes; a point of view which made me very happy, for I have never been able to remember opus numbers and have never seen why I should!

February 19, 1941

Uncle Arnold sprouted a horrendous new idea today: he wants us all, besides our theses and our compositions, to make arrangements of something! I spoke for a two-piano arrangement of the wind quintet, an idea which he heartily approved. Sure, it's an interesting work, and I'd love to do it any other time, but now? When I'm working 14 or 15 hours a day already? No, thanks! (He wants it in 3 weeks.)

Finished translating the *Acht Lieder* tonight.

February 20, 1941

My little talk with "Arnelie" this a.m. as to whether or not I should make the arrangement at once did no good at all, and even did some harm. Now, instead of my original idea, he wants me to get hold of a Handel concerto grosso or other such work in which the *basso continuo* isn't carried out. Dr. Rubsamen says the only place you can get such a thing is in the Clark Library, and it would have to be used there. But my feeble protests only made the old man go into a horrific emotional scene about how I should believe in what he wanted of me, and why do I study with him if I do not believe in him, etc. etc., till I had fairly to throw myself at his feet and protest that he knew I believed in him wholeheartedly, etc. etc. He didn't stay mad at me, thank goodness, and in fact was quite nice aside from his stubbornness on this one point. Trude seems quite herself again and is looking as well as she ever does. (He, by the way, finally wrote my Univ. scholarship letter for me.)

February 21, 1941

U.A. has "changed his spots" again about the arranging business. As everyone with the *basso continuo* assignment was in the same boat as I, about not being able to get to the Clark, he decided to let us use some C.P.E. Bach Sinfonias, etc. (Nagel ed.) which are here in the music library; the b.c. is carried out in them, but very badly. We can't get the music till Monday, now, because it seems he's supposed to sign out for it, and he forgot to do it before leaving today. But, once we get it, we ought to be able to do it in a week—an uninterrupted week, that is.

Hal told me of a terribly funny incident in the counterpoint class. The old man suddenly saw a chair with a loose seat standing in the corner, took a wham at it with both fists in order to mend it, and sent it flying in a half-dozen pieces all over the room and got a splinter in his finger! He screamed and yelled bloody murder, made the most terrifying faces, pleaded for somebody to open his finger with a needle, and pulled on it till the blood came. I guess he must have finally got it fixed all right, for there wasn't a mark on his hand when I saw him. Later in the class, his easel fell on him, so he must have had a thoroughly unnerving two hours!

February 22, 1941

Fine reception for the Werfels at Krakowski's. I thoroughly enjoyed my conversation with them. They are really first-rate . . . and now that they are going to stay in L.A. I hope to see them more often. I guess they've been visiting off and on a good bit with the Schoenbergs. Alma, in particular, said they'd seen them only a few days before. She's quite taken with the baby; says it's pretty in spite of looking like its papa. I had quite a long talk with her about him as a young man (she says he looked just as now), and about Zemlinsky, who was her teacher too, and about the late lamented Gustav Mahler, of whom she spoke quite freely. After lunch, "Franzl" (her pet name for Werfel) responded to ever so many requests by reading several of his poems in German . . . He did *Der Mensch ist stumm* and several others . . . such wonderful reading I've never heard in my life. Even if one did not understand a word of German one could not help feeling the beauty and force of it. As I told him very sincerely, after hearing those poems read in that way I couldn't help wanting to go home and set every one of them to music . . .

February 24, 1941

Uncle Arnold wasn't as annoyed as he might have been at our not being able to have our music for orchestration over the weekend. When I told him the tale of woe, he scratched his newly-cropped head sadly and muttered, "Is this sabotage?" He devoted the whole hour to looking at my sketches for the Serenade, and was surprisingly undestructive. Of course, some things were wrong: the march is not march-like enough in character, the harmonies of the Gavotte are a little *affektiert*, the appearance of an unaccompanied theme at the beginning of the Scherzo suggests that I might not have had an idea for accompaniment, the Gigue looks too much like a second-rate fugato, etc. But his criticisms weren't the devastating kind at all.

He liked the Portnoff concerto[38] pretty well; he should, because,

[38]The Piano Concerto of Mischa Portnoff (1901-) had been broadcast by the New York Philharmonic the day before. Titles of some of his other works (*Brief Flirtation, From Temple to Tepee, Lodge Fire Tales*) do not bespeak the Schoenberg pupil, nor does his ASCAP biography credit him with such study. Cf. *The ASCAP Biographical Dictionary of Composers, Authors and Publishers* (New York, 1966), p. 578.

according to the radio announcer at least, P. studied with him for a while. He found it too long and too repetitious, but liked the independence of the orchestral voices and of the piano part.

February 26, 1941

Uncle Arnold looked at my 9 pages of orchestration of the K.P.E. Bach (3rd Sinfonia) and didn't rip it to pieces. His chief criticism was that my orchestration was a little too old-fashioned, and too thick sometimes on account of too many doublings. He thought, too, that some of it was rather superficial in its transcription; attributed this to my having done it a bit too fast, which I'd done only because I thought he was in a hurry to see results! But he wasn't a bit nasty; in fact, he seemed in quite good humor today. Alas, I won't be able to come to him tomorrow, for he's very busy studying for his citizenship exam. I'll go out on Saturday, though. I offered him the translation of the *Acht Lieder*, but he told me to bring it on Saturday instead, as he might otherwise mislay it.

He was telling the Structural Functions people about his wonderful idea for notating *arco* and *pizz*. He thinks the former should be represented by the symbol of a bow, and the latter by that of a hand with extended thumb. Really, he ought to put out a kiddies' edition of the violin concerto with all those cute little pictures in it!

February 28, 1941

Uncle Arnold was in top form. He spent the class time discussing problems of orchestration, especially that of the relative weights of the instrumental groups and the importance of a *pianissimo* in every orchestral instrument. In connection with this, the following tale: in 1902, Strauss invited the then-young Arnold to a Wagner performance under his direction in Berlin. Afterwards, the two were talking about it, and Strauss remarked that in Wagner it was so difficult for the singers to make themselves heard—whereto our fresh young squirt replied, "Oh, maybe; but when Mahler conducts Wagner, I never have any difficulty hearing the singers!" "Well," commented the sixty-six-year-old on this youthful *boutade* of nearly 40 years ago, "I was young then, and perhaps I was a little rough!"

Mr. Carfagno says that *Pierrot* has been released for 2 weeks but U.A. doesn't know anything about it. Hope C.'s right!

March 1, 1941

My lesson with Arnelie this morning was about as private as if I'd had it in Grand Central Station, what with a.young typist in one corner of the front room typing away on the mailing list for his lecture, and receiving his friendly attentions every 5 minutes; Mamma and Ronnie acting out *Little Red Riding Hood* in the next room (Ronnie was doing a good job as the Wolf, too!); the telephone ringing every now and then; a sewing-machine serviceman popping in at a most inopportune time; Trude and Nuria returning from school and requiring some more of the old man's attention; and the Strangs dropping in for a friendly visit! I got my lesson, all right, but it was spaced out over about twice the usual time; I left home at 10 and didn't get back till 2!

March 3, 1941

Mr. Stein broke a record today by bringing one measure of orchestration. Uncle Arnold had to spend nearly the whole hour explaining what was wrong with it! S. had the melody scored for 2 flutes, and the thickest possible kind of accompaniment underneath, marked *forte*. U.A. wrote 12 *p*'s over it and crossed out all the notes, remarking, "Even if they played only the 'pianos' and not the notes, it would still be too loud!" Mr. Stein: "Well, ah, but what should I do then?" Uncle Arnold: "Something else!" Later on, talking about transposition of the horns, he said that he regrets very much having used E and Eb horns in *Pelleas*. It was due, it seems, to a Straussian influence which he's long since outgrown.

March 4, 1941

Got a surprise from Rubsamen today when he blithely told me that on Monday afternoon the music department had assembled in conclave and (apparently at the inspiration and suggestion of Uncle Arnold) had decided that, in addition to the thesis, a comprehensive oral examination will be required of each candidate for the M.A. Ouch! . . . I guess if it was Uncle Arnold's idea he must have some good reasons for it, and I shall cheerfully submit to his will.

March 5, 1941

Uncle Arnold comes a-breezing into advanced composition this afternoon, his face fairly glowing with malice, and burbles, "Oh, I just found out that all of you will have to take oral examinations for your degrees!" Such duplicity, tut tut! He devoted most of the hour to attacking, and quite rightly, the proportions between the instruments which Rimsky establishes in his orchestration treatise. So wrong are these proportions that you wonder however it happens that R. and his pupils are such super-orchestrators!

This tale is a little long, but it's so funny, and so typical of the old man in his best vein of humor, that I think it worth recording. Hal, writing a sequence on the board in Structural Functions, was suddenly interrupted by U.A. making a very strange request of Mr. Stein: namely, that he should go to the office and fetch a certain old yellow pencil which could be found in such-and-such a place. Indicating the pencil he was holding, he remarked, "This one too good!" I didn't understand his meaning, but still less explicable was his subsequent conduct: having received the required yellow pencil from Mr. Stein, he took his pocket-knife out, sharpened the pencil to a fine point, and then deliberately broke it against the side of the piano! "Now," he asked the class, "what was unintelligent in this?" We concurred that the unintelligent thing was to take so much trouble to sharpen the pencil, only to break it. Well! and after all this had been laboriously found out, what was the point of the demonstration? To show that Hal had notated wrongly, in a certain measure, C double sharp before C sharp! Paradoxically enough, after all this rigmarole—in which were included many other amusing details which I haven't time to transcribe—he asked no less than three times if he had offended anybody!

🖋 *March 6, 1941*

At my lesson, U.A. gave me some more gory details about the pro-jected exams; made it very clear that they were all his idea, and con-fessed that it is his desire to make it as hard to get a degree from him as possible; all of which I received with a devout "Yes, Master," "How wonderful!" or "How right you are!" For the rest, he looked again at the first movement of the quintet, which is *almost* right now. As he was through with me before bus-time, he let me stay and play the records of his Septet (with the score) . . .

🖋 *March 7, 1941*

U.A. spent class time analyzing Brahms' G major sextet and C minor quartet, with Mr. Stein and me "at the concert Baldwins." Now, by the way, he no longer thinks our orchestration is important!

🖋 *March 9, 1941*

N.Y. Philharmonic intermission today included Deems Taylor's "prevue" of Uncle Arnold's lecture, which I thought was a very good job of "prevuing" indeed: eminently fair and unbiased and perfectly understandable. He called the old man "Doctor" all the way through, which should please him much. You should have heard the suppressed "maleece" in U.A.'s letter to Taylor! and I think T. got the point, being a pretty shrewd fellow.

🖋 *March 10, 1941*

Uncle Arnold looked at my orchestration this afternoon; had many suggestions, but no basic criticisms, except of certain superficialities of K.P.E. Bach, of whom he said succinctly, "For this his father would have spanked him—and he would have deserved it!" But, of course, I'm not held responsible for K.P.E.'s mistakes! Mr. Stein tells me that the old man was tickled to death with Taylor's speech yesterday. After it was over, he bowed to the radio and said "Thank you!", and even sent a congratulatory telegram.

Uncle Arnold set a new record by being *40* minutes late in coming to his dear Composers; but apparently there was some good reason, for he and Mr. Stein were muttering darkly about some blueprinting job which he wanted done and the department was afraid to pay for, or something—I don't know just what. But nevertheless, he was in a good humor among us (though professing himself "disgusted" with the blueprint episode); especially was he gay and sparkling during Structural Functions. You should have seen him practically in stitches, and as red as a beet, when Mr. Stein and I were slogging away at the final movement of the Brahms C minor String Quartet in that class. At the end, though, he applauded—so did the whole class!—and commented that of course it was very difficult for two people to play on one piano from such a tiny score, and that the music was difficult anyway, and that really we'd done a good job! In Structural Functions, he took up a good bit of time trying to figure out some kind of mechanical, visual device by which modulations in elaboration sections could be charted according to the scheme of the related keys. His notions ranged from a complicated machine with slots in which wooden letters and numbers might be placed, through a central square of cardboard trimmed with overlapping pieces of transparent paper, to a system of graphs "on this little paper with the boxes." And if anyone has some more practical ideas on the subject, they're to be brought to him the next time. Shades of the progressivists' "visual education!" He admits that the whole thing will be something of a game. [39]

Because of a routine school physical exam, was 10 minutes late for Uncle Arnold. He wasn't mad, though; in fact, he didn't even ask me what had been the matter, so I guess he knew I had a good reason. He spent the time correcting Jane's arrangement for two pianos of the Menuet from his String Suite. In connection with it,

---

[39]The "charts of the regions" in *Structural Functions of Harmony* (pp. 20 and 30) grew out of this.

he kept bringing up the point, which I thought well taken, that such arrangements should always have the character of original compositions for two pianos, and never of reductions. The poor man had hurt his hand in some way . . . and had it bandaged in the most amazing fashion, with a small piece of dirty-looking cotton fastened down by two pieces of Scotch cellophane tape that had apparently been used once for something else and torn off as a makeshift bandage. Whoever was nursing him this time sure did a funny job of it!

March 21, 1941

Schoenberg didn't seem angry with me for my AWOL departure to Palm Springs . . . He continued looking at my orchestration of the K.P.E. Bach, and, of course, found many finesses to add. Incidentally, we discovered one place in the original that sounds terribly like *Chopsticks* . . . [40]

March 22, 1941

Went out to Uncle Arnold's bright and early this morning for my postponed lesson. It had to be early, for Mr. Stein was supposed to come out later in the morning to put some last-minute touches on The Lecture. He came, but I didn't stick around to see what touches were put on. Alas, the coda of the first movement of the quintet is still not perfect! Now if it's wrong next time I'll be very angry with myself! He analyzed the codas of the first movements of all his quartets, for my benefit: something that, to his knowledge, he hadn't done before.

[40]Music example (mm. 24-27) not in diary. The symphony, one of a group of six which C.P.E. published in 1773, is in *Nagels Musik-Archiv* No. 73 (ed. Ernst Fritz Schmid).

🖎 *March 23, 1941*

Hope came out this afternoon to rehearse the *Kindertotenlieder*. Oh, what a wonderful time we had with them! They are of the most exquisite beauty . . . Really, I grow fonder of Mahler ever day, and do not know how I could have gone so long without appreciating him.

March 24, 1941

Uncle Arnold wasn't at school today—getting plastered at the Charter Day luncheon, I understand—but in his stead there was some wonderful news from Mr. Stein. It seems that, after I'd left the old man on Saturday, he and Stein had a Council of War and decided that the demonstration numbers for the lecture (squibs from the orchestral variations, the wind quintet, *et al.*) should be played on two pianos, four hands . . . Who but I should be the logical candidate for the position of extra pair of hands? We tried some of the things over, and found that they went off very easily. I'll be at the old man's rehearsal in Royce Hall tomorrow afternoon to polish them off some more. By the way, I got my first squint at the text of the lecture this p.m. It's all written in ten-dollar words and filled with high-flown references to God and the Word. I was amused to notice that some hand, Arnelie's apparently, had marked in the accentuation of most of the difficult words![41]

🖎 *March 25, 1941*

Had the great rehearsal with Uncle Arnold this afternoon . . . You should have seen Trude gotten up in an outfit of brightest red that would have been becoming to *me*! I never saw her dress that way before. The old man was quite well pleased with our playing. He told me afterwards that he thought I played excellently, but with "too much technique" and a little too freely in rhythm . . . We won't dare play any wrong notes, because the slides (in A's almost illegible handwriting) of what we are playing will be right up in front of the audience to refute our version!

[41]The lecture ("Composition with Twelve Tones") is in *Style and Idea*. It still remains the most lucid exposition of its subject.

What a wonderful, great day! First of all, I learned of my University Fellowship for next year—I was the indubitable first out of 142 applicants. Called Mrs. Schoenberg about it in the afternoon, but she surprised me by saying that "they could have told me that already if they'd realized I didn't know!" Arlt must have told them.

About The Lecture: I am still enjoying the doubly sweet sensations of the old man's unqualified triumph and of my own. I was there fully a half-hour in advance, attired in my red evening dress, prepared to hold Uncle Arnold's hand to calm his nerves if necessary. As a matter of fact, though, I was more excited than he! He was a little nervous at the very beginning of his speech, when he was responding to Knudsen's introduction; but once he got into it, all was well, and there were no slip-ups of any kind in the presentation of slides and records or in our own playing. During that whole ultra-abstruse two hours, you could have heard a pin drop in the whole place, the big audience was that attentive! A nice audience, too. Plenty of familiar faces: all U.A.'s students, of course, and the music department, and The Relatives (Mrs. Seligmann and Mother Kolisch), and the Weisses, and even, in the front row, my dear Werfel (*sans* Alma). After the lecture, as Mamma and I were sprinting down the corridor in a mad dash for Kerckhoff Hall and the reception, he came tripping up to exchange a few words with me. The few words were these: "You don't compose in the 12-tone scale, do you?" "Oh, no," says I, "Schoenberg won't let me." Werfel: "Well, that is good. I am surely glad to hear that!" And off he trotted.

As for Uncle Arnold's after-reactions, at the reception he was positively luminous, and I don't mean "lit up," either! Every time I brought him another cup of non-alcoholic punch or approached him with the cake-tray, he fairly radiated that childlike happiness of his. Of course, all the local lights present were making much of him, and of me too, I'm happy to say. He must have felt exhausted inside, but outwardly, at least, he seemed to have stood up to the strain magnificently . . .

Uncle Arnold was unable to have me come by for my lesson; he was tired, I suppose, and a bit let down. He's glad it's all over, but when

he asked me if I was, I had to say, well, yes and no; it's something
I've been looking forward to so long, and when you've looked forward to a thing that way, you're always a little let down when it's
all over and you don't have anything more to be expectant about!
(Just the way I felt for a little while after baby Lawrence came.) He
seemed touched and pleased by my feelings in the matter, especially
when I reiterated that I knew it had been a great personal triumph
for him. Well, I'm sorry I couldn't see him today, but will do so
tomorrow when he's feeling more rested.

March 28, 1941

Uncle Arnold in good mood today, still basking in the afterglow of
his great triumph. He tended to business all right in my class (not to
my business, though, alas) but I hear that he came to counterpoint
class an hour late and never breathed a word of counterpoint! . . .

March 31, 1941

At long last I got Uncle Arnold to look at the summary (not the
text) of my thesis this afternoon. He was very nice about it; said I'd
made some good points, and left the substance and plan intact. But
what, if you please, should he start criticizing but my use of the
English language!!!! He'd stand there questioning my use of this
or that word, and then turning to the class with an "I am right, no?"
You should have seen twelve heads sagely nodding! (Not but what
I'm one of the nodding heads myself, when it suits my convenience,
but I don't like to be the one to be nodded down!) Then the dear
man added insult to injury by asking me when I will start composing
and orchestrating again? Well???? What can you say!

April 2, 1941

I'd hoped to get Uncle Arnold to look some more at my thesis
today—but no . . . He did, though, analyze things which had a direct
application to what I am doing: Brahms' G Minor Piano Quartet,
and Mozart's G Minor String Quintet. We had a funny experience
with that last one: I was peaceably playing the upper parts on my
piano, and Mr. Stein the lower ones on his, when I suddenly became

aware of an echo of my part from the other piano! I suspected what was going on, but didn't say a word until afterwards, when I was alone with Mr. Stein. Yes, sure enough, the old man had been banging out that melody right along with (or a little behind) me. He loves it so, he couldn't help it!

He called his orchestration of *Pelleas* "al fresco" instrumentation à la Strauss, where every note need not be played. How quickly he grew away from this! Of course, it was all the fashion at that time.

April 12, 1941

Had my [private] lesson this a.m. Many events of interest. He had with him translations of some of the *Pierrot* verses which Erwin Stein had sent him, and asked how I liked them. I found them quite similar to my own, very good in general, but with a few faults of English. Well, now he wants me to write at once to Lieberson[42] of the Columbia Recording Co. and tell him how much I want for my translation. I guess the records have not been issued yet and there is still hope that my work may be used. Maybe Columbia got disgusted with Slonimsky on account of that *Heldenleben* business.[43]

April 14, 1941

Went to see Arlt this morning about fixing a date for Uncle Arnold's Royce Hall program (the one with my quartet and quintet). We set the date of May 23, 8:30 p.m., which pleases U.A. all right. Also asked A. about *Harmonielehre*; ascertained that he'd already done 50 pages and was proceeding steadily with the work. Also asked

[42]Goddard Lieberson (1911-1977) had become a staff member of Columbia Records in 1939. He rose to the presidency of the organization.

[43]It is my recollection that Columbia objected to some rather sarcastic album notes which Slonimsky had written for *Ein Heldenleben*. (In *Music Since 1900*, 4th ed., p. 1426, he uses the words "notorious" and "egocentric" concerning it—appropriately enough.) The *Pierrot* recording appeared with only brief summaries of the texts, prepared by Slonimsky.

him about that plan for having three young artists on the concert series next year. There is a definite opening for me as the pianist hasn't been selected yet . . .

Uncle Arnold was very glad to hear about the Royce Hall concert and about *Harmonielehre*. I got him to sign my petition to change my thesis title, but only with great difficulty, for my handwriting annoyed him! He looked at the new beginning of the thesis, and at various other points of it; criticized some picayunish things, but I guess the plan is now all right, for the nonce . . . By the way, there was a nice little article about his citizenship in the *Bruin*.

April 16, 1941

Saw Uncle Arnold today, of course, but he didn't get around to looking at my Serenade. He looked at the beginning of A's quartet and found a measure lifted (accidentally I suppose) right out of *Kammersymphonie*. He advised her not to use it; if there could be a better continuation for it than the one he'd already written, he'd have written it! I'll be with him tomorrow again and I suppose we'll have a good hashing over of this and that.

April 18, 1941

U.A. looked at what I'd done with my Minuet of my *Serenade*; had many suggestions, and showed many examples of Mozart's finesses in Minuets. "This should be a stimulation to you," says he to me, and then, turning to the rest of the class, "even to the rest of you who will not be composers!" After he'd analyzed all the most complicated examples, he said to me, "Now you see what I expect from you in a Minuet!" A compliment? I think so!

April 23, 1941

Uncle Arnold damn cute in class today, analyzing the finale of the Brahms F Minor Piano Quintet (especially the introduction, 'cause he doesn't believe in introductions) and telling more about the good old days when he learned to play the violin, then the viola, then the 'cello (he bought it on a Dec. 5, he said—a Saturday—and played it in a quartet the day after). We've heard these tales of his before, but he added some new touches: how, before he had his 'cello, a friend of his borrowed, begged or stole a viola . . . , strung it with zither-strings, and played 'cello parts on it; how he, in his twelfth year, didn't know any music but violin duets and didn't realize that every harmony had a bass, until a good friend of his tipped him off about such things (advised him to go to the Prater and listen to the military bands, especially the bass . . .); how he subscribed to some Book-of-Knowledge affair[44] and waited impatiently for the volume "S" so he could learn to write a Sonata! . . .

April 24, 1941

Sorry to say that he was very cross this morning, on account of having found out from Arlt that I was going to try out for the concert series. He thinks I'm not ready and resents my not having asked his advice. I won't detail his words or actions, but he worked himself up into a terrible hysteria, brought me to tears, and said things I imagine we will both regret. I'll have to go to Arlt, I think, and explain the situation; to Hilsberg too.

April 25, 1941

Hilsberg thinks I'm perfectly right in taking a firm stand about going on with the concert series auditions . . . Uncle Arnold passably well-behaved today, though he made some remarks about maybe deciding the works to be played on the May 26 program by lot or by vote! He took my thesis from me and promised to let me come out tomorrow or so, to talk with him about it . . . I suppose he'll mow me down like a weed.

---

[44]*Meyers Konversationslexikon*, a popular German encyclopedia.

🖋 *April 27, 1941*

Ran out to Uncle Arnold's this noon to talk about the thesis. Am gratified, and surprised, to report that he was moderately nice about it. I'm having to rewrite only two pages (in which I used character-istic terms of his, which he took an oath he'd never uttered!) and to recopy one plate. I stayed with him pretty late as we wanted to listen to Churchill's speech . . .[45]

🖋 *April 28, 1941*

Well, I'll be darned if Uncle Arnold doesn't up and say, in class this afternoon, that Monday the 19th at 4 is to be the date of a pre-liminary performance of "our" concert, at which works to be played will be judged! And he wants Mr. Stein and me to play my quartet four hands! This shows I'm still in the doghouse. I spoke to Arlt before seeing the old man. A. thinks I'm perfectly right about want-ing to carry on; was horrified at what I told him of U.A.'s reactions; also denied U.A. had told him I couldn't play, or any of that stuff. He wants to talk about it to U.A., but I discouraged him.

🖋 *April 29, 1941*

Hoping and praying that Arlt will not talk to U.A. about "you-know-what", as there might be reprisals. The auditions aren't until the end of next month. The whole thing should be allowed to blow over and never mentioned again—unless I win!

🖋 *April 30, 1941*

Had a good bit of the *Serenade* for Uncle Arnold to look at this afternoon, but he didn't get to it. He seemed in a good humor, and

---

[45]We were thrilled by this rousing speech, delivered at one of the war's darkest moments. Churchill ended dramatically with an inspiring quotation from Arthur Hugh Clough: "But westward, look, the land is bright." See *Winston S. Chur-chill: His Complete Speeches, 1897-1963*, ed. Robert Rhodes James (New York, Chelsea House, 1974) Vol. VI, 1935-1942, pp. 6378-84.

didn't jump all over me for asking to have my tomorrow's lesson changed. I'll have to have it on Monday, though, for Saturday he'll be busy with Mr. Strang working on the composition textbook, and Sunday he's conducting the studio orchestra, at Fairfax High, in the *Five Orchestra Pieces*. Will I be there? You bet I will! I asked him, too, if he objects to my entering the *Werfel-Lieder* in the Gamma Phi Beta contest. He didn't; seemed flattered that I'd ask his permission. I guess he thinks he has me where he wants me.

May 4, 1941

Hal, Mamma and I went to Fairfax High School this morning to hear Uncle Arnold conduct the *Five Orchestra Pieces*. He did only the first two; he hasn't had time to study the score of late, so found it too difficult to go on with the rest. After the intermission, he ran through the orchestral parts of *Natur, Wappenschild, Sehnsucht* and *Wenn Vöglein klagen*. My favorite of all was the *Vöglein*, but of course I liked everything I heard. Mrs. Schoenberg and Nuria were there, and very friendly. Also, many friends of ours and theirs: the Weisses, Achron, *et al.* Sorry to say that Achron made a terrible *gaffe*: spoke up to me about the broadcast on Thursday![46] Hope Uncle Arnold didn't hear him, but of course he did. Got U.A. to autograph my copy of the *Five Orchestra Pieces*; he didn't want to do it, but did it anyway.

May 5, 1941

Now Uncle Arnold is beefing about the quartet performance; says it must be perfect, otherwise he won't have it, etc. etc. He wants the quartet to come to his house Friday night and rehearse for three or four hours. That's the night of the first Brahms concert, though I didn't dare say so. Well, if players in the quartet have tickets for the Brahms series, this session will just have to be postponed . . . I

---

[46] I had performed with my teacher Ignace Hilsberg in a broadcast sponsored by Barker Bros. Furniture store.

suppose much of this carrying on is the fruit of Achron's indiscreet remark yesterday. The old man was supposed to have me this morning for the lesson he didn't give me last week; but he was too tired, so now I'll have to wait until tomorrow.

May 6, 1941

Very hot day; sirocco off the desert, high wind and dust. Took the final thesis to Uncle Arnold this a.m.; had to put up with much unpleasantness and many insults, but anyway I got my "approval" papers signed, which is the essential thing. It seems now that the whole latter part is wrong, but he insisted only on the alteration of three examples . . . and promised to let the rest go if I would take the whole affair as a salutary lesson, i.e., believe in him and follow his advice from now on (as if I didn't !) All this was delivered with a rich dressing of "sob-stuff," for which there was only one reason: he was staggering drunk. Trude was telling Mamma that only yesterday he drank too much, wandered out of the yard and got lost, and she had to go out and hunt him and bring him home like a lost puppy. This morning he would read a simple paragraph of mine three times and not know what it said. He accused me of using too many words, which I explain by his seeing double!

May 7, 1941

Uncle Arnold in a pleasant humor today—Nuria's ninth birthday—in contrast to his ferocious mood of yesterday. He spent most of the class hour trying to help C. with the difficulties of the 1st violin part of my finale by suggesting impossible fingerings to him. When he was about to leave at four o'clock, he stuck his head into the room where we were practising and favored me with the sweetest smile imaginable! He didn't know, but does now, that before going to school this afternoon I'd had a little book about Siegfried sent special delivery to Nuria, wrapped prettily as a birthday gift. I suppose that'll put him in a better humor yet. He decided, by the way, that we'd better postpone the concert till June 6. That should work out all right. He probably hoped that I would have to leave before that date, but I won't!

May 8, 1941

Was supposed to have my lesson with U.A. this morning, but when I called up he was so "tired" that he wanted me to wait 'til Saturday. He was very friendly on the phone, asking how our rehearsal went yesterday, when we could come and play at his house, etc. Hope he's nice tomorrow! Possible reason for his change of heart: while he was blitzing me inside on Tuesday, Mamma was laying it on thick to Trude outside about how "I might have a nervous breakdown before the end of the year," and maybe that got back to him.

May 10, 1941

. . . at the lesson, he was nice enough, particularly about the quintet, which is all but finished now; but muttered some dark things about having the Master's exam after finals are over, and about "troubles with the thesis." He wishes I were staying here through the summer, as he would like to have Mr. Stein and me play *Kammersymphonie* with him when he goes to Stockton on July 1 to speak for some national music teachers' convention; but I told him I didn't think that would work out.

May 12, 1941

The burden of today's thoughts is "What's the matter with Schoenberg?" He came to school today with his cheeks sunken in, several more lower teeth missing, and something the matter with his upper plate, his hand constantly over his mouth to hide his injury, his nerves on edge, his manner morbidly mild, his eyes hurt-looking, and hardly able to talk. Query of the moment: did somebody "paste him one"? If so, who so? Nobody knows.

May 14, 1941

I guess Uncle Arnold's injuries have really laid him low, as he wasn't at school today (though Mrs. S. said over the telephone that he'd probably be able to see me tomorrow . . .). So Mr. Stein and I practised *Kammersymphonie* for Sunday's workshop . . .

May 15, 1941

Uncle Arnold and Trude picked me up this noon on their way home from the dentist's, and drove me out to their place. The old man was plenty sick; spent about five minutes glancing at the last measures of the quintet, which he was so anxious to get rid of that he accepted them. So now that work is *fini.* The rest of the time was spent grumbling about the thesis and asking confused questions of the sort he'll put to me on the Master's examination. I don't know whether he'll come to school tomorrow or not.

May 21, 1941

Uncle Arnold tied into the Minuet this afternoon, and made a good many suggestions, not all of them in the most courtly form (a typical comment was, "This *mess*!") However, he didn't cut my favorite finesse, the beginning of the recapitulation of the Minuet while the Trio is still going on. Sorry to say that he had to go out in the middle of class to answer a call from Mrs. Bailiff of Lectures, Drama and Music, and came back smiling like the cat that had, etc. Could he be getting ready to put on the screws about my Concert Series application?

May 23, 1941

Uncle Arnold spent three quarters of our class time beefing about the players in my quartet and telling me I would have to get other ones if I didn't want the performance cancelled! We had a quartet rehearsal right after he left and it went well, too; likewise, practised the *Kammersymphonie* for Sunday. I delivered Ronnie's birthday present, a book of dog pictures, just as the family was ready to leave school, and they were suitably grateful. When getting off the bus in the Village an hour before I'd happened to run into Trude and her mother with the car; she'd given me a long spiel about how they'd been talking to McManus about me and how he (who hardly knows me) had agreed with them that I was working too much. I've an idea she was warning me that the old man had been trying to tamper with M. *re* the Concert Series auditions, of which M. will be one judge; but of course I can't swear it.

🖋 May 24, 1941

Telegram from Columbia Records asking me to change my *Pierrot* translations to correspond with the original French texts, because of wartime copyright problems. Wired them I would if I could get the French book, but can't find it anywhere in L.A. . . .

🖋 May 25, 1941

Our *Kammersymphonie* performance on the Roof was successful. The Great Man wasn't there, but that didn't surprise us much. The rest of the program: Frances Mullen playing the *Piano Suite* . . . and Helen Swaby in the first two movements of that incredible *Violin Concerto*, which I'd never heard before. I was sorry she couldn't play the third movement too, with its wonderful percussion-accompanied cadenza, but suppose she did well to get through the two. She was a bit short on tone-quality, but did hit all the notes, which in that concerto is a very creditable performance. (The old man had heard her a week before at his house, and had, so she said, been pleased.)

🖋 May 26, 1941 (Ronnie's 4th birthday)

. . . As for Uncle Arnold today, he was very nasty. He picked on the Andante of my Serenade; didn't like the theme; these sixths did not liquidate, but only annoyed; that chunk of Brahms had no excuse for cropping up; these syncopations were cheap; etc. etc. Also, by the grace of God, he asked me about *Pierrot*, so I had to tell him of the telegram and he got absolutely furious. Said I must wire Lieberson at once COLLECT that he forbids the use of the French; added that if he found I'd paid for the wire he would make me pay HIM double! Well, I didn't send a wire, but a special delivery letter . . . What a coincidence for him to think of *Pierrot* at this time! Sometimes I think he must be either inspired or informed.

🖋 May 27, 1941

Uncle Arnold was infernally diabolical at our evening rehearsal at his place; practically threw me out of the house. When the quartet, the trio (Carfagno's) and I were late, through a concatenation of unfortunate circumstances but through no fault of our own, he insulted us all and said we wouldn't have gotten away with this in Germany! He praised C.'s music and said nary a word of mine. Finally, he found some trifling error in my score, and called me over to ask me if the score was correct. Not seeing the mistake, I said "Yes." Whereupon he threw the score in my face and gave me such a bawling-out for my rudeness and insubordination during the last twelve months (!) as I've ever heard! Well, at least he didn't put my quartet off the program, but that will come!

May 28, 1941

Letter to A.S. from D.N.:

Dear Mr. Schoenberg:

I cannot thank you enough for the great trouble you went to last night in rehearsing my quartet; it meant a great deal to all of us, and it helped me to see mistakes of my own which I will not repeat in the future. I am sure that from now on our rehearsals will be much more valuable to us, thanks to your suggestions.

I want to apologize, too, for anything that I may have said or done during the evening to offend you. I know that I sometimes get excited and confused and perhaps say things that sound different from what I really mean, but I can assure you that I do not mean to be impolite or annoying. Nobody could be more devoted to you than I am, and if I have contradicted you when you were trying to tell me something for my own good, I am really sorry for it, and I hope that you will forgive me.

I forgot to speak about my lesson last night, but I assume that you will not want me this week because of examinations, and the same may be true next week. If not, you can let me know. I expect to be starting for Michigan right after the examinations as my father is very anxious to have us home. I wish that I could stay on in the summer and continue with my lessons, but I know you want a vacation, and I do not get any more money to continue my studies until September.

Since our last conversation about my work on the piano I have been thinking over very seriously what you said to me, and have discussed it with my parents. I think perhaps I had never explained that part of my musical scholarship is for piano lessons and they naturally expect me to be able to make some public appearances to demonstrate my progress. The reason that I applied for an audition for next year's concert series was in the hope that I might win a chance to make the debut which they expect me to make, without any expense to myself, thus saving the money toward my lessons. Of course my career as a composer is far more important to me and most of my time is devoted to this work and always will be, but I do depend on the money that I get from this musical scholarship and from the French scholarship at the University to finance myself, and that is why I am working on these other lines too. Of course I enjoy all my work, but the composition is my life.

I wanted to tell you last night, but did not have the opportunity, of the wonderful piece of good luck that came to me yesterday, which I hope will please you as much as it did me. The Coolidge Quartet has offered to play my string quartet next season, probably on one of their Library of Congress concerts. A friend of mine happened to speak to them of my work, and they asked me to call yesterday and bring the quartet, which I did. They were really enthusiastic about it, and asked to see the quintet too just as soon as I can get it copied, and said they were quite sure that they would be interested in performing it later. This great honor makes me very happy, and makes me realize all the more what I owe to you. I know that without your wonderful help and guidance I would never have been able to achieve any success worthy of the name, and that everything I can hope to be I owe to you. I cannot even begin to say how grateful I am to you.

Thank you again for helping me rehearse the quartet. From now on we will work on it as hard as possible so as to make next Friday night's performance really worthy of you and all you have done for me.

Sincerely yours,
Dika Newlin

✒ *May 29, 1941*

Got a reaction to the letter. At nine, we'd had Mrs. Berry call him up to say that I was sick and couldn't come (he had an examination in the afternoon anyway, so I figured he wouldn't want me). At ten-thirty, Trude called up to say in a very strained voice that Mr. Schoenberg had received my letter and is very happy about it, and will I come Saturday morning and bring my quartet? I have a feeling that this bodes only ill. Probably I shouldn't go to him, but will do so this time, to give him a chance to redeem himself if he cares to. And if he insults me, I shall just leave, for the time being.

✒ *May 31, 1941*

Had expected almost anything from Uncle Arnold this morning, but he was very meek and mild. Didn't jump on Mamma's handwriting in her copy of my score, spoke only favorably of the Coolidge affair, and confined his criticism of the quartet to constructive suggestions which can be carried out. He did have a couple of outbursts, one about the lack of a bibliography in my thesis, and the other about our "hiding things from him" as to our difficulties in rehearsing; but he didn't get really violent. He wasn't feeling very well—had a devilish stiff neck; the children, too, seemed to be catching slight colds.

✒ *June 2, 1941*

Went over to Hollywood for my quartet rehearsal this morning. Had a good bit of trouble with it, as Uncle Arnold's continued attacks on me have put the players in such a state of mind that they don't want to do anything I say, even play the music! Of course this is what the old man has been working for all the time, so that he could cause me embarrassment and keep my music from appearing on the program. Well, I never did want it on the program anyway, so that's all right with me! I'll tell him about it tomorrow and let him enjoy the delightful mess he's made.

June 3, 1941

Had expected Uncle Arnold to give us a long hard examination this afternoon (in composition) but it was short and easy. A rather pointless thing, though, and just organized to annoy. He was in a nasty mood, and my telling him that I didn't want the quartet on the program under present circumstances made him no less so. Finally he prevailed on me not to withdraw it, on condition that Mr. Stein will take the remaining rehearsals, as I want no more of it. Well, we'll see what happens. He promised me "a very hard oral exam" in two days. "Good!" I cried. "That's just the way I like 'em!" He looked a little taken aback . . .

June 5, 1941

The oral exam is triumphantly past! (passed). I had prepared for it with great care by making myself up to look interestingly ill. But I needn't have bothered, for U.A. was positively angelic! Right at the beginning of the exam (which lasted barely an hour, not including the easy written part) he announced that he would let the others question me because he knew I would "do it good," and if he asked me too hard questions it would have no meaning, and likewise if he asked me too easy ones! Well, he did ask me some, but just on things about my thesis which he knew I knew. Every time I answered the simplest question, he would cry, "Good! Good! Now I want to let her show you how much farther she can go!" Of course, the others were flabbergasted, but followed suit admirably. (Some asked me a few sticky opera questions, which I parried with a marvelous air.) Well, after it was over they all, especially Uncle Arnold, congratulated me extravagantly and assured me that I'd given them a very pleasant hour indeed. Whew!

June 6, 1941

The quartet performance (three movements) took place tonight, and was done very well, too. I had thought of staying away, to give Uncle Arnold a well-deserved punch, but let my better nature get ahead of me. At that, I gave him another good scare by not showing myself to him at all until after the performance, instead of coming backstage ahead of time as he thought I would. No evidence of my presence was to be seen. I sat in the back of the auditorium by myself, and wore a hat with a veil, so he got scared for fear I'd left town without bidding him a fond farewell! He introduced my quartet very nicely; told my age and all that, and said that he expected me in the shortest time to have the *most* brilliant career both as composer and pianist! (Wow! Is he getting afraid of hell!) In fact, he refrained from insulting anybody all evening. He congratulated me sweetly enough afterwards, and so, for the matter of that, did everyone else (there was quite a fair-sized audience).

So now *that's* over, and will never be repeated.

June 9, 1941

This was the day of the preliminary Concert Series auditions. I think I acquitted myself quite well with the first movement of Beethoven's *Les Adieux*, and Debussy's *Poissons d'or*. There were eighteen pianists (including some of my friends), all of whom really did outstandingly well. Schoenberg was a judge! (but of singers, not pianists, thank goodness).

June 11, 1941

Worst news of the day: called up early this morning to find out if Uncle Arnold still wanted me to come and see him at ten, and found out from Trude—he wouldn't come to the phone—that he didn't want to see me now, then, or any time before I left! She tried to argue with him, too, but got nowhere. His excuse was that it would take him longer than an hour to check the thesis if I brought it to him, so I should mail it to him and let him send it back to me with corrections. Gr-r-r!

June 13, 1941 (a Friday the 13th, and my last full day in L.A.)

Spent most of the day at the beach. On the way there, had Hal drop me at Schoenberg's just long enough to leave the thesis (and a little note on my best paper). I hadn't expected the Great One himself to see me, but he did, and so I could tell him a last *adieu*, or *au revoir*, I hope. He wasn't particularly cordial, but he wasn't nasty, either. At least, when I said to him, "Well, I'll be seeing you in September," he didn't reply, "Like fun!" But no, today's was not as tender a moment as the partings of other years. I hope it won't be the last.

June 14, 1941

Did not attend commencement. We're pulling out tonight after a very pleasant last hour (turkey dinner with friends at the Fred Harvey station restaurant) ... Good-bye, Arnold Schoenberg. I won't stay away too long!

The Final Decade
1941 - 1951

There are people with whom it is not easy to live, but to leave impossible.
Thomas Mann, *Doctor Faustus*

This summer was not as previous summers. Outwardly, all was as before: the usual visits from and to family friends, composing, practising, taking summer courses, enjoying Michigan summer fun. But it wasn't the same, for underlying everything was a deep apprehension about the future of my relationship with Schoenberg. Even events which would normally have been joyous for a young composer were poisoned by this anxiety (which still makes my heart beat faster as I relive this time). On June 23, I wrote:

> Got a letter from Bak, a note from Lorin, and a postcard from Mrs. Voorsanger today, and they all told me the same, namely, that Lorin will conduct *Cradle Song* on the

329

> NBC Summer Symphony series on Saturday night, July 5.
> Boy oh boy! Wait till Uncle Arnold hears this one! Of
> course he can't blame me, for I didn't arrange the per-
> formance.

And on June 30:

> ... today I got a letter from Mrs. Irish[1] informing me
> that Barbirolli will conduct *Cradle Song* in the Bowl on
> August 7 . . . Will A.S. be thrilled to learn of this (I DON'T
> THINK)!

The NBC broadcast duly took place:

> ... performance well received with much applause and
> my name mentioned plenty of times . . . But I certainly
> was embarrassed when the announcer said in capital letters,
> "DIKA NEWLIN IS A PUPIL OF ARNOLD SCHOEN-
> BERG." Now if the little man heard that . . .!

Favorable reviews poured in, and letters from all my friends
who'd heard the broadcast. But no word, of course, from Schoenberg. On July 25, I heard that my grant from Independent Aid had
been raised to $1500 yearly, and that this would be continued until
I became self-supporting. "Nice going! I'm not saying a word to
'Arnolt.' " But all this secrecy was beginning to get on my nerves.

On August 4, I travelled to Interlochen to meet Henriette. In that
peaceful atmosphere, at last I could talk about what was on my
mind. I loved Schoenberg as much as ever, but the intensity of the
relationship, his harsh treatment of me for what I often felt to be
insufficient reason, and the constant need to conceal important
happenings from him, were beginning to have an adverse effect on
my health. My emotional and intellectual dependency on him was
becoming too great. I badly needed, not to break permanently with
him—that would never be, unless he wished it, which I thought
unlikely—but to get away for a time and establish my life on a new
basis. Could Henriette help? Would my sponsors buy the idea of my
finishing my education in New York?

[1]Mrs. Leiland Atherton Irish was, for many years, the executive chairperson
for the summer concerts in the Hollywood Bowl. For an interesting survey of
Bowl history to 1952, see Howard Swan, *Music in the Southwest* (San Marino,
Calif., Huntington Library, 1952, repr. New York, Da Capo Press, 1977), pp.
237-244.

She could; they would. To poor Papa fell the unenviable task of writing to Schoenberg about my thoughts (the decision was not yet 100% final). The answer came on August 16: a letter alternately pathetic and sarcastic, obviously showing deep hurt. It broke my heart, but confirmed me in my resolution. On August 24, I wrote

> . . . to Uncle Arnold, assuring him of my devotion, regrets, and so forth. I suppose I should feel either sad or glad about it, but I don't feel anything but indifferent, or maybe glad at least to know what I am going to do.

The arrangements for me to be admitted to Columbia University as a doctoral candidate in musicology went rapidly. On September 7, 1941, we left for New York. Thus began for me four years of new adventures. This is the place for me to pay tribute to Columbia's director of graduate musicology in those years, later music critic of the New York Herald Tribune, now enjoying a well-earned retirement: Paul Henry Láng.

Paul Henry made no bones about it: he hated Bruckner, couldn't stand Mahler, and didn't care all that much for Schoenberg. He was confronted with a stubborn 18-year-old who wanted nothing better than to write a dissertation on Bruckner, Mahler and Schoenberg. His response did him—and me—honor. He knew that, because of my studies with Schoenberg, I was uniquely qualified to do this job. If I felt that I could do an objective piece of work on the subject—and that was my intention—I should go to it! Such a stance called for more moral courage—not always a common quality in academic circles—than one might suppose. For one thing, writing a dissertation on a still-living composer was, in the '40's, just not done! For another, because of a variety of circumstances, having mainly to do with the demands of military service on the male students, I would be the first candidate ever to complete the Ph.D. in musicology at Columbia. Thus, both Láng and I would be placed in an unusually exposed position. He would be subjected to much criticism by his musicological colleagues in other universities for having allowed me to do this outrageous thing; but he stuck by his decision. Our persistence paid off when the book, finally published in 1947, became something of a classic. (In 1978, my revised and updated edition of it was published by W.W. Norton.)

I had laid down some ground rules for myself. Above all, I would not show the work to Schoenberg at any stage in the proceedings. This had to be my view, as objective as I could make it, of him and his forebears. After the work was done, he might see it as a completed entity. Through it, I hoped to show him that my leaving him had not been a wanton desertion, but a necessary prerequisite to my performing this important task: important not only to my career, but to the better comprehension and acceptance of his music. I hoped that he would understand and accept this.

Another decision: that the book would not be a mere analysis of music, but a cultural history of the place and of the times in which this music lived. As the African musicologist Fela Sowande was later to say,

> ... an analytical approach can give us, at best, only the anatomy and physiology of the music concerned; it can tell us nothing about the informing life of the music, nothing about its essence, nothing of what it meant to its creators and why, and we are left with the mere skeleton of what was a living art.[2]

To this end, I steeped myself in all the Viennese atmosphere that I could find in New York of the '40's—and that, thanks to the influx of refugees in those years, was considerable. I spoke, read, and ate Viennese whenever and wherever I could. I devoured books on Austrian art, history, literature. Sometimes I even dreamed in Viennese! It worked; when my book appeared, many readers did not guess that it had been written by a native American who had never seen Vienna. (During my wanderings through that city in 1951-52, when I was retracing Schoenberg's steps for the purposes of my future writings about him, I would often be visited by a strange sense of *déjà vu*.)

Of course, not all of my time was spent with the dissertation. I sought out other people who, to some small degree, helped fill that Schoenberg-sized hole in my daily life. For piano study, there was Rudolf Serkin, hardly a systematic teacher, but a charming and brilliant performer who would, in later years, attain unexpected profundity; Mieczyslaw Horszowski, quiet, mouse-like, and thorough; and the greatest of all, Artur Schnabel, a true philosopher of

---

[2]Quoted in Bill Cole, *John Coltrane* (New York, Schirmer Books, 1976), p. 39.

the piano with a devastating wit and a flair for horrible puns equalling my own. (When he saw *Fantasia*, he was "Disneypointed.") I had wanted to study composition with Bartók, but he would have none of that idea, preferring always to teach piano. Roger Sessions proved a fine teacher; his criticisms seemed gentle after Schoenberg's, but were always to the point and insightful. (He could be sarcastic, too; when I brought him a grandiloquent operatic hymn of which I was rather proud, his only comment was, "Humph! Sounds like Grand Central Station!") With such teachers as these, intellectual stimulation and emotional enjoyment were never lacking.

During these four years I was not out of touch with Schoenberg (the "real" Schoenberg, that is, not the "historical" one). I wrote to him briefly from time to time; always, at birthdays. A typical little note from him was sent on September 21, 1943:

> Many thanks for thinking about my birthday. I am sure—if only I had more time, I would have written you already. But keep me informed about your career. It will always interest me to hear from you.

After his seventieth birthday in 1944, a "form letter" went to all friends who had sent him greetings. With typical Schoenbergian irony he remarked, "at this age, if one is still capable of giving once in a while a sign of life, everybody might consider this already as a satisfactory accomplishment." On my copy, he scribbled:

> Thanks for your nice letter.
> Of course you may name me to the Guggenheim Fellowship jurors. They then will ask me to write about you. I hope you will be successful.

I wasn't—any more than he would be the following year. I was, however, successful in securing, for the following fall and thereafter, an interesting job at Western Maryland College in Westminster, Maryland. There, in a quiet small town set in pleasantly rolling hills, not far from Baltimore, I put his precepts to work in my classes, using his *Models for Beginners in Composition* as the textbook for my composition students and his (as yet unpublished) counterpoint examples as teaching material for my lone counterpoint student. (Counterpoint hadn't been taught in the school till I arrived.) In 1948, I was able to adopt the abbreviated English translation of his

Harmonielehre as my harmony textbook. Between classes, I put the finishing touches on my book (being revised for publication by King's Crown Press of Columbia University). On its publication, I sent him an affectionately inscribed copy—and sat back waiting for the fur to fly.

He fooled me! His response to the work was friendly and enthusiastic. He had been unable to read it himself because of eye-trouble, but Trude had read a substantial portion of it aloud to him. (That pleased me especially, because I always like to think of how my prose will sound when read aloud.) On the strength of it, he now asked me to get in touch with the Philosophical Library in New York, with a view to my possibly translating René Leibowitz' *Schoenberg et son école*. They sent me the book; I was delighted at the way in which Leibowitz' evolutionary presentation of Schoenberg, Berg and Webern linked perfectly with what I'd done in my work. Pitching into the task of translation with enthusiasm, during a stay at the MacDowell Colony in Peterborough, New Hampshire, I finished the job in two weeks! The debonair author showed up in New York that fall and we worked together on a few last-minute revisions. René won many friends among the Schoenbergians, though this would abruptly change when it came out that, on the strength of having copied the score of *A Survivor from Warsaw* for Schoenberg, he was claiming to have assisted him with the orchestration! This was a worse crime than visiting Stravinsky when in Los Angeles (a deed which, if discovered, would always lead to instant ostracism in Schoenbergian society!)

1948 saw me helping Schoenberg with editorial work on *Structural Functions of Harmony*. He approached W.W. Norton with it; they would eventually publish it, though, because of disagreements with some of his standpoints at this time, not until long after his death. He wrote me on April 25 concerning this matter:

> Thank you very much for your letter. I think some of your suggestions go too far, or, from the standpoint of art and theory, no changes are necessary at all. But perhaps you and the publisher are right with respect to conventional attitudes and I am not in the position to judge such matters.
>
> . . . I hope you will be a faithful defender of my artistic

and personal interests. You know me, you know what I like and dislike and you should find a way of not proposing things which offend my feelings.

This I expect from you.

On December 19, his essay *On revient toujours* was published in *The New York Times*. It elicited instant response, including a rather stupid reply by the Bartók disciple Tibor Serly, featuring untrue statements such as "no outstanding creator ever went back to a previous style." My rejoinder to this was also published. For the peroration, I found suitably warlike words:

> Schoenberg has quoted himself not so long ago in these pages: "Only one who deserves respect himself is capable of respecting another man." Let us try listening with a little more respect when a great mind chooses to tell us something about its philosophy of creation. Then, perhaps, our own opinions will be worth taking seriously.

(I was still getting negative feedback on this one from friends of Serly in 1976!)

Meanwhile, the sandbox-squabble between Schoenberg and Mann, over Mann's attribution of the 12-tone method to Adrian Leverkühn in his *Doctor Faustus*, had erupted in the *Saturday Review of Literature* (January 1, 1949). I had to mix into this affair too, of course! Taking the 'retrograde" name of "Joyce Jameson" (during this time I'd become a great fan of James Joyce's *Ulysses*, still one of my favorite bedside books), I fired this off to *SRL*:

> When hearing of himself as Faust
> Herr Arnold S. did sulk and frowst.
> He stands on view as Leverkuehn,
> Who must have been a clever loon,
> But who, alas, expired of paresis,
> A circumstance which must embarrass us.
> His tale's adorned by Wiesengrund,
> Whom S. berates as *Schweinehund*
> Since he, to lend the book some chic ritz,
> Betrayed his Master's twelve-tone secrets.
> So war's declared on Dr. Thomas
> (Alias Serenus Zeitblomus)

With flying bombs and hand-grenades
'Twixt Brentwood and the Palisades,
Until our hero rings the bell
With letters to the SRL,
Exposing, in terms most uncareful,
The views of self and Madame Werfel.
If NOW his feelings this form took,
WHAT WILL THEY BE WHEN HE'S READ THE BOOK!

Schoenberg and I were now very busy getting the book of essays *Style and Idea* into shape for publication by Philosophical Library. We were back to our old tricks again; I'd correct his Germanic English; he'd respond bristling with offended pride; I'd apologize abjectly; we'd start all over again. Mamma, my efficient if sometimes bemused typist, sometimes acted as go-between when I could take no more. Somehow *Style and Idea* did get edited amidst all this, and appeared in 1950. In my brief introduction (dropped from the 1975 enlarged edition) I quoted one of Schoenberg's letters, to explain the work's stylistic peculiarities: "I do not plan to hide the fact that I am not born in this language and I do not want to parade adorned by stylistic merits of another person."[3] Unfortunately, not all critics agreed with this standpoint or with my acceptance of it in my role as editor. But "I could do no other."

Summer of '49; at last I had time and money to visit Los Angeles once more. It was great to see the Schoenbergs again. The children were growing up strong and beautiful; Trude looked well enough, though a little frayed around the edges; the old man had even gained a little weight! Living with them was a young New Zealand relative, Dick Hoffmann, who was helping Schoenberg with his musical chores. Schoenberg delighted in calling Dick, me and himself "*dick, dicker* [Dika] und *am dicksten*," i.e., fat, fatter, and fattest; both Dick and I were definitely on the skinny side!

We arranged a reading of my twelve-tone (!) Piano Trio.[4] Schoen-

[3] Editor's Preface, *Style and Idea* (first edition, New York, Philosophical Library, 1950), v. (Note: this preface was not reprinted in the second edition; such an explanation no longer seemed necessary.)

[4] Later recorded by the London Czech Trio for Composers Recordings, Inc. (CRI 170).

berg liked it, though he chid me mildly for having adopted the uninterrupted one-movement (many movements in one) form which he'd so often used. Breaks between movements would, he now felt, refresh the audience and ease comprehensibility.

He was full of snappy one-liners, as always. On the *Doctor Faustus* controversy: "If Mann had only asked me, I'd have invented a special system for him to use!" On Webern, tersely: "Webern always exaggerated." An amusing episode came when I talked to him about arranging payment for the *Gustav Mahler* article which he was allowing *The Canon* in Sydney, Australia to publish in their Arnold Schoenberg Jubilee Issue (September, 1949). The magazine could pay but little. New Zealander Dick was now called into consultation. The following colloquy ensued:

> Schoenberg: Dick! What do they produce in Australia?
> Dick: Well, sheep . . .
> Schoenberg: Dick! Could he not send us a sheep?

I am sorry that this never happened; an Australian sheep would have looked fine grazing on the Brentwood lawn among the bunnies, chickies, kitties and doggies who were usually disporting themselves there or inside the house. (Schoenberg and I shared this taste; most of this book has been typed with the "warm snoot" of a Russian Blue cat nudging the typewriter carriage . . .)

Schoenberg would now celebrate his seventy-fifth birthday; it elicited one of his best "birthday letters."[5] I would move to Syracuse, New York, where I would spend the next two years at Syracuse University, teaching a large-scale survey of contemporary music as well as interdisciplinary courses. It was a special joy to have Louis Krasner as a colleague; at this time he was head of the Syracuse violin department. I remember, too, coaching young Bette Wolf in the voice part of Schoenberg's Second Quartet for what turned out to be a moving, brilliant performance.

Summer of '50: a brief visit to California. I spent a little time with the Schoenbergs. The old man had now discovered TELE-VISION! Typical of many "intellectuals" at this period, he talked grandly about having bought it "for the children." However, no one

---

[5]Published in Schoenberg, *Letters*, p. 290.

was more enthralled than he as we sat in front of Hopalong Cassidy with our TV trays in our laps. Perhaps he was remembering the Karl May Wild West novels of his youth, a memory of which still lived in his essay *New Music, Outmoded Music, Style and Idea*, wherein he foresaw, too, the exploits of the astronauts:

> Would it not be easy to find numerous youths to fly to the moon in a rocket plane if the opportunity were offered? Is not the admiration of people of all ages for our Tarzans, Supermen, Lone Rangers and indestructible detectives the result of a love for romanticism? The Indian stories of our youth were no more romantic; only the names of the subjects have been changed.[6]

I returned for another academic year at Syracuse. It was difficult, because of the brutal winter climate (Syracuse is the only city I know where the streets have grab-rails for the use of the unwary winter pedestrian!) as well as because of unpleasant encounters with a number of colleagues. But somehow, one made it through till June.

Summer of '51: I was 27, Schoenberg was 76. I was feeling a bit battered; he was mortally ill, though I didn't know it.

> Life was so easy
> Suddenly hatred broke out
> a grave situation was created
> But life goes on[7]

Or so I thought . . .

---

[6]*Style and Idea*, p. 119.

[7]Schoenberg's "program" for the Piano Concerto, Op. 42, written to explain the moods of the work to Oscar Levant, for whom it was originally intended. Rufer, *op. cit.*, p. 71.

July 13-14, 1951

*Mahler was allowed to reveal just   so much
of his future; when he wanted to say more,
he was called away.*

Arnold Schoenberg, *Gustav Mahler*

I spent the day of July 13, 1951, quietly, teaching a few of my Syracuse summer students in composition. One, I recall, was just starting a twelve-tone piece. I believed, now, that it was best to allow interested students to make an attempt at this method, even if they weren't quite "ready" for it. Only in this way, I reasoned, could they gain some practical understanding of what it was all about.

This summer, I'd decided to omit the usual trip to California. I knew that Schoenberg was ill; I thought little about it, for over the years there'd been so many illnesses . . . So, on this day, he wasn't particularly on my mind.

In the evening, I corrected a few student papers, started reading Theresa Weiser's new Bruckner novel *Music for God*, and chuckled over some of its absurdities. I laid out my clothes for the outing I'd have tomorrow with Nan Andrews, wife of the dean of Syracuse

Law School and sister of my old teacher Roger Sessions. I laughed as I recalled Schoenberg's reaction to this friendship. Hearing of my connection with the Law School, he'd written asking me if I couldn't find him a young graduate who would be willing to devote his entire time to handling HIS lawsuits! I'd left the question tactfully unanswered.

I went to bed early, but sleep wouldn't come. Finally I dropped off. Confused dreams; then, a vivid scene. I am at a large social gathering; there's much chatter, drinking, fun. Suddenly, Schoenberg walks in the door. I rush towards him: "Oh, I'm so glad to see you! It's been such a long time!" He does not speak. He looks me right in the eyes with an expression of ineffable sadness. Then, he turns his back, slowly walks away.

I woke up with a start, checked the bedside clock. The time: 2:45 a.m. (Eastern Time).

The dream disturbed me strangely. Arising early to get ready for my outing, I knew that I had to write it down in detail before doing anything else. Usually, I liked to start the day listening to radio news while sipping my morning coffee. This day, I didn't want the radio; it seemed as if I dreaded that intrusion.

I was ready early; plenty of time to stroll over to the University and pick up my mail. The oppressive feeling of the dream had lifted somewhat as I enjoyed the brief walk. I entered crazy Gothic Crouse Hall, approached the mailboxes. Suddenly, a friend's voice: "Oh, Dika! I just heard the news this morning and I'm so terribly sorry!" "Why, what news?" "Oh, didn't you know? Schoenberg is dead!"

No, it can't be; the guy just made a mistake. I met Nan at our appointed time: "Have you heard such a story?" "No, not a thing. We'll listen to the radio later; maybe there'll be something." We did; still nothing. Finally, on the way home, we bought a late paper. Yes, there it was, a brief obituary: "Arnold Schoenberg, 76 . . ."

So it's true, then.

Many years later, I was to read Trude Schoenberg's account of that last night:

> On the 13th (he and I had a great fear of this), he insisted that I should get a sitter-in for the night. He was a German doctor who was not allowed to practise here. I was very tired, but woke up every hour and we had the light on.

Arnold slept restlessly, but he slept. About a quarter to twelve I looked at the clock and said to myself: another quarter of an hour and then the worst is over. Then the doctor called me. Arnold's throat rattled twice, his heart gave a powerful beat and that was the end. But I couldn't believe it for a long time afterwards. His face was so relaxed and calm as if he were sleeping. No convulsions, no death struggle. I had always prayed for this end. Only not to grieve![1] [sic]

The time: 11:45 p.m. (Pacific Time).

On the day of his funeral, I sat for a long time in the large quiet cemetery behind the University. I'd often brought my lunch there, or gone on bird-watching expeditions. Now, I finished reading Theresa Weiser's novel, visualized the scenes of Vienna among which Bruckner—and Schoenberg—had lived and which she evocatively described. I had imaginatively reconstructed them in *Bruckner-Mahler-Schoenberg*. Would I ever see them in reality?

Finally I went home. There, a special-delivery letter awaited me. I had received a Fulbright award to spend the next year in Vienna studying the life and work of Arnold Schoenberg.

Oh, Arnold. If only you could have known.

But maybe you do.

[1]Gertrud Schoenberg to Ottilie Blumauer-Schoenberg, August 4, 1951, in Stuckenschmidt, *op. cit.*, p. 521. (Note: Searle's translation of the final sentence seems wrong; surely the real meaning is that Trude had prayed Arnold would not *suffer*?)

Rückblick: 1951 -1977
(February 19- 22, 1977)

🌸🌸🌸

What a life! Didn't it pass like a wild dream?
Wasn't it quick? Fight and again fight. Greatest
happiness and deepest grief. We couldn't say
that it was boring. It changed like a thrilling
movie piece and there was always surprise.

Hans Nachod to Arnold Schoenberg

Over a quarter of a century had passed since Schoenberg's death. Now, in the city where he'd died, a unique memorial to him had taken shape. The Arnold Schoenberg Institute, devoted to the needs of Schoenberg scholars and performers, would officially open on February 20, 1977. In company with many other longtime friends and associates of Schoenberg, I'd be an honored guest.

Much had happened in those twenty-five years. Schoenberg's work was gradually finding its proper public. *Moses and Aaron*, which he had not lived to finish or to hear performed, had enjoyed triumphant productions in many cities throughout the world. I had

343

seen it at Covent Garden, under Sir Georg Solti, in a brilliantly realistic production with a sensational orgy scene; in Boston, directed by Sarah Caldwell who had the courage to bring this masterwork to the American stage for the first time; and in Caesarea, performed by the Hamburg Opera in the old Roman amphitheatre against the unforgettable backdrop of the Mediterranean. Much more of Schoenberg's music had been recorded. Robert Craft's recorded performances had made most of his major works accessible to a wider listening public. On the night of February 19, I'd learn whether one of the most recent Schoenberg records, the *Cabaret Songs (Brettl-Lieder)* performed by Marni Nixon and Leonard Stein, would receive the Grammy for which it had been nominated. (It didn't.)

My quadruple career as composer, writer, performer and teacher had continued to grow. The style of my music had undergone some radical changes in recent years. From "classic" twelve-tone composition, I'd moved to multimedia production (using, often, very eclectic musical means) and, later, to electronic and computer composition. As I used the computer facilities of Bell Labs in Murray Hill, New Jersey, I often thought of what Max Mathews, director of the music project there, had told me: it was my performance of some Schoenberg piano music at Drew University which had suggested to him that computer music might be used to produce such musical patterns.[1] I remembered, too, how often Schoenberg had spoken of a dream: wouldn't it be wonderful if he could inscribe his music "right on the soundtrack" so that he would no longer have to bother with those pesky performers! Since then, his dream had been fulfilled by Norman McLaren, John Whitney and other experimental filmmakers.

Most recently, I'd joined *Sounds Out of Silent Spaces*, a SoHo (New York City) group devoted to the practice and study of group improvised composition. Here was a new area of exploration for me, and one which I was finding unexpectedly stimulating. Many of the composers in this group—especially Phil Corner, its leader, and Dan

---

[1]The story got into Joan Peyser, *The New Music* (New York, Delacorte Press, 1971), p. 78, but without my name attached: "The project at Bell Labs began in 1957 when Max V. Mathews, a Ph.D. in electrical engineering and director of the behavioral research department of Bell Laboratories, attended a concert of Schoenberg's 12-tone works."

Goode—were by philosophical persuasion "minimalists," believers in using the absolute irreducible amount of musical material for the maximum emotional and spiritual effect. We spoke often of "elementals," of going "beyond systems" (including Schoenberg's) to the most basic "givens" of music. Phil wrote, in the verbal score for his *Day in A Life of This Musician*:

Yes it's true that one does not ever reach any limit what's value no matter how much might be stripped away.
One can go as far as possible towards reduced means yet not arrive at the edge of interests.
—Play so a piece off such purity—

Hurrying home one night after a heated discussion of Schoenberg and his teaching, I'd slipped and broken my right arm. Seeking to write something that I, a temporarily crippled pianist, might successfully perform with my friends, I came up with my own version of a one-tone piece for my left hand, other instruments, and voices. I called it *Atone*:

Atone
by Dika Newlin

A single tone (or tone with its octave doubling) is to be played in a low register of the piano, repeatedly, slowly, at a medium-loud dynamic level, for as long as the performer wishes. Dynamics should be as "steady-state" as possible.
To this may be added:
1) Voices, each singing the chosen tone steadily in his/ her most convenient register. If voices are used, the pianist should choose a tone that most easily accommodates all the singers in the group. In the course of the piece, there may be slight pitch deviations by the singers. These need not be corrected, but can form a halo effect around the original tone.
2) Instruments, such as guitar, oboe, clarinet, trombone, or whatever other instruments are played by members of the group. Instrumentalists should play the chosen tone in a manner compatible with the total sound of the piece. Any semblance of flashy individual virtuosity should be avoided.
One need not reject any reminiscences of "classical"

compositions that might come to mind while playing the piece. ("A", the beginning of Mahler's First Symphony; "Eb", *Das Rheingold*; "B", the murder scene in *Wozzeck*.) These evocations might or might not affect one's spiritual attitudes while playing the piece.

The longest performance thus far has been 45 minutes. I dream of a weekend-long performance with relays of performers and constant flux of audience members (who may or may not be participators).

Wasn't this what Schoenberg and Mahler had been talking about in the conversation reported by Alma Mahler,[2] in which Schoenberg demonstrated the possibility of creating a melody merely by allowing one tone to be sounded by various instruments? Schoenberg himself hadn't pursued this idea to its furthest extent; clearly, then, it was time to do so.

During all these years, I'd been writing about Schoenberg and concerning myself with the writings of others about him. One work, however, stubbornly refused to take shape: the biography that I'd planned for so long. Treatment for "writer's block" by Dr. Theodor Reik, the eminent analyst whose *The Haunting Melody* is a unique contribution to Mahler literature, elicited plenty of interesting psychological insights, but no biography.[3]

What was wrong? Borrowing a thought from Schoenberg's ideas on the non-completion of a Tenth Symphony by Mahler and other composers ("Those who have written a Ninth stood too near to the hereafter. Perhaps the riddles of this world would be solved, if one of those who knew them were to write a Tenth. And that probably is not to take place.")[4], I speculated for the readers of a Schoenberg centennial issue of *Perspectives of New Music*:

---

[2]Alma Mahler, *Gustav Mahler, Memories and Letters* (rev. ed. Mitchell, 1968), p. 182: "I remember a discussion Mahler once had with Schoenberg about the possibility of creating a melody from one note played successively on different instruments. Mahler strenuously denied that it could be done."

A slightly different concept of what I suggest in the final paragraph of *Atone* was later realized by Corner under the title *Elementals*, in a week-long performance at The Kitchen, New York (November 1977).

[3]The case is described in Theodor Reik, *Voices from the Inaudible* (New York, Farrar, Straus, 1964), pp. 182-83.

[4]*Style and Idea*, p. 470.

But what has this to do with writing a biography of Schoenberg? Could the would-be biographers really be equating a deeper study of Schoenberg's life with an approach to higher things? Am I really afraid that my completion of the Schoenberg biography could prove as fatal as the composition of the Ninth Symphony that I'm not going to write?

It sounds too simple. But I know—leaving my own personal experience out of it for a moment—that a majority of Schoenberg pupils looked up to him as a super-Father-Figure—maybe even quasi-divine? They were overawed by him, while often resentful of the "thought control" which he exercised over them. For proof, read the letters of Alban Berg to his wife, especially those in which he discussed the problems that Webern experienced in trying to break away from Schoenberg's overwhelming influence. How to avoid being artistically paralyzed by Schoenberg yet at the same time not to reject him—it is a conflict that we all went through!

Perhaps these speculations answer no questions, not even mine. Yet I want to share them with the readers of *Perspectives* on the occasion of Schoenberg's centennial. In so doing, maybe I'm partially answering the question of so many friends, "When is your Schoenberg biography going to be finished?" And maybe, too, with this public self-analysis, I am bringing closer the moment when I can say (like Byron in the *Ode to Napoleon*), "'Tis done!"[5]

More and more, I found myself returning to my diaries of 1938-41. Here, I knew, was a story of Schoenberg that nobody else had written or could write. Here—I suddenly realized in 1976—was where my real book had been all along! Thank God that the old spiral-bound school notebooks and their contents had remained, but for a few pages, intact during all these years. With editing and annotation for the reader of the present day, this would become my life of Schoenberg—or, maybe, the story of Schoenberg *in my life*.

I wrote to my old friend Donald Mitchell, now music editor of Faber and Faber in London, long ago co-editor with Hans Keller of the pioneering British magazine *Music-Survey*, for which I'd written my first studies of Schoenberg in America.[6] I sent a sample of the

[5]Newlin, "Why is Schoenberg's Biography So Difficult to Write?", *Perspectives of New Music*, Fall-Winter 1973/Spring-Summer 1974, p. 42.
[6]Newlin, "Schoenberg in America," *Music-Survey*, I, 5/6, pp. 128-31, 185-89.

diaries. Would he like to publish such a book as companion-piece to some of the books of similar interest that I'd already translated for Faber: Rufer's *The Works of Arnold Schoenberg* and Natalie Bauer-Lechner's *Recollections of Gustav Mahler*? In a month, the answer came. He loved the material, but thought it "too intimate" for book publication; bringing out portions of it in periodical form would be, he believed, the best plan.

Strategically, then, arrived the first issue of the *Journal of the Arnold Schoenberg Institute* (October, 1976), existing for the publication of just such Schoenberg material as this, and boasting a dedicated editorial staff. Would they be interested in a chapter of my diary? They would. Negotiations had already begun by mail, and would continue this February as I visited the Institute. (As I type these words, Issue 3 of the Journal, containing that chapter—a prelude to this book—is on its way to me.)

I flew to Los Angeles on February 19. Quickly calling Leonard Stein from my hotel to express my regret at having arrived too late for the champagne reception at his home, I heard his familiar, slightly dry voice: "We're having a *little gathering* of the clans . . ." How that favorite expression of his took me back to our school days! I asked him how to find the Institute on the USC campus the next day: "Just ask for the funny-looking building!" (Its unique prow-like façade—pictured on the cover of each issue of JASI—is indeed distinctive.)

For the events of February 20, I turn once more to my diary:

> Well, the Institute has now been christened with multi-magna (not to say jeroboa) of champie and the participants can all go home and suffer from acute jerebitis!
>
> Not too many of my old classmates were to be seen, or, if so, not recognizable by me. Leonard is semi-bald and white-whiskered. Clara is gray, plump and the perfect librarian. The blond, rather slender Gerald Strang is full-faced and gray. Nuria, Ronnie, Larry . . . grew up to be very good-looking people . . . I visited with Nuria who remembered well when we were "children together" . . . She is a straightforward and attractive person.
>
> The reconstruction of the studio is well done except *too neat*! There were more papers on the desk and more books on the shelves in those days! The view into the front yard

is shown, the golden mullioned window just as it was; you could almost step through that window into a land of forty years ago and see the kids and dog playing! A strange feeling. I was talking of the studio to another on-looker who suddenly asked me, "are you Larry's sister?"! Someone said "No one looks old enough for it to have been 40 years ago!" . . .

Many of his quaint gadgets and inventions shown—also "old razor blades" lovingly preserved in a box on which he had written "in two or three years they will be good again." *Not* exhibited was his flyswatter with address stamp on brown paper wrapper! Various types of row-charts (on rollers, miniature easels, etc.) called "12-tone accessories." No case for his missing tooth!

This is the kind of memorialization of "the dear departed" which could become a living death. I could have kissed Boulez for saying just what I have been saying to my friends in the East: namely, if the Institute is to have any value it must come to terms with music *now*. He elu-cidated to my satisfaction his infamous "Schoenberg est mort" sentence. He meant: "mannerism *after* Schoenberg is dead, and was from the start; invention *through* Schoen-berg is living!" In other words, work *through* Schoenberg and then come out on the other side with "your own thing"! Well, what else have I been doing? I hope the others took it to heart!

The music: (on the whole there was "too much cackle and not enough cruggle"[7] [more words than music]; "aus-picious occasion" was said too often . . .)

1) Incomplete Hollywood Bowl Fanfare, completed by L. with orchestration of final measures of *Gurre-Lieder* . . . the total effect was moving.

2) Songs, sung a bit "preciously" I felt; however, *Dank* did finally come off with the appropriate *panache* and was properly cheered. *Gruss in die Ferne* (not previously heard by me)—a mild-romantic Eb cruggle.

3) Finale of Wind Quintet . . .

---

[7]Since conservative thinkers have objected to the use of the word "music" to describe certain contemporary sound-works, I invented the all-purpose word "cruggle" to describe *any* type of organized sound-experience.

Interesting point: the word "Jew" was not *once* spoken all afternoon, even by Stuckenschmidt expressing the guilt of the Berliners. How odd.

. . . Catering was fine, the champie and sparkling Rhine wine flowed freely, plenty cheese, fruit, hot canapés (miniature spinach pies, grilled mushrooms, mini cheese/ pepper quiches, and the like). Reminded me of the Schoenberg birthday parties except there we would have had quite a few gift bottles of Scotch lurking about . . .

And now it was time for me to fly home from this trip into the past. High above the clouds, relaxing after good food and drink, insulated from the outside world by earphones as my eyes flicked lightly over Sean Connery's latest exploits on the screen. I began to muse on what I had seen and heard on the visit, and on the happenings of nearly forty years ago which it had brought to mind. How, I wondered, did that yesterday fit with this today? What, after all, had Schoenberg meant, not just in history, but in my life?

He had given me a sense of history; taught me how to respect composers of the past without being enslaved by them. Without him, I never would have come to know the music of Bruckner and Mahler, would not have understood how what these great men accomplished had helped to prepare for his achievements. In turn, I could see how what he had done made possible what I and my composer-colleagues were doing today. To perceive oneself as part of the flow of history—what an exalting experience! Too few of my students today, I thought, had a feeling for history (of music or anything else), perhaps because it was often so abominably taught. I must continue to try to bring it to life for them, to make them understand the present through the past as I had learned to do. ("Did you really know Mahler?" a student had once asked me. I had been flattered, not affronted, by the chronological mistake.)

He had given me a discipline of work for all seasons. One with such discipline, and with the technique to back it up (which he also gave us in full measure) need rarely be at a loss, given ideas, in any compositional situation.

He had refrained from coddling me; had forced me, sometimes with harsh treatment and ridicule, always to perform at my best. By being tough with me, he had prepared me beautifully for tough situations that I would meet in later life. This was done with pedagogical purpose. Once, he was asked if his brutal methods didn't sometimes cause a student to drop composing for good. Yes, indeed they did, he replied; but, if the student couldn't "take it," he may not have belonged in that demanding career in the first place. I would not necessarily recommend that today's teachers emulate Schoenberg's Spartan teaching methods. In fact, the teacher who tried it, at least in some institutions with a passionate and legalized commitment to mediocrity, would probably find him/herself out on his/her ear in short order. But, by overprotecting students against any hint of frustration or failure, aren't we making it that much more difficult for them to face the real problems of their later careers?

He had taught me, by example and action, to stick by my principles at whatever cost. Even when this brought me into violent conflict with him, he'd always respected me for defending my beliefs. In later life, when there might sometimes have been a temptation to let things slide for the sake of surface harmony in a personal or professional situation, I was inspired by the steadfastness which he'd displayed in the face of much worse problems. There is no doubt that this stance cost him, as it has cost me, both friends and money, on many occasions. I don't think that either of us ever seriously regretted it.

Setting to music Byron's stirring *Ode to Napoleon Buonaparte*, Schoenberg had found equally stirring strains for the final stanza in tribute to George Washington:

> Where may the wearied eye repose
> When gazing on the Great;
> Where neither guilty glory glows,
> Nor despicable state?
> Yes—one—the first—the last—the best—
> The Cincinnatus of the West,
> Whom envy dared not hate,
> Bequeath'd the name of Washington,
> To make man blush there was but one!

Flying high above America on Washington's Birthday, 1977, I could enthusiastically apply many of these words to their composer. Yes, *there was but one* who, living barely into the second half of the twentieth century, had yet made most of its musical innovations possible. For what he had given me—and what he had given the world—I could say, as I say again on this, the twenty-sixth anniversary of his death:

THANK YOU, ARNOLD SCHOENBERG.

Madison, New Jersey
July 13, 1977

Afterwits

Afterwits, Miss Douce promised coyly.
                    James Joyce, *Ulysses*

A pleasant custom of Victorian novelists was to round off a tale by letting the reader know what eventually happened to the characters whose absorbing adventures had filled so many pages.

Unlike Dickens, I could not trace the destinies of all my "characters." Don Estep, Gene Meltzer, Simon Carfagno—where are you? Nor could I keep some of my favorites alive for the final roundup. Alma, Franzl, Trude, Tammy, Snowy, Rudy Kolisch, Eduard Steuermann, and so many more; all gone! (Nadia Boulanger and Roy Harris died even as this book was in the final proofreading stages.) Neither Mamma nor Papa lived to know that I would publish this story of a time in my life to which they had contributed so much. Both did live to enjoy the success which they had worked so hard to help me achieve.

Of some people in this book, it might be said, as Hans Nachod said of himself in relation to Schoenberg: "I will enter history in the trace of you." A few have been unjustly forgotten; may what I have written of their part in Schoenberg's life and mine revive their memory.

353

I have gone on to new adventures. In August, 1978, I chose to leave the worsening climate and creeping blight of New Jersey to assume a new position at Virginia Commonwealth University, Richmond. Here, besides teaching many courses on Schoenberg, hearing students put together some remarkable Schoenberg performances, and sharing with them the techniques of preparing this book, I have the special pleasure of seeing one of Schoenberg's prophesies fulfilled. In that famous lecture of March 26, 1941, on *Composition with Twelve Tones*, he proclaimed, "The time will come when the ability to draw thematic material from a basic set of twelve tones will be an unconditional prerequisite for obtaining admission into the composition class of a conservatory." Today, at VCU, one of the requirements in the first year of Comprehensive Musicianship (without which no freshman can proceed to more advanced study) is the successful completion of a twelve-tone piece.

Yes, Schoenberg could have said, as Mahler did: "My time will yet come . . ."

Richmond, Virginia
December 1, 1979

Schoenberg's Textbooks and Essays: A Chronological List

Note: Schoenberg's American textbooks grew specifically out of his classroom teaching needs and experiences at UCLA. *Models for Beginners in Composition* originated in the first-year composition class; *Structural Functions of Harmony*, in the class of the same name which Schoenberg devised (listed in the University catalog, much to his annoyance, as *Harmonic Construction*); and *Preliminary Exercises in Counterpoint*, in the first-year and second-year counterpoint classes. I do not associate *Fundamentals of Musical Composition* with a specific class I took; but it, like the other textbooks, was carefully designed to meet the needs of his students, with shrewd evaluation of their good qualities as well as their deficiencies.

Harmonielehre. Vienna, Universal-Edition, 1911. 3rd revised and enlarged edition, 1922; 4th edition, 1949. Abbreviated translation by Robert D.W. Adams, New York, Philosophical Library, 1948. Complete translation by Roy E. Carter, London, Faber & Faber, Berkeley and Los Angeles, University of California Press, 1978.

Models for Beginners in Composition. New York, G. Schirmer, 1942; revised edition with corrections by Leonard Stein, Los Angeles, Belmont, 1972.

Structural Functions of Harmony. Completed in 1948, but first published, New York, W.W. Norton, 1954; revised and with corrections by Leonard Stein, 1969.

Style and Idea. New York, Philosophical Library, 1950, translated and edited by Dika Newlin. Enlarged edition by Leonard Stein, including most of the first edition plus many additional items, London, Faber & Faber, 1975.

Preliminary Exercises in Counterpoint. London, Faber & Faber/ New York, St. Martin's Press, 1963; edited by Leonard Stein.

Fundamentals of Musical Composition. London, Faber & Faber/ New York, St. Martin's Press, 1967; edited by Gerald Strang and Leonard Stein.

Dika Newlin's Writings

on Schoenberg

BOOK:

Bruckner-Mahler-Schoenberg. New York, King's Crown Press, 1947; revised and enlarged edition, New York, W.W. Norton, 1978; German translation by C. Nemeth and H. Selzer, Vienna, Bergland-Verlag, 1954.

TRANSLATIONS OF BOOKS BY OTHERS:

Leibowitz, René. *Schoenberg and His School*. New York, Philosophical Library, 1949. Reissue, New York, Da Capo Press, 1970; paperback edition, 1975.

Rufer, Josef. *The Works of Arnold Schoenberg*. London, Faber & Faber/New York, St. Martin's Press, 1962.

ARTICLES:

"Arnold Schoenberg," encyclopedia articles in:
The Academic American Encyclopedia (for high school and beginning college students)
Encyclopedia Britannica (15th ed., 1974)
Encyclopedia Judaica

McGraw-Hill Encyclopedia of World Biography
The New Book of Knowledge (for young people)

"Arnold Schoenberg," *The New Book of Modern Composers* (ed. David Ewen), New York, Alfred A. Knopf, 1961, pp. 334-346.

"Arnold Schoenberg as Choral Composer," *American Choral Review*, VI/4(1964), pp. 1, 7-11.

"Arnold Schönberg in Amerika," *Österreichische Musikzeitschrift*, VII(1952), pp. 160-63.

"Arnold Schoenberg's Religious Works," *Reconstructionist*, January 23, 1959.

"C.P.E. Bach and Arnold Schoenberg: A Comparison," *The Commonwealth of Music* (eds. Gustave Reese and Rose Brandel), New York, The Free Press, 1965, pp. 300-306.

"A Composer's View of Schoenberg's *Variations on a Recitative for Organ*," *Organ Institute Quarterly*, VI/1(Spring, 1956), pp. 16-18.

"Four Revolutionaries" (Schoenberg, Hindemith, Stravinsky, Bartók), *Choral Music* (ed. Arthur Jacobs), Harmondsworth, Penguin Books, 1963.

"From the Tree of Life—A Master and His Pupil," *American Record Guide*, XXXVIII(May, 1972), pp. 464-66.

"Impressions of a Fulbright Research Scholar in Vienna," *Pan Pipes*, XLIV(March, 1952), pp. 13-15.

"*Die Jakobsleiter*: Its History and Significance," BBC Third Programme Booklet, November 8, 1965 (British première of *Die Jakobsleiter*), pp. 5-8.

"A Life in Letters," *The New Leader*, XLVIII/10 (May 10, 1965), pp. 38-39.

"Moses and Aaron," *Reconstructionist*, December 10, 1965.

" 'Moses' in England," *Pan Pipes*, LVIII/3(1966), p. 17.

"The Piano Music of Arnold Schoenberg," *Piano Quarterly*, Spring, 1979.

"The Role of the Chorus in Schoenberg's 'Moses and Aaron'," *American Choral Review*, IX/1(1966), pp. 1-4, 18.

"Schoenberg and Wagner," *Bayreuther Festspiele* 1967 *(Siegfried* program), pp. 15-25.

"Schoenberg in America," *Music-Survey*, I, nos. 5-6, pp. 128-31, 185-89.

"The Schoenberg-Nachod Collection; A Preliminary Report," *Musical Quarterly*, LIV/1(January, 1968), pp. 31-46.

"Schoenberg's New Fantasy," *The Canon, Australian Journal of Music*, III/2(September, 1949; Arnold Schoenberg Jubilee Issue), pp. 83-85.

"Schoenberg's Personality as Reflected in His Music," *The Sinfonian*, Fall, 1951.

"Schoenberg's String Quartet in D Major," *Faber Music News*, Fall, 1966, pp. 21-23.

"Les Schoenbergeries," in "Music Chronicle," *Partisan Review*, XVI/4(April, 1949), pp. 414-415.

"Secret Tonality in Schoenberg's Piano Concerto," *Perspectives of New Music*, Fall-Winter 1974, pp. 137-39.

"Self-Revelation and The Law; Arnold Schoenberg in his Religious Works," *Yuval*, I (1968), pp. 204-220.

"Some Tonal Aspects of Twelve-Tone Music," *American Music Teacher*, III(November-December, 1953), pp. 2-3, 18.

"Why is Schoenberg's Biography So Difficult To Write?", *Perspectives of New Music*, Fall-Winter 1973/Spring-Summer 1974 (Double Issue), pp. 40-42.

Index